PENGUIN BOOKS

FRESH-AIR FIEND

Paul Theroux was born and educated in the United States. After graduating from university in 1963, he travelled to Italy and then Africa, where he worked as a teacher in Malawi and as a lecturer at Makerere University in Uganda. In 1968 he joined the University of Singapore and taught in the Department of English for three years. Throughout this time he was publishing short stories and journalism, and wrote a number of novels, including *Fong and the Indians*, *Girls at Play* and *Jungle Lovers*. In the early 1970s he moved with his wife and two children to Dorset, where he wrote *Saint Jack*, and went on to live in London. During his seventeen years' residence in Britain he wrote a dozen volumes of highly praised fiction and a number of successful travel books. He has since returned to the United States, but continues to travel widely.

Paul Theroux's many books include *Waldo*; *Saint Jack*; *The Family Arsenal*; *Picture Palace*, winner of the 1978 Whitbread Literary Award; *The Mosquito Coast*, which was the 1981 *Yorkshire Post* Novel of the Year, joint winner of the James Tait Black Memorial Prize, and was also made into a feature film; *My Secret History*; *Millroy the Magician*; *Kowloon Tong*; *The Great Railway Bazaar*; *The Old Patagonian Express*; *Riding the Iron Rooster*, which won the 1988 Thomas Cook Travel Book Award; *The Happy Isles of Oceania*; *Sir Vidia's Shadow*, a memoir of his friendship with Sir Vidia Naipaul; *Fresh-Air Fiend: Travel Writings 1985–2000*; and *Hotel Honolulu*. Most of his books are published by Penguin.

PAUL THEROUX IN PENGUIN

FICTION
Waldo
Saint Jack
The Black House
The Family Arsenal
Picture Palace
The Mosquito Coast
O-Zone *
My Secret History: A Novel *
Chicago Loop
Millroy the Magician
On the Edge of the Great Rift
(*containing* Fong and the Indians,
Girls at Play *and* Jungle Lovers)
My Other Life: A Novel
Kowloon Tong
Hotel Honolulu

SHORT STORIES
The Collected Stories

TRAVEL
The Great Railway Bazaar
The Old Patagonian Express *
The Kingdom by the Sea
Sunrise With Seamonsters *
Riding the Iron Rooster *
The Happy Isles of Oceania
Travelling the World
The Pillars of Hercules
Fresh-Air Fiend: Travel Writings 1985–2000

AUTOBIOGRAPHY
Sir Vidia's Shadow

*NOT AVAILABLE IN THE USA

PAUL THEROUX

Fresh-Air Fiend

TRAVEL WRITINGS, 1985–2000

PENGUIN BOOKS

PENGUIN BOOKS

Published by the Penguin Group
Penguin Books Ltd, 80 Strand, London WC2R 0RL, England
Penguin Putnam Inc., 375 Hudson Street, New York, New York 10014, USA
Penguin Books Australia Ltd, 250 Camberwell Road, Camberwell, Victoria 3124, Australia
Penguin Books Canada Ltd, 10 Alcorn Avenue, Toronto, Ontario, Canada M4V 3B2
Penguin Books India (P) Ltd, 11 Community Centre, Panchsheel Park, New Delhi – 110 017, India
Penguin Books (NZ) Ltd, Cnr Rosedale and Airborne Roads, Albany, Auckland, New Zealand
Penguin Books (South Africa) (Pty) Ltd, 24 Sturdee Avenue, Rosebank 2196, South Africa

Penguin Books Ltd, Registered Offices: 80 Strand, London WC2R 0RL, England

www.penguin.com

First published in Great Britain by Hamish Hamilton 2000
Published in Penguin Books 2001

5

The moral right of the author has been asserted

Extracts from 'The View', from *Collected Poems* by Philip Larkin,
'A Voyage IV (Hong Kong)', from *Collected Poems* by W. H. Auden,
reproduced by permission of Faber and Faber Ltd

Set in Monotype Sabon
Printed in England by Clays Ltd, St Ives plc

'A man sets out to draw the world. As the years go by, he peoples a space with images of provinces, kingdoms, mountains, bays, ships, islands, fishes, rooms, instruments, stars, horses, and individuals. A short time before he dies, he discovers that that patient labyrinth of lines traces the lineaments of his own face.'

Jorge Luis Borges, Afterword, *El Hacedor*

Contents

Introduction:
Being a Stranger

For long periods of my life, living in places where I did not belong, I have been a perfect stranger. I asked myself whether my sense of otherness was the human condition. It certainly was my condition. As with most people, my outer life did not in the least resemble my inner life, but the exotic place and circumstances intensified this difference. Sometimes my being a stranger was like the evocation of a dream state, at other times like a form of madness, and now and then it was just inconvenient. I might have gone home except that a return home would have made me feel like a failure. I was not only far away, I was also out of touch. It sounds as though I am describing a metaphysical problem to which there was no solution – but, no, all of this was a form of salvation.

I was an outsider before I was a traveler; I was a traveler before I was a writer; I think one led to the other. I don't think I was ever a scholar or a student in the formal sense. When I mentioned this notion of being a stranger to Oliver Sacks, he said, 'In the Kabbalah the first act in the creation of the universe is exile.' That makes sense to me.

Exile is a large concept for which a smaller version, the one I chose, is expatriation. I simply went away. Raised in a large talkative and teasing family of seven children, I yearned for space of my own. One of my pleasures was reading; reading was a refuge and an indulgence. But my greatest pleasure lay in leaving my crowded house and going for all-day hikes. In time these hikes turned into camping trips. Fortunately our house was at the edge of town – so I could leave the front door, and after half a mile of walking be in the woods, attractively named the Mystic Fells. On my own, I had a clearer sense of who I was, and I had a serious curiosity about what I found in the woods; the taxonomy of the trees and flowers and birds was a new language I learned in this new world.

When I went to Africa, young and unpublished, I became a *mzungu*, or white man, but the Chichewa word also implies a spirit, a ghost-figure, almost a goblin; a being so marginal as hardly to be human. I did not find it at all hard to accept this definition; I had always felt fairly marginal, with something to prove. So, speaking about myself as a traveler is the most logical way of speaking about myself as a writer.

As for my apprenticeship as a writer, I am sure that my single-mindedness was helped by my being out of touch. Both ideas – being a stranger, being out of touch – seem to me to be related. I believed myself to be a stranger wherever I was – even when I was younger among my family at home; and for much of my life I have felt disconnected. You think of a writer as in-touch and at the center of things, but I have found the opposite to be the case.

A variation of this concept was once a great topic in colleges. When I was a student it was the obsessive subject – the alienated hero or anti-hero, the drifter, epitomized by the figure of the casual and detached murderer Meursault in Camus's *L'Etranger*, or Raskolnikov in *Crime and Punishment*, or the trapped and ineffectual Josef K. in Kafka's *The Trial*, who is a total stranger to the process which is for no apparent reason blaming and victimizing him. There seemed to me something freakish about these men and something formulaic about their predicament. I found these characters and this discussion less persuasive because the characters seemed like stock figures in a morality play. I could not identify with,

> I, a stranger and afraid
> In a world I never made.

I have been much more affected when an apparently whole, round character described a sense of loss or deep isolation. It is no surprise when the hero of a post-war French novel is said to be alienated, but how much more affecting when the anguish is that of someone instantly recognizable, like Nicole Diver in Fitzgerald's *Tender is the Night*, or Peyton Loftis in William Styron's *Lie Down in Darkness*, or the 'whiskey priest' in Greene's *The Power and the Glory*. It is almost a shock when one of the great serene masters of the novel speaks of alienation, as these three men have done – Fitzgerald on alcohol in *The Crack-Up*, Greene on manic-depression in *A Sort of Life*, and Styron on suicidal depression in *Darkness Visible*. Even Henry James, the intensely sociable and inexhaustible dinner guest, experienced several breakdowns and many depressions. Jorge Luis Borges wrote, 'I speak in a poem of the ancient food of heroes:

humiliation, unhappiness, discord. Those things are given to us to transform, so that we may make from the miserable circumstances of our lives things that are eternal, or aspire to be so.'

There are few more explicit descriptions of the pain of isolation than that confided by James in a letter to a friend, who had asked mildly, using a travel metaphor, what had been his point of departure – what 'port' had he set out from to become a writer. James replied:

The port from which I set out was, I think, that of the essential loneliness of my life – and it seems to be the port also, in sooth, to which my course again finally directs itself! This loneliness (since I mention it!) – what is it still but the deepest thing about one? Deeper, about me, at any rate, than anything else; deeper than my 'genius,' deeper than my 'discipline,' deeper than my pride, deeper, above all, than the deep counterminings of art.

The English writer V. S. Pritchett spoke about this condition of otherness in his autobiography, how it was not until he began to travel far from his home in south London that he began to understand himself and his literary vocation. He said that he found distant places so congenial that he became an outsider at home. Travel had transformed him into a stranger. He wrote, 'I became a foreigner. For myself, that is what a writer is – a man living on the other side of a frontier.'

For various reasons it is not so easy to be a foreigner now – I am using the word in a general sense. Yet it was very easy for me to be a foreigner less than forty years ago, when I was an impressionable teenager and amateur emigrant. Then, a person could simply disappear by traveling; even a trip to Europe involved a sort of obscurity. A trip to Africa or South America could be a vanishing into silence and darkness.

The idea of disappearance appealed to me. For about ten years, the whole decade of my twenties, I was utterly out of touch. I went to Central Africa in 1963 and stayed for five years, and then instead of heading home I went to Singapore, from which I emerged late in 1971; and at that point buried myself and my family in the depths of the English countryside, nowhere near a village. In this entire period, living frugally, I did not own a telephone and the few calls I made were all in the nature of emergencies – reporting births and deaths, summoning doctors, all on borrowed phones. This decade of being off the phone, which is the most extreme condition of being cut off, was formative for me. In most respects it was one of the best things that could have happened in my passage toward becoming a writer, because it forced upon me a narrow sort of life, from which there was no turning back. I was isolated and enlightened. I learned to cope, I read more, I wrote more, I had no TV, I thought in a more concentrated way, I lived in one place, I studied patience.

'Connected' is the triumphant cry these days. Connection has made people arrogant, impatient, hasty, and presumptuous. I am old enough to have personally witnessed the rise of the telephone, the apotheosis of TV, and the video, the cellular phone, the pager, the fax machine and e-mail. I don't doubt that instant communication has been good for business, even for the publishing business, but it has done nothing for literature, and it might even have harmed it. I think in many ways connection has been disastrous. We have confused information (of which there is too much) with ideas (of which there are too few). I found out much more about the world and myself by being unconnected.

And what does connection really mean? What can the archivist – relishing detail, boasting of the information age – possibly do about all those private phone calls, e-mails, and electronic messages. Lost! A president is impeached and in spite of all the phone calls and all the investigation, almost the only evidence that exists of his assignations are a few cheap gifts, a signed photograph, and residue on a dress. So much for the age of information. My detractors may say, 'You can print e-mails' – but who commits that yakkety-yak to paper?

As for the video revolution, the eminent Pacific archeologist Yoshihiko Sinoto told me that the most rapid deterioration he had ever seen in human culture took place when video machines, powered by generators, became available in the outlying islands of the Cook Group in the Pacific. Now villagers were watching *Rambo* movies and pornography, with disastrous results to the fragile society. Last year I was in Brazil. A woman in Rio mentioned that she was flying to Manaus on the Amazon to meet her husband who worked there. She was eager to go, she said, because *Titanic* was showing at an Amazonian theater. Four months later I was in Palawan, a somewhat remote island in the Philippines, and walking along a beach I heard a Filipino boy humming the *Titanic* theme song, 'Our Love Will Go On.'

Nothing I can say in protest against the proliferation of the creepier manifestations of popular culture will change the continuous innovation in electronic media, which seems more and more to me like a cross between toy-making and chemical warfare. Having lived through the whole electronic revolution, I know that much of what I have seen is not progress but *folie de grandeur*. It is misleading, creating the illusion of knowledge, which is in fact the most profound ignorance. Obviously advances in communication are traveling so fast that you can accurately characterize people as writing at the speed of light – throughout the world.

But of course not the whole world. The most aberrant aspect of the delusional concept of globalization is the settled and smug belief that the world is connected, and that everyone and every place is instantly accessible. This is merely a harmful conceit. The colorful advertisement for cellular phones or computers showing Chinese speaking to Zulus, and Italians speaking to Tongans is inaccurate, not to say mendacious. There are still places on earth that are inaccessible, because of either their geography or their politics or their religion. Parts of China are off the map, and for that matter parts of Italy are too – there are villages in the hinterland of the province of Basilicata in southern Italy that are as isolated as they have ever been.

For the past ten years, since the disputed and disallowed election of 1991, the entire Republic of Algeria has been a no-go area, where an estimated 80–100,000 people have been massacred. Algeria – a sunny Mediterranean country, the most dangerous place in the world, with the worst human rights record on earth – is right next to jolly Morocco and colorful Tunisia, the haunts of package tourists and rug-collectors. This bizarre proximity highlights the paradox, which is an old one, that close by there are areas in the world that are still forbidden, or *terra incognita*, where no outsider dares to venture. In spite of all our connectedness we have very little idea of what passes for daily life in Algeria.

Distant and arduous travel is not always required to find a no-go area. For many years Northern Ireland was a complex of forbidden towns and neighborhoods, based on interpretations of Christianity. If you were the wrong sort of Christian you might be killed. There are New Yorkers who think nothing of traveling to Tierra del Fuego but who would not set foot in certain areas of New York City. I am not saying all these places are equally dangerous but only that they are perceived to be so.

And while some people in the world are accessible, many are not – many live in closed cultures, the sort of hermetic existence that has not changed for centuries. For well over forty years, travelers were forbidden to enter Albania, and Albanians were forbidden to leave. This isolation ended ten years ago, and because the confinement had been involuntary Albanians have found it hard to adjust – have 'decompensated' to use the clinical term – and have suffered a decade of chaos and a sort of political dementia, which has in part fueled the Kosovo conflict. I was in Albania a few years ago. It was a glimpse of the past for me and, by the way, a place without telephonic connection to the outside world.

There are many such places. Zambians in their capital, Lusaka, find it much easier to communicate with, say, people in Los Angeles – just pick up the phone or log on to the Internet – than with Zambians, the Lozi people, in their own Western province, who live without electricity or telephones and in some cases without roads. Life goes on for the Lozis, and though they suffer drought and disease, their lives are in many ways richer, more coherent, for their isolation. Some hinterlands in the world still exist, neglected if not inviolate. Thank God for them; but of course it is only a matter of time before they are violated, with predictable results. I have personally witnessed this in a number of countries. When I first traveled in Sicily in 1963, Uganda in 1966, Afghanistan in 1973, Honduras in 1979, the Upper Yangtze in 1980, Albania in 1993, I felt in each place that I was off the map; but after me came a deluge – soldiers, tourists, developers, or the complex cannibalism of civil war – and the inhabitants of those places have been profoundly changed, if not corrupted in new and uninteresting ways, as though turned into gigantic dwarfs.

Anyone with money for a ticket can fly to any other big city in the world – an American airport is a gateway to Vladivostok and Ouagadougou. My reaction to this is, *Big deal*. Cities did nothing for me; it was the hinterland that made me.

In Africa as a *mzungu*, I was a stranger among The People, which is what the word *Bantu* means. I was not a person but rather a sort of marginal spirit-like being, and what I spoke was unintelligible to most of them. That was a good lesson. Until then, I had not known that most people in the world believe that they are The People, and their language is The Word, and strangers are not fully human – at least not human in the way they are – nor is a stranger's language anything but the gabbling of incoherent and inspissated felicities.

I should have known this purely on the basis of Native American terminology. *Bantu* meaning 'The People' has its counterpart throughout the world's cultures. The name of virtually every Native American nation or tribe or band – Inuit, Navaho, and so on – translates as The People, the implication being that they are human and the stranger is not. For example, the earliest people in what is now Michigan called themselves 'Anishinabe, 'The First People.' Strangers named them the Chippewa, which was corrupted to Ojibway, a variation of 'Those who make pictographs' – because of the elegantly engraved birch-bark scrolls they produced.

The early French travelers who were the first to encounter these Anishinabe were blind to these scrolls – could not read them, were interested purely in the furs the people could supply. There are distinct disadvantages to being a stranger. The stranger is always somewhat at sea and, like such a castaway, faced with unusual, unexpected problems.

Otherness can be like an illness; being a stranger can be analogous to experiencing a form of madness – those same intimations of the unreal and the irrational, when everything that has been familiar is stripped away. The stranger can feel like someone wounded or disabled. In *The Wound and the Bow*, Edmund Wilson used the Greek myth of Philoctetes as a metaphor to describe the relationship between art and illness. The underlying idea in the myth is that Philoctetes' wound is part of his character: 'the conception of superior strength as inseparable from disability.' It is not only Philoctetes' wonderful bow alone that makes him superior, but also his fortitude, a power derived from his bearing the pain of his wound. His unhealed injury gives him nobility. This notion of the idea of the link between trauma and art (or sickness and strength) was not new with Edmund Wilson; it exists throughout literature. It is in part the basis of the heart-sick artist-lover of the Romantic Movement as well as much of what we understand as modern, too. Borges, who was blind, wrote, 'Blindness is a gift.'

The greatest exponent today of this interpretation of illness as a possible source of imaginative power – though he has never referred specifically to the myth of Philoctetes – is Dr. Oliver Sacks. His patients are classic strangers. In the case histories collected in *The Man Who Mistook His Wife for a Hat* and *An Anthropologist on Mars*, Dr. Sacks has explained how an apparent disability in one area of a person's life can grant an access of strength or inspiration in another area. More recently, in *The Island of the Color-Blind*, Dr. Sacks has described how achromatopes develop a keen understanding not of color but what he calls 'a polyphony of brightnesses.' The non-color-blind person is as helpless as the sighted man in the Wells's story 'The Country of the Blind.' Dr. Sacks describes encounters in which the physician is revealed as less acute, less capable and perceptive, than the patient.

To be a stranger is to be childlike, a bit defenseless and dim, and having to acquire a language. In *Seeing Voices*, his study of the deaf, Dr. Sacks compares St. Augustine's description, in his *Confessions*, of his learning to speak as an infant, with the deaf learning sign language. Wittgenstein's analysis of this experience relates this to the stranger's dilemma: 'Augustine describes the learning of human language as if the child came into a strange country and did not understand the language of the country; that is, as if it already had a language, only not this one.' This is precisely what the stranger feels: an inner sense of helplessness, almost infantilism, in this new place, as though the stranger had passed through the looking-glass.

Living in the African bush for so long meant that I was dependent upon the hospitality of the Africans, the Nyanja people in Nyasaland. They could have managed very well without me, but I needed them. My first task was to learn their language – Chinyanja, also known as Chichewa. After that my life was much easier. My isolation was increased by my having only a bicycle for transportation for my first two years; I had no phone, and for long spells of time – hours or days – no electricity. On the plus side I had access to a vegetable market and a distant post office. I raised pigeons and ate them. I liked my students, I had friends in villages nearby. Except for the periods of time when there was political trouble in the country and rifle muzzles were pointed at my face, I did not feel I was in much danger, because in general I understood the risks. In spite of my sympathy and goodwill, I knew I lived apart, but that was not a new feeling. In terms of being a writer, I felt very lucky.

Another important and old-fashioned fact was that in the Africa I knew, and even the South East Asia I knew, local people did not think of solving problems by uprooting themselves and emigrating. They accepted that they would live and die in their own country, indeed in the village where they had been born. They did not have relatives or families elsewhere. A person who is in a country for life tends to see himself or herself as part of a community, with responsibilities. Because fleeing was not an option, the people I knew had a well-developed sense of belonging. They took the long view:

they had been there forever, the land was theirs, they were part of a culture, with a long memory, deep roots, old habits and customs. Living among such people intensified my sense of exclusion, of being a stranger, and it fascinated me.

Haunted by the restless dead, these places are more populous than they appear, for most people share their existence with the unseen world of spirits. Ancestors live within us. There is an Inuit notion that a new baby, born after a recently deceased grandparent, is actually the incarnation of the person, and the infant will be referred to as 'Grandad' or 'Grandma' and treated with the respect accorded to an elder. In most of the places I lived for my decade of being cut off, there was an accepted belief that the dead were not dead and not even absent; for many people in the world no one dies, no one really goes away. The dead are present, friends are present, ancestors are present. Recognizing this, Lévi-Strauss wrote, 'There is probably no society which does not treat its dead with respect.' At my present age I am more prepared to entertain the concept of ancestor worship and the proximity of the spirit world than of monotheism. Anyone who has grieved for the loss of a father or mother understands what I am saying, but it extends to all areas of time passing.

Turning up twenty-five years after leaving Malawi, I met people who reminded me that I had not been forgotten. As a friend, I had not really left. For them not much time had passed. Is this because we in the West tend to measure time in terms of a single lifetime? Perhaps in places where the life expectancy is very short (it has just been calculated at thirty-eight years in Zimbabwe) a life-span is a useless unit of measurement.

Toward the end of a long day paddling in the Trobriand Islands off the north-east coast of Papua New Guinea, I put ashore at a tiny seaside village, intending to ask permission to camp on a nearby beach. 'Stay here,' the goggling villagers insisted. 'You will be safe.' That also meant they could keep an eye on me. No one ever asked me how long I intended to remain in the village, though they were bewildered that I should prefer my tent to the hospitality of their huts. Fear of malaria – endemic and often fatal in the Trobriands – was my only reason. After two weeks of utter contentment I paddled away.

They yelled, 'Come back some time!'

A long time, six months or more, passed before I returned, and when I did, without any warning, dragging my kayak out of the lagoon, a woman on the beach smiled at me and said, 'We were just talking about you.'

Her casual welcome delighted me. There was nothing remarkable about my reappearance, it was as though I had hardly left the village. I had thought of the intervening months as full of incident in my life. That same time was not long for them; it represented one harvest, and one storm, and several deaths. But no one truly dies in the Trobriands, they simply go to another island: the spirits of the dead reside on Tuma Island, just a bit north.

Their own notion of the passage of time made my return less stressful. There was Trobriand protocol – ritual greetings and presents – but there was none of the drama and forced emotion that characterize an American homecoming. It pleased me to think that I figured in their consciousness. Death or departure was part of an eternal return.

And the friendship of people who come and go for whatever length of time is not diminished by their absence. What matters in the Trobriands is your existence in the consciousness of the village. If someone talks about you, or if you appear in their dreams, you are present – you have reality.

The most dramatic example of otherness occurs when two radically different cultures meet for the first time. This encounter is summed up in the expression 'first contact.'

In *First Contact*, their 1987 account of a series of such events in New Guinea, the authors, Bob Connolly and Robin Anderson, found people in the New Guinea Highlands in the 1980s who had been present when Australian gold prospectors first came to the Highlands in 1930. The Australians were in a hurry, looking for gold, but seeing them cross a river in their valley the villagers believed that these white men were the ghosts of their ancestors. All used the word 'spirit' to describe the strangers.

One of the witnesses, Kirupano Eza'e, said, 'Once they had gone, the people sat down and developed stories. They knew nothing of white-skinned men. We had not seen far places. We knew only this side of the mountains. And we thought we were the only living people. We believed that when a person died, his skin changed to white and he went over the boundary to "that place" – the place of the dead. So when the strangers came we said, "Ah, these men do not belong to the earth. Let's not kill them – they are our own relatives."'

'I asked myself: who are these people?' another man, Gopie Ataiamelaho, said. 'They must be somebody from the heavens. Have they come to kill us or what? We wondered if this could be the end of us, and it gave us a feeling of sorrow. We said, "We must not touch them!" We were terribly frightened.'

They had to be from the sky – where else could they have come from? Also some people took the white men to be incarnations of a mythical being, Hasu Hasu, associated with lightning.

This parallels the Hawaiian belief that Captain Cook, in the year of First Contact, 1778, was the God Lono – he seemed to have all the attributes, and he was feared until he too was discovered to be mortal. On an earlier voyage, in October, 1769, when Cook arrived at Turranga Nui in what is now New Zealand, the Maori thought these Englishmen were *atua*, supernatural beings, or perhaps *tipuna*, ancestors who were revisiting their homeland. Cook's ship, the *Endeavour*, was taken to be a floating island, the sacred island Waikawa, and the crew to be *tupua*, or goblins. In 1517, the year of their First Contact, the Aztecs took the Spaniards to be avatars of Quetzalcoatl, the Plumed Serpent, God of Learning and of Wind.

Even today the word for foreigner or white man in Samoan is *palangi* (a related word, *papalangi*, is used in Tonga), meaning 'sky burster', a person who came from the clouds, not a terrestrial creature. *Haole* – white person in Hawaiian – means 'of another breath.' The polar Inuit assumed that they were the only people in the world, so when they saw their first white stranger, the explorer Sir William Parry, upon first meeting him in 1821, they said to him, 'Are you from the sun or the moon?'

'*Dim-dim*' in Trobriand has the meaning of someone not human, nothing at all like the Trobrianders, who trace their origins to original ancestors who rose from holes in the northern part of the main island. The Naskapi Indians of Labrador thought the first white men were ghosts, because ghosts were white, too, and fairly common. The writer Larry Millman, who collected oral accounts of the Naskapi around Davis Inlet in Labrador, told me that as a result of this belief, 'the Naskapi kept bumping into their white visitors, who were Oblate Fathers, because they thought they could walk right through them, as in fact they could walk through ghosts.' Today in Hong Kong, the word *gweilo* is used for a white person or foreigner; it means 'ghost-man.'

The more isolated a people, the greater the emphasis on a stranger being benign. I am not referring to their near neighbors, with whom they were probably in conflict – as in New Guinea and elsewhere; but rather in the hard-to-account-for person of another color who, invariably, is first seen as a spirit of a dead ancestor, and then as a patron with goods to share, and next as a pest, and of course finally as a threat. As they saw more foreigners, the Inuit began to see them as fellow humans, but different; and the widely used Inuit word for white person is *kabloona* (derived from *qallunaat*), which means something like 'eyebrow stomachs,' probably a reaction to their hairy bodies by the almost hairless Inuit.

In general, from the linguistic point of view, the more contact a people has with foreigners the more they lose their innocence regarding the strangers' motives and this cynicism is usually reflected in their language. The late-medieval book of travels attributed to Sir John Mandeville has proven to be a compilation of travel narratives from many sources, and, with the actual accounts of early (thirteenth- and fourteenth-century) travelers to China, includes many medieval fantasies about cannibals and one-eyed men and dog-headed people. Among others, Shakespeare used the more outlandish details in his work – you can see the result clearly in *The Tempest*, Caliban is straight from Mandeville.

Columbus's descriptions of the islanders he encountered in the West Indies show him to have been heavily influenced by Mandeville. He asserted that he saw one-eyed men, and cannibals, and dog-nosed individuals. He was also influenced by Marco Polo – and using his copy of Marco Polo's *Travels* as confirmation, Columbus thought he might be in Asia. Some islanders he took to be soldiers of the Great Khan. It was important for Columbus to establish the myth of Carib cannibalism, for then Spain could enslave the people on the grounds that they were savages. This same logic applied in the Pacific – New Hebrides is the most dramatic example – the apparent existence of cannabalism justified intense mission activity, or slavery, or both.

Anthropological stereotyping is not new, but one of its symmetries is that when an isolated people are visited and discover that the visitors are not gods or ancestors or goblins, but are people looking for gold, or land, or souls to save – usually all three – they tend to protect themselves, and for defending their homes they are termed 'cruel,' 'brave,' 'bloodthirsty,' 'warlike,' or 'savages.'

The word in Italian for slave (*schiave*) is related to the word for Serbian (*Schiavone*), as in English (from Latin) slave is related to Slav – so many Slavs had been enslaved, the words became synonymous, as barbarian has its roots in 'bearded' – the hairy enemy – and bugger is related to Bulgar.

This European stereotyping is shared by the Arabs and the Chinese. In China there are many words for foreigner, from the generic *wei-guo ren* to words for Red-Haired Devil, White Devil, and Big Nose. It cannot be a mere coincidence that all these people, Europeans, Arabs and Chinese, live in places that have been crossroads for foreign travelers – and enemies. Unlike the New Guinea highlanders and the Inuit, they were well aware that there were others in the world.

The Arabic language reflects this worldliness: 'foreigner' is *ajnabi* and the root means something like 'people to avoid.' Another such word for foreigner is *ajami*, which means 'foreigners; barbarians; people who speak Arabic badly; Persians.' *Gharib* – stranger – is related to *gharb*, the West, in the sense of 'a person from the West.' ('East' appears to have more friendly connotations in Arabic.) But the point is clear, from the linguistic point of view. First Contact exemplifies a kind of innocence, and nothing intensifies xenophobia more than seeing strangers as a threat.

'Every stranger is an enemy,' a notion I have encountered in my travels in various cultures, achieved its cruelest expression in Nazism. In his Preface to *Survival in Auschwitz* (also titled *If This is a Man*), Primo Levi discusses this delusion. He writes:

For the most part this conviction lies deep down like some latent infection; it betrays itself only in random, disconnected acts, and does not lie at the base of a system of reason. But when this does come about, when the unspoken dogma becomes the major premiss in a syllogism, then, at the end of the chain, there is the Lager [the Nazi extermination camp].

It is rare to find the opposite view, but not long ago Tenzin Gyatso, the Fourteenth Dalai Lama, wrote (in his essay 'Compassion and the Individual'), 'All that is necessary is for each of us to develop our good human qualities. I try to treat whoever I meet as an old friend. This gives me a genuine feeling of happiness. It is the practice of compassion.'

But I was not embraced as a traveler; I was seen as a stranger, sometimes a dangerous one. My experience of that conflict made me a writer.

One of the paradoxes of otherness is that in travel each conceives the other to be a foreigner. But even the most distant and exotic travel has its parallel in ordinary life. Every day we meet new people and are insulted or misunderstood; we are thrown upon our own resources. In the coming and going of daily life we rehearse a modified version of the dramatic event known as First Contact. In a wish to experience otherness to its limit, to explore all its nuances, I became a traveler. I was as full of preconceived notions as Columbus or Crusoe – you can't help it, but you can alter such thoughts. Non-travelers often warn the traveler of dangers, and the traveler dismisses such fears; but the presumption of hospitality is just as odd as the presumption of danger. You have to find out for yourself. Take the leap – go as far as you can. Try staying out of touch. Become a stranger in a strange land. Acquire humility. Learn the language. Listen to what people are saying.

It was as a solitary traveler that I began to discover who I was and what I stood for. When people ask me what they should do to become a writer, I seldom mention books – I assume the person has a love for the written word, and solitude, and disdain for wealth – so I say, 'You want to be a writer? First, leave home.'

Except for 'Down the Yangtze,' all the pieces in this book were written since my last collection, *Sunrise with Seamonsters* (1985). I have placed them thematically, in a way that seems right to me, rather than putting them in chronological order.

Part One

Time Travel

Memory and Creation:
The View from Fifty

One of the more bewildering aspects of growing older is that people constantly remind you of things that never happened. Of course this is also the case when you are younger, but it is only with the passage of time that you're sure of the lie. I was driving up to Amherst with my parents a few years ago to collect an honorary degree and my mother, who was excited and talkative, said, 'I always knew you were going to be a writer.'

I said to myself, *No, you didn't. You always said I was going to be a doctor.*

My father said, 'Yep, you always had your nose in a book.'

I said to myself, *No, I didn't.*

When I got to Amherst one of the officials said, 'Remember when we arrested you at that demonstration?' And he laughed. 'That was something!'

I said to myself, *It was horrible. About fourteen people on the whole campus protesting what was the beginning of the Vietnam War, and everyone else calling us Commies. The so-called Student Left was composed of freaks, misfits, kids with glasses and hideous haircuts, dope smokers, a jazz pianist, and a handful of Quakers. I had the glasses and the haircut. It was no joke. My uncle in Boston heard about my arrest on the radio and he called my parents, and people said, 'This is going to affect your whole future.' My whole future!*

Someone else that weekend said, 'Well, when you were editor of the student newspaper . . .'

I said to myself, *I was never editor of the student newspaper, which was actually quite a prestigious post and much more respectable than anything I would have chosen or been given.*

I think perhaps that I have made my point, and I don't want to labor it. But the subject has been on my mind a great deal lately: I have just turned fifty years old. Who wrote this?

3

Fifty: it is a dangerous age – for all men, and especially for one like me who has a tendency to board sinking ships. Middle age has all the scares a man feels halfway across a busy street, caught in traffic and losing his way, or another one blundering in a black upstairs room, full of furniture, afraid to turn the lights on because he'll see the cockroaches he smells. The man of fifty has the most to say, but no one will listen. His fears sound incredible because they are so new – he might be making them up. His body alarms him; it starts playing tricks on him, his teeth warn him, his stomach scolds, he's balding at last; a pimple might be cancer, indigestion a heart attack. He's feeling an unapparent fatigue; he wants to be young but he knows he ought to be old. He's neither one and terrified. His friends all resemble him, so there can be no hope of rescue. To be this age and very far from where you started out, unconsoled by any possibility of a miracle – that is bad; to look forward and start counting the empty years left is enough to tempt you into some aptly named crime, or else to pray. Success is nasty and spoils you, the successful say, and only failures listen, who know nastiness without the winch of money. Then it is clear: the ship is swamped to her gunwales, and the man of fifty swims to shore, to be marooned on a little island, from which there is no rescue, but only different kinds of defeat.

I wrote that in my novel *Saint Jack* when I was twenty-nine years old, and I think it is inaccurate as it applies to me – I cannot identify that person or relate to that state of being middle-aged and clapped out. Nor can I share even remotely the sense of loss Philip Larkin expresses in his fiftieth-birthday poem, 'The View:'

> The view is fine from fifty,
>   Experienced climbers say;
> So, overweight and shifty,
>   I turn to face the way
>   That led me to this day.
>
> Instead of fields and snowcaps
>   And flowered lanes that twist,
> The track breaks at my toe-caps
>   And drops away in mist.
>   The view does not exist.

> Where has it gone, the lifetime?
> Search me. What's left is drear.
> Unchilded and unwifed, I'm
> Able to view that clear:
> So final. And so near.

These sentiments give me the willies. Larkin at fifty seems to regard his life as just about over. I do not feel that way; I hope I never do. I have always felt – physically at least – in the pink, no matter what my age. One line in *Saint Jack* goes, 'Fiction gives us the second chances that life denies us,' and this remark, which I regard as prescient, is one of the themes of this excursion today.

When I began writing *Saint Jack* in 1970, one of my friends was turning fifty in Singapore and it seemed to me, I suppose, salutary to observe that climacteric, for, as I say, one of the strangest aspects of growing older is that people constantly remind you of things that never happened – and worse, they ignore what actually took place. The invented reminiscence of 'I'll never forget old what's-his-name' has a cozy quaintness and seems harmless enough, but the element of self-deception in it can lead you badly astray.

Lately I have been wondering about the relationship between memory and creation; and between memory and perception – and behavior, too. It all seems scrambled together. I say 'lately' partly because of this half-century birthday and also because of several dramatic changes in my life – becoming separated from my wife, traveling extensively in the Pacific, resuming residence in my American house. My life has been full of changes, all of them unexpected. When I was young and felt a bit down-trodden I thought, *My life will be pretty much what it is now* – because people were always prophesying – saying they knew exactly what was going to happen to me, even if I didn't – another example of people alarming me with their lies.

I often think that I became a writer because I had a good memory. When I say 'a good memory' I do not mean that it is a totally accurate memory, only that it is a very full and accessible one, packed with images and language. Montaigne, who discusses the question of memory in his essay 'On Liars,' claimed to have had a terrible memory. He makes the case for the virtues of having a bad memory (such an afflicted person is less worldly and less ambitious and less garrulous), and asserts, 'an outstanding memory is often associated with weak judgment.' There are other treats in store for the deeply forgetful person: 'Books and places which I look at again always welcome me with a fresh new smile.'

Montaigne suggests that he is utterly helpless. And while it is true that remembering depends upon habit, it also depends upon the use of deliberate techniques. I agree in general with Dr. Johnson's observation, reported by Boswell, that 'forgetfulness [is] a man's own fault.'

Yet often the very drama of events prints them on our memory.

At the age of two I started a fire under my crib – I put a match to some newspapers, as I had seen one of my older brothers doing just a few days before. Without any alarm I was a spectator to a great confusion in the house, as my burning mattress was flung out of the back window, onto the lawn.

Not long after that I squeezed through the loose picket in a fence and cut my scalp on a rusty nail on the top bar. The scar was a white crescent, and for a long time after that, whenever I got a short haircut, people said, 'What's that on your head?' I must have been very young – how else could I have got through that small opening in the fence?

A few days after my sister Ann Marie was born, in 1944, when I was three, I was being looked after by a neighbor, while my mother stayed in the hospital. I began to look for my father. Believing that he was at church – it was a Sunday – I eluded the baby-sitter and walked there, a quarter of a mile away, and I distinctly remember the long crossing of a four-lane road known as the Fellsway. I was so small I could not see over the hump in the middle to the other side of the road. I sat on the church steps, calling out, 'Daddy,' and there I was found by my panicky father. A search party had already been sent to a nearby brook, believing I had fallen in and drowned. I suppose this was my first attempt at independent travel.

The first book that was read to me was *Make Way for Ducklings* (it had a Boston setting), and the second was *The 500 Hats of Bartholomew Cubbins*, by Dr Seuss. As soon as I could read I wanted to be a hero.

I can name nearly every child who was in my first grade class, Miss Purcell's, at the Washington School, in Medford. We wrote with big thick pencils; in the third grade Miss Cook introduced us to ink – we had inkwells and we used sharp steel nibs – the difficulty of forming letters with those sputtering nibs is vivid to me even today. I know

Psalm 23 because it was Miss Cook's favorite when I was eight. I knew the distinct odor of everyone's house, friends and relatives, where I was taken as a child: the assertive and often offensive smells of strange cooking and different people. Blindfolded, I could have identified thirty of those smell-labeled households.

I have more recollections of this kind, which go under the name 'episodic memories' (remembering a specific event), and I am well aware of their approximate truth. As Sir Frederick Bartlett wrote in *Remembering*:

Remembering is not a re-excitation of innumerable, fixed, lifeless, and fragmentary traces. It is an imaginative reconstruction, or construction, built out of the relation of our attitude towards a whole active mass of organized past reaction or experience, to a little outstanding detail which commonly appears in image or in language form. It is thus hardly ever exact, even in the most rudimentary cases of rote-capitulation, and it is not at all important that it should be.

I have altered my memories in the way we all do – simplified them, improved them, made them more orderly. Memory works something like this: stare at a square and then close your eyes; the after-image gradually softens into a circle – much more symmetrical and memorable. The poet Goethe was the first to write about this phenomenon.

'Few have reason to complain of nature as unkindly sparing of the gifts of memory,' Dr. Johnson wrote in *The Idler* (No. 74). 'The true art of memory is the art of attention.'

That observation is vividly illustrated in the life of the Italian Jesuit Matteo Ricci, who traveled and proselytized in China in the late sixteenth and early seventeenth centuries. He is known to Sinologists as the man who drew the first map of the world for the Chinese – and in so doing conveyed many facts disturbing to the Ming court: that China might not be the Middle Kingdom, that other large countries exist on the planet, and that the earth is round.

Ricci developed a highly complex memory system, which served him well as a missionary (he carried a whole library of Christian theology in his head), and as a linguist (he became so skillful in the language that he wrote a number of books in Chinese). His memory also endeared him to the Chinese and won him Christian converts. In his brilliant study of the man and his times, *The Memory Palace of Matteo Ricci*, Jonathan Spence described how 'Ricci wrote quite casually in 1595 of running through a list of four to five hundred random Chinese ideograms and then repeating the list in reverse order.'

The memory palace that Ricci advocated was an imaginary mental structure that might be based on a real building. This construction, great or small, was the best repository for knowledge. It could be vast, full of rooms and halls, corridors, and pavilions, and in each chamber we could place the images of the things we wanted to recall. Ricci wrote, 'To everything that we wish to remember we should give an image; and to every one of these images we should assign a position where it can repose peacefully until we are ready to claim it by an act of memory.'

The scholar Francesco Panigarola, who may have taught Ricci in Italy, and who wrote on memory arts, could remember as many as 100,000 images at a time. And as a Jesuit, Ricci was well aware of the importance Ignatius of Loyola attached in his *Spiritual Exercises* to memory as a means of contemplation. Ricci himself credited the concept of the memory palace to the sixth–fifth-centuries-BC Greek poet Simonides (of Ceos). But the arts of memory were a part of classical learning, and in listing the memory experts of the past, Pliny's *Natural History* was as powerful an inspiration to Ricci as it was to Jorge Luis Borges 400 years later – the result in Borges's case was his wonderful story 'Funes the Memorious.'

Ireneo Funes, the eponymous hero, has a marvelous memory, and one day the narrator loans him a copy of Pliny. Later, he visits Funes, who begins by reciting the book by heart – in the darkness of his room.

. . . enumerating, in Latin and in Spanish, the cases of prodigious memory recorded in the *Naturalis historia:* Cyrus, king of the Persians, who could call every soldier in his armies by name: Mithridates Eupator, who administered the law in twenty-two languages of his empire; Simonides, inventor of the science of mnemonics; Metrodorus, who practiced the art of faithfully repeating what he had heard only once.

But Funes is unimpressed by any of this. His own memory is as good but much stranger, for after a fall from a horse he became paralyzed; yet in his waking from the trauma of the fall he discovered he had the gift of an instantly imagistic memory:

He knew by heart the forms of the southern clouds at dawn on 30 April 1882, and could compare them in his memory with the mottled streaks on a book in Spanish binding he had seen only once . . . Two or three times, he had reconstructed a whole day; he never hesitated, but each reconstruction required a whole day. He told me: 'I alone have more memories than all mankind has probably had since the world has been the world . . . My memory is like a garbage heap.'

Borges describes one of Funes's bizarre projects, how he has invented an original system for numbering, giving every number 'a particular sign, a kind of mark.' The number one might be *the gas* and two might be *the cauldron*, and so on: '. . . in place of seven thousand thirteen he would say (for example) *Maximo Perez*; in place of seven thousand fourteen, *The Railroad*; other numbers were *Luis Melian Lafinur, Olimar, sulphur, the reins, the whale* . . . in place of five hundred he would say *nine* . . .'

Assigning a bizarre image to a word, Funes has reached the number 24,000. The narrator is at pains to point out that Funes is almost incapable of sustained thought or of generalizing. Funes can't understand why the word dog stands for so many shapes and forms of the animal, and more than that, 'it bothered him that the dog at three fourteen (seen from the side) should have the same name as the dog at three fifteen (seen from the front) . . .'

In this oblique story, describing the memory palace of Ireneo Funes, Borges gives final expression to the clear link between memory and creation.

As a schoolboy I had no memory palace, but I had a manageable sub-Funes system of converting anything I wished to remember into an image. My intelligence was emphatically pictorial; in this I was buoyant, but I foundered whenever a subject became unreasonably abstract. I still regard the best sentences as those which throw up clear images, and the worst as opaque, abstract, unvisualizable – like this one!

I performed well in school because rote-capitulation was so important; in fact, reasoning was far less important than remembering. 'Semantic memory' – knowledge of facts – was demanded. Learning was memorizing: history was names and dates, geography was capitals and cash crops, English was learning poems by heart ('The sun that bleak December day/Rose cheerless over hills of gray . . .'), biology was the simplest of all for me – not just a memory exercise but a new vocabulary: nictitating membranes, epithelial cells, osmosis, and the exotic-sounding islets of Langerhans (in your pancreas). Early in my life, on the basis of my easy grasp of biological nomenclature, and what I consider aesthetic reasons – all those euphonious names – I resolved to be a medical doctor. Even after I had abandoned the ambition I told people that it was my chosen profession, because, being respectable and money-making, no one would question the choice.

I survived school because I remembered everything: my memory saved me. It was an odd, undemanding and unsatisfactory education, and I think – because so little writing was involved in it – that its oddness helped make me a writer. For one thing I read whatever I liked – in a jumble, preferring adventure stories about fur trappers, or castaways, ordeal stories that involved cannibalism (*Boon Island* by Kenneth Roberts comes to mind), and books considered smutty or outrageous in the 1950s – *Generation of Vipers*, *Tropic of Cancer*, *Lady Chatterley's Lover*. Because of the censorship and repression of the period, language itself was a stimulant – seeing certain forbidden words on a page was a thrill. I avoided anything literary. I was not taught any formal approach to essay-writing. I was forced to invent my own writing technique.

This home-made reading list and my impressionistic method of writing did not serve me particularly well at college – I was criticized for not being rigorous or trenchant. *Who says?* was a frequent comment by my teachers in the margins of my essays. I was offering personal opinions not literary judgments. This did not worry me. My academic aim was never to excel but only to get it over with and move on. I was impatient to graduate; my reading had given me a taste – not for more reading, nor writing, but for seeing the wider, and wilder, world. I had felt small and isolated living in the place where I had grown up. I had read to find out about the world, I despaired of surviving being swallowed up by my home town – and Medford still seems to me one of the strangest places I have ever known; I wanted to leave.

There was another obstacle. I was, I think, curious and energetic, but there was a weariness in the novels I read, in life in general, a sense of Doomsday, when I was in college. The post-war dreariness had penetrated into the 1950s and even overlapped the 1960s, and in the vogue for the placeless novel or play or poem the dominant emotion was frustration and anger expressed as exhaustion. It was a sense of powerlessness, and it was almost certainly political: this was an age of racial segregation, of deep conservatism, of domineering religious views, and a denial of women's rights. Books were banned and put on trial. The literary expression of the period was a kind of confusion. It was the era of *Waiting for Godot*, the setting of which is an almost bare stage. Bare stages were in vogue. Novels without much sense of place were in vogue – I am thinking of the French *nouvelle vague*, but there were British and American imitators. Naturally Eliot's 'The Waste Land' was extremely popular.

I found this all unhelpfully abstract. My main objection, although I did not know enough to formulate it at the time, was that my own memories were of no use, my own experience somewhat irrelevant to the metaphysics of the modern novel or poem. Apart from blackouts and the shouts of air raid wardens – but why would the Germans want to bomb Webster Street? I wondered – I had no useful memory of World War II. That set many of us apart in the 1960s. I had no sense of the waste land – I came from Medford, after all, which was a frustrating but funny place. We used to say Medford was famous because Paul Revere had ridden through it in 1775, but in fact we were more proud of the tough gangs of South Medford who slugged it out with the gangs from Somerville. Medford had particularities – my teacher Mr. Hanley, who had a wooden leg; Harry Walker, the drunken policeman, who once lost his badge (and gave us a quarter when we found it); hangouts – Joe's Poolroom and Brigham's Ice Cream Parlor and Carroll's Diner; the dank, muddy smell of the Mystic River.

It is true that I could share some of the feelings of the spiritual crisis in the literature of the 1950s and 1960s, but I had no strong belief that God was dead. In any case, God was like Banquo's ghost, popping up at every riotous occasion, to my great shame. I had been raised a cultural Catholic, and so religion had a strong ethnic coloration, depending on who was saying mass or giving the sermon – perhaps an Irish priest (St. Patrick, Mother of God, boozy funerals) or Italian (St. Anthony, the muscular Christ, boozy weddings).

Now and then I recognized my own world in fiction: in the stories of J. F. Powers (*The Prince of Darkness*, for example), in José Maria Gironella's Spanish trilogy – I have no idea how it came to be in the house – *The Cypresses Believe in God* (sex and syphilis figuring in a large way), in Joyce's *Dubliners*. But in general I never recognized anything in fiction as resembling the world I knew. I rather envied the prosperous families with prep-school kids; or the Jewish families trying to look respectable; or even the struggling blacks: their worlds appeared, to a greater or a lesser degree, in popular fiction. Stereotypes of them existed. They were written about. My own mongrel world had gone unreported. It was like being denied my own experience, and without a model – with nothing to imitate, with the mistaken notion that my own world might not even be worth writing about (after all, there seemed nothing specifically literary about the life I knew) – I devised my own remedy, I fled – I went away – as far as I could: with the Peace Corps to Central Africa.

Africa was a lucky choice for me, because distance in terms of both space and culture produced in me feelings of alienation that only memories could ease. I could not live in a culture that was utterly foreign, and so my solution was to live in my head. I needed to remember the past in order to be calm, and retrieval was not easy; I needed to be in touch with things that were familiar. I was in Nyasaland, which at that time was a British protectorate. The African towns were superficially English, like English culture made out of mud. In the absence of stimuli – I went to Africa with one small suitcase; I had virtually no possessions – I had to devise ways to gain access to my memory.

Does this seem a very deliberate process? It was nothing of the kind. It was not a calculated act. Like almost everything in my life it was haphazard, accidental, and I was seldom conscious of what I was doing. Writing is to me only superficially deliberate – it is much more like digging a deep hole and not quite knowing what you are going to find; like groping in a dark well-furnished room (surprises everywhere, and not just remarkable chairs but strange people murmuring in the oddest postures). I am inclined to agree with the novelist-narrator Bendrix in Graham Greene's novel *The End of the Affair* when he says (and Greene himself believed this), 'So much of a novelist's writing . . . takes place in the unconscious; in those depths the last word is written before the first word appears on paper. We remember the details of our story, we do not invent them.'

This is why writing takes such patience. I had that, and determination – a great stomach for the job. And why? Because my life depended on it. I had nothing else – no one to support me, encourage me, or pay my way; if I faltered, or failed, or if I took a year off, I was shafted.

For years I had been practicing the craft of writing, but what is the craft? It involves rumination, mimicry, joke-telling. It requires long periods of solitude – I have always managed to be happy alone. Many writers I have known talk to themselves. I have this mumbling habit; it has served me well not merely as a mnemonic device but as an imaginative rehearsal for writing – it is image-making of a serious kind – and I nearly always mutter as I write.

Nothing is truly forgotten – there is no forgetting – Freud said; there is only repression. In *Civilization and Its Discontents* he wrote how 'in mental life nothing which has been formed can perish . . . everything is somehow preserved, and in suitable circumstances (when for instance regression goes back far enough) it can once more be brought to light.'

All his life Freud was concerned with retrieving early memories. This preoccupation led him to develop theories of repression, and eventually to write his wonderful paper 'Creative Writers and Day-Dreaming.' A Freudian might explain my creativity in Africa as follows: when I had ceased to be affected by repression at home, and in the United States generally, and was living entirely on my own, unaffected by the scrutiny and the ambitions of my somewhat censorious parents, I was able to recapture in these suitable circumstances the early memories that gave me an impetus to be creative. Perhaps.

Writing in Africa gave me access to the past, it helped me cope with long periods of isolation in a foreign place, it made me reach specific conclusions about the people I was among – in a word, it enabled me to see Africa clearly. This plunge into my own memory inspired in me feelings of a oneness – with Africans and their landscape. Our lives in many respects were utterly different, but on closer examination I saw how much we had in common, and how these people shared many of my fears and hopes.

I am speaking of an early period in my writing life, but the most crucial one. I was in my early twenties. I had begun to deal with reality. It was no longer the literature of the Waste Land, the Theater of the Absurd, minimalist poetry, the barren and featureless narrative. I do not belittle them; I am simply saying they were no help to me. I may seem to criticize certain types of writing. No; only they are not my type. 'The house of fiction has many windows,' Henry James said.

From the vantage point of Africa, I was able to see that where I came from seemed to have merit and was a worthy subject. Africa, too, was an immediate subject – after all, hadn't Conrad and Hemingway written about it? Nevertheless, I arrogantly felt that these great writers had not done Africa justice. It irritated me that although *Tarzan of the Apes*, *Henderson the Rain King*, *The Unbearable Bassington*, and *Devil of a State* were partly or wholly set in Africa, neither Burroughs nor Bellow nor Saki nor Burgess had ever set foot on the continent.

Conrad and Hemingway had no such excuse, yet in their fiction they ignored Africans or else made them insubstantial figures in a landscape. Conrad could be terribly ponderous and vague; Hemingway, remote and rather privileged, was the sort of man who hadn't the slightest clue to the human activity – the politics and culture – in the country. He was a big-game hunter – the sort of rich and complacent *bwana mkuba* we saw in Land Rovers heading for the herds of kudu or the migrating wildebeest.

As a resident there, not a tourist, I had the settled belief that any slob could kill big game in Africa – they were big and they were everywhere; nothing was easier than bagging a zebra – there were herds of them; and an animal like the coveted (and now seriously endangered) bongo was the easiest of all – you just set dogs on this broad-horned antelope and when it was preoccupied with this pack of savage mutts you shot the poor creature in the heart (to preserve its head as a trophy). Hemingway's Swahili was notoriously bad and laughable. And as for Africans themselves – they are like a well-kept secret: no one had really written about them except sentimental settlers like Karen Blixen (who wrote from the point of view of a colonial memsahib). Doris Lessing came a bit closer in *The Grass is Singing* but even she seemed to be writing about an earlier period.

I was not writing particularly incisively, but I had started along the right road – a narrow and empty side road. I had a sense of being freer, of growing stronger, and my belief in myself had nothing to do with success or failure, but only with writing well. Of course, I wanted to be recognized – I wanted to be a hero – but that desire was not incompatible with the various fanciful roles I had chosen for myself, growing up: the traveler, the hunter, the explorer, the lion-tamer, the forest ranger, the scientist, the surgeon – they were all brilliantly solitary and somewhat heroic. I can honestly say – and it was a great help to me – that I had no driving ambition to be wealthy. If so, I am sure I would have given up writing and done something that was more immediately profitable. I knew many people who did just that.

'The opposite of play is not what is serious but what is real,' Freud writes in his paper 'Creative Writers and Day-Dreaming.' And he goes on to describe people's fantasies and their relationship of these day-dreams to the reality of their lives. 'We may lay it down that a happy person never fantasizes, only an unsatisfied one.' Time is of course a crucial factor, because of the relationship between memory and fantasy. The fantasy is linked to three 'moments of time' (not very different from the 'spots of time' to which Wordsworth alludes in *The Prelude*):

Mental work is linked to some current impression, some provoking occasion in the present which has been able to arouse one of the subject's major wishes. From there it harks back to the memory of an earlier experience (usually an infantile one) in which this wish was fulfilled; and now it creates a situation relating to the future which represents a fulfillment of the wish. What it thus creates is a day-dream or fantasy, which carries about it traces of its origin from the occasion which provoked it and from the memory. Thus past, present and future are strung together, as it were, on the thread of the wish that runs through them.

Normally, a day-dreamer conceals his fantasies, but if these fantasies should be revealed to us, Freud says, we would be repelled or unmoved by them. When the creative writer, on the other hand, discloses his fantasies we experience pleasure. 'How the writer accomplishes this is his innermost secret; the essential *ars poetica* lies in the technique of overcoming the feeling of repulsion in us which is undoubtedly connected with the barriers that rise between each single ego and the others' – that is, in artistic alteration, the writer softens and disguises his day-dreams; and with style or wit he gives us aesthetic pleasure. It is all in the telling, Freud says, which is true enough, and this 'enjoyment of an imaginative work proceeds from a liberation of tensions in our minds.' He goes on in a more interesting aside to say that 'not a little of this effect is due to the writer's enabling us [as satisfied and enlightened readers] thenceforward to enjoy our own day-dreams without self-reproach or shame.'

In a word, reading is liberation. We are vindicated in our dreams. The same is true of writing, since a dream is being fulfilled in its artistic recreation. And the dream has a complex time-frame – past, present, and future. Something in the present provokes an impression that rouses a wish that is linked to an earlier memory.

Being in Africa certainly liberated me, and I did remember a great deal that I had thought I'd forgotten. This access gave me a sense of conviction; it calmed me and in that reflective mood I was given greater access. I discovered, for example, that if I was very calm, at a point of resolution, I could write well. It might be truer to say that

I needed to be calm – my mind clear – in order to remember. My sense of freedom grew. The joy of writing made me more joyful, because at its best it has always demanded a mental journey and led me deeper into my unconscious mind. There is a paradox in this: the deeper I have gone into my own memory the more I have realized how much in common I have with other people. The greater the access I have had to my memory, to my mind and experience, searching among the paraphernalia in my crepuscular past, the more I have felt myself to be a part of the world.

The political dimension of this creative process was something that I had not expected. There was a dissatisfaction among Africans, a hankering for something better in their lives. That yearning, and that confusion, were familiar to me. They felt as I had growing up, and in many ways their condition, the way they had been patronized by colonial powers, recapitulated the condition of children in a large oppressive household. Imperialism is like a big unhappy family under the control of domineering parents. It was the way I had felt, growing up. This was a powerful stimulus to me; contemplating the conditions of Africans stimulated my own childhood memories – the frustrations, the longings, the fantasies. Consequently, in this atmosphere, writing about Africans, and recalling my own past, I could truly express myself.

The provocative occasion that Freud mentions as stimulating the memory and producing a creatively useful fantasy might also be the simple contemplation of an object, or chance association of music or an odor. A phrase of music stimulates the memory in Proust's *Jean Santeuil*, the famous memory-unlocking taste of the cookie in *Remembrance of Things Past*.

I developed internal ways of stimulating my memory. It is possible for a writer to think creatively only if he or she manages to inhabit a mood in which imagination can operate. My need for external stimuli inspired in me a desire to travel – and travel, which is nearly always seen as an attempt to escape from the ego, is in my opinion the opposite: nothing induces concentration or stimulates memory like an alien landscape or a foreign culture. It is simply not possible (as romantics think) to lose yourself in an exotic place; much more likely is an experience of intense nostalgia, a harking back to an earlier stage of your life. But this does not happen to the exclusion of the exotic present; in fact, what makes the whole experience thrilling is the juxtaposition of the present and the past, Medford dreamed in Mandalay.

It was a deliberate dream for me. In the dark, in distant places when I needed the consolation of memory – in Africa and Singapore – I used to calm myself and reflect on the past by mentally getting into my father's old Dodge and driving from home through Medford Square, up Forest Street, down to the Lawrence Estates, past the hospital where I was born, and then drive the long way home, around Spot Pond, taking in all the scenes of my early youth.

Who are the great travelers? They are curious, contented, self-sufficient people who are not afraid of the past. They are not hiding in travel; they are seeking. Recently I was on the northern Queensland coast of Australia, in an Aboriginal reserve. In the most unlikely spot I encountered a beachcomber, who had been living there for several years. He was looking for floats and bottles, building a raft that would take him around the top of Cape York in one of the most dangerous channels in the world for current and wind – the Torres Straits. I asked him if he knew the risks.

'I'm not bothered,' he said. 'You can go anywhere, you can do just about anything, if you're not in a hurry.'

That is one of the sanest statements I have ever heard in my life.

So many times over the years, in the most far-flung places, I have heard people exclaim, 'This reminds me of home' or 'This reminds me of' – and name a place where they have been very happy. It might be said that a great unstated reason for travel is to find places that exemplify where one has been happiest: looking for idealized versions of home – indeed, looking for the perfect memory.

Friends are also reminders of where we have been, what we have seen: they are a repository of our past, and friendship and love enable us to retrieve memory. The most human emotions and activities put us in touch with the past – which is another way of saying that neurosis frequently distances us and makes the past ungraspable. When Freud says that only the unsatisfied person has fantasies he is not saying that the more unhappy you are, the more access you have to memory; on the contrary, he states that if 'fantasies become over-luxuriant and over-powerful, the conditions are laid for the onset of neurosis or psychosis.'

You know how much friendship matters to memory when for whatever reason a friend leaves the orbit of your existence. Losing a friend to death or absence or misunderstanding is not only a blow to our self-esteem but a stun to memory. The sad reflection that we are losing a part of ourselves is true – part of our memory has departed with the lost friend.

One of the extremes of this is marital woe – separation and divorce. My wife and I separated in 1990 in London. The pain of that loss had many causes. It was an emotional trauma, but it was more – it was as though I had been lobotomized, part of my brain cut away. My wife had been a repository of our shared experience, and I could count on her to remind me of things I had forgotten. When she read something I had written she had a unique ability to judge it – she always knew, even when I didn't, when I was repeating myself, or being a bore. Her presence stimulated my memory, because her memory was an extension of my own; we had lived together and loved each other for more than twenty years.

It is easy for a writer to think, because of the solitary nature of the profession, that he or she is in this alone. But is that so? A writer cannot be the solitary figure in the waste land, the actor on the bare stage. 'Everything I have written has come out of a deep loneliness,' Henry James wrote – lonely, yes, but he was not alone, he could not have been and written as he had of such a complex world, so many landscapes, so many levels of society. The paradox is that the writer is involved both in society and in the world, and yet alienated from it. It is simply not possible to remove yourself from the society of people or the flow of events, yet the very things that stimulate writing are frequently obstacles to the writing process. Travel is a great stimulant, as I said; but it is hell to write while you are travel-ing.

I separated from my wife in London and quickly realized that I could not live in the city anymore. That very day I flew to the United States. I needed the comfort of my childhood home, I needed reassurance, the stimuli of those landscapes and sounds; the weather, the temperature, the odors. It was winter: frost, rattling branches, wood planks shrieking in the house, night skies, dead leaves.

I also needed the artifacts in that house, simple objects, such as pictures and knickknacks. My chair. My desk. My books. With these, I felt, I could begin again. Once, about six years ago in London, we were burgled. People have many responses to news of a burglary: you feel violated, they say; the thieves must be desperate, they say; they come from awful homes, they're on drugs, they need your stuff. You might have been killed, is another response.

Mine was none of these. I felt: they stole my memories – they removed a portion of my mind! The insurance people said: How much were these things worth? I told them truthfully: They were priceless. I would never look upon those objects again and remember. For this reason, for a period of time, I felt like the Ayatollah. I am not talking about a video recorder or a radio. I am speaking of a small silver box which had the camphor wood odor of Singapore, of the pen with the worn-down nib with which I wrote seven or eight books, of the amber necklace I bought with my last twenty dollars in Turkey. All of it gone, flogged to a fence somewhere in London. 'Sentimental value,' people said – yes, but to me there is no other value. If all we were talking about was money then these things could have been replaced and I would have had no problem. What was removed from me by these thieves were the stimuli for some of my dearest memories.

Freud, interestingly, was just such a magpie in the way he collected little objects – his house and his study were crammed with pots and statues and artifacts, most of them classical, Egyptian, Greek, and Roman. He never wrote about them, but there is no question but that these stimulated him, for his work is full of classical allusion and historical detail. In many ways it is a great pity that Freud's house was never burgled, because I would love to read his analysis of his own emotions as the victim of a theft of his treasured possessions.

I aspire, where material possessions are concerned, to the Buddhist condition of non-attachment. That is my ideal. I am not so acquisitive that I am possessed by these objects, though I do feel dependent upon them at times. I think one must practice ridding oneself of them, but that requires a concentration and great mental poise – I want to learn how to give them away; it must be my confident decision. I don't want them torn out of my hands. Obviously, the happiest person is that Buddhist who sees (truly) that such objects are illusion, and who owns nothing – all these possessions are in his or her memory.

The act of writing – artistic creation – dependent on memory, is itself a mnemonic device. And what is strangest of all is that drawing on memory, writing a novel – say – I am giving voice to one set of memories while creating a structure for remembering the circumstances of writing that book. Looking at almost anything I have written I can remember the room, the weather, my frame of mind, the state of the world, or whatever, while I was working on that piece of writing. For a reader or critic this can be deceptive. For example, it was in Dorset in the west of England that I described the hot cloudy tropics in *Saint Jack*, and in Charlottesville, Virginia, that I wrote about Dorset in *The Black House*. I look at *The Mosquito Coast* and see south London, I glance at *Jungle Lovers* and hear the cooing voice of the Chinese amah feeding my children in our Singapore house.

My books mean as much to me for what they are, for their narrative, as for those personal scenes and circumstances that they have the power to evoke. Often, the memory of writing the book overshadows the work itself. This is not an aspect of writing that has been explored or analyzed, and yet most novelists when asked to introduce a particular work reminisce at some point about the surroundings of their creation – the house, the family, the weather, the writing room. It is almost a conventional digression in any introduction. I think I can truthfully say that nearly everything I have written carries with it the circumstances of its creation. *Picture Palace* happened to be my twelfth work of fiction but the title might have served for any of them.

Such books are in the widest sense histories – of my world and myself. In spite of my conscientious work, they are probably full of inaccuracies, but they are as true as I could make them. I lost patience with the Waste-Landers and the purveyors of whimsy, the people who used language for its own sake, its own sound. 'It's like farting "Annie Laurie" through a keyhole,' as Gully Jimson says in *The Horse's Mouth*. 'It's clever, but is it worth the trouble?' The opposite of play, Freud said, is not seriousness but reality.

The political implications of this ought to be obvious. Having lived through the 1950s and 1960s, and having heard all the canting conservatives, I am well aware of our national tendency toward revisionism. If the 1960s was a time of disruption and unruliness by students and others, it was because they faced an almost overwhelming, and much more vocal, number of people who were saying, 'Bomb Peking . . . Bomb Hanoi . . . Mine Haiphong harbor . . . Give white South Africa a chance . . .' The Vietnam revisionists are legion and the issue has been flogged to death. But to take a recent example of revisionism, I was amused by the reception that Nelson Mandela was accorded when he was released after twenty-six years in a South African prison. I remember when he had received his life sentence – I copied his courtroom speech in his own defense into my notebook; I remember reading this eloquent affirmation of human rights to a friend, who dismissed it, actually laughed, saying, 'He's dreaming.' Every industrialized country continued to trade with South Africa, and the apartheid regime officially declared the Japanese white – and

Japan gladly accepted the reclassification in their eagerness to trade. Mandela's reputation grew because a few people clearly remembered him, and because Mandela had the good luck to survive – he was one of those South African prisoners who were not tortured to death. Mandela's greatest achievement was that he himself was loyal to his memory. Hitler said, 'Who remembers the Armenians?' – referring to their massacre by the Turks in 1911 – when he was challenged in his decision to exterminate the Jews. It was only recently that Americans remembered who the Palestinians are, when we were forcibly reminded by the intifada.

Memory can be a burden, and can seem a bore. In Sinclair Lewis's novel of the future *It Can't Happen Here* one of the hero's perorations about remembering sounds tedious to his listeners until America falls apart under a fascist dictatorship. Most Yankees who travel to the South are struck – I certainly have been – by the Southerner's memory for detail in a war the rest of us have mostly forgotten. Faulkner makes the point in *Absalom, Absalom!* – the Southerner lives in a state of constant remembrance of the past. This is generally true, though this lamentation for the old South does not always embrace the memory of slave-holding or the sort of apartheid, the Whites Only signs, that I saw myself on a visit to Virginia when I was ten. The Civil War was fought in the South, but I also think that the humiliation of defeat is more memorable than the euphoria of victory; and emphatically, the winners have the most authority when they publish their version of history.

That is why it is often better to look at the past, or at the reality around us, through the window of fiction. A nation's literature is a truer repository of thought and experience, or reality and time, than the fickle and forgettable words of politicians. Anyone who wishes to be strong needs only to remember. Memory is power. I said earlier that in choosing to be a writer I felt that I was on the right road – but a narrow and lonely one. I remember most of the way, and now I see that it has been the long road home.

The Object of Desire

I remember the hot day by the lake, and the half-finished summer house, its rough-cut timbers still holding the tang of the saw blade, and the wooden floor, and my friend's barefoot mother standing in her shorts and bra. I was so small I saw her long legs rising into her loose shorts. Damp wisps of hair framed her face, which was bright with a blush in the day's heat, and she was playing Hawaiian music on a flat guitar. Never mind the music. I was almost asthmatic with lust.

'I haven't played this for such a long time,' she said.

She was smiling. Her hands lowered to play the instrument left the cones of her bra exposed, and all her concentration was on her playing. She was a lovely woman and must have been in her early thirties, and although she had yellowy Latin skin her eyes were pale blue.

My mouth was gummed shut in panic and pleasure. I was nine or ten. I had returned to the house for something and saw her. There were just the two of us in the house, and I sensed that I was part of something that was somewhat illicit – my very desire was a proof of it.

My friend had a habit of complaining about his mother. Each time he did I thought, *You fool.*

In the pistol imagery I associate with desire I know the hammer was cocked on my libido that day. It was so sudden it left me breathless, and ever after whenever I have run across that sequence of imagery I am helpless.

How can I speak for all men? But it seems to me that many men fix on their object of desire at a place that is deep in the recesses of childhood, their libidos are coded at an early age. It is the childish aspect of lust that is for most men the hardest to admit or come to terms with. It is the childishness that all prostitutes and role-players know. Locate that imagery in a man's libido and he is yours.

*

Being away from home, at my friend's summer house, was all part of the thrill. Being away is almost in itself a thrill – liberating, freedom, different rules, away from the strictness of home. Is it any wonder I have spent forty years wandering?

But that experience of the strange, the unusual, the forbidden, had been inspired by other sensual episodes at home.

Another woman, an unmarried college friend of my mother's, used to visit two or three times a year. She was attractive, Irish, pale skin, dark hair, and very kind and attentive. She talked to my mother, and smoked and drank coffee, and then she left.

But not quite. Her cigarette butts, never more than three or four, remained in the ashtray; and there was smoke in the air – pleasantly pungent, and mingled with the odor of her perfume. All of this was unusual and arousing to me. No one smoked in my family, the perfume was distinct. And the keenest thrill of all was seeing the lipstick on the cigarettes, not a solid color, but the fine lines of her puckered lips imprinted in crimson on the paper, and sometimes on the rim of the coffee cup.

Lipstick, cigarette smoke, perfume, are all mingled in my mind as aphrodisiacs.

Like most men, I find myself staring at strange women, and the way they are dressed, and try to account for the fact that I am aroused. Growing up in the 1940s and 1950s, my experience of sexual subtlety and obliqueness was created by repression. Inevitably the woman who is the object of my desire is wearing a sort of slinky dress, with cleavage and high heels, an image of which Marilyn is the apotheosis: the 1950s. That is the era when I began creatively noticing women. The key was cut all those years ago, and though it is inevitably a bit nicked and blunted now from constant use, it still unlocks my libido.

The human sexual imagination may be circumscribed by the instinctive urge to create a master race, or insure the survival of the fittest, but it also is – intensely – about recovering the onset of sexuality, fixing upon a desirable image. It is about seeking joy. Most of all, it is the recognition of a love object.

Once in Hollywood I marveled at a particular actress's amplitudes – Thomas Hardy uses that nice word. 'It's all wire,' a producer friend said. I did not know that breasts could be plumped and supported with wire, like roses on a trellis arch. The eroticism is often contained in the secret of our not knowing; in our speculation. A dress is what it is; but it has other functions – what it hides, what it reveals. Nevertheless it is almost universally the case that a man looks at the woman's face first, and then what he can discern of her body through her clothes, and last of all, almost as an afterthought, looks at her clothes, except when they seem familiar and address (in a sweet voice) something in his past.

Men fix on their object of desire at a place that is deep in the recesses of childhood. I cannot speak for women, but most men's libidos are fixed at an early age. Speaking for myself, I can recall the first flicker of sexuality – the sense of something important happening in my body, a chemical reaction that was producing heat. It was that summer day at my friend's house in the country, by the lake, the sight of his mother in her white bra and shorts, barefoot.

We are the only animals which blush – or need to, Mark Twain said, in disparagement; but I think that remark is a tremendous compliment to the human imagination. Shame is a complex reaction, and what causes it is even more complicated. Far from being the only animals which blush, we are the only creatures to contrive a satisfying sexual act exclusively from toe sucking, sodomy, bondage, being a whipper or whippee of the object of desire. The intense non-tactile voyeuristic contemplation of another person is sexually fulfilling for some lovers.

Animals, much more predictable, are not only capable of sexually harassing each other, and of serious molestation, but they spend quite a bit of time doing it. Look at dogs and cats and pigeons; other creatures manifest tendencies toward grossness or exhibitionism – obvious examples are giraffes, who are habitually interested in each other's urine, and the ape female on all fours, flashing her humid glowing pudendum at the passing male. But these arousal activities are nearly always related to estrus and procreation.

At some time in human evolution we were programmed to produce offspring, but this is clearly not an instinctive priority for some people (few of whom obey cycles of 'heat'), who have turned such foreplay into an end in itself. That's unnatural, some people say. Of course it is! If all that people required to satisfy their libidos was foot fetishism or sodomy or coprophilia or spanking, the human race would expire. That does not make it wrong, except to many of the world's religions, which have a vested interest in keeping us living in an orderly animalistic fashion – pairing up, mating, nesting and rearing our young. It is rather funny but typical of the odd and unpredictable nature of humanity that religion itself with its insistence on taboos has frequently created desires where none existed. And the very fact that something is forbidden or deemed wicked has made it more pleasurable, especially for those of us who grew up in an atmosphere of repression. That such acts are unnatural is part of their appeal. Half the country breaks state laws in the bedroom. Obviously that is part of the fun in living in places like Alabama and Georgia.

Our behavior is determined to a great extent by the kind of responses we have learned, the libidinal trigger, which varies from person to person. It is not the same as the stimulus-response of an ape female habitually exhibiting her rump to a potential mate. This usually works on ape males, but the human response, easily desensitized, needing variation, would eventually be, There she goes again.

It is a fact of life that what is regarded as human perversity is our most specific humanity; what separates us from animals is our individual weirdness. 'Each of us is unique and special' is a common enough platitude, and is intended to acknowledge human individuality. Put another way, what makes us human is our capacity for deviant behavior. Please don't tell me to define 'deviant' – it means anything that prevents the human race from continuing, and can be as harmless as voyeurism, or an overindulgence in cheeseburgers, or as deadly as war or firing heroin into your foot. We are strange and unpredictable – that is what makes us unique, bless our twisted hearts; and deviation can give pleasure.

I am perhaps prejudiced in thinking that men are much stranger than women. Men, no matter which ones, invariably look at women and begin to solve the sexual equation, that goes something like this: *Is she displaying sexual interest, and if so, is it directed at me, and –* these facts having been established – *am I interested?*

Most of us men look at women and think: *Yes* or *Maybe* or *No.* Those are just questions as simple as blinking lights. Women know this, fashion designers know this, advertisers know this. The questions are not the determiners of the man's desire. One of the fundamental causes of crime in the world is that where women are concerned no is a sexual turn-on for men – a personal challenge. It perhaps originates as much in a dated female coquettishness as in male aggression. I am not making any judgment on this; perhaps I am old-fashioned in believing that a woman saying 'No' is the biggest turn-off in the world, and yes to me is an aphrodisiac. I have the weight of literature on my side, Molly Bloom at any rate:

yes when I put the rose in my hair like the Andalusian girls used or shall I wear a red yes and how he kissed me under the Moorish wall and I thought as well him as another and then I asked him with my eyes to ask again yes . . . and his heart was going like mad and yes I said yes I will Yes.

From the male point of view, the nature of women's fashion is all about indicating a general sexual mood, specifically a woman's willingness. (And when I say 'male point of view' I mean my point of view.) Unlike the ape exhibiting her parts to a passing male, there is no single gesture or act, nor any single item of clothing, that expresses willingness. There are conventional clothes – variations of underwear; and there are various forms of nakedness.

Evolution has ravaged the mechanism that causes the estrus cycle. In the absence of that (which makes animals sexual predators or pleaders) we are nearly always looking for a willing partner, not always to have sex with but for many other complex reasons, of which male acquisitiveness, ostentation, pride and vanity are just some. Willingness is the key – in ourselves, in the other. It is obvious that a woman who dresses up wants to be observed. Men, less subtle, more single-minded, cannot rid themselves of the notion that a woman who wants to be observed and desired also wants to be possessed.

Fashion itself – the enthusiasm for dressing up, no matter what clothes the woman is wearing – is a specific signal to a man. Women say to each other, *You look fabulous!* Men cannot say that without investing the exclamation in either coy or overt sexual innuendo, because men cannot separate fashion from sexual plumage. The *reductio ad absurdum* of this is the utter bluntness of the women in Orwell's novel *1984* who wear a red apron on the days they want to get laid. The majority of men would be delighted if instead of an expensive dress women simply wore a little button on their lapel that read *Yes*. In reality such a button exists, but it is not button-shaped, it is made of silk or lace, and it is called a dress.

Women's ambiguous not to say secondary role in the world has forced them to be artful, watchful, sometimes over-alert. Clothes are a classic example of this over-alertness, and appear to have a variety of motives: clothes might indicate attention-seeking eroticism, but they might also be plumage or uniforms, displays of beauty, wealth or power. Men, far less conscious, less deliberate, more confident and at the same time more conservative, are unimaginative slouches compared to women and find it hard to read them.

Men, who are fairly stupid when it comes to women's clothes, are seldom interested in fashion for its own sake. But sometimes a style catches on, nearly always erotic – slips, bras, slit skirts, fur, feathers, whatever – and men go weak at the knees.

Isn't it so that when women dress mainly to impress other women (who are in any case more knowledgeable than men in these matters), the men lose interest? Women's fashion (an easy target for a male satirist) is generally more oblique than women's makeup. And while most women can talk intelligently about men's fashion, it does seem to me that men are more conservative in their reactions and deal with their insecurity by being anonymous in fashion. Insecure women seem to do the opposite by studiously following trends that single them out and distinguish them. A woman's dressing in an outrageous way is a kind of extravagant dare, a bid for attention being a bid for power. That way of dressing, which is a way of life, is closed to men.

It goes almost without saying that women's fashion seizes a man's attention when it is motivated by eroticism. Because sexuality whips up the blood and vibrates so near to the surface in so many man–woman encounters, it is impossible for a man to consider what a woman is wearing without at the same time wondering what is underneath. This is not necessarily the imagining of a naked body, but perhaps whatever lies next to her skin. Men of a certain age were stimulated by female sexual images before they became aware of the struts and buttresses and technical underpinnings.

Fashion that is utterly new and unfamiliar, that does not echo an image from a man's sexually impressionable period, is doomed to failure from the man's point of view. For some men the image is sufficient to provide sexual fulfillment. This is also the reason men are more fetishistic than women. One of the more pathetic generalizations you can make about men is that some of them are perfectly happy nuzzling a woman's shoe. In fetishism the donut is mistaken for the hole. That women are rarely fetishists is yet another difference between the sexes and the manner in which their libidos are awakened.

The object of desire is the Rosebud we carry within our imagination. In each man there is a variant image, or some set of associations comparable to the lipstick-smudged and perfumed cigarette, or the barefoot woman in her bra standing in total concentration; the image needs to be answered in the present. It is exquisite in its tiny way, and overwhelmingly significant.

At the Sharp End:
Being in the Peace Corps

My record was so bad (they sent the FBI to check up on you then) that I was first rejected by the Peace Corps as a poor risk and possible troublemaker, and was only accepted as a volunteer after a great deal of explaining and arguing. The alternative was Vietnam – this was 1963, and President Kennedy was still muddling dangerously along. I was sent to Nyasaland; soon it became Malawi. And then a month before my two-year stint was over I was 'terminated' – kicked out – fined arbitrarily for three months' 'unsatisfactory service,' and given hell by the Peace Corps officials in Washington. Of course they believed the truth – that I had been framed in an assassination plot against Dr. Hastings Banda, the President-for-Life ('Messiah,' 'Conqueror,' and 'Great Lion' were some of his lesser titles). But the case against me looked bad. I was debriefed. There was Central Africa to Washington airfare deducted from my earnings and I ended up with 200 dollars. Out I went – it was now 1965. I still had the draft to contend with.

It was a mess, and for a long while afterwards I hated the Peace Corps and laughed at their pious advertising campaign, 'The toughest job you'll ever love.' Ha! I hated the bureaucracy, the silliness, the patronizing attitudes, the jargon, the sanctimony. I remembered all the official freeloaders who came out from Washington on so-called inspection tours, and how they tried to ingratiate themselves. 'You're doing wonderful work here . . . It's a great little country,' they said; but for most of them it was merely an African safari. They hadn't the slightest idea of what we were doing, and our revenge was to take them on long bumpy rides through the bush. 'Sensational,' they said. They went away. We stayed. Most Peace Corps volunteers know that feeling: the smug visitor leaving in the Jeep and the dust flying up; and then the dust drifting slowly down and the silence taking hold.

On the subject of Vietnam these Peace Corps bureaucrats were surprisingly hawkish and belligerent. Most of them, including the reps, believed Vietnam to be a necessary war. The volunteers were divided. This was an important issue to me, because I had joined the Peace Corps specifically to avoid being drafted, and I was dismayed to find so many Peace Corps officials advocating the bombing of Hanoi or the mining of Haiphong harbor. As a meddlesome and contentious twenty-two-year-old I made a point of asking everyone his views on Vietnam. I believed the war was monstrous from the very beginning and I have not changed my views. What astonishes me today is how few people remember the ridiculous things they said about Vietnam in the 1960s.

But we are a country of revisionists, and the chief quality of the revisionist is a bad memory. No one now remembers how confused Kennedy's Vietnam policy was or how isolated the student movement was. I had been involved in student protests from 1959 until 1963 – first against the Reserve Officers Training Corps, then against nuclear testing, and then against our involvement in Vietnam. How could I have been inspired by Kennedy to join the Peace Corps? I had spent years picketing the White House – and in doing so had made myself very unpopular. When I applied to join the Peace Corps this career as an agitator was held against me. It was all a diabolical plot, I felt. And there was the president with such style – money, power, glamour. He even had culture! And I didn't know the half of it, for somewhere Marilyn Monroe was dialing his number and somewhere else a Mafia moll was painting her nails in expectation of the president's visit. I had to fight my feeling of distrust and alienation in order to join. There were many like me – anti-authoritarian, hating the dazzle and the equivocation. And when the news broke that the president was shot, halfway through a lecture in Peace Corps training – something about land tenure in the Nyasaland Protectorate – we were all properly put in our place. More revisionism, more guilt, and I thought, *Get me out of here*.

Nyasaland – soon to become the independent republic of Malawi – was the perfect country for a Peace Corps Volunteer. It was both friendly and destitute; it was small and out of the way. It had all of Africa's problems – poverty, ignorance, and disease. It had only a handful of university graduates. It had lepers, it had Mistah Kurtzes, it had Horatio Alger stories by the score. It had a fascinating history that was bound up not only with early African exploration – Livingstone himself – but also one of the first African rebellions, Chilembwe's uprising. It was the setting for Laurens van der Post's *Venture to the Interior*. The people were generous and extremely willing, and as they had not been persecuted or bullied, and had been ignored rather than exploited, they were not prickly and color-conscious like the Kenyans and Zambians. There was a pleasant atmosphere of hope in the country – very little cynicism and plenty of goodwill. The prevailing feeling was that the education we were providing would lead to prosperity, honest government, and good health.

An added thrill was that many British settlers were still in residence. Some of these were old-timers – 'wog-bashers,' as they sometimes called themselves – who remembered the place when it was even wilder and more wooded. They had little contact with Africans – the place had never been a colony in the strict sense, only a backwater – and they resented us. Most of us hated them and mocked them, and we had a special loathing for the few PCVs who began moving in settler society. These pompous little creeps – so we said – went to gymkhanas and cocktail parties at the local club and dated the settler children when they returned from their Rhodesian boarding schools. We saw them as social climbers and traitors, and feelings were very strong on the same issue. It was not uncommon for a Peace Corps Volunteer in town for supplies to approach a group of settlers in a bar and say something crudely provocative such as, 'The Queen's a whore' (her portrait always hung over the bottles), and nearly always a fight would start. To Africans these antagonisms were very exciting.

We had arrived in the country speaking Chinyanja fairly well, and we had plunged in – made friends, taught school, run literacy programs, coached sports, and generally made ourselves useful. We were, as the English say, 'at the sharp end' – on our own, and exposed, and doing the toughest jobs. The Africans were eager. Afterwards it occurred to me that over the years of British rule the Africans had become extremely lonely and curious – always seeing whites at a distance and wondering what the hell they were like. The Peace Corps Volunteers were the first foreigners to offer them a drink. They were amazed that we were interested in them, and they repaid our interest with hospitality.

In addition to my teaching I collaborated with a man at the Ministry of Education on writing two English textbooks to replace the miserable ones that had been standard (but they had been written for schools in Ghana many years before). Foundation Secondary English, Book

One and Book Two, is still being used in Malawi twenty years after it appeared, and I am still receiving royalties on it.

We were pestered by Israeli soldiers who had been taken on to train our students to become single-minded cadets in a goon-squad, but apart from them the school ran well. I planted trees and we put a road through. I was proud of the place; I liked my students, I enjoyed working with my colleagues. And the country affected me as no other country has, before or since. I felt I belonged there, I was happy, I was committed. I was having a good time as well as doing something worthwhile – what could have been better?

Now and then I remembered that I was in the Peace Corps. That gave me an odd feeling. I disliked the idea that I was with an outfit, and I rejected the suggestion that I was an American official working abroad. I had never been easy with the concept of the Peace Corps as an example to spineless Marxists, and the implications of fresh-faced youngsters wooing Third Worlders away from communism. I was well aware that American officialdom used us to deflect criticism of Vietnam and more robust and spread-eagled diplomacy.

I wanted the Peace Corps to be something very vague and unorganized, and to a large extent it was. It did not run smoothly. The consequence was that we were left alone. I was glad to be able to call my soul my own. The Peace Corps was proprietorial only when it suited them and, generally speaking, they took an interest in volunteers only when an official visitor arrived in the country. Then we were visited, or invited to parties. 'You're doing wonderful work . . . They're saying great things about you.' But I didn't want attention. I didn't want help. I wanted to be self-sufficient. Anyway, most of our jobs were too simple to require any back-up, and we seldom wrote reports.

We were not trusted by the embassy personnel or the State Department hacks – all those whispering middle-aged aunties who couldn't speak the language. We felt embassy people were overpaid and ignorant, always being fussed over by spoiled African servants. We were, we felt, independent spirits – English teachers, health workers, answerable only to our students and patients. I regarded the Peace Corps as a sort of sponsoring organization and myself as an individual who had only the most tenuous link with it.

I had met many Peace Corps officials, and it seemed that the higher you went in the Peace Corps the less you knew, the less you accomplished. The officials were ambitious and political and it often seemed to me that they hardly knew us and had little idea of what we were doing in the country. I think I am typical in believing that the Peace Corps trained us brilliantly and then did little more except send us into the bush. It was not a bad way of running things. After all, we were supposed to use our initiative. And I think we were never more effective as volunteers than when we were convinced that we were operating alone, at the sharp end, putting our own ideas into practice, far away from the bureaucrats.

Because we were on our own, the Peace Corps officials regarded our situation as delicate. The Peace Corps did not want us to be too visible, too friendly, or too involved. Keep a low profile, was the advice we were always offered; I did not follow it and so eventually I got the boot. I was insulted when I was sent out of the country. It seemed like the act of an absent parent, someone I hardly knew asserting his authority over me.

That is why I do not associate my years in the Peace Corps with group photographs, and horse-play, and heart-to-heart talks with the rep, and images of President Kennedy showing me the way, and soft-ball games with the other volunteers, and the sort of hands-across-the-sea camaraderie that you see on the posters. It was not 'the dream – the vision.' It was much more interesting.

It was to me most of all the reality of being very far from home and yet feeling completely at home in this distant place. It was a slight sense of danger, the smell of wood smoke – blue-gums burning; hearing the Beatles for the first time in a bar in the town of Limbe. In the States there was a sort of revolution in progress, but it had started partly as a result of the first Peace Corps group that had gone to Nepal. Those volunteers returning from Kathmandu had blazed the hippie trail.

In Malawi we had all of that, too – good people, wilderness, music, ganja, dusty roads, hard-working students, and a feeling of liberation. Things were on the move, it seemed. In Malawi I saw my first hyena, smoked my first hashish, witnessed my first murder, caught my first dose of gonorrhea. One of my neighbors, an African teacher, had two wives. My gardener had a gardener. Another neighbor and friend was Sir Martin Roseveare, who liked the bush. He was principal at the nearby teachers' college and he died only in 1985, in Malawi, at the age of eighty-six. (He was knighted in 1946 for designing the foolproof and fraud-proof ration book.) With two servants I moved into an African township, where I lived in a semi-slum, a two-room hut – cold water, cracks in the wall, tin roof, music blasting all day from the other huts; shrieks, dogs, chickens. It was just the thing. The experience greatly shaped my life.

When I think about those years, I don't think much about the Peace Corps, though Malawi is always on my mind. I do not believe that Africa is a very different place for having played host to the Peace Corps – in fact, Africa is in a much worse state than it was twenty years ago. But America is quite a different place for having had so many returned Peace Corps Volunteers, and when they began joining the State Department and working in the embassies, these institutions were the better for it, and had a better-informed and less truculent tone. The experience was an enlightening one for most volunteers. I still do not understand who was running the show, or what they did, or even what the Peace Corps actually was, apart from an enlightened excuse for sending us to poor countries. Those countries are still poor. We were the ones who were enriched, and sometimes I think that we reminded those people – as if they needed such a thing – that they were left out. We stayed awhile, and then we left them. And yet I think I would do it again. At an uncertain time in my life I joined. And up to a point – they gave me a lot of rope – the Peace Corps allowed me to be myself. I realized that it was much better to be neglected than manipulated, and I had learned that you make your own life.

Five Travel Epiphanies

I was in Palermo and had spent the last of my money on a ticket to New York aboard the ship the *Queen Frederica*. This was in September, 1963; I was going into Peace Corps training for Africa. The farewell party my Italian friends gave me on the night of departure went on so long that when we got to the port a Sicilian band was playing 'Anchors Aweigh' and the *Queen Frederica* had just left the quayside. In that moment I lost all my vitality.

My friends bought me an air ticket to Naples, so that I could catch the ship there the next day. Just before I boarded the plane an airline official said I had not paid my departure tax. I told him I had no money. A man behind me in a brown suit and a brown Borsalino said, 'Here, you need some money?' and handed me twenty dollars.

That solved the problem. I said, 'I'd like to pay you back.'

The man shrugged. He said, 'I'll probably see you again. The world's a small place.'

     * * *

For three days in August, 1970, I had been on a small cargo vessel the *M.V. Keningau*, which sailed from Singapore to North Borneo. I was going there to climb Mount Kinabalu. While aboard, I read and played cards, always the same game, with a Malay planter and a Eurasian woman who was traveling with her two children. This ship had an open steerage deck, where about 100 passengers slept in hammocks.

It was the monsoon season. I cursed the rain, the heat, the ridiculous card games. One day, the Malay said, 'The wife of one my men had a baby last night.' He explained that his rubber tappers were in steerage and that some had wives.

I said I wanted to see the baby. He took me below, and seeing that newborn, and the mother and father so radiant with pride, transformed the trip. Because the baby had been born on the ship

34

everything was changed for me and had a different meaning: the rain, the heat, the other people, even the card games and the book I was reading.

* * *

The coast of Wales around St. David's Head has very swift currents and sudden fogs. Four of us were paddling sea kayaks out to Ramsey Island. On our return to shore we found ourselves in fog so dense we could not see land. We were spun around by eddies and whirlpools.

'Where's north?' I asked the man who had the compass.

'Over there,' he said, tapping it. Then he smacked it and said, 'There,' and hit it harder and said, 'I don't know, this thing's broken.'

Darkness was falling, the April day was cold, we were tired, we could not see anything except the cold black chop of St. George's Channel.

'Listen,' someone said. 'I think I hear Horse Rock.' The current rushing against Horse Rock was a distinct sound. But he was wrong – it was the wind.

We kept together. Fear slowed my movements, and I felt quite sure that we had no hope of getting back tonight – perhaps ever. The cold and my fatigue were like premonitions of death. We went on paddling. A long time passed. We searched; no one spoke. This is what dying is like, I thought.

I strained my eyes to see and had a vision, a glimpse of cloud high up that was like a headland; and when I looked harder, willing it to be land, it blackened. It was a great dark rock. I yelped and we made for shore, as though reborn.

* * *

We were driving in western Kenya, under the high African sky, my wife beside me, our two boys in the back seat. Years before, not far from here, I had met this pretty English woman and married her. Our elder son had been born in Kampala, the younger one in Singapore. We were driving toward Eldoret. Sixteen years ago, as a soon-to-be-married couple, we had spent a night there.

The boys were idly quarreling and fooling – laughing, distracting me. My wife was saying, 'Are you sure this is the right road?' She had been traveling for three months alone in southern Africa. We were in an old rental car. Cattle dotted the hills, sheltering under the thorn trees. We were just a family on a trip, far away.

But we were traveling towards Eldoret, into the past; and deeper in Africa, into the future. We were together, the sun slanting into our eyes, everything on earth was green, and I thought, *I never want this trip to end*.

* * *

Just before Independence Day in 1964, when Nyasaland became Malawi, the Minister of Education, Masauko Chipembere, planted a tree at the school where I was teaching in the south of the country. Soon after this, he conspired to depose the Prime Minister, Dr. Hastings Banda. But Chipembere was driven out of the country.

As time passed I often thought of the little tree he had shoveled into the ground. When Chipembere died in Los Angeles ('in exile' as a CIA pensioner) I thought of the tree.

Twenty-five years after I left the school I traveled back to Malawi. Two things struck me about the country. Most of the trees had been cut down – for fuel. And no one rode bicycles anymore. Most buildings were decrepit, too. Dr. Banda was still in power.

It took me a week to get to my old school. It was larger but it was ruinous, with broken windows and splintered desks. The students seemed unpleasant. The headmaster was rude to me. The library had no books. The tree was big and green, almost forty feet high.

Travel Writing:
The Point of It

I used to have some sympathy with the bewildered browser in a bookstore who, seeing the stacks of travel books, asked, 'What are they for?' Until recently I felt that was a fair question. The travel book had always seemed to me a somewhat insufficient form. Why write about that country? What's the occasion? What's the point? So often such journeys appeared little more than excuses for authors in search of material – rather suspicious outings, I always thought.

Travel books are hardly a form at all. They come in every shape and size, ranging from bloodlessly factual guides (*Discovering Turkey*) through stunt and ordeal books (*Skiing Down Everest*, *Survive! 116 Days in a Rubber Dinghy*) and what I think of as the human-sacrifice ones, to the highly imaginative works of someone like the late Bruce Chatwin, who was never quite sure whether he was writing travel books or novels. Not that he cared much – the question nearly always produced his loudest and most desperate laugh, as though he was being tickled in the ribs by a complete stranger.

An unlikely source, Nabokov's novel *Laughter in the Dark*, contains a passage that amply illustrates a justification for this sort of travel writing. One of the characters says:

'A writer for instance talks about India which I have seen, and gushes about dancing girls, tiger hunts, fakirs, betel nuts, serpents: the Glamour of the Mysterious East. But what does it amount to? Nothing. Instead of visualizing India I merely get a bad toothache from all these Eastern delights. Now, there's the other way, as for instance, the fellow who writes: "Before turning in I put out my wet boots to dry and in the morning I found that a thick blue forest had grown on them ('Fungi, Madam,' he explained) . . ." and at once India becomes alive for me. The rest is shop.'

In six long travel books and an assortment of shorter ones I have been, figuratively speaking, putting my wet boots out to dry and describing what the morning brings. I've taken people as I've found them. When I described Iran in 1974 as backward, unreliable, dusty, and fundamentalist – a wilderness of mud houses and scrimmaging mullahs – I was set upon in New York by a shrieking woman named Mrs. Javitz, who ran the Shah's publicity machine in the United States. She had persuaded herself, but she was unable to persuade me, that Iran was a showcase of Western democracy and modernity. The passage of time has revealed an Iran – bloodstained, and ringing with the cries of vindictive clergymen – that I more easily recognize.

Events ought to prove the worth of the travel book. V. S. Pritchett's *The Spanish Temper*, written in 1955, is both topographical and psychological. Reading it, you are prepared for anything, the death of Franco, the reinstatement of the King, the rise of the Social Democrats, or whatever. V. S. Naipaul's analysis of Hindu caste in *An Area of Darkness*, Henri Fauconnier's anecdotal sociology of planters in *The Soul of Malaya*, or the Mexican anticlericalism recorded by Graham Greene in *The Lawless Roads*, all these say something that makes the immediate future of the particular country coherent. The books are also, incidentally, the adventures of individuals. Ella Maillart's *Forbidden Journey* is exactly the same trip as Peter Fleming's in *News From Tartary*, since they were traveling companions. But the books read like different trips, as anyone who compares them will see. (Hers is clear-sighted and down to earth; his is often facetious.) The same thing goes for Greene's *Journey Without Maps* and his cousin Barbara Greene's *Land Benighted* – two versions of one traipse through Liberia.

Until recently I was happy enough to regard the travel book as an unclassifiable artifact – like the distant journey. Then the events in Tiananmen Square unfolded, and now, in the aftermath, I have started to reassess the genre. I think that any travel book about China written in the last few years ought to have prepared us for those events – maybe even prefigured them. I have always felt that the truth is prophetic, and that if you describe precisely what you see and give it life with your imagination, then what you write ought to have lasting value, no matter what the mood of your prose.

'Cantankerous' is the lazy reviewer's word for my handling of this complex process. 'Mr. Theroux didn't like [the Chinese people] much,' a *New York Times* reviewer observed about my China book, *Riding the Iron Rooster*. 'Grouchy Traveler Back on the Rails Again,' one headline ran, and another, 'Theroux Grumpy in New China Travel

Book.' There were several more, and they are still fresh in my mind (though I must say that sales of half a million books have the effect of neutralizing even the most ill-natured and silly review). The thrust of many of these reviews was that I was a sour and impatient intruder in a socialist paradise, and that I had an irritating and impolite habit of bringing up unwelcome subjects while interrogating the Chinese with a kind of unreasonable gusto.

In the book I gave an account of how, in an anti-crime campaign, the Chinese government had executed 10,000 people, not, I pointed out, during the Ming dynasty, but between 1983 and 1986, when tourists were sailing down the Yangtze and skipping around the Forbidden City and remarking on how 'Westernized' the Chinese were. This enthusiasm for shooting hastily convicted criminals in the back of the neck, I went on, was supported by the bridge-playing, lovable little Deng Xiaoping, an energetic hangman who clings to the Chinese belief in 'killing a chicken to scare the monkeys.' During a pep talk to the five-man standing committee of the Politburo, I continued, Mr. Deng summed up his attitude by saying, 'As a matter of fact, execution is the one indispensable means of education.'

The victims of such instruction might be murderers; but they might also be pimps, arsonists, prostitutes, gamblers, procurers, rapists, white collar criminals, thieves, muggers, or members of Chinese secret societies. In other words, disrupters of life. The Chinese (I said in many places) have a horror of *luan* – chaos. A suitable candidate for capital punishment is anyone who goes against the grain. The people who engage in such activities are regarded by Politburo – indeed by chain-smoking, 'Westernized' Mr. Deng – as hippie scum, whose only cure is a bullet in the neck.

Every railway station in China (I passed through hundreds of them in every province and region) displayed portraits of executed people: there they were on the wall, the haggard faces of the condemned persons, looking doomed. A red 'X' over the face meant the individual had been dispatched. I was told that many were students, and that roughly 3,000 malefactors a year were executed.

I decided in my book to keep away from the Forbidden City, to give short shrift to the Great Wall and to talk to the Chinese – to the working people, officials, and students. The working people complained about inflation, the officials complained about students, and the students said reforms were not happening quickly enough. 'There will be more demonstrations,' one student told me, referring to student demonstrations in six Chinese cities, including Beijing and Shanghai, that had taken place only weeks before. 'Many more.' This was in early 1987.

Meanwhile, American television was filming the grand opening of the Kentucky Fried Chicken outlet at Tiananmen Square, and the fashion shows, the Japanese cars, the terracotta warriors, the mass-produced back-scratchers, the arrival of American business executives, the bowling alleys in Canton, and so forth. What else could they do? Television cannot film corruption. Television cannot spend five days on a rattling railway train, talking endlessly. Television needs excitement, it needs an angle, it needs a 'soundbite.' So television did not prepare us for the massacre of the students in Tiananmen Square.

Nor did the American businessmen, junketing politicians, accountants, lawyers, or bankers. They were making deals, not trying to capture a mood. The poor jet-lagged tourists couldn't do much either: they were being hauled from one repainted monument to another, and told that this Disneylandish-looking place was an ancient tomb or temple.

I believe I have a sunny disposition and am not naturally a grouch. It takes a lot of optimism, after all, to be a traveler. But a travel writer must report faithfully on what he or she encounters in a country, and *Riding the Iron Rooster* is full of the voices and complaints of Chinese students, who seemed to me very similar in outlook and alienation to American students of the 1960s, of whom I was one: impatient for change. I also faithfully reported official cant, the fall of Hu Yaobang, the rise of Zhao Ziyang, the dismissal of Fang Lizhi (who, confined to the American embassy in Beijing, is looking more and more like Jozsef Cardinal Mindszenty, the Hungarian prelate who spent fifteen years in the American Embassy in Hungary). In China, I felt I was seeing one paradox after another. To understand the country, you need to write about more than its pseudo-spiritualism or its clumsily reconstructed temples. Nor is it a question of liking or disliking the Chinese. The job of the travel writer is to go far and wide, to make voluminous notes, to tell the truth. There is immense drudgery in the job. But the book ought to live and, if it is truthful, it ought to be prescient without making predictions.

I had been seriously wondering what use the travel book has. And then, with the events in Tiananmen Square, I saw that it performs a unique function. A book has the capacity to express a country's heart

– as long as it stays away from vacations, holidays, sightseeing and the half-truths in official handouts; as long as it concentrates on people in their landscape, and its dissonance as well as the melodies, the contradictions, and the vivid trivia – the fungi on the wet boots.

Part Two

Fresh-Air Fiend

Fresh-Air Fiend

Normal, happy, well-balanced individuals seldom become imaginative writers, and generally, writers tend to be notoriously unhealthy. There are reasons for this, the most compelling of which are that a writer works alone, indoors, in a room, on a chair, with the door shut. Any young person who wonders what his or her chances are of becoming a writer ought to assess their ability to deal with solitude and, figuratively speaking, an entire working life thrashing around in inspissated darkness.

The writer is odd from day one and in the course of pursuing this maddening profession becomes distinctly odder. There are not many exceptions. Only unfunny non-writers were surprised when Art Buchwald announced a few years ago that he had been treated many times for depression, or that William Styron wrote in *Darkness Visible* of being suicidal. It is a commonplace to say that creative people tend to be irrational, or manic-depressive, or hard to get along with. It is not unusual for a successful writer – your favorite, the one you think of as full of sunshine, wisdom and laughter – to spend great portions of his or her life in a state of fury, hideously disappointed, or even raving mad.

The loneliness of the long-distance writer concerns me, because writing a large book is a daunting task, requiring time, silence, and space. It is a condition summed up in the image of a two-pound chicken trying to lay a three-pound egg. It can be very irritating when writers are told how they might manage their lives better ('You should get yourself a computer!'). The more imaginative and ambitious the writer, the greater his or her solitude – and, you might say, the greater the likelihood for the person's being eccentric.

You might deduce from the foregoing that writing is my hopeless passion. Perhaps it is, but it is not occasional, nor is it work in any conventional sense; it has no limits, it is simply my life.

I feel a need to emphasize the seriousness of the writer's dilemma, because of the radical nature of my solution. I am not dealing with the fanaticism of the literary passion, but the problems it poses – the way it may consume a person or wreak havoc on their health. I take writing for granted as a fact of life, so I am more interested in the opposite of writing, which is a counter-life and a consolation and also a passion.

I have always lived near the water, and for forty-five years – since I learned to row a small boat at the age of ten – I have found refuge in the bosom of small boats. Scarcely realizing why, I took my frustration outdoors and gave it an airing. When I was eleven at Scout camp, I learned to paddle a canoe. At my school, team sports were the thing, and strong talented players were chosen over weak inexperienced ones like me. I did not mind being rejected. I knew that the school, like most American schools, hated losing teams. It would have been a humiliation to be regarded as having helped the school lose; nor was any school inclined to teach me the fine points of the game – any game. As a result I lost interest in all ball playing; never played, never went to games, still don't.

The sense of liberation that I felt on the water, alone in a boat, was comparable to the freedom I had felt expressing myself in writing. Navigating on a trip in a small boat is like a reenactment in the open air of being a writer. 'The Open Boat,' Stephen Crane's short story, is only superficially about seamanship; there is hardly a boat trip or ship journey in literature that is not also a metaphor for the active life. On lakes and rivers in Africa, in sampans and sailboats for three years in Singapore, and seventeen years of boating in Britain – on the Thames, along the coast, on the elongated lochs of Scotland – I felt I had found a way of freeing myself from the intensity of writing, and the sense of suffocation of being confined indoors. I never owned an engine or outboard motor: my interest is in non-polluting self-propulsion, not speed; in sailing, rowing, paddling.

The passion became stronger as I grew older, more aware of my health and, especially, more conscious of a growing inwardness. Being outside, away from my desk, I found inspiring, and some of my best ideas have come to me in the most unliterary circumstances – offshore, in the invigorating trance that the aerobic exercise of rowing continuously can induce.

I had always spent summers on Cape Cod, even when I was resident in England. I kept a rowboat and a small sailboat on the Cape, for my own benefit, and so that I could teach my children how to use them as well. Such skills, I felt, would stand them in better stead than chucking a ball or swinging a bat or risking brain damage by tackling a muddy oaf. I don't despise such sports. I merely feel they have limited use as a person grows older, and I know that men and women can row and paddle and sail well into their eighties.

The solitariness of boating is not a disadvantage; for a writer it is almost essential to pursue a solitary passion in the open air. Long ago I accepted the absence of congeniality in a writing life. Small boats I found to be perfect companions, and the longer I played about in them the more possibilities I began to discern. The Thames, as rowers and sailors know best, is tidal as far as the first lock, at Richmond. That makes it more challenging, even treacherous, but you can turn the tidal flow to your advantage and, with good timing, it is possible to coast home on an outgoing tide.

Rowing on a sliding seat is wonderful water-beetle exercise, and after I had done it in London using borrowed boats (I was a member of the Thames Rowing Club) I took a major step in 1982 and had a sixteen-foot wooden rowing skiff custom-made for me by Lowell's boat shop in Amesbury, Massachusetts. This boat can be rowed using a fixed thwart, or a sliding seat; or – equipping it with a dagger board and a rudder and a sprit-sail – it can also be sailed. I named the boat *Goldeneye* (after a seasonal duck). The year it was delivered to me I rowed it around the whole coast of Cape Cod and to Martha's Vineyard, as a sort of maiden voyage.

I wrote about that trip, but the trip was the thing not the essay, which I called 'Sunrise with Seamonsters' after a sunny Turner painting of a madly littered seascape. I sought small boats for the exercise and the experience, not in search of material. I regarded the effort – and still do – as a rest for my imagination, and a way of undoing the frowstiness and creeping rigidity of spending hours at a desk. Of course, many people are stuck at a desk – I know that, I am not gloating. I am merely describing one man's escape, which is passionate in the classical sense, like the impulse of a person who vanishes from home or work to a secret and revitalizing assignation with a lover.

After a while messing about in small boats ceased to become a sport or a recreation. It was a physical necessity, and when winter came and my boats were dry-docked or garaged for the winter I got restive. A rowing machine may keep you in shape, but exercise had been only one of my objectives. I needed air and space and light, and the challenges of wind and open water. I had not minded being suddenly fog-bound and having to use my compass. My best trip ever had been from the Cape to Nantucket, way beyond the horizon, setting off south-east into the blue water of Nantucket Sound using dead reckoning – a chart, a compass, and vectoring on the incoming tide by my estimated speed. Nothing on this earth can compare in unearthly intensity with the experience of being alone in a small boat with 360 degrees of watery horizon around you. Yet there are months of the year on Cape Cod and in Britain when no sane person ventures out in a small boat. Even the harbors are empty. The ferries and fishing boats come and go, but a New England winter is simply too cold for the rowing or sailing of a small boat.

The sea in winter is unforgiving – much worse than any wilderness of snow-laden trees, more merciless than a mountainside, harsher than any desert. If you go down in cold water and lose your boat you are doomed as soon as your core temperature drops, and it drops in minutes in a winter sea.

It was during a period of winter withdrawal in 1984, returning from a skiing trip, that I stopped at a sporting goods store and saw a kayak hanging from the ceiling. The boat seemed reasonably priced. I bought it on the spot, with paddles and a life jacket. A few days later, on a cold Cape afternoon, I paddled it down Scorton Creek to its mouth and then into the sea. The boat was much more stable than I had imagined, and I marveled at how it easily tracked through a heavy chop. Most of all, in this enclosed banana-shaped craft, I was warm.

From that day onward, I realized that, sea-kayaking, I could go boating all year round, in almost any weather, even on the coldest day. The paddling muscles are the same upper-body ones you use in cross-country skiing, so I was prepared for the physical effort. I worked on learning to paddle in heavy seas, on landing in surf, and I studied safety – self-rescue in a kayak is essential. The so-called Eskimo roll is only one of many methods of righting a kayak. A paddler who does not have a rescue plan has no business venturing out in a small boat. A detail in winter boating can mean the difference between life and death.

Kayaks look pretty much the same, yet every one is different, not only in speed and weight but in handling. In a rowboat these would be almost unnoticeable nuances, but since a kayak is something you sit in the differences are significant. The kayak is attached to the paddler, who is snug in it, filling the seat, feet jammed against the footrests, waterproofed further by a spray-deck which encloses the paddler in the cockpit as tightly as a drum-head. The Inuit were sewn into their kayaks, and there they stayed for seal hunting trips of several days and nights. For that period they were warm, leak-proof, and unsinkable.

Traveling in various countries in Africa and Asia, I realized how much I was missing by not having a boat. I had no way of going down a river, or seeing a coastline; small boats were never readily available. On my second visit to China in 1986 I saw how much better off I would have been if I had had a boat in my luggage.

This is not a crack-pot idea. There are many companies that make collapsible or folding kayaks. The two best are the German 'Klepper' and the Canadian 'Feathercraft.' These boats come in bags that can be checked in with other luggage. In each case the single-person version weighs under sixty pounds and is just under sixteen feet long when assembled. The Klepper's frame is made of wood, the Feathercraft's is high-quality aluminum and plastic; the hulls are similar, canvas and hypalon rubber.

I own both models and have gone thousands of miles in them, sailed as well as paddled them, in every sort of weather, watching seabirds off the coast of Wales, threading my way among the harbor seals on the Cape in winter, and the vigilant ospreys of Florida's barrier islands, as well as bouncing around the fifty-odd islands I visited for my book *The Happy Isles of Oceania*. Some of those islands were inaccessible to any but a small boat. People fly to Tonga, hire a yacht, and cruise the islands of the Vavau archipelago. But because of the shifting sands there are islands that are unreachable even to a yachtie with a tender. A collapsible kayak is the answer. They are the small-boat choice of the Navy Seals and the British Special Forces, and of sea-going commandos all over the world. They go anywhere. That is obviously the small boat to own.

If passion implies escape, and I think it does, embodying secrecy, fantasy, intense emotion, and a flight from the ordinary that fills us with a sense of well-being, then passion is the right word for how I feel about setting off in a small boat. About sixteen feet of deck and just a few inches of freeboard are all I need. I give thanks for this little craft, because without it a career of writing would be like a life sentence of solitary confinement. So it was writing that forced me to become a fresh-air fiend, and that madness, that passion, has enlightened me, as the greatest passions ought to.

The Awkward Question

When my French publisher, Robert Laffont, asked me who in the whole of France I wished to meet, I said, 'D'Aboville,' whose book *Seul* (*Alone*) had just appeared. The next day in the shadow of Saint-Sulpice I said to d'Aboville's wife, Cornelia, 'He is my hero.' She replied softly, with feeling, 'Mine too.'

Almost anyone can go to the moon: you pass a physical and NASA puts you in a projectile and shoots you there. I once met Buzz Aldrin. He said to me, 'Your grandmother could go to the moon' – a bewitching thought, Granny's handbag, Granny's space suit, Granny's, 'Oh dear.' It is perhaps invidious to compare an oarsman with an astronaut, but rowing across the Pacific Ocean alone in a small boat, as the Frenchman Gérard d'Aboville did last year, shows old-fashioned bravery. Yet even those of us who go on journeys in eccentric circles simpler and far less challenging than d'Aboville's seldom understand what propels us. In 1988 an American named Ed Gillet paddled a kayak from the harbor at Monterey, California across 2,200 miles of the blue Pacific, to Maui in the Hawaiian islands, the world's longest open-ocean crossing. He almost died – he was without food and water for the last three days of this sixty-three-day trip. He was without radio contact. And afterwards all he ever wrote about his epic ordeal was a modest and somewhat self-mocking two-page piece for a New Zealand kayaking newsletter. He cursed himself much of the way for not knowing why he was making such a reckless crossing. Astronauts have a clear, scientific motive, but adventurers tend to evade the awkward question why.

The forty-eight-year-old d'Aboville single-handedly rowed a twenty-five-foot boat of his own design from Japan to Oregon. He had previously (in 1980) rowed across the Atlantic, also from west to east, Cape Cod to Brittany. But the Atlantic was a piece of cake compared to his Pacific crossing, one of the most difficult and danger-ous in the world. No one had ever done it before. For various reasons

50

d'Aboville set out very late in the season and was caught first by heavy weather and finally by tumultuous storms – gale-force winds, forty- and even forty-six-foot waves. Many times he was terrified, yet halfway through the trip – which had no stops (no islands at all in that part of the Pacific) – a Russian freighter offered to rescue him. 'I was not even tempted.' He turned his back on the ship and rowed on. The entire crossing, averaging seventeen strokes a minute, took him 134 days. I wanted to ask him why he had taken this enormous personal risk.

D'Aboville, short and compactly built, is no more physically prepossessing than another fairly obscure and just as brave long-distance navigator, the paddler Paul Caffyn of New Zealand. Over the past decade or so, Caffyn has circumnavigated Australia, Japan, Great Britain, and his own New Zealand through the low-pressure systems of the Tasman Sea in his seventeen-foot kayak.

In a memorable passage in *The Dark Side of the Wave*, Caffyn is battling a horrible chop off the North Island and sees a fishing boat up ahead. He deliberately paddles away from the boat, fearing that someone on board will see his flimsy craft and ask him where he is going. 'I knew they would ask me why I was doing it, and I did not have an answer.'

I hesitated to spring the question on d'Aboville. I asked him first about his preparations for the trip. A native of Brittany, he had always rowed, he said. 'We never used outboard motors – we rowed boats the way other children pedaled bicycles.' Long ocean crossings interested him, too, because he loves to design highly specialized boats. His Pacific craft was streamlined – it had the long, seaworthy lines of a kayak, and a high-tech cockpit with a roll-up canopy that could seal the occupant in rough weather. A pumping system, using sea-water as ballast, easily righted the boat in the event of a capsize. The boat had few creature comforts but all necessities – a stove, a sleeping place, roomy hatches for dehydrated meals and drinking water. D'Aboville also had a video camera and filmed himself rowing, in the middle of nowhere, humming the Alan Jackson Country and Western song 'Here in the Real World.' D'Aboville sang it and hummed it for months but did not know any of the words, or indeed the title, until I recognized it on his video.

'That is a very hard question,' he said, when I asked him why he had set out on this seemingly suicidal trip – one of the longest ocean crossings possible, at the worst time of the year. He denied that he had any death wish. 'And it is not like going over a waterfall in a barrel.' He had prepared himself well. His boat was well found. He is an excellent navigator. 'Yes, I think I have courage,' he said when I asked him point blank whether he felt he was brave.

It was the equivalent, he said, of scaling the north face of a mountain, the most difficult ascent. But this lonely four-and-half-month ordeal almost ended in his death by drowning, when a severe storm lashed the coast of Oregon as d'Aboville approached it, upside down, in a furious sea. The video of his last few days at sea, taken by a rescue vessel, is so frightening that d'Aboville wiped tears from his eyes watching it with me. 'At this time last year I was in the middle of it.' He quietly ignored my questions about the forty-foot waves. Clearly upset at the memory, he said, 'I do not like to talk about it.'

'Only an animal does useful things,' he said at last, after a long silence. 'An animal gets food, finds a place to sleep, tries to keep comfortable. But I wanted to do something that was not useful – not like an animal at all. Something only a human being would do.'

The art of it, he was saying – such an effort was as much esthetic as athletic. And that the greatest travel always contains within it the seeds of a spiritual quest, or else what's the point? The English explorer Apsley Cherry-Garrard would have agreed with this. He went to Antarctica with Scott in the ship *Terra Nova* and made a six-week crossing of a stretch of Antarctica in 1912, on foot, in the winter, when that polar region is dark all day and night, with a whipping wind, and temperatures of minus 80°F.

On his trek, which gave him the title for his book, *The Worst Journey in the World*, he wrote:

Why do some human beings desire with such urgency to do such things: regardless of the consequences, voluntarily, conscripted by no one but themselves? No one knows. There is a strong urge to conquer the dreadful forces of nature, and perhaps to get consciousness of ourselves, of life, and of the shadowy workings of our human minds. Physical capacity is the only limit. I have tried to tell how, and when, and where. But why? That is a mystery.

In any event there is no conquering, d'Aboville says. *Je n'ai pas vaincu le Pacifique, il m'a laissé passer.* 'I did not conquer the Pacific,' d'Aboville said after his ordeal. 'It let me go across.'

The Moving Target

A courageous but obscure traveler named Nathaniel Bishop, from my home town of Medford, Massachusetts, rowed a small boat called a 'sneakbox' 2,600 miles from upper New York State to New Orleans in 1877 or so. When he arrived at New Orleans, exhausted, and tied his boat to a jetty a group of young drunks congregated on the jetty near his boat and mocked him and threatened him and swore at him. This, I have come to think, is a very American reaction – rewarding eccentric effort with mockery and violence.

In the 1920s the long-distance horseman A. F. Tschiffely saddled up in Buenos Aires and rode 10,000 miles northward, heading for New York City. He crossed deserts, mountain ranges, jungles, swamps; labored over the Andes, he toiled through Central America, he trotted across Mexico. But the worst was to come. His most dispiriting days on this two-and-a-half-year journey were those he spent traversing various American states. 'I had a great deal of trouble with "road hogs,"' he wrote in *Southern Cross to Pole Star*, and he told how American motorists would deliberately swerve to scare him.

'Off and on different objects were thrown at us, and once even an empty bottle, whilst shouting, "Ride 'em cowboy!"' On a back road in the Blue Ridge Mountains a man calculatedly side-swiped him and injured his horse's leg (the driver then honked and waved in triumph). After two more serious incidents of this kind Tschiffely abandoned his epic trip in Washington, D C, and took the train to New York.

At this point the reader who is a jogger or similar sort of outdoor exerciser will shudder with recognition. Practically every jogger I know has been heckled or threatened in this way. Anyone who runs by the roadside, it seems, is subjected to cat calls, honks, verbal abuse, unwelcome invitations, and guffaws. Objects are flung from cars – coins, food, beer cans. People spit. It is remarkable how forcefully people can spit when there is someone either to impress or to intimidate.

Women joggers occupy a special category of potential victim in which wherever they exercise they can accurately be described as running a gauntlet.

In London, such behavior is less common in my experience – bystanders are more used to eccentricity. They have to be, because people live at such close quarters. Henry James remarked on this 100 years ago in *English Hours*, speaking of the 'tight fit' in England: 'We seem loosely hung together at home as compared with the English, every man of whom is a tight fit in his place.' And he goes on to say, 'It is not an inferential but a palpable fact that England is a crowded country.'

Americans who boast of living in a place with plenty of room for everyone tend to object to any sort of proximity, and at the slightest hint of a loss of elbow room say, 'You're in my space' or 'Get out of my face.' At the same time, the pressure of crowds and the uncertainties of class have made Britain a more tolerant and gentler place. Anglers can be awful to canoeists but that is strictly territorial in a country where fishing rights are sold by the yard on rural rivers. But few people are bothered by joggers, horse-riders, or athletes in outlandish clothes. The British cyclist causes the least comment of all – it might be anyone, a policeman, a schoolchild, a commuter, a racer, or your elderly father-in-law. The British jogger is allowed his or her share of the road.

The American jogger is frequently harassed by people in moving cars, and these antagonists are their single greatest risk, far greater than bone spurs, gut aches, hammered knee joints or hot flashes. I have found no literature on the subject of antisocial behavior toward people who make themselves visible through solitary exercise. What might be perceived as harmless heckling seems to me to express an intention that is related to assault, obstruction, rape and murder.

I don't jog – too tough on my muscles and bones; it makes me feel unwell. But I value solitary aerobic exercise of other kinds, such as pedaling a bike, paddling a kayak, and rowing a boat. I happened to be cycling when I realized that my presence aroused a sort of hysteria in bystanders or people passing in cars. They shouted abuse, they laughed. What's so funny? They threw things. It was actually worse in bad weather, as though there was something in the very nature of adverse conditions that made people gloatingly more abusive, because I was more vulnerable. Rain or cold days brought out brutishness in them. I endured it for a while, and then I asked around. I was not alone. Most cyclists have stories of this kind, and joggers had much worse ones, and women joggers the worst persecution stories.

Fleeing to the ocean doesn't help. Rowing my boat off Cape Cod, I am constantly harassed by speedboats. What is it about recreational motor-boaters (as opposed to fishermen in motor boats) that makes them a callow, facetious, and aggressive breed of people? Something to do, perhaps, with the fact that boozing and boating go together, and so many of the boaters are teenagers, not old enough to drive a car. A rowboat is no match for one of these foaming monsters that goes slapping past. I have lost count of the number of times such boats have almost swamped me. I can only believe that it is deliberate. Is it possible the boaters don't know they throw up a five-foot wall of water in their wake?

The smaller and frailer-seeming the boat, the greater the threat. In my kayak I am frequently yelled at, barracked, hectored, and mocked. Kids on jet skis are unspeakable – they side-swipe, they strafe, and they leave you in no doubt that these machines ('personal watercraft') are simply the latest in a long line of technological atrocities unleashed on a peaceable world by Japanese manufacturers.

Anecdotal evidence overwhelmingly indicates that anyone who jogs or rows or cycles in the open, in this free country, is asking for trouble in the form of some sort of opposition. As I say, it ranges from an obscene gesture to an attempt at murder. It is worth examining as a social phenomenon, partly because we take for granted that it will happen, but also because it is a specifically American occurrence. I have cycled and rowed in other countries, and I have been stared at, but not harassed. The aggression in the American reaction often has a comic veneer, the bullying joshing sort which characterizes a certain variety of our humor and which makes it indistinguishable from sadism. The origin of this kind of heckling might be summed up in the shriek, 'Get a horse!' but it is much more serious than it seems and I believe that it constitutes an actual threat.

In the most common situation the threat comes from more than one person – rarely is it one-on-one. The group of people in the car or speedboat, the phalanx of jet-skiers, are nearly always male. Their response appears to be a reflex of violent envy directed against an isolated and vulnerable person – the skimpily clothed jogger, the madly balancing paddler, the panting cyclist. It is like an objection to the sort of assertive freedom and health implicit in these pastimes, and it might be bound up with the suspicion – in a minority of cases a well-founded suspicion – that someone who exercises this way so publicly is showing off.

Yet the response is so lacking in tolerance that I cannot help but think that at its source is a wild anger, a fear and frustration, at being faced by a free spirit, someone who cannot be controlled. And the instance where the fat foolish person plows by in a speedboat with a loud and stupid remark – I have encountered such people many times on the water – might be explained by his sudden realization that for once in his foolish life he is stronger and faster and apparently superior. Such a person would deny he is a criminal, and yet his reaction is the impulse behind most crime – the eagerness to commit an act of violence because the victim seems weak, ludicrous, exposed, and naked: victims nearly always seem that way. Crime is a monstrous sort of unfairness, and so it is always in the criminal's interest to pick on an especially weak or supine target.

Why does this, as far as I know, mostly happen in America? What is it that rouses us and incites us against people pursuing innocent and healthful objectives? Perhaps that is part of the answer – the very innocence and health implicit in jogging or cycling might be a kind of provocation. As for the shouting – well, Americans tend to think out loud: you get perfect strangers yapping at each other all over America. In our strenuously verbal and competitive culture great stress is placed on self-assertion. The irony is that people jogging or paddling or cycling are exhibiting in a non-aggressive way those same demonstrative characteristics. And as I mentioned, it is more than likely, too, that joggers and other fresh-air fiends are motivated to a certain extent by impure enthusiasm. There are many who could be accurately described as show-offs, seeming to invite comment. It is very hard to see a person cantering on a horse without imagining that person thinking, *I am on a horse and you're not.*

Even so, that is no reason for the person to be violently harassed. We are described as a nation that respects the rights of individuals, but I have seldom found this to be the rule. Eccentricity – even the healthy eccentricity in these one-person pastimes – is commonly perceived as a threat. I suspect that we are much more deeply conservative and threatened by novelty than we can possibly imagine; generally speaking we don't want to believe that we are, and we cling to a mostly mythical notion of ourselves as tolerant and liberal-minded. I think our tolerance is mostly posturing. It is unpleasant to contemplate, but this swift impulse to harass the jogger or to swamp the small-boater seems like a specifically American trait, one of our worst, arising from the pack mentality of our competitiveness, our vocal masculinity, our contempt for eccentricity, and our self-justifying humor in which the butt of the joke is always a weak victim.

I wonder whether it is possible to widen this argument and make it political. So much in American foreign policy is related to implied threat or the wish to control. I think our irrational reaction to any number of countries which have chosen an unconventional path to political or economic fulfillment is an example of this envious bullying. We are always talking about freedom as though we valued it. If we truly valued it and practiced it, we would probably talk about it less often instead of treating it like a mantra in the hope of overcoming our baser instincts.

Dead Reckoning to Nantucket

I set out one morning in my kayak, facing the open sea, intending to paddle thirty-five miles or so from Falmouth on Cape Cod to the island of Nantucket, stopping at the Vineyard on the way. I felt waterproof, buoyant and portable, with a sleeping bag and food for four days. It was a lovely morning but I was already in a sunny frame of mind, knowing that in order to paddle to Nantucket and camp on the way I would have to trespass and break the law.

For me the best sort of travel always involves a degree of trespass. The risk is both a challenge and an invitation. Selling adventure seems to be a theme in the travel industry, and trips have becomes trophies: wealthy people pay big money to be dragged up Everest on ropes, or go white-water rafting down the Ganges, or risk death for photo-opportunities with gorillas in war-ravaged Rwanda. The element of hardship in this sort of travel has either been down-played or eliminated – still, the risk factor is so great that such ambitious tourists are often injured or even die on such trips.

Adventure travel seems to imply a far-off destination, but I think a nearby destination can be scarier, for nowhere is more frightening than a place near home that everyone has warned you against. You can dismiss ignorant opinion – 'Africa's dangerous!' or 'India's dirty!' or 'China's crowded!' – but when someone you know well, speaking of a place near home, says, 'Don't go there,' it sounds like the voice of experience. This does not usually deter me. The idea is to devise a way of going, as when in 1853 Sir Richard Burton learned colloquial Arabic, grew a beard, darkened his skin, and gave his name as Mirza Abdullah, and his occupation as 'dervish,' in order to take the Haj as a born Muslim to the holy city of Mecca, forbidden to infidels. When the Chinese told me a place was forbidden – a word they love and use often – I merely smiled and thought of ways to disobey.

Warnings applied to the ocean surrounding the Cape sound especially dire. But if you took all advice and heeded all warnings and obeyed the opinion of scare-mongers you would never go anywhere. Most people who hand out advice are incapable of putting themselves in your shoes: they fear for their own safety, and they impose this fear on you; and when they are speaking of a place with a bad reputation near home they can be bullies. There is no terror like the terror of what is nearby. The vaguely familiar can be worse than the unknown, because any number of witnesses have supplied spurious detail, the hideous certainty of specific fatal features, and the lurking idea that if you go you will either die or be horribly disappointed.

Such opposition can be stimulating, perversely inspiring. Everybody and his ocean-going brother told me not to try to paddle to Nantucket. I listened to them and then, that morning, I rose before dawn and got the latest weather report for Cape Cod and the islands, and prepared my kayak for the trip I was determined to make.

Cape Cod is vast. It is not one little jig-jog of land. It is composed of all the seas around it, the water, the sounds, the channels; the fetch and chop of the tide-races, the sand bars, the islands so small they appear only twice a day at low tide and have scarcely enough room to serve as a platform for a seagull's feet.

The sea is a place, too, and it is not empty either; it contains distinct locations, shoals, rocks, buoys, cans and nuns – and wrecks that stick up with the prominent authority of church steeples or bare ruined choirs. The angler facing south from the jetty at Hyannisport sees just an expanse of blue water, yet there are nearly as many features on the nautical chart of Nantucket Sound as there are on the adjacent map of Hyannis. These are not only the sites of nameless wrecks and gongs and bells, but memorable and resonant names. Crossing to the Vineyard from Falmouth you pass L'Hommedieu Shoal, Hedge Fence (a long narrow shoal), and Squash Meadow, and if you cross from there to Edgartown there are many named rocks. The current – its changing speed and direction – is another serious consideration; and the water depths range from zero to over 100 feet. But it is misleading to think that because the sea is a place it is safe and hospitable. In his book *Cape Cod*, Thoreau wrote, 'The ocean is a wilderness,' and he went on to say that it is 'wilder than a Bengal jungle, and fuller of monsters . . .'

In bad weather you can't see the Vineyard from the Cape shore, and even on the clearest day you can't see Nantucket. The challenge to the paddler is more than open water; it is also a swift and changeable current, a strong prevailing wind, and scattered shoals that send up a steep chop of confused waves. Nantucket Sound has a long history of being a ship-swallower, one of the most crowded graveyards of any stretch of ocean in the world. It was not uncommon in the nineteenth century for a whaling ship to leave Nantucket and to spend two years sailing around the world, crossing the southern ocean and going around the Horn and through the Roaring Forties, only to be smashed to bits on the rocks or shallows at Nantucket, within sight of the harbor.

None the less, I was thrilled by the warnings. For a number of years I had wanted to cross the Sound, head for Nantucket through open water, and get there in one piece, in my own craft, by using dead reckoning. I knew it wasn't simple. Nantucket lies far below the horizon, and only its 'lume' – the flaring halo of its harbor light – shows at night from the nearest part of the Vineyard.

Whenever I spoke about paddling there, people tried to put me off. They were sailors with boats that drew five feet of water, or else fellows with speedboats who had never been out of sight of land, or tourists and party-goers who knew the route only from the long, cold ferry ride from Hyannis.

My dream of paddling through the wilderness of open water was of course the dream of an Eagle Scout (Troop 24); but it was also the dream of someone who had had enough of foreign travel for a while, of places that were crowded and thoroughly tame, of the tedium and sleep-deprivation of long plane journeys, and of the yappy turbulence of other travelers. I had recently been to Tibet, Polynesia, northern Scotland and the southern island of New Zealand; I had not been alone. Tourists have penetrated to the farthest, wildest parts of the world. An article I would prefer not to write, about the spread of tourists, might be titled *They're Everywhere*.

But they are not in the Muskeget Channel. I knew I would not run into anyone on the way. I had never heard of anyone making this crossing, or even wanting to. Small Craft Warnings are frequent. The *Eldridge Tide and Pilot Table* shows a four-and-a-half-knot current running in some places in the Muskeget Channel, and with a strong wind and tide it could obviously be much greater than that. To cap it all, it is illegal to camp on any of the outer islands. It was dangerous, it was trespassing, it was foolhardy, it was forbidden.

Catnip, I thought. *Who wouldn't choose to paddle a kayak to Nantucket?*

*

I left Green Pond Harbor in East Falmouth, paddling my folding kayak, the nearest thing there is to an Eskimo kayak.

An Oriental man and woman were fishing from the breakwater.

Perhaps to amuse the woman, the man shrieked at me, 'You'll never make it!'

I considered this remark and kept paddling into the slop of the Sound. Among the Klepper's many virtues are its seaworthiness and stability, its lightness, its storage space, and its portableness – it can be taken apart in about fifteen minutes and stuffed into two bags. It can't be rolled over easily, and if you fall out you can climb back in – this is almost impossible in other kayaks.

It was one of those beautiful mornings in early September, after Labor Day, when the Cape has a bright, vacant look – no traffic, no pedestrians, no swimmers, and only fishing boats on the water. The sky was clear, the wind was light; a low dusting of haze prevented me from seeing the Vineyard distinctly. My plan was to head for East Chop lighthouse, continue on that shore for a few miles, and have lunch on the beach below Oak Bluffs. My afternoon plan would have to depend on the wind and weather; but the outlook was good.

Crossing Nantucket Sound is the Cape sailor's first psychological barrier. I had rowed and sailed across it before I paddled it, but paddling was the simplest of the three. It can be dangerous to vessels of any size. On August 20, 1992 I was crossing from Green Pond to Oak Bluffs and saw a passenger liner anchored off East Chop. I paddled toward it, and the rising tide, flowing east, gave the illusion that this ship was moving slowly west. In fact, I was being tugged away from the anchored ship. Approaching it I saw that its main deck was as tall as a twelve-story building, and rounding its stern I saw *Queen Elizabeth II – Southampton*. Passengers were being taken ashore to Oak Bluffs a mile and a half away in whale boats. I paddled to the gangway and struck up a conversation with the mate.

'I've never see the *QE II* here.'

'We call here every few years.'

'Where are you headed?'

'New York City. We're sailing tonight.'

'I just paddled from the Cape and crossed several shoals. I know there are plenty up ahead. How does a big ship like this manage?'

'No problem. We come through here all the time.'

That night the *Queen Elizabeth II* ran into an uncharted rock at the western edge of the Sound, near Sow and Pig Rocks, causing millions of dollars' worth of damage to the hull. The passengers were taken off the ship and ferried to New Bedford, where they were transported by bus to New York City. It was a whole year before the ship was repaired and put back into service.

The tide can also be a problem. On the morning of my dead-reckoning departure it was against me: I knew it would be, because I needed it in my favor this afternoon. The tidal current creates the strangest effects. A mile off Green Pond there was a tide rip – a mass of spiky white waves drawing me toward them from my patch of clear water. The thing to do is stay upright. I paddled through them and after a while I saw that I was way off course – nearer West Chop than East Chop (these are the separate arms of Vineyard Haven, and each indicates a patch of rough water). I struggled against the current, feeling that I was paddling upstream, and about an hour and a half after leaving the Cape I was at the Vineyard shore. Thirty minutes later I was at Oak Bluffs, lying on the beach, drinking Chinese tea and eating a cheese sandwich.

Here as postprandial reading, I looked at the *Tide and Pilot Table* and saw that everything was in my favor: the tide had just turned, I would have a cooperative current to lead me toward Edgartown and Katama Bay. And if I eluded the Ranger and camped on the beach at the southern point of Chappaquiddick I would have a merciful current tomorrow on the way to Nantucket: that is, it would carry me safely north-east. But it was not endlessly merciful. If I were delayed, or if I didn't paddle fast enough, I would be carried into the Atlantic Ocean when the current reversed in the mid-morning.

The great fear that everyone had expressed to me was the Muskeget Channel, which is a sort of teeming drain that was capable of sluicing any craft into the Atlantic. No boats enter it. How could they? If the currents didn't get you, the sand bars or the rocks would. But a kayak draws only a few inches of water. And anyone could see that the dangers of the channel had to be set against its advantages – it was only an eight-mile crossing to the nearest piece of land, the uninhabited Muskeget Island, where I could trespass if the weather happened to deteriorate. What tempted me most to cross the channel was that no one I had met or spoken to, and no one I had heard of, had ever done it. It meant that I might be the first non-Indian to do it alone in a self-propelled boat; and I might discover that it was not dangerous at all.

The traveler is essentially an optimist, and in that hopeful mood I paddled all afternoon, south to Edgartown. This is one of the loveliest and snuggest harbors in the world, a tidy town of brilliant white and slightly haughty houses and brick walls and shady streets. Just across the harbor is Chappaquiddick Island, with low woods and sandbanks and expensive and rather buried and furtive-looking houses, the seasonal haunt of fleeing New Yorkers.

I pulled my kayak onto a town landing and walked into Edgartown to buy some beer and to verify tomorrow's weather report (sunny, scattered clouds, light winds 10–15 kts). I considered staying the night at a hotel, but that would have complicated my trip. I needed the earliest possible start from an advantageous position on the coast, and this I had designated as my camp-ground: Wasque Point, on the south-eastern corner of the island.

So, although I had been paddling for more than seven hours, I crawled back into my kayak and paddled another hour through Katama Bay. The sun was setting, and the air was turning cool; it was twilight and chilly by the time I got to the sand spit. I was so tired I could not pull my loaded kayak over it. I sat and rested among some nervously bleeping oyster catchers, and then I gathered armfuls of slimy seaweed and spread it on the sand and pulled my kayak up this slippery track into the dunes.

A few four-wheel-drive vehicles – fishermen – were leaving the beach; and there was a tawny Bronco with *Ranger* lettered on its door. I ambled around the beach until sunset, and then tipped my kayak on its side and spread out my ground sheet and my sleeping bag. I drank beer and had dinner in the starry moonless dark as the waves monotonously dumped and broke on the sand, with the sound of someone sighing. I wanted to be invisible, so I did not build a fire. Just before I turned in I walked to the edge of the beach and looked east-south-east with my binoculars and saw the lume of Nantucket – no land but a definite light, like the dim flash of a thunder storm or the glow of a distant fire in the sea.

Then I lay down in my sleeping bag and murmured,

> Oh, God, make small
> The old star-eaten blanket of the sky,
> That I may fold it round me and in comfort lie.

I woke often in the night – listened to the waves, listened to the wind in the sea grass and the drizzling sand grains – and I felt like a savage, just as portable, just as naked and vulnerable to attack. I lay there like a dog on a rug. I was exposed but I was in an out-of-the-way place – no one came here except fishermen, and they wouldn't be returning until after sun-up. By then I would be gone.

With good food, in my expensive sleeping bag, lying alongside my unsinkable kayak, as an early September dawn was breaking, I did not feel that I was roughing it. This merely seemed an eccentric form of luxury: I was comfortable, I was alone, and I was successfully trespassing.

Sunrise was a messy reddened eruption out of the sea, and it kept spilling garish light everywhere and draining the redness into the water as the sun rose like a squeezed blood-orange. A cloud the shape of a huddled animal soon smothered the brightness and the sea turned the bluey-white color of skimmed milk.

By then there was no sign of Nantucket, which lay below the horizon. The wind was light, though the sea swell was pronounced, and the waves were still dumping steadily. I ate a banana, drank the last of my tea, took a bearing with my compass, and headed east-south-east into a wave that broke over my deck and into my face. There were no other people on the beach, no other boats in the water. The sea was clear, the sky was empty. The Chappaquiddick shore was just a sandbank, a bluff with a whiffle of sea grass on top. Light and water and sand: it was a minimalist landscape, three bands of light, dawn still breaking over it, and all of it looking like a just-emerged corner of a continent, bobbing at the surface of a watery planet, without a soul in it, a sort of prologue to Paradise.

The rest was oceanic – endless and eternal: I was paddling into nothingness. Behind me Chappaquiddick had begun to drop into the sea. I was nervous, of course, because I am not much of a navigator and because I could see rough water ahead and beyond it only more water. But it was not even seven o'clock in the morning. I had a whole day to get where I was going. If something went wrong I had twelve hours of daylight in which to save myself.

Rough water ahead looked like a river flowing swiftly through the sea. This jumble of steep breaking waves was the result of the tidal stream being pushed upward by a shoal. The vertical current produced an 'overfall' of turbulent surface water. The waves broke over me and drenched me as the current pulled me sideways. I braced myself with my paddle and didn't fight the current. I had included it in my crude calculations. That is what dead reckoning is – getting to a hidden destination by figuring your average speed and true course after leaving a known point of land. I was counting on the current taking me north-east as I paddled four knots an hour east-south-east, and I assumed I would get a glimpse of Muskeget Island after an hour or so. Traveling hopefully into the unknown with a little information: dead reckoning is the way most people live their lives, and the phrase itself seems to sum up human existence.

I had not known that Muskeget Island was so flat and hard to spot. On all charts certain prominent landscape features are indicated – a dome, a water tower, a radio antenna, a steeple. There was nothing shown on the chart for Muskeget Island. From my boat I thought I saw a smudge, which could have been an island; but I kept losing it as my boat slid from the crest of a wave into the trough. Then it was like sitting in a box, unable to see over the sides. What might have been obvious from the deck of a sailboat was impossible to see from my kayak, so low in the water.

And what water. Now I understood why larger boats never crossed this channel. There were more waves, breaking in the middle of nowhere, indicating a sand bar or some rocks. I crossed at least three more overfalls – one was fifty yards wide and had the look of a maelstrom. In the distance I saw waves breaking, and no land in sight. That seemed ominous – I might find myself surfing out to sea. But I was still paddling hard. I did not want to turn back. And the smudge in the distance was definitely a piece of land. Now it was off to the far right, which meant that I was being carried faster by the current than I had calculated.

By mid-morning I was paddling off Musgeket, the flat island that is one of the most remote and least visited pieces of land for hundreds of miles – just a low ledge in the sea. Shaped like an anvil lying on its side, it is about a mile long and half a mile wide. No trees grow on its windswept surface, only blowing grass and rose bushes. At its western end sits a single unoccupied house. I paddled to the back of the island, out of the wind, and went ashore. There was no need for me to shelter here. It was not even noon, and I could see Nantucket through the smoky haze, the western tip of it, Eel Point, the north arm of Madaket harbor; and ahead, as Robert Lowell writes in 'The Quaker Graveyard in Nantucket,' 'a brackish reach of shoal off Madaket . . .' That was about five miles away, beyond another island, Tuckernuck, beyond two shipwrecks hulking out of the blue sea, ochreous with rust.

My nervousness about the open water crossing was gone. Having gained confidence in my use of dead reckoning, I felt stronger. Now I could see where I was going. I paddled through the miles of shallows off Tuckernuck and onward to a beach, where I lolled in the sand and had lunch. The tide had long since shifted: the current was against me; I battled it all the way to the long breakwater that guards Nantucket harbor, and I glided past Brant Point to the landing.

I had been to Nantucket on the ferry many times. But because I had come this way – plowing through the waves alone, seeing no one, not saying a word, only trespassing on the beaches and on the notorious channels – the place seemed utterly new. I now had some sense of its distance and its uniqueness; of how much of it there was; and how from the sea it seemed to stagger westward in a succession of sinking fragments.

Yachts were bobbing in the harbor, and people were strolling among the bright white houses, buying ice creams and T-shirts. There is always a state of high excitement in Nantucket town, because so many of the visitors have come for the day and want to make the most of it by the time the ferry leaves. The place is full of fishermen and millionaires, it is Yankees and Ivy Leaguers. It is, as Melville wrote, 'a mere hillock, an elbow of sand' and yet if you somehow delete all the Jeeps and sport utility vehicles it has one of the most beautiful main streets in America; as for the rest of the island, it took Melville a whole chapter of *Moby-Dick* to describe it properly – its look, its meaning, and its moods.

I was salt-crusted and sunburned. No one noticed me beach my boat. I walked urgently because I had hardly used my legs in two days. I bought an ice cream and a souvenir T-shirt and became part of the crowd. But I had the sense of having discovered Nantucket in my own way, and – through dead reckoning – had discovered something in myself. That to me is the essence of the travel experience. Is there any point in going across the world to eat something or buy something or to watch poor people squatting among their ruins? Travel is a state of mind. It has nothing to do with distance or the exotic. It is almost entirely an inner experience. My particular way of getting to Nantucket – alone, almost blindly over water – seemed to transform the destination. The Nantucket I had arrived at was a different place from the Nantucket of the ferry passenger, and I was different, too – happier, for one thing. The trip had done what all trips ought to do. It had given me heart.

Paddling to Plymouth

A man fishing is not easy to distract, but when this wading one saw me he lowered his tackle and called out, 'This I've got to see!' It was a November day on the Cape and the surf was up. I was heading out of an inlet into cold three-foot dumpers, in a kayak.

I was grateful to him for a remark which seemed to celebrate my departure. And I was pleased that he had noticed me, because in a vainglorious way I was proud of setting out on such a cold morning. I was also a little apprehensive: the turbulent after-effects of Hurricane Kate were still in the air and on the sea. Because writers are mainly sedentary people we have a tendency to overdramatize physical effort. The non-writers I know, who are travelers, take things pretty much in their stride and seldom make a meal of their adventures. The fisherman's attention made me self-conscious, and I took a formal sort of care in negotiating the waves, going up and over them and punching with my paddle. Then I was beyond the surf zone, bobbing along in relative safety.

This trip had not been a casual decision. A month before I had spent some time in South East Asia. That had been a casual decision. But kayaking alone in a November sea off Cape Cod had required quite a lot of forward planning. I needed equipment and practice; I had to study the weather; and I had to overcome certain fears. I felt weak and ignorant, and I was afraid of tipping over in a cold sea and having to make what kayakers call a 'wet exit.'

My fear of falling in was so great that the first chance I had I decided to tip over my boat and throw myself into the sea – to break the suspense. I was wearing a wet suit, but even so the shock of the cold sea-water gave me a lasting headache. I was also worried by high waves. To prove to myself that I could maintain my balance in them I went out one day and paddled in a sea that was producing four- and five-foot waves near shore. I had also been fearful of the cold, but I quickly discovered that in a well-found kayak one is almost impervious to the cold – in fact, perspiring and overheating are much greater problems.

As it was a week before Thanksgiving I decided to paddle to Plymouth. I estimated that with detours it would be just about thirty miles. I was especially eager to get close to a blurred gray bluff on the off-Cape coast that I could see on clear days from my kitchen window. That was about fifteen miles away; but I had never been there. I liked the idea of visiting my view. After a month or more of practice and nerving myself for the trip, I set off, passing that slightly mocking fisherman at the inlet. Then I continued, staying just offshore, and plunging up the coast, fighting a twenty-knot headwind. In *The Survival of the Bark Canoe*, John McPhee writes, 'If the human race has one common denominator, it is hatred of a headwind.'

The sea was scattered with white-caps. Apart from the fisherman, there was no one else on the beach; and except for a distant ship there was nothing on the sea. I was alone and rather excited at the prospect of this unusual outing. It was like answering a dare. I was certainly trying to prove something to myself, and I was enjoying the pleasure of having ignored dire warnings. Most people are only too happy to discourage you from anything that looks risky. Whenever I mentioned that I was going to spend the fall kayaking on the New England coast, people tried to put me off. Too cold, too windy, they said; too dangerous alone, and what about the sharks? I suppose people say those things because they don't want to be held responsible for another person's foolishness, and because they cannot imagine anyone doing something they would not do themselves.

The dire warnings filled me with resolve and seemed as hearty to me as a salutation. They made me think I was doing the right thing. The Cape in winter is bleak and unvisited and yet it is less convincing as a backdrop for adventure than, say, Thailand. A person flies to Bangkok and returns with a pile of snapshots and a few yards of raw silk and believes that to be the very stuff of travel. Why am I not persuaded of it? Travel is supposed to be swimming pools and sunshine and the whole supine experience of feeling very rich because everyone else in the travel destination is colorfully poor. I don't condemn such travel as a vice, though I think it is helpful to recognize that there is an implied snobbery in this sort of vacationing. At its best it is harmless, but it is also thoroughly predictable. The adventure of travel is something else, something personal and enigmatic, and I usually associate it with risk. This might mean an assault on the north face of the Eiger, but it could also mean a rainy afternoon in Redhook, or the choppy seas off Scusset Beach, in Massachusetts.

Adventure may be deliberate. There are travel companies that organize trips – comfortable trips – to the North Pole and to Cape Horn. Yet adventure is more likely to be accidental. Classically it is the picnic that turns into an ordeal – the 'Please, George, drop the keys!' of the Charles Addams cartoon (George aloft in the talons of an enormous bird); the hunting expedition that becomes a nightmare – the *Moby-Dick* experience that is more simply served up in efforts such as *Deliverance*; or the jolly, away-from-it-all sea voyage that is interrupted by killer whales and is later retold in *Survive the Savage Sea*, or that other favorite reversal of fortune, about the man and wife who stay afloat for months in a rubber dinghy, before the inevitable Korean freighter sights their last flare.

Circumstances are everything. In the summer, tiny tots thrash around in inner tubes on the sunny sea off Sagamore; but in winter no one goes very close to the water for fear the waves will rise up and snatch them away. The winter wind is north-westerly, cold and hard and blowing directly from Plymouth. Sailing is impossible in such seas; rowing is out of the question; and even the large yachts are in dry dock for the winter. Next year, people say, and stuff their hands deeper into their pockets, as they go on surveying the wild sea from the shore – the breakers and dumpers, the hurrying white-caps and the clash of clapotis, the flying spray, and the claw-shaped overhanging wave crests that look like something out of Hokusai.

November had dripped into my soul. My remedy from that gloom lay in battling through the surf, from my house in East Sandwich across the bay and around the corner to Plymouth. The season made it difficult and therefore rewarding. Half the thrill of it was that I had never done it before. I also liked the idea that I was alone, that the trip involved maps and planning, consultation and even a degree of secrecy. In spite of planning, the unexpected usually occurs. True travel is launching oneself into the unknown. There is no excuse for it except that one offers oneself in a spirit of experiment. To me one of the most compelling trips holds the prospect of the unknown near home.

And yet paddling a kayak off the New England coast, even in winter, is not very strange. Sea-kayaking, which has been carried on by the ice-bound people of Alaska and West Greenland, has caught on as sport and a recreation in recent years. This little craft has allowed people to travel to places that were unreachable in any other sort of boat. A kayak can go almost anywhere in practically any weather. In the right hands it is probably the most adaptable and sea-worthy vessel afloat. Kayaks have been paddled across the Atlantic and through the Caribbean and up the Alaskan coast and down the Nile and the Amazon. In 1979 Charles Porter of Maine rowed his Klepper kayak around Cape Horn – incidentally making him the first man to go around the Horn backwards.

There have been paddlers in kayaks at the Horn for almost as long as there have been humans. When Darwin first saw the boats he was scornful. He concluded that the kayak proved that these people were savages. These Indians were no better than animals, he said, because they had not improved their kayaks. 'The canoe,' he wrote in 1837, 'their most ingenious work, poor as it is, has remained the same as we know from Drake, for the last two hundred and fifty years.' Darwin was mistaken in his conclusion, though. Four hundred years later the kayak is still unchanged in its basic design, because for its size it is as near as possible to being a perfect boat.

That first day I paddled to the east end of Cape Cod Canal. This wonderful trench, proposed by early settlers in the seventeenth century and finally opened in 1914, passes from Cape Cod Bay to Buzzards Bay. When I crossed the eastern entrance a strong current was running out of it, because the tide was rising – the canal current floods east and ebbs west. With both the wind and the tide against me, I was pushed a distance offshore and had to paddle hard to get back near land, out of the wind. I had lunch farther on at Sagamore, under a cliff. There, a dog-walker told me he had seen a shark that morning.

'Its dorsal fin was about this size,' he said, measuring two feet with his mittens. 'And it wasn't flopped over, so I know it wasn't a sunfish. Must have been ten–twelve foot long.'

Soon after that, night fell. It came quickly, like a shade being yanked at four o'clock, and then there was nothing I could do but put in.

I did not see any sharks the next day, but I saw hundreds of eider ducks, and grebes, and canvasbacks, and goldeneyes. And cormorants gathered on rocks, looking as though they were posing for German medallions as they held their wings up emblematically to dry. The beach had an empty scoured look, and it was bleak and curiously lifeless – in great contrast to the waves just offshore and the foamy corrugations on the horizon. At times I could not see over the tops of the waves when I paddled in troughs between them.

Eventually I was close to the cliffs that I saw from my kitchen window – the long eroded headland near Center Hill Point. The waves broke over my bow, and now and then over my head, and streamed over my spray-deck. I did not tip over and I stopped worrying about it. It was heavy going in such a strong wind, but I was in no particular hurry. I knew that my destination was merely my excuse to take the trip.

If I needed any justification, I had it on the third day. Paddling in a shallow rocky bay near a place the chart said was Churchill's Landing, I saw half a dozen dancing boat-moorings – or were they lobster markers? The buoyant lumps began to disappear. Then some returned, bobbling; then there were ten. Soon I saw that these heads were unmistakably seals. They came closer and surrounded me, and I counted seventeen of them. They were funny, friendly, and nimble, their whiskers dripping, their smooth heads gleaming, like enchanted beach toys. Their odd upthrust and swiveling heads made me laugh out loud and I was delighted when they followed me toward Manomet Point.

Seeing those harbor seals and creeping up on them and being followed were worth my month of preparation and all this effort. The whole point of travel is discovery, and few experiences can match the satisfaction of such an extraordinary discovery near home. That vision of rollicking seals stayed with me and gave me zest for the next leg into Plymouth.

It was not much of a distance, of course, but the trouble was that as soon as I rounded the point I received the full unimpeded blast of the north-west wind. I was off White Horse Beach, and struggling through the surf. I reminded myself that I was not in a hurry. I had chosen an unusual means of getting to a familiar place; when I was younger I headed for unusual places by conventional means. This time I was lured by what was visible and the prospect of entering the unknown; and on the way I had seen marvels.

To avoid the breakers smashing on Rocky Point, I detoured into Plymouth Bay and headed for the breakwater at the harbor. Here I was sheltered by the high ground of the mainland, and with the wind deflected I paddled into Plymouth. If I had come in a car I probably would have driven through without stopping. But because I had come in a kayak, I was grateful for this safe arrival and this pleasant landfall. I visited the Rock, and then I made a tour of *Mayflower II*, on which people dressed as Pilgrims explained their ship and the colony with effective mimicry in the accents of mythical Mummerset. A man dressed as the ship's master described the rough passage; Mrs Brewster was there to expound her husband's theology; and so were some of the crew, all dressed the part and well informed. In Plymouth proper, someone dressed as a chicken stood by the roadside gesturing to a sign that said, 'Order your turkeys for Thanksgiving.'

I went into the post office to send a postcard. I was wearing sunglasses and a splashed wetsuit and rubber booties. I had paddling mitts called 'pogies' on my hands. I was windblown and on my suit were rimey stripes of sea salt. In a secret, self-dramatizing way I felt like Ishmael.

The woman at the counter sized me up and said, 'Where have you been?' I said, 'Out there, paddling a kayak.'

'What are you doing that for – a coffee commercial?'

Fever Chart

In many countries you remember your meals, while in other – and I think more interesting – places you remember your illnesses. High on my chart of unforgettable afflictions is dengue fever, also known as break-bone fever, which is endemic throughout most of the tropical world. I first came across dengue during Peace Corps training in Puerto Rico in 1963 – it was common on the island. But I was not bitten. Nor was I bitten in Africa over the next five years. But in 1969, in Singapore, the attractive woman who lived next door came down with a severe case of dengue. One hot night a few days later I fell ill, actually collapsed – my knees buckled, my temperature shot up to 103, my nerves burned in my skin, I felt paralytic. Very soon, I exhibited other symptoms: my hair began falling out, my joints ached, I became depressed, and for several days sobbed uncontrollably. And I hallucinated, fantasizing extravagantly that the mosquito that had bitten the voluptuous woman next door had also bitten me – two feverish people, one mosquito.

The expression 'virtual sex' was not in my vocabulary then, but my head was full of metaphysical poetry (I taught in the English Department), which amounts to the same thing – John Donne is the poet of virtual sex, particularly in 'The Flea.'

> Mark but this flea, and mark in this
> How little that which thou deny'st me is;
> It sucked me first, and now sucks thee,
> And in this flea our two bloods mingled be.

This was precisely my dengue conceit, and it has a scientific basis. As an arbovirus infection, dengue requires only humans and mosquitoes to cast its pall. The same mosquito had visited the woman and me.

Illness is nearly always dramatic in imaginative literature – look at Tolstoy's 'The Death of Ivan Ilych' or Camus's *The Plague*, or Greene's *A Burnt-out Case*; so much of fiction is a fever chart. But illness is very tedious in a travel book. When I wrote about my dengue fever it was in a short story of the same name (in *The Consul's File*). I am proud of the fact that in six lengthy travel books I have never recorded a single instance of having diarrhea. This is not delicacy on my part, and my stomach is as susceptible as anyone else's – but who wants to read about it? A great personal sense of accomplishment can be derived from overcoming illness abroad, but no sensible reader of a travel book wants to hear the gory details of your amoebic dysentery, or bout of malaria, or resident jigger.

This reminds me that on leave from Africa in the 1960s I went to a family doctor in south London and told him that I suspected that I had the larvae of a jigger flea living under my toenail. 'You Americans,' he said. (We are the world over perceived as hypochondriacs and alarmists.) But I swore it was so, and when he dug the horrible squirming maggot out from under my toenail he made a face as though he had gouged an extraterrestrial from my body and had the grace to say, 'Blimey.'

The principal difference between fleas and flies are wings. Fleas are wingless, they leap from victim to victim on strong hind legs. Flies fly. The 'tumbu fly' referred to in handbooks about tropical diseases is known in Central Africa as a 'putzi fly' – *putzi* means maggot in the Chichewa language. But 'maggot infestation' or *myasis* would be a painful nuisance by any name. Using evasive action I had succeeded in avoiding putzi flies for almost two years when I happened to take a trip up-country. It was October, known in that region as 'the suicide month' for its intense heat.

All I lacked on this trip was Corporal Jika Chikwawa, lately of the King's African Rifles, who normally did my washing and ironing. One day up-country I washed a shirt and hung it out to dry. Putzi flies laid eggs on the shirt. I wore the shirt afterwards, and the warmth of my body hatched the eggs, from which maggots emerged and burrowed into my skin. A day or two later I had boils all over my shoulders and back. At first I had no idea what this hideous outbreak was, and then I popped one of the boils and a maggot wiggled out. My body ached with forty-odd more, nearly all of them out of my reach. I owe it to my friend 'Malawi Bob' Maccani, formerly of Likuni (Central Province), now of Los Angeles, for staying up one hot night in 1965 and holding a match over each boil until the maggot squirmed, and then squeezing the things out. We did not know that a less disgusting method is to spread oil over the boil (and the maggot's breathing apparatus), forcing the creature to crawl out of your body for air. Reflecting on this later, I was reminded of the disease that overwhelms the main character in Edmund Lucas White's little-known horror story 'Lukundoo' (an African explorer breaks out in boils that contain tiny black men), and used this putzi fly episode to good effect in my *World's End* short story, 'White Lies.'

In Malawi, I had no personal experience of African eye-worm, though my students knew it. The strangest aspect of this filarial infection (caused by a fly bite) is that one day the victim sees the worm crawling across the surface of his or her eyes and they know they are afflicted. How can the traveler prevent this happening? Avoid the lovely and inviting shaded forest pools where the large chrysops flies breed and bite. Don't swim in Africa, is a good general rule. If you do the chances are excellent that you will emerge from Lake Victoria, or Lake Edward, Lake Albert, the Congo River, or your local swimming hole with bilharzia (schistosomiasis). And the cure – big needles in the gut – is more painful than the illness. Except for splashing in the waves at Mombasa I never seriously swam in Africa.

Malaria is one of the worst and most persistent problems in the tropics. The prophylactics are not terribly effective and all types of malaria are painful and some are fatal. Using a well-made tent with a mosquito net in New Guinea has probably helped me more than daily paludrine. It has become common for many sunny republics to under-report their cases of malaria (or dengue) so as not to discourage tourism. This denial regarding the AIDS risk is certainly common throughout East and Central Africa, where AIDS patients are seldom treated and almost never hospitalized. Regarded as doomed no-hopers, a waste of hospital space, they are sent back to their villages to die. The Kenyan, Ugandan or Malawian secretaries of health are technically correct when they say there are no AIDS patients in their hospitals. But no one ought to be fooled by this smiling assurance. Keep your immune system away from Ugandan and Kenyan prostitutes, an inordinate proportion of whom, according to World Health Organization estimates, carry the AIDS virus.

AIDS is avoidable. So is gonorrhea, yet through sheer stupidity I did not avoid it. I have given fictional expression to my venereal episodes in my novel *My Secret History*. Malaria is very hard to avoid. But the trouble with most equatorial fevers is that they are almost impossible to diagnose or name. Many people have flu and think it is malaria – the initial symptoms are often similar. The worst fever I ever endured was at a leper colony in a hot, low-lying place in Malawi called Mua. This was a mission hospital run by Dutch White Fathers. I fell ill. One priest told me I might have blackwater fever, another said it could be malaria. Yet more priests speculated and prayed for my soul. I assumed it was malaria and dosed myself with chloroquine. I sweated for three days, hallucinating, my ears ringing. After the fever had broken I could barely walk upright. Diarrhea came next, and I had to negotiate the latrine, a long-drop privy, where bats attached themselves to the edge of the toilet seat. When I entered they let go and flapped in loud batty circles in the pit beneath me.

Compared to this ghastliness the leprosy was almost a trifle. It was common in Mua – 1,000 lepers in this one hospital compound – but it was not dangerous to me, nor to the priests. Leprosy is not particularly contagious, nor infectious, and though it leaves permanent and unmistakable scars, it has a straightforward cure – sulfa drugs. My experience of the leper colony at Mua was a paradox, a sort of golden period of innocence, my Eden almost. It was 1964. I loved this clearing in the jungle: the simplest bush conditions, the lepers from all over the country, many different people brought together by a blight called *khate*, not Hansen's disease. AIDS was unknown then, we played cards by lamplight and listened to the lepers drumming; the only urgency was the constant bandaging. I have often thought of writing a novel about this strangely happy place.

Most ailments go with the territory. I remember an American I met in India who boasted of his constipation – he was unique in Delhi, city of squitters and bowel-shattering meals. Cut yourself on coral anywhere in the Pacific and you often end up with a serious infection. One of my memorable foreign lesions was a septic knee in Hawaii. What we used to call 'dhobi's itch' or 'Rangoon itch' in Singapore (in Rangoon it is probably called 'Singapore itch') was a fungal infection, and everyone had it, as everyone eventually had sand-fly bites, or lice of some sort.

'Grab lice or bhodhee lice?' an Indian pharmacist asked me much too loudly in the Victoria Chemist Shop on Serangoon Road in Singapore in 1971, and every customer at the shop turned to stare at me.

It is not possible to travel without coming down with something, yet no one should stay home for that reason. Apart from terminal boredom, Twinkie overload, and severe trauma to the brain from watching television, there are plenty of illnesses available at home. Paranoia. Nits. Dog bites. Bedbugs. Botulism. Sexually transmitted diseases. Lyme tic seizures. Rocky Mountain spotted fever. Whatever. I was made miserable by a paronychia (infection at the base of a fingernail) in London, and several years later got the same thing in New Guinea. The first bout I cured with antibiotics, the second, in a village in the Trobriand Islands, I cured by boiling my thumb twice a day for a week, much to the puzzlement of the local children.

As I write, a funeral is being held for a Seattle youngster who died having eaten nothing more exotic than a hamburger at his local Jack-in-the-Box fast food outlet. Obviously that ought not to deter anyone from traveling to the Pacific Northwest. And simple accidents are much more common than infectious diseases, at home and abroad. Thomas Merton left his Trappist monastery in Kentucky after twenty-seven years of seclusion, only to fall victim to a faulty fan which electrocuted him in Bangkok. That, like the frequent tourist drownings in shore-breaks, is a far more common story than, for example, the celebrated cases of Lassa fever – a grotesque, often fatal, but rare disease – which tend to mislead potential travelers to West Africa, who are much more at risk from, say, malaria or dysentery or injuries sustained from being mugged.

It can be extremely dangerous for a kayaker to perform an Eskimo roll in an English river. In the past decade, many kayakers in England have contracted Weil's disease, also called leptospirosis, from being infected with spirochaetal bacteria. These picturesque rivers are tainted with large amounts of rat urine. It is not unusual to read of an English kayaker making a so-called 'wet exit' and successfully swimming to shore, only to fall victim to Weil's disease from the short swim. The consequence is often kidney failure, a hook-up to a dialysis machine, and a long convalescence – all this from a few minutes splashing in a pretty tributary of the Avon.

It is true that some doctors today resemble the overweight and chain-smoking golfers and scare-mongers who, thirty years ago, gave me shots and then sent me abroad with facetious warnings of crocodile bites and beri-beri. The enigmatic quack who measured the size of Marlow's head before his Congo journey in *Heart of Darkness* ('Some heads are different when they return') was until recently a fairly common general practitioner. But many doctors are travelers, as well as skiers, paddlers, rock-climbers, trekkers, as interested in preventive medicine as in doling out antibiotics. This has been an immense help in replacing the fear of illness in travel with an instinct for sensible precautions.

I sometimes think I have caught almost everything catchable (and curable) in thirty years of travel.* AIDS is the nightmare, but there is another illness that is mentioned only in whispers, and that is *kuru*. This disease of the nervous system is found in eastern New Guinea, principally among the Foré people. The word *kuru* means 'trembling' – one of the symptoms. You go mad, and then you die. And the unique feature of *kuru* is that it is contracted by people only after they have eaten human flesh.

---

* A hubristic and, it turns out, inaccurate assertion. Since these words were written, severe dehydration on a long trip down the Zambezi River in 1997 traumatized my kidneys and brought on my first experience of gout; and in 1999, squinting miserably, I was diagnosed as suffering prematurely from severe cataracts, because of exposure to the ultraviolet rays in the tropical sunshine that I have encountered as a fresh-air fiend.

Part Three

A Sense of Place

Diaries of Two Cities

AMSTERDAM

Tuesday, April 10, 1990

Today is my 49th birthday. I knew I would be traveling to Amsterdam today, so last Saturday I pedaled my bike from London to Brighton, 49 miles. It was a terrible trip, because of the absence of cycling paths. I had to cycle by the side of the road, with the trucks and cars beeping their horns at me and roaring past. At roughly the 40th mile I felt 40, but by the 49th I felt 49. I dismounted and drank two pints of beer, ate an Indian meal alone, and then took the train back to London. Happy birthday. I keep thinking of my 50th, next year. George Orwell once wrote, 'At 50, every man has the face he deserves.'

Going from the bombed and rebuilt suburbs of London to the bombed and rebuilt suburbs of Amsterdam, there is no change: it is visually the same awful post-war architecture – budget-conscious, blighting the landscape. It is not until one is in Amsterdam proper that one feels one is in a different country. In the plane the pretty woman (Dutch) next to me said, 'So you are going to spend your birthday all alone? How terrible.' But she didn't offer to cheer me up tonight.

I am met at Schiphol airport and brought directly to a radio station, where we have a lively discussion of my new book, *Chicago Loop*. That is, after all, the reason I am here. I wonder whether authors should be paid to go on publicity tours – perhaps paid by the hour?

Dinner at a restaurant in Hilversum, and I eat some *sliptong*. No one knows the name for this in English, but it's a small sole. We then go to the TV studio, another discussion, this one videotaped so they can put subtitles on it. The host of the program is intelligent and well dressed, and I feel stupid, slow, and badly dressed. Will the Dutch think I am showing contempt by my looking so scruffy? And yet one of the great virtues of traveling in Amsterdam is that a visitor can dress casually. Here, I always think, neckties are superfluous.

A taxi back to Amsterdam in the rain, and at 10 p.m. we arrive. I was up at 6 a.m. And yet I am not very tired. I walk until midnight around the red light district, marveling at the monotonous meretriciousness of it all. But how motherly the prostitutes look. A woman in Amsterdam tells me the same thing. She says, 'All these whores look as though they are saying, "Come to Mummy!"'

April 11

Woke at 7 a.m. and listened to BBC World Service. Trouble in the Chinese province of Xinjiang – Muslim Uighurs revolting against Han Chinese domination. I mentioned this as a very strong possibility when I wrote my book about China in 1987, and I added, 'The Chinese would suppress such a revolt without mercy.'

Breakfast with Dr. Mulder of *Handelsblad*. He wonders whether I would keep a diary of my visit to Amsterdam. I told him that I keep a diary every ten years – in 1970, 1980, and now 1990. I write all sorts of trivia, and then marvel at it years later – at the prices and the minute details of life. I can't be bothered to keep a diary the rest of the time. After all, I have books to write, and a diary is simply an interruption. It is something that non-writers ought to do, for the edification of their grandchildren.

Dr. Mulder has a background in criminology. I interrogate him about this although he continually steers the conversation back to books. His insights on the prison riots in Britain convince me that the British have one of the least enlightened prison systems in the Western world – still basically rooted in nineteenth-century ideas of penal servitude. Indeed, most British people would like to ship prisoners to Australia or Devil's Island.

An interview was supposed to take place at 9.30. The interviewer was late – about the rarest occurrence in Holland. But she mistook the time. Still, we talked for half an hour. I said I tried to be truthful. She said, 'But what is truth?' implying that there is no such thing. I told her this is more or less the sort of discussion that schoolchildren have, about truth, beauty, and the meaning of life. I would rather talk about sex and violence – or about cooking.

Dr. Wolffers is shown in. He is a medical doctor. He also has an interest in books, my fiction, and the Third World. He has traveled in many parts of the world that I have, so it is a pleasure to talk to him. I try to steer him around to the subject of medicine. My great regret in life is that I did not finish my medical studies. I think I am like a woman who knows that she is no longer able to have a baby, at age 40 or so; I am past medical-school-age, so to speak. Dr. W. encourages me to study medicine. On the other hand, his interest is alternative medicine. I ask him a traveler's question – does he ever carry antibiotics on his trips? He says flatly no – never.

'What do you do about diarrhea in the tropics?' I ask.

'The important thing is to rehydrate yourself. Most of these other preparations are simply cosmetic.'

Then he gives me the formula. Let's say you have diarrhea in Bangladesh and have no medicine. You mix a pinch of salt with several spoonfuls of sugar in about a half-liter of water. This will help do the trick. Brown sugar is the best, because it contains potassium.

I am delighted by this non-literary conversation.

Lunch with the Board of Trustees of the John Adams Institute. One woman I met ten years ago in Washington, another man is a colleague of my brother, a lawyer, the rest are distinguished and all the men wear neckties. So I again feel scruffy and badly dressed. In spite of this, the director of the Concertgebouw offers me tickets to Verdi's *Requiem* tomorrow. The last time I was in Amsterdam I heard the same piece in the same place.

I feel I am seeing very little of Amsterdam, so I suggest to the next interviewer from *De Morgen* – he is a Belgian called Samiel van Hole, a travel writer himself – that we go to the Van Gogh exhibition. At the same time, while I am looking at the paintings I will answer his questions, mumbling into his tape recorder. In this way I will have a glimmering of pleasing my aesthetic sense. Samiel says that he is too nervous to look at the pictures. He reads his questions from a piece of paper, I carry his tape recorder and I mumble. It is satisfactory, but exhausting. His wonderful news is that he has just signed a contract for his travel book with a distinguished publisher in Amsterdam. I am convinced he is probably a great traveler when he tells me that he is unable to drive a car.

Returning to the hotel to prepare my lecture, I lie down and fall asleep. I am wakened by the telephone. Too late to prepare, but I am so well rested that I am clear-headed. If I had notes or a lecture prepared I would feel dull and earnest. As it is I feel bright and eager. The Kuplezaal is filled – about 450 people. But Dutch audiences always do their homework; they buy and read your books, they ask good questions; they are attentive. So after a 40-minute talk and a short break for coffee I answer questions. The best is, 'Have you ever experienced evil?'

A short walk, and then dinner alone, which I spent writing a fax to the States.

My bedtime book is *The Aspern Papers* by Henry James. I read it 20 years ago, but am happy to return to it each night. One chapter a night before I sleep.

April 12

After my first sound sleep I am interviewed by an Australian for the World Service of Radio Nederland. After the interview he tells me stories about Australia, and I tell him about my kayak trip to North Queensland. He has been living here for 20 years, and like other aliens has taken root. But he was part of the profoundly international '60s culture, which deeply affected Amsterdam, even if it did not make much of an impression in provincial bourgeois Holland.

I am picked up and driven to Rotterdam to sign books. On the way I learn a curious fact: the Dutch have taken to using mountain bikes. *Mountain bikes in Holland?* This is an example of the Dutch susceptibility for fads, the Dutch eagerness to be part of world culture. Sometimes it is overdone – you have to know when to stop. And the American junk food places all over Holland make me sad.

Rotterdam: lots of book buyers at Donners, 'the biggest bookstore in the Western world' (so I am informed). I sign books. I eat a *broodjie*. I return to Amsterdam, and I reflect that I have spent 5½ hours going to Rotterdam to sign books. If I were the Pope or Michael Jordan I would understand the mechanism which requires a personal appearance. But I am a near-sighted writer who hates long car journeys as a passenger.

A photo session ('Put your hand to your cheek') and two more bookstores – signing, talking – and finally, at 8.15, the Concertgebouw – Verdi's *Requiem*.

There are nearly as many performers as spectators – a whole choir, a huge orchestra; it is beautifully, thrillingly performed. But just after the thunderous second *Dies irae*, when the choir is singing

> *Lacrymosa dies illa,*
> *Qua resurget ex favilla,*

a man in the choir suddenly collapses! There is drama: the choir and the quartet continue to sing the lugubrious verse, as the man gasps for breath, and to the sad strains of Verdi's *Requiem* he is carried out by four members of the choir and a man from the audience. Everyone present is a witness.

April 13

I wake early, write in my notebook for the first time since I arrived – the beginning of a story – I feel at last settled enough to write; and then I ask the next interviewer to conduct the interview at the Yoshitoshi Exhibition, at the Rijksmuseum. This turned out to be a pleasant conversation with a knowledgeable woman, as we were passing from one picture to another, looking at what the Japanese call *Ukiyo-e* prints – pictures of 'the floating world.' The Japanese these days are also susceptible to novelty. While they are buying modern furniture and pictures they are selling their antiques and prints.

The 'Night-Watch' is closed for restoration – a lunatic threw acid on it. The fact that he was shrewd enough to throw acid makes me think he's not a lunatic.

Another interviewer: 'The problem in Holland is not the young people. They spend 1.3 hours a week reading, is that bad?'

I said, 'Not necessarily. Their parents spend 6 hours reading *De Telegraaf*. Is that good?'

I am now preparing to leave Holland, to return to London. I would like to stay longer in Amsterdam. And the fact is that it is only when I go home that I get culture shock.

LONDON

Sunday, October 3, 1993

Arrived at 7 a.m. after a ten-month absence, but really I have not lived in England for almost four years. And the last time I stayed in a London hotel was 1971, at just this time of year. The lovely clouds, the wet pavement, the penetrating dampness all bring back memories of that arrival, a little shivering family of four fresh from Singapore, without a job or a house, or much money. Then eighteen years passed and everything happened, and now I feel like a ghost, slipping back into the country, to haunt and be haunted.

The view from the Stafford in St. James's is rosy. There is an article about me and my new novel, *Millroy the Magician*, in the *Sunday Times*. I sound absurd. I put this down to the young English journalist's discomfort with being frankly appreciative. He knows that if he is nice to me he will be accused of arse-creeping, and so his admiration is turned into sniping. But who cares? The article will be lining the bottom of your budgie's cage tomorrow and so will this diary the editor at the *Guardian* asked me to write.

October 4

London traits: lowered voices, lateness, pessimism, pallor, a look of fatigue, rumpled clothes, bad haircuts, the stillness of tube passengers. But this seems to me to be the least threatening city in the world; even on a good day, New York is a hellhole. Thirty thousand people dead in an Indian earthquake, but that is yesterday's news, now on an inside page, because today the headline concerns Russia, '500 Dead as Tanks Go In' – confrontation at the Russian parliament. I no longer live in a city and so I have forgotten how world news energizes city slickers.

A sign of the times on an ornate Victorian public dustbin in Kensington: 'Thank You for Keeping the Royal Borough Tidy – Sponsored by Coca-Cola.' A journalist refers to a previous book of mine, 'Written in your blue period.' Another one compares my character Millroy with Wilhelm Reich; my man proposes a vegetarian diet, based on the Bible; Willy had his Orgone Box. 'Established science finds it threatening.' In the evening I give a talk at Waterstone's in Hampstead; it is a form of evangelizing, with alert, attentive listeners, literary piety, just the thing for me with my book about a religious nut.

October 5

No breakfast, a tuna fish sandwich for lunch, dinner with the Spanish ambassador, Señor Alberto Aza, who has just been Spain's ambassador to Mexico. The differences between Mexican bullfights and

Spanish ones: Mexican bulls are smaller, Spanish ones braver, Mexican matadors often stick the banderillas into a bull's neck – this is regarded as a menial task in Spain, and so forth. Señor Aza was a low-level diplomat in Africa when I was a low-level school teacher there. That was in the nineteenth century, when Franco and Salazar were alive. Señor Aza: 'They say that Galicians are so secretive that if you pass one on the stairway, you will not know whether he is going up or going down.'

I have been to Easter Island and New Guinea, but I have never been to Spain. Talking with him I conceive the idea of going to Spain, but starting in Gibraltar; grinning like a dog and wandering aimlessly along the Spanish coast.

October 6

Nothing will irk me today, because Victoria Glendinning praises my novel in *The Times*. And a little glimpse of Waterloo International, which I had never seen before, gives me a thrill: you will soon be able to go from there on a succession of trains, to Kowloon or Hanoi. On the other hand, a return air ticket to Gibraltar is 149 pounds – probably cheaper than the return rail fair to Edinburgh. I head for Leadenhall Market. Business at the bookshop there has not been so brisk since that cowardly bombing by political scumbags in April displaced 100,000 office workers.

Literary postscript: A woman visiting the shop says that a gigantic drunk who called me a 'wanker' and tried physically to attack me while I was speaking at a literary dinner in Fremantle, Australia, was a friend of a friend. I wrote about this in my *Happy Isles of Oceania*. Everyone said I was exaggerating and slagging off the Aussies. This Digger's name was Kester, and he was thwarted by a woman named Prue Dashfield. Interesting: a man would not have dared to try and stop him, but this woman did. I made a nervous joke of it, and when the drunk heard the applause from the corridor he said, 'Hear them? They agree with me! They wanted me to kill the wanker!'

I am reading *Tender is the Night* and find this: 'Often people display a curious respect for a man drunk, rather like the respect of simple races for the insane. Respect rather than fear. There is something awe-inspiring in one who has lost all inhibitions, who will do anything.'

October 7

Toni Morrison has won the Nobel Prize. I met her once in Paris when we were on a literary panel with James Baldwin and she laughed in a resonant, rumbling way. Why didn't Baldwin win it? Why didn't Borges and James Joyce? 'I see the Nobel Committee is pissing on literature again,' V. S. Naipaul once remarked to me.

'Why is your book so grim?' a journalist asks me in an interview. She then reveals that she has only just started reading it. I tell her that Victoria G. called it 'very funny' just yesterday. Next question: 'Why do you always travel in a bad mood?' I challenge this: what book are you referring to? She collapses, confessing that she has never read anything I have written.

In the evening to Broadcasting House. Another sign of the times: the BBC recently sacked all the underpaid men who used to show guests to the studio. You are now given a map on a piece of paper and asked to find your own way. I got lost. Then I found the studio. No one there except a man speaking about 'conkers' into a mike. He leaves, and I sit alone among litter in a tiny room, and ring a number on an old Bakelite phone, and am connected to Radio Scotland. An hour later I leave, not having seen another human being in the building. False economy is one of the most destructive English vices.

October 8

Does anyone watch Sky TV? I am in the studio with Frank Delany, the Buck Mulligan of our time, and Margaret Atwood, and Robert Waller, who is the most famous novelist in America at the moment. He is carrying a guitar, an ominous sign, a bit like William Burroughs fondling a pistol. You want to say, Get that goddamned thing away from him! Margaret, a Canadian, says, 'I live in the only safe country in the world.' I challenge this. New Zealand, Costa Rica, Eire, and Mongolia are much safer in my experience. I head for J. Walter Thompson to discuss the merits of Rolex watches with a copywriter named Charity-Charity, 'because when I got married I decided not to take the chap's name. I wanted my own name.'

To Cheltenham and the glorious countryside where I always wanted to live (and now it is too late). I am ten minutes late for my lecture. No one has panicked. I slide from the car to the podium. More evangelism and literary piety. Afterwards, a man says, 'You should read the poem by Gavin Ewart called "American Fatties." ' I wish I could find it. Another man follows me out to the street and shyly asks, 'Where did you get those wonderful shoes?' They're Mephistos, made in France, bought in Hong Kong.

October 9

Cosmo Book Day, at Church House, Westminster, where one of the *Cosmopolitan* covers announces, 'Big Growth Areas! Fellatio on the upswing!' A chat with Sue Townsend, whose husband, Colin, manufactures canoes. This book event is all young women with jobs who buy and read books. It is a thousand times more interesting than a literary lunch, usually attended by elderly people wanting to kill time ('in self-defense' as DeVries remarked) – I hear someone say of a friend, 'Oh, she went to the College of Short Planks . . .'

In the evening to the South Bank to hear Baroque music. People in my face all week, but this is heaven. London music is what I miss most. Never mind, I am off to Gibraltar in the morning.

Farewell to Britain:
Look Thy Last on All Things Lovely

Living in Britain, I used to believe that I would never get lost, nor would I ever find an unknown place in this peaceable but much-trampled kingdom. Yet people got lost all the time in the Welsh hills, or froze to death in the Lake District, or drowned off the coast; and many rural places had the look of wilderness, even if they weren't wild. And for all its tameness, Britain was difficult to leave and often hard to travel around. On a clear day the French coast was visible to the south-east, yet Britain was not Europe. It was not America, either; it was much more than England. It had edges; cold water lapped its shores. As time passed Britain seemed larger to me, not smaller, some parts of it almost unreachable; though in eighteen years I never lost the sense that I was on an island.

The breadth and subtlety of English literature, perhaps the greatest literature in the world, endows a foreign bookworm – which is what I was, and am – with a distinct sense of what Britain is like; the complex power of its monarchy, the labyrinthine nature of its cities, the grandeur and diversity of its coastline, the misleading folksiness of its villages, the almost Oriental complexity of its manners and society. As for the beauty of its seasons, there is a whole library of English literature on the subject of spring alone; but it helps to live through the darkness and uncertainty of an English winter to appreciate it.

I cannot say that I went to visit Britain to indulge myself in verifying its literature. I left teaching in Singapore and headed for England because in 1971 a house in the English countryside could be rented for the equivalent of about ten US dollars a week. I found a cottage in west Dorset, not far from the sea. As a self-employed writer, with a wife and two children, I could live in a lovely place without feeling any financial pressure. So, although it was bargain-hunting that sent me to that village, and not the work of Thomas Hardy, inevitably, among these deeply rooted people, I discovered the truth of Hardy's writing. His descriptions of the folk, the farms, the hills, the wild flowers, the villages, even the forms of cruelty, still held. It was my lesson. I resolved to be as faithful to what I experienced.

When people in London said 'the North' they meant Manchester or Newcastle, but for me north always meant Scotland, because I had a distinct sense that I was on an island. One of the many oddities of subdivided Britain is that one of the northernmost regions is called Sutherland – so it was for the Vikings, for whom it was south. When I took a train I never had a notion of crossing into Wales, or into Cornwall or Scotland; it was just more stops and smaller stations. The tribal warfare of Britain, with its teasing as well as its injustices, its enduring aggression and sense of grievance, is something I regarded with a detachment I had learned in observing the Baganda and the Acholi quarrel in Uganda.

After a time we moved from Dorset to London, but I never lost the feeling that I was a castaway. As a foreigner I was determined not to die there and be buried in a gloomy churchyard under a blackish dripping yew tree. One day I would sail away. I never guessed that I would leave alone, feeling as portable and insignificant as when I arrived. I landed in Britain on November 4, 1971; I left on January 19, 1990. The years that these dates enclose are among the happiest as well as the saddest I have ever known: joy bordering on rapture, misery at the very edge of despair.

I knew I did not belong – no foreigner can in Britain – nor did I want to. Anyway, I quite enjoyed the experience of being at once alien and anonymous, like 'The Man Who Fell to Earth', a Martian who looks like everyone else. This condition seemed to me to epitomize the writer's dilemma. But on an island of such unselfconscious literacy and library-going it seemed natural to be a writer. Because of our peculiar attitude toward money, a writer is an oddity in the United States, but not in Britain.

I was always a taxpayer but never a voter, so I had no sense of belonging, of supporting a political party, or even of being an English resident. My home was a house in south London, on this island of Britain. I often felt physically uncomfortable or socially constrained, and yet I was intellectually freer and better appreciated than I ever felt before or since. I was never entirely at home in Britain and yet I never had a sense of being unwelcome. Seeing people on the street, I used to think, *You are home and I am not.* I constantly prayed, *I don't want to die here.*

After eleven years in Britain I grew restless. To gather more experience to write about this island I set off to circumambulate the coast – on foot, and by train and bus and boat. When *The Kingdom by the Sea* appeared, with all its breezy generalities and affectionate mockery, the reviews were robust – British literary journalists practice harmless cruelty – yet the fuss meant my book was taken seriously, and so was I, because I still lived there. What American Anglomaniacs don't understand is that the British will listen to the opinions of almost anyone who lives on the island; but generally speaking, if a writer doesn't live in Britain they have no interest in his or her opinions. When I left Britain, ceasing to be a resident, I lost my nit-picking license.

One day I made a list of all the things I liked in Britain: bread, fish, clouds, beer, country pubs, clotted cream, flower gardens, apples, newspapers, woolen cloth, radio programs, parks, Indian restaurants, amateur dramatics, the Royal Mail, the trains, and the patience and modesty and politeness of people.

'Look thy last on all things lovely/Every hour,' I used to murmur to myself when I lived in Britain. I loved paddling the coastline of Wales in my kayak, and cycling from London to Brighton, hiking the South Downs, listening to a symphony concert in the Royal Festival Hall, visiting one son at Oxford and the other at Cambridge. *What luck*, I thought. *I have planted my family here and it has flourished.*

After I left I looked back and saw that to a large extent England had made me, but not in the way I had imagined. I had resolved to be frugal, and living among frugal people I had not lost the habit. I saw how the difficult road had rewarded me. I began to cherish, and still do, times of adversity and disappointment and hardship. And I began to understand what hardship is. It is not, for example, the long, vividly difficult road over the Tibetan plateau, from Golmud to Lhasa – which I have traveled; it is the eighteen years I spent on the South Circular Road, which is almost indescribably depressing, and who's interested? Hardship can be a lively subject, but nuisance is something that no one wants to hear about.

Britain is beautiful, but Britain can also be bleak – not ugly or picturesquely dangerous, but with stretches of enormous monotony that seemed to nibble at my soul. The heart-sinking housing estates by the motorway in Huddersfield; the look of my children's pale faces among all the others in the schoolyard of their primary school; the crowded bus stops, sadder for being orderly; the bleakness of certain reaches of the Thames at low tide; and nothing on this earth that I have seen is bleaker than a drizzly winter afternoon in Catford – brown sky, gray bricks, black street. But I never regarded it as failure – it was reality, an opportunity, and my discomfort made me look more closely and gave me something to write about. Then I moved on and closed the book on it.

Gravy Train:
A Private Railway Car

I was sitting in the sunshine on the rear car of a train heading west feeling utterly baffled and thinking, *I have never been here before*. It was not just the place (early morning in the middle of Colorado); it was also my state of mind (blissful). I was grateful for my good fortune. To think that riding a train, something I had done for pleasure all my traveling life, had been improved upon. In the past, what had mattered most in any long train journey through an interesting landscape were the motion, the privacy, the solitude, the grandeur. Food and comfort, I had discovered, are seldom available on the best trips: there is something about the most beautiful places having the most awful trains. But this was something else.

My chair was on the rear observation platform of a private railway car called 'Los Angeles,' formerly part of the Southern Pacific Railway. My feet were braced against the brass rail; the morning sunshine was full upon my face. I had woken in Fort Morgan, and after a stroll in Denver had reboarded to have breakfast with family and friends in the private dining room of this car: orange juice, home-baked blueberry coffee cake and muffins, scrambled eggs and fresh juice and coffee. Then the morning paper in the private lounge, and finally settling myself in the open air on this little brass porch on the rear as we started our climb through the foothills of the Rockies, and an hour out of Denver it was epic grandeur, past frozen creeks, and pines and rubbly hills, destination San Francisco. I was very happy.

From this position on a train, eye contact is possible, and as we passed through Pinecliffe, in Gilpin County, a woman stopped at the level crossing, stuck her head out of her car, and waved at me, making my day.

'Anything I can get you?' That was George, the steward, holding the rear door open. 'Coffee? Cookies? More juice? Hot chocolate?'

There were four armchairs and a big sofa in the parlor just inside; and off the corridor, four bedrooms, two with double beds, and hot showers. Farther along, the dining room, and the gourmet kitchen, and beyond that a big long Amtrak train, the California Zephyr, pulling us on its usual route, from Chicago to San Francisco, via Denver and Salt Lake City.

As for the rest, I was ignorant. Happiness has no questions; bliss is not a state of inquiry. Whatever squirrely anxieties I possessed had vanished a long way back, probably soon after we boarded in Chicago, or else at Galesburg. Bliss had definitely taken hold as we crossed the Mississippi, because I remember standing right here on the rear platform and gawking at it, the chunks of ice gleaming in the lights of Burlington, Iowa, on the distant riverbank, the clattering of the bridge, the sense that I was in the night air, hearing and seeing the water, and smelling it too, a marshy muddiness this damp winter night of the great river.

We had left Chicago the previous afternoon in fog so thick that airline passengers had turned O'Hare into a gigantic dormitory and departing flights were so thoroughly canceled that there was a slumber party at each gate. The fog was news, and so there was a certain sense of excitement in slipping out of it. I glanced from time to time at the Amtrak route guide, which gave helpful information. We passed Princeton, Illinois ('Pig Capital of the World'), and Galesburg (associated with Carl Sandburg, and the Lincoln–Douglas debates, and 'Popcorn was invented in Galesburg by Olmstead Ferris'), then through Monmouth (birthplace of Wyatt Earp). But all I saw were dark houses and dim lights and the vast Midwestern sky, and here and there a small nameless town, not noticed by the guide, and a filling station on a side road, or a bowling alley, or the local diner filled with eaters.

It is easy to understand the envy of the traveler for the settled people he or she sees, snug in their houses, at home. But I could not have been snugger here in the private railway car. Thinking of the days that stretched ahead, all of them on the rails, I was put in mind of Russia, of long journeys through forests and prairies, past little wooden houses half buried in the snow, with smoking chimneys. It was like that, the size of the landscape, and the snow, and the darkness and the starry night over Iowa.

After hot showers, we assembled for pre-dinner drinks in the parlor and toasted our trip and talked about the train.

'This was the car that Robert Kennedy used for his campaign in

1968 – he made his visit to Los Angeles on it,' Christopher Kyte said.

Christopher was the owner of the 'Los Angeles,' having bought it some eight years ago and restored it at great expense to its former glory. It had been built and fitted out at the height of the boom in the 1920s, and finished just in time for the crash in 1929.

That Robert Kennedy had used it, and made whistle-stop speeches from the rear observation platform, was a solemn thought, but it had been used by many other people: actresses, tycoons, foreign royalty. Sam Rayburn and Lyndon Johnson had made hundreds of trips on it, between Texas and Washington, DC. It had seen drunks and lovers and millionaires; it was not a mere conveyance, any more than a ship was – people had spent a part of their lives on it.

'Los Angeles' was for weeks at a time Christopher Kyte's own home, one of the mobile aspects of his California-based company. A humorous, self-mocking fellow, whose innocence and innate goodwill made his humor all the more appealing, Christopher Kyte reminded me of Bertie Wooster. He was all the more Woosterish when he was in his double-breasted dark suit, recalling a scandalous episode, and George, the steward, was at his elbow, helping with a name or a date. George was Jeeves to his fingertips – efficient, helpful, silent, good at everything, eighteen years on Southern Pacific. 'I've looked after Tom Clancy,' he told me. He was as kindly as Christopher, and it was a wonder, given their dispositions, that the company made any money at all. But it has more than prospered.

Nostalgia is not the point; nor is it the glamour of an antique railway car. The idea is comfort, and privacy, and forward motion. It is a grand hotel suite on wheels, with gourmet food and fine beds, and a view of the Great Plains, and any stop-over you like.

'I'd like to spend a day skiing,' I had told him, a few weeks before we left on the trip. I knew we were passing through Colorado and Utah and snowy parts of California. 'What if we stopped for a night somewhere in Utah?'

We decided on Provo, just about sixteen miles from the narrow snowy canyon in the Wasatch Range where Sundance is located. That would be our second night.

'We'll drop you in Provo,' Christopher said. 'A car will meet you at the station. Stay at Sundance that night and ski the next day. Then meet us at the station in Salt Lake City and plan to have dinner on board. The chef will have something special.'

Meanwhile the Iowa plains were passing and we filed into the dining room for our first night's dinner, six of us around the table, feasting on pot roast, braised Southern-style. The conversation was enlivened by a meal-time quiz show of guessing celebrities' real names (significant answers: Reg Dwight, Gordon Sumner, Malcolm Little, Bill Blythe, Newton McPherson).

That night the Zephyr pulled 'Los Angeles' through Nebraska, from Omaha ('Boys Town . . . is west of town') to Benkelman near the Colorado border ('one hour earlier if going west'). But I was still asleep in Colorado. I roused myself around Fort Morgan, in the high plains, and a little later watched people gathering for the Annual Stock Show and Rodeo outside Denver, just next to the tracks – cattle, cowboys, stock-pens – the year's big event. I got off to buy a newspaper in Denver, and soon after, in the clear bright day, was sitting on the rear observation platform in the sunshine, for the long climb through the foothills of the Rockies, through the pines and aspens.

Snow and cold drove me inside around lunch time, and soon we came to the small town of Winter Park, not far from Fraser (which 'proudly calls itself "the ice-box of America"'). That afternoon we had a long snowy ride under the steep pinnacles of shale in Glenwood Canyon, to Glenwood Springs, and where the rock was uncovered it was the color of honey in the fading daylight. Skiers got off the train to make their way to Aspen and Vail. We followed the course of Spanish Creek which flowed toward the Colorado River.

'Who has been your oddest passenger?' I said to Christopher over dinner, as we clattered down the canyon.

'Most of our people are wonderful,' he said. But he was smiling, remembering.

There was, for example, the man traveling with five strangers who showed up in the dining room one morning stark naked, just as the wife of a tycoon was saying, 'Pass the sausages, please.' The naked man was five foot four; he weighed 300 pounds. This was not a welcome sight at the breakfast table.

'You have no clothes on,' Christopher said to him.

'I always eat breakfast like this,' the naked man said, and began to sip his coffee, while the rest of the diners averted their eyes.

Ever the diplomat, Christopher suggested that he would be more comfortable having his breakfast served on a tray in the privacy of his room.

Oh, yes – Christopher was still smiling gently – and there was the transvestite who was a rather sedate man during the day, and at night put on a wig and a dress and mascara and drank far too much Drambuie and turned cartwheels on the rear platform with such energy that Amtrak threatened to uncouple 'Los Angeles' and leave it on a siding in Omaha.

And the man who bedded down with his stuffed giraffe and teddy bear. And the man who celebrated his divorce by boarding in Reno and setting off on a ten-day trip in the car with a little harem of five young women who took turns visiting him in his room. And the large, ill-assorted family who used a cross-country trip as the occasion for a noisy three-day binge.

'The minute they boarded I knew there'd be a problem,' Christopher said. 'They were the sort of people who use the word "party" as a verb. Very bad sign.'

We were by now on dessert, and also near the top of the Wasatch Range – Soldier Summit, almost 7,500 feet high, snow everywhere. From here we traveled in loops and through tunnels to Provo, where a little van was waiting. It was round about midnight.

'Have a good time skiing,' Christopher said.

'Dinner will be served at eight tomorrow,' George said. 'We'll be waiting for you.'

The mist at the station gave way to sleet outside of town, and before we had reached Sundance it was snow, drifting down the canyon. But there was so much snow already that we could see the slopes and the lifts and the stands of snow-clad pine gleaming in the lights of the resort.

All night the snow fell, and it was still falling the next morning. Fortified by the late dinner, we had juice and two set off to the downhill slopes and two to the wooded cross-country trails. We rented skis, poles, and boots; we had all the rest of our gear. After the eating and drinking of the train this was perfect – kicking and gliding cross-country through the meadows and woods of Sundance. A break for lunch, and then a whole afternoon of skiing. The snow still fell, the air was mild – hardly freezing. Except for a flock of crows and one invisible woodpecker, the woods were silent.

At dark we handed back our ski gear and were taken to Salt Lake City train station, about an hour away. And there, solitary, detached, at a platform in the middle of the train-yard, its lights blazing, was the 'Los Angeles.'

A movable feast, I was thinking, as a woman in a white smock greeted us.

This was the chef, Regina Charboneau, just in from San Francisco, where she owned a restaurant and a blues bar. The Southern cuisine was Regina's inspiration, but it was Southern cooking with a difference, traditional ingredients served with a flourish – the sweet potatoes and crab cakes and buttermilk biscuits we had been eating. Tonight we were being served pheasant and okra gumbo, and salmon with potato crust over creamed hominy grits and warm chocolate bread pudding. The pheasant and okra gumbo, hearty and flavorful, was meant to restore us after our day of skiing. The gumbo, the bread pudding and the biscuits were full of her own innovations.

'My sous-chef said, "What about lentils with the salmon?"' Regina said. 'I told him, "Everyone does that. Let's rethink the lentils."'

The grits they tried had come from Regina's childhood. She had gotten to San Francisco by way of Natchez (where she was one of nine children, her father a chef and restaurateur), Missoula, Montana (where she gained a sense of reality), the settlement of Chignik Lake, Alaska (where at the age of twenty-three she was camp cook), Paris (Cordon Bleu school), and Anchorage (several successful restaurants). Her stories could not top Christopher's naked passenger, cartwheeling transvestite, and cross-country harem; but they were very good, and included a plane crash in Alaska, strange times at the work camp, and at least one marriage proposal by a young Aleut male: 'Marry me,' the man said. 'You damn good cook. You paint the shanty any color you like. I not beat you very much.'

Later, in my room, full of food and warmth and a pleasant fatigue, I began to understand the meaning of the expression gravy train, not the sinister implication of voluptuous self-indulgence but a friendly journey where everything is rosy.

Sometime during the night the westbound Zephyr snatched us from Salt Lake City station and whisked us across the Great Salt Lake Desert at ninety-five miles an hour. We were still in high desert in the morning, a landscape like Tibet, arid stony ground with the peaks and ridges of snowy mountains showing in the distance on almost every side.

'Those are the Ruby Mountains,' Christopher said, indicating a great white wall to the east. A bit later, about eighteen miles out of Reno, 'And that's Mustang Ranch.'

It was, pinkish and sprawling, three or four one-story buildings by the side of the tracks; not very glamorous, it had the look of a boys' camp, which in a sense it was. Reno itself, part circus, part residential, seemed a complete blight on the landscape, 'kitsch in sync,' in the words of one wag. Those people who boarded the Zephyr here did not look like winners; in fact, no one looked like a winner here at all.

Some friends of mine and their child had been driven from their home in Colfax, farther down the line, to join us here. They got on board, and all the way along the route of the Donner party we ate and drank. One of them brought me a copy of *Ordeal by Hunger*, the story of the Donner tragedy, by George Stewart, and there I sat as we clunked past Truckee – deep in snow – and Donner Peak and Donner Lake, where the awful events of death and cannibalism unfolded. I sat all afternoon reading and stuffing myself with coffee cake.

It was downhill after that in every sense, through the foggy forests of ponderosa to Colfax and farewells; to Sacramento in the dusk; and the moonrise at Martinez, where Howard Hughes's *Glomar Explorer* was riding at anchor.

'Joe DiMaggio was born here,' Christopher said. 'And so was the Martini. Maybe.'

Then we were rolling through the Bay Area's backyard.

'May I suggest we put the lights out?' Christopher said, with his usual grace. 'The last time we came through here some young people threw rocks at our windows. I'd pay each of them 200 dollars not to! But this way no one will see us.'

The darkness inside 'Los Angeles' revealed everything outside – the lights of the bay, the distant bridge we had just crossed, the muddy little docks in the foreground, Oakland just by the tracks, the skyline of San Francisco, Emeryville up ahead, where we glided to a stop.

I hated separating myself from the snug comfort of 'Los Angeles.' Taking nothing for granted, I travel hopefully; but I am not surprised when everything goes wrong. I am very grateful when things turn out well. If bliss can be described as an exalted state of not wishing to be anywhere else, then this had been bliss.

The Maine Woods: Camping in the Snow

Through the cold late-afternoon forest, down a long looping slope that looked like a trail, I glided on my cross-country skis, bumping tree trunks with my elbows, until the trail narrowed to nothing – just dark shadows of huge trees patterning the snow. But I had been misled. It was not a trail at all, and within minutes I was lost.

I had to remove my skis to struggle onward through the dense groves of yellow and silver birch and the stands of pine so thick they were black and looked impenetrable. The early sunset broke through blindingly to show me another clearing, and I saw large tracks in the snow, the length of my own ski boots, but wider – the prints of a black bear. They were unmistakable: I could make out the claws and see the pads of the paws indented in the snow. And they were recent – they had not iced over. So I was not alone.

There are shaggy distracted black bears in the north woods of Maine known as 'beggar bears.' They have had some experience of humans – they have raided a camper's garbage pit perhaps, or they might have been clumsily fed by a bemused hiker. In any case, they are cautious but not afraid; they have learned by association that there is sometimes food in the vicinity of human beings. American black bears tend to be oblique: they do not look for trouble, there is plenty for them to eat in the forest. They feed placidly and they retreat when they hear an unfamiliar sound. But the beggar bear is dangerous when it is hungry. It may turn predatory at the sight of a person. In America, the urban counterpart of a beggar bear is a mugger with a knife or a pistol.

With that sort of degenerate bear in mind, I turned and skied back the way I had come, on the tracks I had left. A person on cross-country skis can always eventually find the way back. And perhaps I should not have feared this animal.

'There is nothing in the Maine woods that will hurt you, except another human being,' a man had told me the day before I set off.

He knew what he was talking about. He was Irvin Caverly, Director of Baxter State Park in northern Maine, which is one of the most important wilderness areas of New England. These 193 square miles are unique in America for being privately endowed, the gift of one man, Maine millionaire and former governor Percival Baxter. Before he died at the age of ninety in 1969, Baxter provided a trust fund to support the park. He specified that it should be kept out of the control of politicians and that it should never become a national park. The vast forest he bequeathed contains many mountains, including Maine's highest peak, Katahdin (5,216 feet), which was sacred to the Indians – it was where their gods dwelled, their equivalent of Mount Olympus. It is a lovely mountain – remote, solitary, and most serene on winter afternoons, when its snow is deeply tinted with the gold of the setting sun. All around it are the tall trees and trackless hills of Baxter's wilderness.

'The works of men are short-lived,' this far-sighted man said. 'Monuments decay, buildings crumble, and wealth vanishes, but Katahdin in its massive grandeur will forever remain the mountain of the people of Maine.'

The whole of northern Maine is one enormous logging operation for the pulp and paper mills that provide income and employment in the state. But this forest, especially in winter, is a place apart, in which there is no human sign – no footprints, nothing but the crush of trees, the sound of wind and birds, and in winter deep snow, successive layers of it that first descend in November and continue to accumulate for four or five months, only thawing in April. In May, there are still large bright patches of snow all through the forest which from a distance look as pure and as soft as spilled cream.

Entering the forest on skis on my first day in mid-March, I had seen that the snow was so deep I would be wearing the skis all week. I had chosen skis over more traditional snow-shoes that are made of bent wood and rawhide webbing and make you unsinkable. Though many hikers use them, I find wearing them is like walking with a tennis racket strapped to each foot.

A snowy wilderness is a problem, but cross-country skis are only part of the solution. I had been concerned about finding places to pitch my tent – there was no bare ground anywhere. Wet, windy weather had been forecast. I did not have a sled – wilderness campers often ski in a harness, dragging a sled loaded with as much as 110 pounds of gear. I would be carrying all my gear in my backpack. I wanted to travel light and see as much of this wilderness as possible, sleeping each night in the snow.

But, because of the cold and the possibility of emergencies – a person becoming lost, frostbitten, injured – it was a park rule that in the winter season only teams of three or more well-equipped adults were allowed to camp in the forest or climb Katahdin. As an individual, I could ski into the wilderness area each day, but at sundown I had to leave – signing in and out in the logbook of the gatehouse, which was over an hour's skiing from the main road, where I had left my car.

When I asked the director whether I could camp just outside the park he took pity on me and said, 'I think I can do better than that,' and gave me the use of a rugged one-roomed cabin which was an occasional shelter for stranded rangers, and was in a snowy pine wood at the fringes of the wilderness, at the shore of a wind-swept pond.

I skied to the cabin the first day just to see what I would need: it contained a bare mattress and a chair, and a pot-bellied stove, but no water, no lanterns, no cooking facilities. I left a bucket of snow inside the hut to thaw. When I returned the next day the snow was still frozen. Yet I had all I needed in my backpack – a small camp stove, a sleeping bag, some spare clothes, candles, a flashlight, maps, a compass, a knife, a first-aid kit, and enough fruit and dehydrated food to last six days.

Prepared for the worst, I felt happy, confident, more than that – almost euphoric, with a sense of independence and self-sufficiency. I had skis and camping gear and food. All around me, there was an endless supply of water in the form of pure meltable snow. The weather was pleasant, in spite of the forecast – the daytime temperature just above freezing, the nights very cold. There were birds in the trees – chickadees, woodpeckers, sparrows, jays – and animal tracks in the snow. At the edge of the park there were signs of humans – the grooves of skis and the flatter, wider tracks of snow-mobiles – a few miles into the forest where the wilderness began, the only sound was the moan of wind in the treetops. Just before sunset the forest took on an atmosphere of utter strangeness – the silence and cold of limitless forest, as though I had entered a time-warp, an earlier period on the planet before the emergence of humans.

'It is difficult to conceive of a region uninhabited by man. We habitually presume his presence and influence everywhere,' Henry

David Thoreau wrote in *The Maine Woods* – and he was writing about these very woods, on the slopes of Katahdin, where he had hiked and camped in 1846. He was overwhelmed by the wilderness: 'Nature was here something savage and awful, though beautiful . . . This was the Earth of which we have heard, made out of Chaos and Old Night . . . the fresh and natural surface of the planet Earth.'

It was impossible for me to travel except on skis. The rangers used snow-mobiles for emergencies, or to traverse the back-country, but these vehicles were useful only on the flatter and more thinly wooded areas. Skis were more versatile, and mine brought me to the brink of rocky precipices, and across frozen ponds, and through trackless woods.

The first days I ventured farther and farther from my cabin, with emergency supplies in my pack, some food, my water bottle – first skiing up the eastern edge to a camp called Roaring Brook, and then to the west, to Abol Falls. I was looking for moose – which are numerous and fearless – or for evidence of more black bears; for coyotes; or lynx or deer. I saw tracks of each of these animals, but not the animals themselves.

Later, when I told a local man that I hadn't seen any of the creatures, he said, 'Maybe not. But they saw you.'

In the winter, skiing cross-country through the forest, the greatest difficulty is not the cold – not initially. It is that such an effort makes you perspire heavily. I was warm – too warm – most of the time, even wearing a minimum of clothes. At noon when I stopped for lunch, the perspiration would freeze on me and stiffen my clothes with ice. So my lunches were short, and later when I got back to my camp I got such a chill from my cold, wet layers of clothes that I shivered for hours – long after my feeble stove was blazing. My clothes never really dried, and they were still clammy in the morning. In a tent this would have been much worse: traveling light, you never really dry out, and it is this that makes the winter wilderness dangerous – skiing hard and coping with wet clothes.

All this time the mountain loomed above me – a great rocky camel's hump, some of its contours still giving it a resemblance to the volcano it had once been – forced out of the ground by fire, and then carved by ice – the monumental glaciers that covered this part of Maine during the Ice Age.

It was so warm one day that some birds were particularly lively, jays and ravens and crows, frisking and flitting in the daytime warmth, and tentatively uttering their mating calls. Strengthened by the sunlight, I skied toward a location on the slope of the mountain known rather ominously as Avalanche Field, but before I reached it I saw a team of climbers skiing slowly in my direction, descending through the forest. They had camped near the mountain a week, staying in shelters, and had climbed to the ridge of Katahdin and to several peaks.

We talked awhile, and the team leader spoke of the precipitous trails, the icy cliffs, the snowdrifts and one serious fall, when a man tumbled backwards into the rest of the team. It had been a breathless all-day climb, from their camp to the main peak and back, and they had been involved in technical climbing on rock, ice, and drifted snow. They were somewhat intimidated by my numerous nosy questions and at last, feeling – I suppose – defensive, the team leader said, almost apologetically, 'We had a nice view from the top.'

I knew exactly what he meant. It seems absurd for anyone to spend a week in a wilderness of snow, skiing and climbing, and at the end of this exhaustion – cold hands and feet, extreme fatigue, aching muscles, and nothing to eat except hurriedly rehydrated cuisine – at the end of it all, sum up the crowning achievement with the murmur, 'a nice view.'

It is simply impossible to explain except in metaphysical terms, yet who wants to hear a camping trip deconstructed as a critical aspect of enlightenment? The motives of this effort are a personal matter; yet no bystander – and no reader – ought to be subjected to a pompous discussion of the wilderness experience and the Meaning of Life. None the less, it is nearer to the truth to understand this passion of solitary skiing along narrow forest trails in the winter as an exploration of the heart and mind – an inner journey.

As the days passed, my familiarity with the forest deepened, and I came to recognize birds and land features and the vagaries of the weather. My competence grew. I could ski greater distances, and I enlarged my territory in the forest, claiming more and more of the territory, becoming bolder. So I grew. It helped to be alone. I developed certain routes through the woods as my own, I discovered short cuts across frozen ponds, I ranged more widely and was better able to judge the risks of the distance and the cold.

I liked the thought that as long as my little gas stove worked I would always be able to melt snow and have a supply of drinking water. And it was a satisfaction to me that I learned to work my stove in a high wind and have a hot, energizing meal in the middle of the day, in a remote snowfield or in the forest. It made me feel that I had more than survived in this inhospitable place – that I had begun to enjoy the privilege of being a citizen of the wilderness.

My conceited feeling lasted for a while – perhaps two more days. And then the weather deteriorated. From days of sunshine and nights of profound cold, the temperature rose, the sky darkened, the clouds lowered, and in their place was a fine mist of ice chips and rain. There was no mountain anymore. The trees had no tops – they ended obscurely in a ragged ceiling of mist. I had been prepared for this from the weather report on my tiny radio. Yet the effect was worse than I imagined.

I woke in the morning to a demoralizing sound, the steady patter of rain, spitting against the snow and eroding it, giving the surface the irregular and rotten-looking surface of old battered styrofoam, as though the snow had begun to decay. It was not the spring thaw, it was a meteorological anomaly – the deranged weather of New England, in which anything might happen.

The mist and fine rain were beautiful – giving a haunted look to the forest, a wraith-like aspect to the pines – but they were deadly. Just a short trip on skis was a frustrating experience, a sort of blinding baptism – poor visibility in a drenching downpour. To compound it, the surface of the snow was almost unskiable. There was no other way to travel, so I stayed in the cabin, feeling captive – the empty forest all around – and listened hard, hoping the rain would stop.

It did not stop. It eased. But the temperature dropped again and on the second day of this dreary storm, in which the entire forest was transformed from a brilliant kingdom of tall trees into a forbidding place, the word 'wilderness' acquired for me a more ominous meaning. The forest had been a region of sunlight and snow, overlooked by a mountain that seemed to have a benevolent shape. Now the mist veiled the mountain; a darkness penetrated the woods, picking out every tree as though traced in an etching; and the rain froze hard.

In New England, we have a macabre expression for a large patch of ice on a ski trail. This unexpected frozen puddle – often greeny-yellow, from the color of the earth erupting just beneath it – is called a 'death cookie.' It is usually circular, a disc of ice, and it is rare for a skier to cross one without falling.

It seemed to me that the frozen rain had turned the whole of Baxter Park into a death cookie. Every surface was glazed, every tree, every twig thickened with glassy frozen layers of ice. And the surface of the snow that had once broken easily under my skis had become a hard shell. It was like skiing on endless smooth slopes of crystal – my skis had no edge for this, they would not grip, and predictably enough I fell several times. The ice crust was so hard that in places when I fell I hardly broke through it.

What was most maddening was its beauty. The frozen rain that had coated the whole forest – each trunk and twig and pine needle glistening individually – this magic prevented me from venturing very far. More than that, it prevented me from escaping.

I made several attempts to ski out, and then I calmed down. Be prepared and be patient: these are the lessons of all winter travel in the forest. I was lucky to have a cabin, even if it was drafty by day and like a refrigerator at night. I wrote my notes by candlelight, and before bedtime, holding a flashlight to the page, I reread *Madame Bovary* ('Accustomed to the peaceful, she turned in reaction to the picturesque'). And now and then I looked out of the window, at the wilderness encased in ice, like an old preserved carcass – a mammoth entombed in a glacier.

I kept thinking how, after a week of skiing and climbing and at last reaching the summit of the snowy mountain, the men I had met had said, 'We had a nice view.' That oversimple summary illustrated the impossibility of describing the euphoria one felt in the open air of a remote wilderness. At the end of each day I had felt a sense of achievement and exhaustion – a thrill, yes, but why? Because I had spent the entire day alone in a vast, simple landscape of snow and cold. There is a species of large-pawed rabbit in this forest called a Snowshoe Rabbit – I had seen their tracks: the creatures managed beautifully in the deepest snow. They had adapted and prospered. On my good days I had felt like one of them.

Continuing rain and sleet, the weather report said, and so, leaving my spare food behind so that I could move more quickly, I packed my knapsack and waterproofed myself with my parka and gloves, and headed out. I had an early start. It was an amazing jaunt – three hours of cross-country skiing in the most slippery woods I have ever ventured through.

Still, I was leaving with regret, because I felt I was being driven out by the terrible weather. And I had no single image for this place – only the sense of the wilderness as an enormous natural labyrinth in four dimensions. But skiing that morning back to civilization, I saw a bird chirping in a tree. I had time to study it – it was wild and fearless and took no notice of me. It was a rare bird for these parts, an Evening Grosbeak – looking like an overgrown goldfinch, with a yellow visor over its eyes. It was a stroke of luck. It was hard to describe the experience of the wilderness, but this bird was the answer – it was rare, it was beautiful, I had never seen one before, and so it could stand to sum up the trip. What was your trip like? people might say. And I could reply, I saw an Evening Grosbeak – a goldfinch bigger than my whole hand.

Trespassing in Florida

I was trespassing on the coastal wilderness of an Aboriginal reserve in northern Queensland in Australia recently when I met a middle-aged beachcomber. He looked sunburned and furtive. He had a small, nervous-looking dog under his arm, and he said that they – he and his mutt – had been living there in the dunes, under a piece of flapping canvas, for several years. Today he was out on the beach, he said, looking for bottles and net-floats that the tide had thrown up.

'Flotation,' he said. 'That's what I'm looking for.'

He explained that he was building a raft that would take him and his dog across the top of Cape York. This is one of the worst channels known for current and wind. I asked him if he knew the risks.

'I'm not bothered,' he said. 'You can go anywhere, you can do anything, if you're not in a hurry.'

Who are the great travelers? They are all sorts, of course; an enormous number have been depressive – bipolar types, capable of serious gloom. Livingstone sulked in his tent for days, Vancouver locked himself in his cabin, Speke shot himself, Scott sometimes wept, Nansen was suicidal, so was Meriwether Lewis; but at their best they are curious, contented, patient, courageous, and paragons of self-sufficiency. Their passion is visiting the unknown.

I was not talking to that beachcomber long before he began to reminisce about his old home on the Thames, near Gravesend. It interested me that he was pushing on, planning to raft around Australia. He said as far as he knew it had never been done before. I understood perfectly and I encouraged him. The profoundest satisfaction in travel is a sense of discovery, the private thrill of seeing something new or seeing it in a new way. This is unquestionably egotistical, but such discoveries do not come easy – nothing is harder than that uncertain, Martian-on-earth feeling of being alone in the middle of nowhere. The pay-off is a conceited feeling of having gone to a distant place and unlocked a secret. As far as I am concerned, everything else in travel is a vacation, the view from the chaise longue – horizontal.

I admired the beachcomber's independence, and I admire the intelligent, knowledgeable, map-carrying traveler. Anyone who knows one bird from another, one wild flower or tree from another, is capable of intensifying this feeling of discovery. A landscape looks different when you know the names of things – and, conversely, can look exceedingly inhospitable and alien when it seems nameless. But there is a point where, when a place looks very strange, it is not an indication of its remoteness but simply a mark of your ignorance.

When I was younger I liked traveling in cities, being among mobs of people, seeking out churches and museums. I think it gave me a sense of self-importance, of being big and busy. I have not grown misanthropic, but with the passage of time I have come to value emptier spaces, to seek out the natural world, and the ultimate of what travel has to offer – wilderness. Is this a way of reinvigorating myself with a peek at innocence, and of having trespassed into Eden? It hardly matters – so much in travel is self-delusion.

Look at Florida. Even in the middle of the busiest tourist destination it is often possible to find something resembling wilderness. The road signs in the great empty stretches of south Florida's Alligator Alley saying 'Panther Crossing' are there for a purpose. Occasionally these endangered creatures are seen. The glimpse of one must be like a glimpse of the world before the Fall. Nearer the coast, where the dolphins frolic among the powerboats, there are so many ospreys they could easily be mistaken for pests. You can travel for days among the low and misleading islands on the outer reaches of Charlotte harbor and never see a golfer, which I suppose is one definition of wilderness.

Anyone wishing to understand the meaning of the word 'backwater' should come here. In a tentative and accidental way, I first found this part of Florida almost twenty years ago when I was driving south from Sarasota on back roads looking for January sunshine. Then, after the motels and caravan parks petered out, the land grew spookier and more swampy and the towns were little more than a gas station and bait shop and a post office, all in one weather-beaten building.

Beyond these remnants of roads were tropical vegetation and a network of waterways, the banks held together by the spindly legs and arms of mangroves. It delighted me to think that Florida (even then regarded as spoiled, vulgar, too flat, and too hot) had this stretch of paradise that was like the deep tropics – a jungly coast with glittering, beckoning islands. I kept going back. Even its hidden parts began to be discovered and developed, though some of it is still wilderness in the sense of being a place where you can be lost and never found.

This thirty-mile-long outflung pattern of barrier islands, protecting Charlotte harbor and Pine Island Sound, was charted by Ponce de León in 1513, while he sailed down Pine Island Sound looking for the Fountain of Youth. He saw only Indians, the Calusas, who were such determined warriors – their name means 'fierce' – that they fought to the death. Most of them were killed by the well-armed Spaniards, the rest were dispersed to Cuba and other parts of Florida. But the Calusas had left behind fascinating remnants of their traditional culture, notably their shell mounds, which are impressively high, as much as forty feet, creating actual hills on what were the flattest lands imaginable. The Calusas used these mounds in their rituals; they had a cult of the dead that linked them with the Indians of Mexico.

After the Calusas and the conquistadors and the pirates had come and gone, millionaires and settlers arrived – this was in the 1920s and 1930s. These well-heeled pioneers were so impressed by the Indian mounds that they squatted on them and built their mansions on the ancient heaps of shell and human bones, an act of desecration that gave them – like most acts of desecration – wonderful views.

The large low-lying area of swamps, barrier islands and bays is variously known as the Shell Islands, the Pirate Islands, or the Coconut Coast. It is certainly the most tropical, and one of the most beautiful. Sanibel, the southernmost link on the chain of islands, is the most heavily visited, millions of cars trundling across the causeway link to the mainland in a single season. Or not trundling at all, but rather standing still in a mile-long halted line. The road, a continuation of Route 867, carries on, winding through the pines and the palms, and a bridge to Captiva Island. At the end of the road is a sprawling resort where, on most days, the rambunctious jet skiers vie with the dolphins and the yachts for space at the edge of the intracoastal waterway, all of them captivated, so to speak.

North Captiva, another barrier island of sand and mangroves, lies isolated just across Redfish Pass. It is accessible only by small boats, because of the mud flats and shoals that surround it. North of it is

Cayo Costa, a state park, the prettiest of all, and with almost no population, about four miles long and a mile wide at its thickest point. Cayo Costa, also known as Laccosta Island, is the haunt of ospreys and bald eagles, crocodiles and wild pigs, and a few campers. There is a small, environmentally friendly campsite on the western, Gulf-facing side, near its spectacular beach.

None of this is wilderness in the sense that it has been left unexplored, but it is wild enough, and in the maze of islands that make up this swampy offshore archipelago there are plenty of snakes and gators and herons and tortoises. The endangered gopher tortoises can't burrow in the densely planted lawns of Sanibel, but they have no problem in the dunes of the islands farther north.

Yachts enter the anchorages of Useppa ('A private Membership Island,' a sign warns on the waterway) and most dinghies can get into Cabbage Key, where there is a small hotel – it was once the winter home of the novelist and playwright Mary Roberts Rinehart – but other scores of islands hereabouts stand in such shallow water they are off-limits to almost all boats except those which draw only a few inches of water.

I was once in the house of a friend on Gasparilla Island, near the well-heeled settlement of Boca Grande, when an elderly and very wet gentleman appeared at the front door.

'Just swam to shore – got stuck on a bar,' he said, dripping onto the welcome mat. He held a wet stogie in his fingers – probably force of habit. 'Mind if I use your phone?'

His name was Larry, he was seventy-one. He was out fishing in his small boat and, distracted by a nibble, soon found himself high and dry a half-mile out. He had had no choice but to slosh and swim to shore.

'Happens all the time,' my friend said.

And that was why, when I made my tour of the islands, I used the smallest boat I could find, a flat-bottomed fifteen-footer with a simple outboard motor. A kayak would have been more suitable, and would have given me greater access. Next time, I thought.

If it is (as I think) axiomatic that anywhere pleasant that is easily accessible is eventually spoiled, it should not be hard to understand why the little islands in and around this area remain lovely. Even Little Gasparilla, the five-mile island just north of Gasparilla, is reachable only by boat, which is probably why its shores are full of ospreys and herons and turtles. The beaches here, and on Gasparilla

– an undeniably splendid place with a bottleneck of a causeway (toll: 3.25 dollars) – are long, and rather empty, palm-fringed and with white powdery sand. The proof that the beaches on Cayo Costa are seldom visited is that the ospreys actually nest in the low trees overhead. Elsewhere these big, squeaky-voiced falcons nest on poles put up by bird people.

The tiny humps of land, mostly held together by mangroves, that lie behind these bigger barrier islands still contain old shell mounds under the sturdy gumbo limbo trees. If you have the right boat it is easy to spend a week exploring the small islands that seem to float in the recesses of Turtle Bay and Bull Bay. These bays are about halfway down the western side of Charlotte harbor, but the harbor is so wide you can't see the far side from here: in the middle of it, among the dolphins and the occasional manatee, it is like being at sea.

Nearly everyone in the area has a pirate story – actually, the same pirate story in different fanciful versions, of the buccaneer Gasparilla and his cut-throat crew. It is very likely that Gasparilla did not exist, though Friar Gaspar certainly did – one of the passes was named after him on a Spanish chart made in 1783. Treasure undoubtedly exists but it is less likely to be found in sea-chests buried under the insect-haunted dunes of the islands than in the vaults of the Dupont estate, and those of the surrounding mansions, in Boca Grande.

This part of America was first explored by the Spanish almost 500 years ago. The area has experienced successive waves of people looking for Indians, for gold, for silver, for slaves, for seclusion, and – more recently – for sunshine and game-fish (the annual Tarpon tournament attracts masses of fishermen). It is reassuring that a place so pretty – and so apparently fragile – should still endure and still sparkle.

The people risking sunstroke on the beach, the folks on the yachts, the motorists struggling toward North Captiva, all of them believe they are in the very bosom of the place, but have little idea of just how huge and hidden most of these islands are. That surely is one of the many paradoxes of travel. I spent days in my small boat going from one waterlogged island, and one remote beach, to another, hardly seeing anything move except a heron or gopher turtle or a ruddy turnstone. Yet all I had to do was make a forty-minute detour and I would be within hailing distance of a golfer in green pants or a pot-bellied boy on a jet ski.

The interior islands, and the ones with small populations, resemble the keys of Belize – very similar contours and vegetation, and the same tropical heat and insects. This is 'the Mosquito Coast' in more than one sense. I find it heartening to discover that there are still wild and almost inaccessible places even in so tourist-ridden a place as south Florida. Building is bound to increase, more of the land will be steamrolled by developers, and some of the unluckier animal species are doomed; but it is safe to say that many of these islands, in spite of your trespassing, may never be violated – you'd drown, you'd starve, you'd become marooned if you tried.

I nearly drowned myself in one of the sudden storms that frequently explode over these islands. I was about a mile from shore, and saw the sky quickly blackening with storm clouds that were like the lid of a kettle being slipped over the earth. I soon found myself trying to outrace the storm, and losing, fighting sixty-mile-an-hour winds and gusts of even greater velocity. The storm danger and the mudflats, the mangroves and the mosquitoes, have in their way kept much of the area liberated, obscure, and somewhat empty – in a word, ideal. I left having reached the conclusion that it had passed the ultimate travel test: I wanted to go back.

Down the Zambezi

In the extravagant African sunset the Zambezi River was deep red, reflecting the crimson sky, and it shimmered in oxbows across the dusk-black landscape of the flood plain like a vessel thick with blood.

That vivid arterial image seemed appropriate to the Zambezi, which is teeming with life throughout its 1,633-mile length. 'This magnificent stream,' David Livingstone exclaimed, when he first traveled down it in 1853. More tellingly he called it 'God's highway,' an access route for Christianity and commerce. Livingstone imagined the Zambezi's future as a vast thoroughfare, with good-sized trading ships plying the river, bringing prosperity to the interior of Africa.

From my vantage point in a small plane over the Upper Zambezi in western Zambia I saw old eternal Africa, clusters of mud huts and fishermen in dugout canoes. What could have been clumps of boulders scattered all over the river were pods of hippos, preparing to scramble up the banks for their night-time grazing. And the small villages of thatched-roof huts glowed by the light of cooking fires and candles.

It was pretty much what Livingstone had seen all those years ago, when he traveled hopefully upriver, making charts. He went to Africa from Scotland in 1841 aged twenty-six, and except for brief absences he spent the rest of his life there, thirty-two years. Among his gifts was his linguistic skill (though he spoke with a thick Scottish accent) and his ability to get on with Africans who, having seen so many instances of enslavement, were understandably hostile toward out-siders. Livingstone could be difficult – he often exhibited manic-depressive behavior. Yet his travel was to a great extent a record of his success in charming the African chiefs up and down the river, putting their suspicions to rest.

In the Zambezi twilight, the landing strip looked like a small bandage on the great flank of the flood plain. We descended through the smoky air of the dry-season bush fires and rolled to a halt on this grassy plot.

In the morning I could see that the banks of the river were lush, and that was the first indication I had that, no matter how drought-stricken or starved the rest of the land was, the banks of the Zambezi are green, from end to end.

I had woken to the sounds of the busy bird life of the river, the kingfishers, the bee-eaters, the herons and egrets and fish eagles. From time to time I could hear the warning sounds of hippos, which are misleadingly comical, like a tuba played under water. Now and then there was a sudden splash – a jumping tiger fish, startled by the blowing hippo. Tiger fish, which can grow to thirty-five pounds, have ferocious teeth, and are known for their terrific strength in battling anglers.

'We're off the map here,' said Bernie Esterhuyse, and it was true – I never found this bend in the Zambezi, Ngulwana, on any map. With his wife, Adrienne, Bernie runs a small tent camp devoted to tiger fishing. Like many other South Africans, they had migrated north over the past few years to the Zambezi Valley to start tourist-related businesses. Apart from a few small villages near the river they have no neighbors.

'The Litunga gave us permission to build here,' Adrienne said later, referring to the king of the Lozi people, the dominant tribe in this province. 'Most of this land is his.'

We were driving through deep sand, toward the market town of Lukulu, two hours away.

'Where's the road?'

Strictly speaking there was no road. The idea was to go cross-country, following the riverbank, in the general direction of Lukulu. This Zambezi flood plain, stretching for miles along the river, was very sandy, like a beach that had become detached from an ocean, part of the Kalahari sand-veldt. The surface was pitted all over with the sort of holes you see crabs skittering into.

But these were rat holes. The rain had been so sparse the season before that the river had stayed low and the rats had not drowned in their holes, as usually happened. As we labored on, rats were diving for cover.

At a cluster of huts under some deep-green mango trees I saw a group of women pounding corn in a mortar – taking turns with the log-like pestle. Like many other riverside villages, it was orderly and well stocked. 'We know we are lucky,' one of the women said, acknowledging that they owed their lives to the river.

After we passed the time of day I wondered whether, in leaner times, anyone ate those rats. The word for rat is *khoswe* in Chichewa, which I had learned as a Peace Corps Volunteer in Malawi. *Kodi ichi amadya?* I asked. Are they edible?

'We Lozis don't eat them,' another woman boasted. She understood me. Because of the wide dispersal of Malawians, I was to discover that Chichewa was understood for almost the entire length of the Zambezi. 'But the Luvale and Lunda people like them.'

The Luvale and Lunda are the far-flung and poorer tribes of this immense area of the Upper Zambezi, the Western Province of Zambia, once known as Barotseland, kingdom of the Lozis, who are still loyal to their king.

The river traffic I could see was not motorized, but there was plenty of it – men in dugouts, big and small, paddling slowly upriver. Still speaking in Chichewa, I called out to the paddlers, asking them where they were going.

'To market!' The market at Lukulu was a day's paddle upriver.

These fishermen told me that their villages were distant. In this dry season they lived in the temporary fishing camps of reed-walled huts with thatched roofs that were numerous on the riverbanks.

They had gardens too, fields of corn, which they made into flour. Boiled with a few pints of the Zambezi, this was one of their starchy staple foods (called *sadza*, upriver, and *nsima*, downriver). They ate it with fish or stewed greens. Cassava and beans were also sprouting in these riverside gardens. At a distance from the river, people foraged for wild berries, called *muzawe*, which they made into porridge. Though drought conditions prevailed throughout much of the province, the Zambezi provided the means of life for dwellers on its banks.

All the way to Lukulu we saw people in the distance crossing the sandy flood plain using ox-drawn sleds, with heavy wooden wish-boned-shaped runners skidding through the sand. And sometimes – speaking of appropriate technology – a dugout canoe was pulled across the sand by a pair of oxen.

Some of these conveyances were piled high with vegetables or firewood, to sell at the market, but several held very solemn-looking people.

'*Adwala*,' one of the ox-drivers said to me, of the passenger. 'He's sick.'

They were on their way to see the only doctor for many miles around, Dr. Peter Clabbers, who runs Lukulu Hospital. I made a point of seeing him myself when I got to the town, which was small but sprawling on a bluff that overlooks the river: a Catholic mission, several schools, a busy market, and an even busier hospital.

'I see one new HIV patient almost every day,' Dr. Clabbers told me as we walked through the clean but spartan wards of Lukulu Hospital. Dr. Clabbers, from Holland, has been at the hospital, one of the best on the Upper Zambezi, for three years. He told me that AIDS and HIV cases were continuing to climb ('I used to see two or three a week'), and that TB, cholera, and meningitis patients were also numerous. There were some violent injuries, too.

'I see the victims of land mines occasionally,' Dr. Clabbers said.

The border of Angola was less than eighty miles away, and for almost twenty years the UNITA forces of Jonas Savimbi had been waging a guerrilla war in these outlying provinces against the elected Angola government. Upriver near where the Zambezi looped through Angola from its boggy origin in Zambia, life was still disrupted by the effects of this guerrilla war. There were many explosives scattered near villages and in the bush.

'And now and then I see some young boy who's blown his hand off after finding a grenade and playing with it,' the doctor added.

Leprosy, Hansen's disease, has been largely cured, though there are still some lepers in Lukulu, both out-patients and resident in the local leprosarium. Moses, a man in his sixties, was severely afflicted – he had lost most of his extremities – but he was good-humored.

He said, 'My problem was that I spent fifty-three years in a village being treated by a local doctor.' That was a euphemism for a witch doctor.

As he was a Lunda I asked him whether it was true, as people said, that the Lunda ate rats. 'They do, but I don't,' Moses said.

Lukulu market was bustling, and like many riverside markets on this part of the Zambezi, its bright colors were an effect of the used clothes, lying in enormous piles or draped on racks or else flapping like pennants on long lines. In Zambia they are known generally as *salaula* ('second-hand'), because they originated as charitable donations in the US and Europe. They are sold cheaply in bales and sorted by the clothes vendors – racks of old blue jeans, heaps of T-shirts and dresses and skirts and shorts. They are still serviceable and are so inexpensive their existence has just about destroyed the indigenous Zambian textile industry.

At the fish market, Julius Nkwita was selling small piles of dried fish, about sixty cents for a handful. But sometimes he swapped his fish for cups of flour or an item of clothing. He might have been one of those men in the dugouts I had seen on the river earlier that morning, paddling toward the market in Lukulu.

Julius had five children, ranging in age from three to fourteen. His wife and four of his children were in his home village, some distance from the river, while he stayed in his seasonal fishing camp – just a reed hut – with his son, fishing intensively.

'I camp on the riverbank,' he said. 'I catch fish, dry it at my camp and when I have enough I come here by river to sell it.'

I was curious to know whether he had made his own dugout canoe. No, he said, he had bought it, 'for two cows.' A cow in these parts was used as payment for big-ticket items – for canoes, sleighs, and brides. A twelve-man canoe, a seventeen-footer, might cost three cows.

Julius sold bottle fish and large bream, tiger fish and the catfish known as barbel, smoke-dried like kippers. Fishing remains the primary occupation for the men on the Upper Zambezi. In the course of traveling much of the river's length I was to see not just nets and fishing tackle, but an almost unimaginable variety of fish traps – all sizes, from the smallest, which resemble narrow lampshades, to the largest, five feet long, shaped like large bulging baskets and strong enough to hold the angriest fish. The women use the river to water their gardens, and because there is always water in the Zambezi, it is possible for gardens to flourish year-round.

'Oh, yes, we have many hippos,' Julius told me. He said that hippos gobbled the gardens. Out canoeing, he was occasionally attacked by a hippo.

'What do you do if a hippo goes after you?'

'Swim away from the canoe,' he said, explaining that the hippo concentrates on the canoe rather than the people in it. The animal single-mindedly tips over or destroys the boat when it feels its territory or its attack zone has been entered by something alien.

Down by the river, at a Lukulu landing, people were being ferried to and from the far bank in canoes. Some boys were swimming, and the river's muddy darkness made it seem ominous.

'Aren't you worried about crocodiles?'

They laughed and said, 'It is not deep here!'

That did not reassure me, and yet within a few weeks I found myself looking for midstream sandbanks where I could swim – if my brief, urgent thrashing could be called swimming. Crocodiles tend to ignore canoes, but do attack humans – people bathing, doing laundry, washing dishes – in the river. The very shallow spots and sandbanks are generally free of crocodiles – and hippos, too – though it is rare to see anyone swimming in the Zambezi.

After some days in and around Lukulu and at the fishing camp at Ngulwana, I set off with Petrus Ziwa in a four-wheel-drive vehicle through the Luena Flats.

'My mother was from Malawi,' Petrus said, explaining why he, a Zambian, spoke Chichewa so well. At sixty-two, he had far exceeded the average life-span of a Zambian male, which was a mere thirty-six. A Jehovah's Witness, hoping for my eventual conversion, he tried to hasten the process by quoting scripture. He had an abiding fear of snakes; even on the hottest nights he slept with his face covered – usually wrapped in a towel.

'Egyptian cobras and black mambas,' he said. 'They are strong, Daddy.'

This 'Daddy' was interesting. The term of respect in Chichewa is *Bambo* – Father; but Petrus always translated this 'Daddy,' as in, 'The battery is dead, Daddy' or 'It is too hot, Daddy' or 'Please give me your watch, Daddy.'

In this season, the hot beautiful flood plain was a broad expanse of sand scattered with clumps of fine golden grass. We headed south, through the sand, using a compass. Our destination today was Mongu and the Litunga's royal compound on the Zambezi canals at Lealui. At Mbanga, just a small collection of buildings and mango trees in the middle of the plain, I asked a man, how far to Mongu?

'By foot it is ten hours,' he said. 'By vehicle I don't know.'

There was no bus because there was no road. Wish-bone sleds were passing, going in the opposite direction – one with a load of cassava, another carrying an elderly granny, the last with a sick person, all of them pulled by plodding oxen in the hot sun.

'Going to Mongu,' they said. Mongu was a real town on a real road, with a post office and a hospital and a market. But still it took a whole day to get there from here on foot.

Everything was measured differently, in the currency of cows, or the distance of foot-hours. The separate notion of time and distance was pleasant, and its simplicity was strangely relaxing, modifying my sense of urgency. Here, among people for whom not much had changed in many generations, whose expectations were modest, I was happiest taking one day at a time, as they did, and feeling lucky to be so near the life-giving river, a source of food and water.

'A roller, Daddy.' Petrus was pointing upwards.

It was a racquet-tailed roller, tumbling through the sky toward the Zambezi flood plain to impress a possible mate, as we traveled slowly through the deep sand, in places higher than our hubcaps. Other birds with bright plumage, white-fronted and carmine bee-eaters, flew past us. I had seen their colonies on the vertical sides of the Zambezi banks upriver. Toward noon, as the day grew hotter, we seemed to be the only thing moving across the sand, though of course hawks hovered, and vultures, too. The big game, the lion and elephant and buffalo, were on the far side of the river, ranging across the Liuwa Plain, where the dark line of trees at the western horizon marked the course of the Zambezi.

'This is all the Litunga's land,' a herdsman named Vincent Libanga said to me along the way. Vincent said he walked sixteen miles to the river to buy bream or dried *ndombe*, catfish.

Vincent spoke of the Litunga with great respect, yet he had never seen his king. The Litunga kept to himself, did not circulate even in Mongu, his nearest town, which we reached in the late morning. Mongu was an unprepossessing place – its roads had pot-holes and its shops contained little merchandise; but it is also an administrative center, with schools and fuel depots, and so it is a center of activity. Within minutes of arriving I was offered a leopard skin by a whispering poacher, or perhaps I might be interested in buying some ivory? I said no and before I could register my disapproval the young fellow slipped away.

The center of Mongu is high enough for one to see, across five miles of marsh, the royal settlement of Lealui.

'How will we get down that terrible road?' I asked, looking ahead at the viaduct of crumbly mud.

'We will go through the marsh instead, Daddy.'

It was stickier, and it was slow, but this route worked. In contrast to Mongu, Lealui was a peaceful shady settlement of twittering birds, on the low, level plain which is criss-crossed by canals. This royal compound, dating from about 1866, is near the river, which is central to the Litunga's rule and his rituals, the most elaborate being the annual royal progress, called the Kuomboka, from his summer to his winter quarters. At the end of the rains, when the river is in flood, the royal barge and the attendant canoes are paddled with great ceremony from one palace to the other, Lealui to Limalunga, through the system of canals.

The palace buildings of the Litunga were large and solid, some with tin roofs, others thatched – all of them stately in spite of their plainness. They were surrounded by a tall reed enclosure, like a stockade, with pointed stakes. The gateway was not guarded, but out of respect no one ventured near it. In the leafy center of the settlement the king's subjects and petitioners were dozing under the trees, behind the royal storehouses and the council house. Some people had obviously been there for quite a while and had set up makeshift camps, where they were cooking and tending goats and looking after children.

Virtually the whole of the Western Province, an area the size of New York State, once belonged to the Litunga; to his half-million subjects today, it still does. As a consequence, this province of the Republic of Zambia pays for its monarchist sentiments by being neglected by the Zambian central government in Lusaka. The roads are poor or non-existent, the schools are substandard, and many of the hospitals are run by foreign doctors. The result of this neglect is an air of independence and self-sufficiency, and of course underdevelopment. It looked and felt to me precisely like the rural Africa I had first seen over thirty years ago.

I was eager to see this reputedly urbane king. He had been one of Zambia's ambassadors before the sudden death of his father in 1987 and his subsequent coronation. The Zambezi is a long river, but this man rules a third of it, and there were no other kings on its banks. It seemed to me no small thing to be the King of the Zambezi.

'You must first introduce yourself to the Ngambela,' the court historian, Jonathan Mashewani, told me. 'Court historian' was an informal title. He was a young man in his mid-twenties with a tattered notebook under his arm, hoping somehow to win a scholarship to study abroad.

He showed me to a small compound where a tall man introduced himself. 'I am Maxwell Mutitwa, the Litunga's prime minister.' His title, Ngambela, was translated as 'the king's chief councilor,' and it was his task to interview me to determine whether I had a worthy motive in visiting the king.

He was big and fleshy and heavy-faced, with the easy manner and the soulfulness of a blues singer. His house was poor, just a mud hut with religious mottoes tacked to the wall.

'I am the Litunga's spokesman,' the Ngambela said. 'He is like a baby. I have to speak for him.' He lamented the opportunism of elected politicians and assured me that a monarchy with a chiefly system is the ideal form of government.

'A monarchy is a family, you see,' he said. 'People love their chiefs more than they do their president. Because it is in their blood – the same blood. We are all related. We are one people.'

A chief was not a despot, he said; a chief was controlled by the people.

'Give me an example,' I said.

'Chiefs have to listen. If a chief makes a mistake he will be told so by the people. But if a commoner comes to power it is very hard to convince him that he is wrong when he makes a mistake.' He gestured to the door of his hut. 'Look out there in my compound.'

I looked out the side door and saw fifty people.

'All of them want to speak to me,' he laughed. 'They want to see the Litunga, they need help, they need advice. I am their prisoner!'

The Ngambela approved my visit but said that I also had to be presented to the Kuta, which was the council of chiefs.

'If this is going to take time,' I said, 'I will have to make camp.'

'You must ask the Kuta for permission to camp here.'

It was late in the afternoon before I was granted an audience with the Kuta. This council was nine elderly men, the sentries of a threadbare monarchy, sitting on old creaking chairs propped on ceremonial straw mats, in an unswept stone building, the council house. I sat some distance away on a low chair and thanked them for their attention.

'What is your mission?'

I explained that I wished to see His Royal Highness, to discuss the Zambezi, which they called in their own language Lyambai. Livingstone wrote, 'The term Leeambye means "the large river," or the river par excellence. Luambeji, Luambesi, Ambezi, Ojimbesi, and Zambezi, &c., are names applied to it at different parts of its course . . . and all possess a similar signification.'

Each chief spoke in turn, commenting on my request. They asked detailed questions, such as, 'Who sent you to see the Litunga?' and 'What sort of information will you request of His Highness?'

And then, for a long time, they debated this, each chief and minister in turn, speaking at length, while roosters crowed outside and a skittering and squealing above the thin board of the ceiling was almost certainly a family of rats.

I sat, baffled by the progress of the Lozi debate, making notes to pass the time. What impressed me about this council and about life at Lealui in general was that everyone who lived there did so out of respect for their king. No one was paid for serving the king. The courtiers and servants carried out their duties in the royal administration and from time to time returned to their home villages, where they had families and gardens.

After two hours my petition to camp in the royal village was granted, and so was my request to visit the Litunga in the royal compound. 'Maybe tomorrow.'

It was sadly clear to me from his tone that 'tomorrow' was a metaphor for 'fairly soon.'

But I had permission to stay, and so I pitched my tent near the Ngambela's compound and, after dinner, turned in. Through my mosquito net I could see only candle flames and lamplight. The laughter of children, the muttering of adults, even the barking dogs went silent soon after nine, and then there was darkness that was unrelieved by a small scrap of moon like an orange rind.

The royal drums sounded at nine-thirty and midnight and four a.m., sometimes with chanting and the tripping notes of a marimba. At dawn, as the sun rose over the fifty or so thatched roofs of Lealui, there were cockcrows and the lowing of cattle, and the children laughing again.

'We cannot find the king,' one of the chiefs said to me. 'We have looked everywhere.'

The king's councilors were eager for me to see the royal personage, who wore a British admiral's uniform on ceremonial occasions, a relic of an earlier Litunga's visit to Britain. The chiefs found me sympathetic and friendly; they wondered aloud whether, after my audience, I might pass my findings on to the president of the United States. I said that I would do what I could. They needed help, they said. They hoped to restore Lealui to its former glory, when it was the home of 10,000 people.

Still no Litunga. I spent two days bird-watching, writing my notes, and making inquiries. In the meantime, was I interested in knowing the meaning of the night-time drums? I said yes, and learned from

Jonathan Mashewani, the court historian, that each drum sequence had a specific name and was a signal, the first indicating a curfew, and later an 'All's well,' and so on. Some of the drumming was accompanied by the marimba sound of the *silumba*, with songs praising the king, until sunrise, when a particular kettledrum, the *sinkoya*, was struck, 'to welcome the Litunga to the next day.'

On the third day, seeing that the number of people waiting for an audience with the king had swelled, I made my excuses to the Ngambela and left. My not meeting the king was part of an old tradition of travelers in Africa arriving at a remote royal compound and asking for an audience and then waiting for months. Sir Richard Burton was one who vividly recorded this suspense, but there have been many others. 'One cannot get away quickly from these chiefs,' Livingstone wrote in similar circumstances.

Following the Zambezi bank closely on a parallel road in a south-easterly direction, Petrus and I headed for the only ferry that was operating on the Upper Zambezi that month, at Sitoti, south of Senanga.

'Usually we have no trouble with hippos, but one man was killed last month. He was cut in the stomach by a hippo,' the ferryman, Ivan Mbandwe, told me, as he steered us across the river, near a pod of watchful hippos.

By now I was persuaded that the pinkish buttocky hippo near the ferry landing, with its cavernous mouth and peg-like teeth and tiny ears, blowing sour notes through the grommets in its nostrils, only looked goofy and lovable. Roused by the intimation that its portion of the river was being invaded, it turned swift and deadly, a big bossy brute.

'A hippo can hold its breath and stay submerged for seven minutes,' Petrus told me.

I kept the figure in mind. Not long after, while paddling an open canoe on the river, I saw some hippos ahead and of course gave them a wide berth. They snorted, they complained, they disappeared underwater. I waited for seven minutes and then moved on through the smooth water.

Suddenly, just feet away from my boat, I saw a mottled pinkish head emerging through swirling water. I dug my paddle into the water and thrust it, hearing the flap and blow of the hippo fussing astern. I kept going until I was well downstream.

'That was a mock-charge,' I was told later, by a Zimbabwean river guide.

'How do you know?'

'Because he didn't get you.'

Near Ngonye Falls, south of the Sitoti ferry, crocodiles rested on patches of sand, with their mouths open for ventilation and also to allow ox-peckers and egrets to clean their teeth. Otters plunged, looking sleek, some playing, others clearly chasing fish. And all over the fourteen cataracts of Ngonye, in the rising mists in this broad complex of red cliffs and frothy pools, there were flitting birds.

The whole of the Zambezi is lovely, but it turns dramatic at the beginning of the Middle Zambezi with Ngonye Falls. These falls, not as well known as the much larger Victoria Falls, have become an accidental rendezvous spot, where foreign tourists meet Africans in the presence of crocodiles and otters. The falls are a day's drive south of Mongu, or a day's drive north of Katima Mulilo on the Caprivi Strip of Namibia. Afrikaner families, up from Namibia for the weekend, put on life-jackets and are run out to islands in rubber dinghies for picnics, while Lozi women wash laundry at the river's edge, and children scrub the soot off cooking pots with wet sand, wincing at the sound of the outboard motors.

The Zambezi north of Sioma or Maziba Bay is out of the reach of most travelers, but beginning at these falls, and extending all the way – 700 miles – to Kanyemba at the border of Mozambique, are the sightseers, the safari people, the bungee-jumpers and white water rafters, the canoeists, the game-viewers, the gourmet travelers, the gapers, the vacationers, the men working the timber concessions, and the sort of ignorant strangers who, when told about the poor harvest in the west, say simply, 'That's their problem. The government does too much for these people.'

Petrus and I followed the south bank of the Zambezi out of Zambia and into Namibia, where it flowed muddily past Katima Mulilo and Schuckmansburgh. Soon we were back in Zambia and Petrus was saying goodbye and 'Travel well,' in his own language. I reminded him of the Chichewa saying, 'To travel is to dance.'

The many stamps in my passport – I got one every time I crossed the river – were the proof that the Zambezi was a frontier. The river flows through, or forms the border with, seven countries. We had traveled from Zambia, across the Caprivi Strip in Namibia, and farther on through Botswana, and back again to Zambia through Zimbabwe.

The Zimbabwean town of Victoria Falls is visibly more prosperous than its sister city, Livingstone, across the bridge in Zambia. But I found an older, mellower Africa still exists in Livingstone, and its Maramba market attracts people from miles around – Africans buying clothes and getting haircuts and stocking up on provisions, and tourists from over the border in search of bargains.

This most touristy reach of the river had once been the front line in the bush war that was waged by the African soldiers of the political parties ZANU and ZAPU.

'This Zambia riverbank was all Zipra freedom fighters in the 1970s,' Colin Lowe told me.

Born in Southern Rhodesia, a tobacco farmer when it was Rhodesia, Colin was now a canoe tour operator, guiding groups of tourists down the Zambezi.

He gestured to the Zambian side and added, 'The camps were allowed by Kaunda, and there were quite a few guerrillas dug in on the bank. The Rhodesian Security Forces were on the other side – over there. They would shoot and shoot, and when fire was returned they would pinpoint it and let fly.'

On the Zambian bank where the guerrillas had hunkered down, planning their invasion, there are now farms and small hotels, and on the Zimbabwe bank where the Security Forces had been dug in there is now the Victoria Falls National Park, with its grazing animals.

Threading our way through the pods of hippos, Colin guided me by canoe downriver. At the Zambian bank that was nearest to Livingstone Island, I was taken by a narrow boat – known on the Zambezi as a 'banana boat' – to the island itself.

I regarded it as my good fortune that I was able to approach Victoria Falls by the river, and that night I camped midstream, as near to the falls as it was possible to be, on Livingstone Island. The explorer camped on this small mound of rock and palm he called Garden Island in November, 1855, and afterwards he wrote, 'No one can imagine the beauty from anything seen in England.'

Few sights in Africa can equal, in sheer physical beauty, Victoria Falls. Ahead of me, beyond the rocks and swiftly moving channels, was the same sort of smoke I had seen for weeks from the bush fires of slash-and-burn agriculture. The smoke rose fifty feet above the river and the rocky lip of the gorge, and closer it more resembled vapor from a cauldron, pink in the twilight. But this visual prelude did not prepare me for the sound that rose a moment later as the boat drew near – a low murmuring which grew to a mighty roar, and at last an industrial bellow and an odd grinding sound that was unceasing. It is an ear-shattering engine of collapsing water with a rainbow suspended above it, arching from Zambia to Zimbabwe, and above that rainbow the rising vapor, *musi oa tunya*, 'the smoke that thunders.'

Victoria Falls happens fast: the flat water of the upper river rushes past rocky islets and at the lip of the ravine the sheet of water begins to flutter as it drops, widening to a white slashing skirt of foam and tearing down 200 feet in noisy fury.

The gorge is narrow. If the falls were not so loud it would be possible to speak to the people walking on the opposite side in Zimbabwe. Camped on the island I heard only the sound of falling water, though it was pierced briefly by the whistle of the train on its way across the other end of the gorge. What makes the Victoria Falls so loud, so smoky-seeming, so dramatic, is the slender steepness and the great depth of the chasm. It also means that you have to be almost on top of it in order to appreciate it, but that is easy – it is accessible from either side, and it is possible to go near enough to feel the spray on your face and to get a vertiginous view in the greeny depths of the gorge. The river's shadows and its froth give it the look of marble, like the floor of a palace corridor.

So-called adventure travelers were bungee-jumping off the Livingstone Bridge or on river-rafting trips in the sixty miles of gorge below the falls. The more sedate check into the sumptuous riverside safari lodges, and sit under the trees sipping drinks, wearing fashionable safari outfits and watching wildlife.

I have a vivid memory of sitting at sundown with some travelers, having a drink on the verandah of a safari lodge, while just across the river a crowd of about thirty Chacma baboons were doing the same, crouched at the river's edge, sipping and barking companionably.

Some carmine bee-eaters began to gather on a branch near the verandah. They roosted side by side, their number growing – now there were nine of them. People were counting excitedly. Now there were eleven.

'The record is twelve,' the resident bird-watcher said.

And then I sneezed, and a cry of disappointment went up.

I resumed paddling by joining a downriver canoe expedition

at Kariba, a relatively new town in Zimbabwe, on Lake Kariba.

Until the 1950s, this lake had been a deep gorge, where the Batonka people thrived. But the dam that was finished in 1962 turned Kariba Gorge into a lake, with houseboats and ferries bobbing on its surface, and crocodiles – a notoriously dangerous number of them – gliding just beneath.

The Kariba fish stocks of bream, tiger fish, and kapenta are dwindling according to the latest reports.

'Too many people are catching fish on the lake,' said Professor Christopher Magadza, head of the University of Zimbabwe Lake Kariba Research Station. There are thirty registered fishing companies, as well as many people fishing illegally.

Paddling downstream from the dam, I was accompanied by flights of birds – reed cormorants, darters, ox-peckers. The hippos in the channel snuffled and blew, some tiger fish jumped completely clear of the river. Baboons gathered in the limbs of the tamarind trees to eat the seeds they particularly like. In his *Trees of Southern Africa*, Keith Coates-Palgrave suggests that the river's tamarinds tell a story. These trees were brought as seeds to the Zambezi from India by traders carrying spices – tamarind among them – in the sixteenth and seventeenth centuries.

At dusk, I drew my canoe out of the water at a small sandy island, and pitched my tent. In the morning the river level had dropped so much that my canoe was now thirty feet from the water's edge. During the night the hydroelectric plant at the dam had decreased its power output – possibly to conserve the water in the lake – and the reduced flow of water meant that the river was now lower, with mud banks this morning where there had been water yesterday.

I dragged my boat out and paddled on. Though there is much more human settlement on the Zambian side of the Zambezi, animals do not distinguish one country from the other and the swimmers – elephant and buffalo and hippo, rather than lion and hyena and baboons – often emigrate to find the best feeding grounds.

One late afternoon below Chifengulu I saw a commotion in the middle of the river – many heads and flapping ears. When they came to a sand bar and clambered out and crossed it, I was able to count them – forty elephants. They were big and small, swimming from Zambia to Zimbabwe, enormous bulls up ahead and cows behind nudging the baby elephants. The current was swift once they descended into the deeper water and the babies hesitated, needing encouragement.

I was downwind, but even so I stayed well away. They were panting from the effort. They took little notice of me because they had a larger obstacle ahead, a steep muddy bank rising from deep water. It meant they had to climb, to maintain their balance and tramp upward. This made for a turbulent exit, as they crowded near the bank and splashed and struggled.

The Zambezi made the elephants more elephantine – blacker, bigger, the water streaming from their flanks making their hides shine, and their tusks were washed a brilliant white in the river. It was a procession of gleaming black hides and bone-white ivory, and something about their heavy breathing and the way they were winded from this crossing made them seem hard-working and vulnerable.

Not long after, I discovered just how vulnerable elephants can be in the Zambezi.

'This is like a tour of carcasses,' Mark Evans told me as he drove me in his Land Rover a quarter of a mile from a side channel of the river where a large elephant lay dead, its tusks hacked off. Mark had been a bush guide and ranger in Zambia game parks for most of his adult life. Even so he was shocked. 'Three killings in the past three days.'

At first light we had heard thirty-six shots from what Mark guessed was an AK-47. It was clearly a poaching incident. The rangers were called but by the time they showed up the poachers had killed the elephant, hacked one tusk away, cut off its head and rolled it over to get at the second tusk. By the time we saw it the corpse was covered with vultures, and for the next five days and nights, it attracted wild dogs and hyenas and lions and even crocs from the river which had gotten wind of it.

For over 500 years the elephants here have been plundered. Muslim traders, 'Swahilis' ('coastal' in Arabic) from Zanzibar and Kilwa, were well established at Tete by the end of the fifteenth century, trading cloth and other goods for ivory. One tusk produced three billiard balls, two tusks were needed for a piano. Timothy Holmes wrote in *The Journey to Livingstone*, 'Every keyboard entailed one elephant killed and at least two slaves to carry the tusks.'

In spite of what I saw, the ivory ban has generally been a success. The number of poaching incidents has diminished. Elephants have perhaps suffered more from a loss of habitat caused by an irregular and smaller flow of the river. Before Kariba Dam was built, this vast area below Chirundu was a flood plain, but now that it no longer floods and renews the soil, the land is less fertile and consequently supports fewer animals.

The bird life is hardier and more constant: Egyptian geese, the small jewel-like malachite kingfisher, the seven-foot-tall Goliath heron, the lily-trotter (African jacana bird) actually titupping on the water hyacinths, the stately fish eagle; and even when one cannot see them one can hear their distinct cries – the blacksmith plover with its unmistakable 'tinking,' like a hammer striking metal; the lonely whistle of the bou-bou shrike; the spotted dove calling out 'Work harder!'; and the bratty voice of the gray lourie, snarling, 'Go away! Go away!'

'There were once rhinos here,' Mark said. 'There are now virtually none at all. The world demand is great. The Chinese grind the horn and sell it as an aphrodisiac. The Omanis use rhino horns for dagger handles.'

He then added a sentiment that I heard often on the Zambezi: 'Tourism actively discourages poaching. Rhinos feel safer near the camps and lodges, where the poachers don't dare to go.'

Poaching of Zambezi elephants has caused countries to join hands across the Zambezi. Ambrose Charumbira, Senior Scout at Mana Pools National Park in Zimbabwe, told me that he and his men had held meetings with the Zambian Park Service to eliminate poaching. The fact the poachers were heavily armed was the greatest problem. They offered resistance when they were apprehended and as a result rangers on both sides of the river had died in the struggle to eliminate poachers.

In the evening the lions that had fed on the carcass of the elephant padded to the river to drink and digest their food. I saw them from my boat licking their chops and looking sated. I was safe enough, twenty feet away in the water, since lions seldom enter the river.

I drank the river too. Though I was hesitant at first, only wetting my lips or sipping it, I eventually developed a taste for it on my long trip downriver. On the hottest days I dipped my cup into the water and guzzled it, without ill-effects.

The Zambezi has a different character and personality every ten miles or so: the placid upper river becomes the tumbling river of the falls and the gorges, swells into Lake Kariba, flows swiftly through the gorges and widens again above Chirundu, site of the Otto Beit Bridge.

The bridges at Chirundu, Victoria Falls, and Tete are the only ones that can take motor traffic.

Two more days of paddling past Chirundu brought me to a section of the Zambezi which on the Zimbabwe side is Mana Pools. This national park is another area that was closed during the war of Zimbabwean independence. Mana Pools – 'mana' means four in Shona – is full of wild game. In the dry season, when the pans in the bush have evaporated, the larger animals make for the river to slake their thirst.

I was paddling down this section of the Zambezi with Alastair Macdonald, a Zimbabwean guide, who knew the river well. One day we pulled our canoes into a wooded shore of Mana Pools and walked about half a mile into the bush Then we sat behind a downed tree and watched. Four elephants plodded past us. We followed them back to a boggy area that was adjacent to the river. Gathered near it were more elephants, some waterbucks and elands, three zebras, some Cape buffaloes, as well as baboons, and herons, and wild dogs – eight species peaceably sharing one source of water.

Below Mana Pools there are places where the river is a mile wide. One day, paddling near the middle of a broad stretch of water, we saw an enormous black mountain of seamless storm cloud advancing toward us. Fighting the sudden strong wind that preceded the storm, we made for the closest bank. The wind whipping against the current created a short breaking chop that began to slop into our boats. Within minutes we were swamped, our canoes like brimming bathtubs. Instead of trying to bail, which would have been useless, we kept ourselves upright by bracing with our paddles as we stroked.

The incentive for staying in your boat midstream in such a Zambezi storm is the certainty that crocodiles are attracted by delicious dangling legs.

'Crocodiles are opportunists,' Alastair said, as we draped our gear over hot rocks to dry it in the blazing sunshine that followed the storm. 'I saw a croc bite someone's paddle about a month ago. Must have thought it was edible.'

The red rocks were the first of many that we encountered as we traveled down the stream toward the Mupata Gorge, in places so narrow you can throw a stone from one side to the other. On the Zambian side I saw small clusters of mud huts and some good-sized villages – men in dugouts fishing with nets, women working in gardens, growing corn, children lugging buckets from the river to water the crops. There are no villages on the Zimbabwe bank. This lower part of the Zambezi has been divided into hunting areas where in the dry months hunters – foreigners mostly – go on big-game safaris.

'I take hunters out sometimes,' Alastair Macdonald told me. 'I know it's not politically correct, but hunting is one way to manage the animal populations. And it's profitable for the Zimbabwe government.'

A license to shoot a buffalo is 3,000 dollars, an elephant costs 5,000, a leopard 6,000. There are no guarantees.

'The best hunter on the Zambezi is the hyena,' Alastair said. 'They're much more successful than the lions or the leopards.'

I drifted along with the clusters of floating hyacinth – some like tiny islands – under the high Zambian escarpment. This ridge diminishes from a great green fortress-like wall to an assortment of low hills farther downstream. On my last day of paddling I reached Kanyemba, the place where three countries meet: Zambia, Zimbabwe, and Mozambique. I could see a hill just past the point where the river twisted into Mozambique. The little town beneath that hill is called Zumbo. It was settled by the Portuguese in 1715. After almost 300 years of continuous settlement Zumbo is still just a little town on a bend in the Zambezi, where the Zambezi descends the Central African Plateau to the coastal plain in Mozambique.

The Zambezi flows for almost 500 miles in Mozambique, though for upward of thirty years two guerrilla wars, one after the other, closed this hinterland. There was first FRELIMO's decade-long struggle against the Portuguese. After independence in 1974 an anti-FRELIMO movement called RENAMO was formed – supported mainly by white South Africa and an assortment of right-wing well-wishers. In the RENAMO war millions of people were either killed or displaced, bridges blown up, communications shattered, roads were closed, towns and villages depopulated by massacres. Because of this civil war, the Mozambique Zambezi, from Zumbo to the delta in the Indian Ocean, and the main tributary, the Shire River, were inaccessible to outsiders as well as to many Mozambicans. Throughout the war, the interior of Mozambique was a heart of darkness.

That was a great shame, for this part of the Zambezi is important historically. Livingstone sailed a paddle steamer upriver from the delta to Tete and also up the Shire, the first Westerner to do so, raising his hopes that the whole river could be navigated. The Shire tributary was never explored by the Portuguese, because of the hostility of the Africans on its banks.

The Zambezi and the Shire had allowed Livingstone to penetrate the African interior with all its marvels – lakes Shirwa and Nyasa, the country we know today as Malawi, the labyrinthine marsh on the Shire with its abundant elephants, and the mountain Morumbala, or 'The Lofty Watch Tower,' a solitary 4,000-foot-high sentry post in this riverine fastness. Yet the widespread famine and the crocodiles caused one of Livingstone's men to call the Shire 'literally a river of death.'

One hundred years later, with the armed struggle on the Lower Zambezi and the Shire, that was also true. The rivers remained no-go areas even after a peace agreement was signed between FRELIMO and RENAMO and hostilities ended in 1994. In the dry season of 1995, the first descent in a motorboat down the Shire and into the Zambezi was made by an expedition led by Captain Chris Marrow. Captain Marrow is an Englishman who supervises an aid agency, Mariners, which is dedicated to reestablishing ferry and barge services, virtual life-lines, over the Zambezi in Mozambique.

Two months after Marrow's expedition Alastair and I paddled down the Shire from Nsanje in Malawi through the marshes and into the Zambezi. We were able to accomplish this only with the help of two Malawian paddlers, Karsten Nyachikadza and Domingo Mon, who guided us through the marsh in their dugout canoe.

'Don't walk far,' Domingo said, when he saw me heading into the bush to relieve myself. 'There are bombs all over.'

He meant land mines. The peace agreement had been signed, but there are still thousands of land mines that have not been removed. These mines remain a problem, and the roads are terribly muddy, treacherous, and unreliable. Every bridge I saw in rural Mozambique had been blown up – some had been replaced with flimsier and more functional spans, others had not been replaced at all. The entire north–south railway network that had crossed the Zambezi was a rusty ruin. Whole towns had been demolished – I saw the roofless houses, the old scorched and windowless villas, the deserted farmhouses, the tipped-over locomotives.

In spite of this all the waterways are open. The Zambezi is once more a wide thoroughfare through Mozambique's heartland. The trouble is, it is hardly used except by small dugouts and the occasional motorboat.

We had set off, south of Nsanje, down the Shire River in southern Malawi.

'We go to the Zambezi all the time,' Karsten Nyachikadza told me in Chichewa. His own language was Sena and he said he felt right at home in this region, for the Sena nation overlapped Malawi and Mozambique.

'What are the problems we'll have on the river?' I had asked. 'What about hippos?'

He laughed. There weren't many hippos, he said. The people had eaten most of them during the war. The crocs would not bother us. I was touched when he said, 'The people are good.'

'No problems, then?'

'The wind,' he said. 'Just the wind.'

Each day in the afternoon, the wind came up – the same prevailing easterly that I had cursed upriver, and this head-wind slowed Karsten and Domingo's big dugout and even turned my kayak into a clumsy weather vane at times.

Some of the most dangerous aspects of the Zambezi are almost invisible – the wind, the mosquitoes which carry malaria, the biting tsetse flies, or the innocent-looking fruit called 'buffalo beans' which causes painful welts on the skin. There are also spiders, scorpions, and at some of our riverside camp sites big wet frogs which position themselves near anyone sleeping in the open and then jump with a gulp in a great smothering flop onto your face.

We camped at the edge of riverside villages – always asking permission – woke each morning at four-thirty, folded the tents, and packed the boats. We pushed off before five, at first light, paddling and drinking river water and peeling the small mangoes that were just being harvested on the river. We had lunch in the boats, too, and pushed on until the wind came up. Then we looked for a likely village, introduced ourselves from our boats, and were welcomed ashore.

That was when we pitched our tents and broke out our food boxes and built a cooking fire and had a proper meal – a pot of the plain starchy flour mixture, *nsima*, that we ate with fish or vegetables. As soon as the sun set and the clouds of mosquitoes descended, I crawled into my tent and listened to my short-wave radio. The days were so strenuous I was usually asleep by eight o'clock.

We threaded through the Ndinde Marsh, heading toward the Zambezi on waterways as narrow as creeks, with tall grass brushing us from both sides. The 'vast herds' of elephants that Livingstone saw in and around the Chiromo Marsh no longer existed – indeed, though the bird life was vigorous and there are many crocodiles and some hippos, we saw few large animals along the Shire. They have been killed or displaced by the people who inhabit the small villages along the Shire banks.

'We're going to the Zambezi!' Karsten called out confidently to the people on shore, or in dugouts, as he shoveled at the river with his lollipop-shaped paddle.

The people greeting us here were a community of marsh-dwelling Africans, perhaps 2,000 of them, all of this same sprawling Sena nation, whose precarious settlements were not on any map. There was no road, no school, no church, no hospital here. When they wanted to sell fish or buy nets or cooking pots they paddled upriver to the markets in Malawi; when they bartered their fish for bags of sugar they loaded their flotilla of dugouts and made trips in Mozambique, sometimes as far as the Zambezi.

'We don't need passports, Father,' Karsten said.

They come and go, downriver, from country to country, without passports – without even saying where they are going. But I was more conspicuous. At the international border, the tiny riverside depot of Megaza with its mud huts and its abandoned collection of ruined river boats and its clouds of mosquitoes, I had to go through the strict formality of Mozambique customs and immigration. This was in the open air, under a mango tree. There was a commotion in the tree – ripe fruit dropped onto the official table. It was a rat in the branches, nibbling the fruit, and it kept interrupting the proceedings.

After that, and for many miles, we could see Morumbala, which is more a plateau than a mountain. There were farms and fruit orchards at the top, we were told. How had the Portuguese gotten up and down the mountain? I wondered.

'They were carried by Africans,' the villagers said.

There were abandoned houses and plantations, remnants of the Portuguese colonial presence, at many places on the banks. We camped in villages of the Sena people, who seem as remote today as they were in the time of Livingstone. Certainly people's lives follow the traditional pattern, the men fishing in the river to the cries of the masked weaver birds, and the women and girls grinding corn: that rhythmic thud of the pestle and mortar is like a heartbeat on the river.

After five days of heat and mosquitoes on the muddy, slow-moving

Shire, I looked up one noon and saw the river turning a corner, entering the Zambezi – clearly the Zambezi, for it was half a mile wide and moving swiftly, tumbling down from Tete on its way to the sea. And soon I heard the chugging of an engine – the first since leaving Nsanje.

It was the barge at Caia, big enough to serve as a drive-on ferry for trailer trucks. Made 'from next to nothing,' Chris Marrow told me – twelve 'uniflotes' and four engines that had been assembled from eight scrap engines – this brainchild of the Mariners was the only way across the Zambezi for the 260 miles between Tete and the ocean.

I approached a trailer truck loaded with sacks of beans as it rumbled off the barge at Caia. 'Yes, we are going to Beira,' the driver, Gilberto, told me. And, yes, he said, he had room for my folding boat, my camping equipment, my duffel bag. But he waved his hand when I began to get into the cab.

'You ride on top,' he said. 'Only the owner can ride in here.'

He gave me a freshly picked pineapple as consolation as I threw my gear up, and then climbed to the top of the truck's load. Think of this as a hayride, I told myself, as I shared the pineapple with the twenty or so Africans who also clung to the tarp that had been thrown over the bags of beans.

It was early afternoon when we set off. Then it began to rain. Fourteen hours later, in darkness and drizzle, we arrived in Beira and the air was briny. The distance had not been great, but the road was appalling.

Livingstone believed that the whole Zambezi was navigable. He was mistaken. He would be surprised that no ships ply the river, and probably startled by the hydroelectric schemes at Kariba and Cabora Bassa, and by the towns on either side of the falls. But much of the river would be instantly familiar, for so little has changed. His scrupulous notes, his cartography, his taxonomy of the river's flora and fauna, still stand, and his descriptions of its topographical wonders and its dramatic weather cannot be improved upon.

Livingstone constantly referred to the beauty of the Zambezi, but he was a relative late-comer in this regard. The Africans have always seen the Zambezi as a river of mythic power, something lovely that was also a vital force, endlessly pouring from the heart of Africa.

The True Size of Cape Cod

The Cape Cod that people write about I seldom recognize. I constantly think about the place. It is my home, so it is in my dreams, a landscape of my unconscious mind, perhaps my mind's only landscape. Paddling between islands in New Guinea I often think, 'That's no worse than Falmouth to Oak Bluffs.' Swimming in a bad chop or a swift current anywhere I think of Wood's Hole or the harbor entrance at Lewis Bay. Living on the Cape has given me a good notion of wind speed and air temperature. This complex landscape has taught me ways of measuring the world of risk.

But the world landscape presents a problem on the Cape. I find it hard to separate the land from the water, or the water from the winds. The stranger walks or drives to the shore and looks across to the Vineyard, or on the bay side to Wellfleet, or wherever; always seeing divisions. The local person does not distinguish between land and water, and keeps going, actually or mentally, seeing shoals and eddies and sunken ships and the rocks that are exposed only at low tide – not barriers but features. There are calm days, of course, and the prevailing winds are often reliable; but the weather is eccentric, and it is not unusual for the winds on successive days to blow from all the points of the compass, and these winds determine the weather and the condition of land and water.

To a stranger, the Cape seems like many simple separate places according to the time the person has visited, seeking the jolly, the quaint, the charming, the historical. When such strangers describe the place they are very choosy. It seems odd for a local to hear such selective descriptions of the terminal moraine of the Cape, of the dunes and woodlands and harbors. Or of Nantucket Sound as a sort of moat that protects the island of Martha's Vineyard. Or how Nantucket Island is some distance to sea – too flat and far to be visible. Or how Wood's Hole is like a spillway, and farther south in the Sound there are ship-swallowing currents and the hidden rocks that holed the *QE II*. These are just versions of the Cape, simplified portraits of its peculiarities.

To me, knowing the true size of the Cape means knowing ways of navigating it: finding routes into the marshes and up the tidal creeks; knowing the offshore shoals and sand bars, such as Egg Island off Hyannis, or the Billingsgate Shoal off Wellfleet, or the three serpent-shaped shoals which make the crossing from the Cape to the Vineyard so unpredictable: L'Hommedieu Shoal, Hedge Fence Shoal, and Middle Ground. Even on a flat day with no wind there are standing waves on the shoals, making a specific contour, and the waves range from a foot-high embankment of water, to five or six feet of irregular fury, more like white water in a narrow river than anything in an ocean. Muskeget Channel, between Chappaquiddick and Nantucket, can be terrifyingly swift, full of whirlpools, or rocks; and yet that is the same world of the Cape – just its nether side. These waves and swells have their analog in the dunes of Truro or Sandy Neck, or the wooded ridge of the Upper Cape.

If a place is home, most years it offers 365 faces. Whether it is a Cape marsh, or a creek, or a pepperidge tree, or a dune, or the sea itself, it is different every day of the year. Knowing the differences keeps you fascinated and may make you safe. Not understanding a current or an offshore wind or a shoal in a channel can lead to death. That is also why I have a problem rhapsodizing about the Cape or using the quick-to-fade colors of hyperbole. I would not want to paint a pretty portrait only to mislead someone into thinking they are safe when they are not.

Yet if the Cape were not dangerous it would lose much of its reality for me. The water of the Cape is seen from shore as seemingly featureless and deceptive as moorland, which is why it has claimed so many lives. In a hubristic way, people plant their houses by the shore – nearly always these people are from off-Cape, and when they return in late spring they often see that the house has been undermined if not swept away by the winter storms.

When Henry David Thoreau walked the length of the Cape and wrote about it, he remarked on how the world's true wildernesses lie under the sea. It goes without saying that, like everywhere else, a portion of the marine world of the Cape has been tainted and littered. More and more I have come to see that the single-species fanatics, like the protectors of certain stretches of beach, are missing the point. The Cape is its total sum of land and water. The much-too-big houses and pretensions of Osterville have to be balanced against its rural poverty in the wood-lots of Mashpee; Oak Bluffs is black, Edgartown is white, but both are middle class. The little reckless alewives make their way every April up creeks in Brewster to spawn. The Cape has taught me that we live in one world, fragile and failing, and it is the whole that must be understood, not any fragment of it.

German Humor

It was a complete coincidence that I happened to be reading Freud's *Jokes and Their Relation to the Unconscious* the day I was summoned to West Germany, not long ago. It was just prior to the present eruption of nationalistic feeling, the mutual embrace of the two Germanys, the breach in the Wall. Before I left people kept asking why I was going. It seemed too boring to say I was on the circuit for my own *Das Chinesische Abenteuer* (*Reise durch das Reich der Mitte*), so I lied and said I was compiling an anthology of German humor. The axiom in joking is, a person's favorite joke is the key to that person's character; and so it is for a culture. A traveler profits by such insights, and many travelers recognize the querying faces and the silence that descend after he or she has told a joke in a distant land.

Like most jokes, and especially German jokes, this little wheeze had a serious side. Freud says 'the factor of "topicality" . . . is a fertile source of pleasure in a great many jokes.' I wondered how East Germans might figure in this. What had begun as a piece of frivolity developed into a preoccupation: I found myself asking questions, making notes, and inquiring into nuances. Many Germans maintain that humor is non-existent in their country – the formality of German life and speech does not lend itself to joke-telling, and I suppose one could seriously question (as Freud does) whether jokes constitute humor at all. In my experience most joke-tellers are nags, bores, racists, sadists, boasters, blasphemers, look-at-me types. And since this takes up nearly the whole of humanity, surely such people could not be unknown in Germany.

'One Person in Four in Munich is Unhappy,' the *Suddeutsche Zeitung* announced in its main headline the day I arrived. No one found that the least bit funny, nor did anyone laugh over the enormous student demonstration, thousands of students protesting over inadequate provision for their brass band practice. In Rosenheim at the

Klepper folding-boat factory I was staring at a pair of antlers mounted on a trophy board when Herr Walther, the owner said, 'There are ten mistakes on that thing. Can you guess them?'

The inscription read 'Shot by Enrico Caruso at Monte Gran Sasso 31.11.1876' and there was a certain amount of other detail about Caruso's having been a member of a paddling club in Naples.

'The antlers are upside down,' I said.

'Good. First mistake. Go on.'

'How old was Caruso in 1876?'

'Three years old. Excellent. Continue.'

It was a thunderously labored joke – there is no November 31, there are no elks in Italy, and so forth – but it was the genuine home-grown item.

Political jokes are predictable enough, but in Germany curiously only Chancellor Kohl is the butt of them. There is no mockery for the far-right Republicans, whose leader is a former member of the Waffen-SS and fairly pleased with himself having made electoral gains in the most recent election in Berlin. And there are no West German jokes about East Germans – none about the drabness of their lives, the fanaticism of their Olympians, and not one about the coughing top-heavy Trabant, little more than a metal blister on wheels, one of the most laughable motor vehicles on earth. I elicited only pity or silence when I asked for jokes about East Germans.

Most Kohl jokes depict him as a blunderer, and just the mention of his nickname, *Der Birne* – 'The Pear,' mocking his shape – causes laughter. Another joke has Herr Kohl and Mrs. Thatcher toasting each other with a beer. 'Here's to your health,' Mrs. Thatcher says, and thinking she said, 'Here's to your *hell*' – light beer – he replies, 'Here's to your *dunkel*' – dark beer.

Blunderers and clowns are regarded as very funny, and in Germany they usually come in pairs: Little Erna and Little Fritz (Klein Erna and Klein Fritzchen) or the duo of Tünnes and Schäel, the Laurel and Hardy of Cologne. One day, they are required to sell a shipment of brassières at the market. Schäel is amazed by Tünnes's having sold hundreds. How did you manage to sell so many? he asks. Tünnes replies, 'I cut them in half and yelled, "Hats from the Pope!"'

The fact that it is faintly anti-Catholic and that it must be told in a dialect makes this joke hilarious, but only in Cologne.

East Friesians are the most mocked of Germans in the regional jokes. Why do the East Friesians smile at thunderstorms? Because they think they're being photographed. I met an East Friesian from the island of Juist. I asked him who the East Friesians make jokes about. He said, 'Other East Friesians.' But he went on to say, 'These jokes were invented by East Friesians as a marketing technique to popularize East Friesia.'

'Germans never make jokes about themselves,' a woman told me in Frankfurt. But does any country do that? I assumed that in Saarbrücken on the French border there would be French jokes, but there aren't. They are rather in awe of the French there and have even adopted the French habit of making jokes about the Belgians.

Austrians are also mocked. Did you hear the one about the Austrian bank robber who went into a Munich bank and said, 'Put your money in the air, give me all the hands you have, because I'm a hostage!' The bank teller replied, 'Shall I give it to you in shillings?' because he knew that a fool like that had to be an Austrian.

The commonest jokes, I was told, are jokes about Turks. 'Turkish jokes are now sanctioned, because the feeling against foreigners is very strong at the moment' – and I should say that foreigners also include American servicemen, who are resented these days as much for their presumption as for their nuclear arsenal.

Turks in Germany are the perfect victims: they are dark, they are hairy and sinister, they are Muslim, they stick out like a sore thumb, and in general they are on the bottom rung of the workforce.

People in factories tell Turkish jokes, kids in school tell them.

Everyone I met had heard Turkish jokes, but no one would repeat one. I solemnly said it was for my research. They said – no, the jokes are stupid, I can't tell jokes, I can never remember the punchline. One person said, 'They are unbelievably cruel jokes. They're awful. They're hard. They're like this. What is the difference between a Bavarian and a Turk? And the answer will be that the Bavarian is a human being and the Turk is an animal.'

'I hate these jokes,' a woman said to me with real feeling, and the more I asked the more I seemed to be inquiring not about jokes but about the darker side of the German character. 'The joke,' Freud says, 'is the contribution made to the comic from the realm of the unconscious.' One was risked. 'What are the two Turkish holidays?' Answer: '*Sommerschlussverkauf* and *Winterschlussverkauf*' (the summer bargain sale and the winter bargain sale).

That seemed pretty tame. I persisted. I was told to lay off. At first I took this for German delicacy. When I kept on asking for examples of Turkish jokes I was told that there were no real Turkish jokes.

'They are anti-Jewish jokes with the names changed,' I was told. 'They are horrible. They are even about gas chambers.'

As a matter of fact, many of the jokes in Freud's study are about Jews, and I mentioned this. One woman said she knew many such jokes – Turkish, Jewish, the lot.

Racial, ethnic and xenophobic jokes say a great deal about the teller. I tried to encourage her. *Hear about the* (choose victimized group) *man who claimed his wife was a terrible housekeeper? He said, Every time I pee in the sink there's dirty dishes in it.*

Naturally, she didn't laugh. She said, 'I'm not going to tell you any. You'd just put it into one of your books.'

Part Four
China

Down the Yangtze

There is no Yangtze River. The name is unknown to most Chinese, who call it Da Jiang, 'Great River,' or Chang Jiang, 'Long River,' unless they live above Chongqing – there, the swift silt-filled waters are referred to as Chin-sha Jiang, 'The River of Gold Sand.' That is only a misnomer now. As recently as the 1930s, in the winter months when the level dropped, the Chinese squatted at its edge and panned for gold, sluicing the mud and gathering gold dust. European travelers reported seeing washerwomen wearing thick gold bangles, made of the metal that had been carried from where the river – let us call it the Yangtze – rises in Tibet.

But it has more moods than names. 'I am careful to give the date of each day's notes,' Archibald Little wrote in *Through the Yangtse Gorges* (1887). 'The river varies so wonderfully at different seasons that any description must be carefully understood only to apply to the day upon which it is written.' Captain Little was overwhelmed by it; he compared it to the Mississippi and the Amazon; he said it was indescribable. It has in many stretches a violent magnificence. It is subject to murderous floods, and its winter level creates rapids of such turbulence that the river captain steers his ship through the foam and travels down the tongue of the rapid, praying that no junk will lie in its path, as it is impossible for him to stop or reverse. The Yangtze's four divisions are like four separate rivers: above Chongqing, it is mythic and still associated with gold and landslides; the Upper River (Chongqing-Ichang) is the wildest – here are the gorges and the landscape of China's Walter Scottish classic *The Romance of the Three Kingdoms*; the Middle River (Ichang-Wuhan) is serene and a mile wide; the Lower River (Wuhan-Shanghai) is slow, clouded with silt, and populous.

I sailed 1,500 miles downstream, from Chongqing to Shanghai. Every mile of it was different; but there were 1,200 miles I did not see. It crosses ten provinces, 700 rivers are joined to it – all Yangtze statistics are hopelessly huge and ungraspable; they obscure rather than clarify. And since words can have a greater precision than numbers, one day I asked a Chinese ship captain if he thought the river had a distinct personality.

He said, 'The mood of the river changes according to the season. It changes every day. It is not easy. Navigating the river is always a struggle against nature. And there is only one way to pilot a ship well.' Smiling and blowing smoke out of his nostrils, he explained, 'It is necessary to see the river as an enemy.'

Later, a man told me that in the course of one afternoon he had counted nine human corpses bobbing hideously down the river.

The Yangtze is China's main artery, its major waterway, the source of many of its myths, the scene of much of its history. On its banks are some of its greatest cities. It is the fountainhead of superstition; it provides income and food to half the population. It is one of the most dangerous rivers in the world, in some places one of the dirtiest, in others one of the most spectacular. The Chinese drink it and bathe in it and wash clothes in it and shit in it. It represents both life and death. It is a wellspring, a sewer, and a tomb; depthless in the gorges, puddle-shallow at its rapids. The Chinese say if you haven't been up the Great River, you haven't been anywhere.

They also say that in the winter, on the river, the days are so dark that when the sun comes out the dogs bark at it. Chongqing was dark at nine in the morning, when I took the rattling tin tram on the cog railway that leads down the black crags which are Chongqing's ramparts, down the sooty cliffs, past the tenements and billboards ('Flying Pigeon Bicycles,' 'Seagull Watches,' 'Parrot Accordions') to the landing stage. A thick sulfurous fog lay over the city, a Coketown of 6 million. The fog had muffled the morning noises and given the city an air of frightening solemnity. It also stank like poison. Dr. Ringrose, who was from Leeds, sniffed and said, 'That is the smell of my childhood.'

There were thirty-three of us, including Ringrose. The others were American, most of them millionaires, many of them multi-millionaires. 'If you have 2 or 3 million,' one of them told me in the dreary city of Wanxian, 'you're not a millionaire – you're just getting by.' Another enlarged on this. Not to be a poor millionaire you needed 25 million. 'If you have 25,' she said crisply, 'you're all right.' But Lurabelle Laughlin, from Pasadena, had inherited 50 million dollars. Her husband, Harry, told me this. He said Lurabelle could buy and sell every person on board our ship. He wasn't being malicious, only factual. 'And I'm not too badly off myself,' he said.

'I hate walking,' Mrs Ver Bryck told me. Mrs Ver Bryck, another oil heiress, hailed from Incline, Nevada. 'I never walk. I've been everywhere and didn't have to walk. I pay so I don't have to walk. And stairs are my bugbear. But you look like a walker, Paul. Are you going to walk and do all that crappy-ola?'

I cherish the memory of Ami Ver Bryck and Lurabelle Laughlin walking from the tramway at Chongqing across the muddy paving on the foreshore, with hundreds of Chinese in baggy blue suits watching in utter silence. Lurabelle's mink coat was golden, made from thirty-five creatures of the 'tourmaline' variety; Ami's was a rich glossy mahogany. And here was Bea Brantman, also in mink. 'This is my football coat,' she cried. 'I wear it to all the games.' Bea and her husband, who was known to everyone as Big Bob, had eleven children. Big Bob said, 'I guess they'd put me in jail for that in China! Watch out, Bea, it's kind of slippery here. It looks more like an ocean than a river. You can't even see the other side.'

It was a good companionable crowd, and though it seems a contradiction to say so, these millionaires represented a cross-section of American society. Some had inherited their money, some had got it from divorce settlements, or had married into it, or had made it from nothing. One had earned it from brokering, another from gun accessories, another from burglar alarms, four were oil fortunes, one was advertising, others didn't say. Some struck me as rather stupid, with their cowboy novels and their remarks about building condominiums near Hankow or Ichang and all the talk about Connecticut. Some were very smart about Chinese history or porcelain, and they knew the various dates in the Cultural Revolution. They were Democrats and Republicans, Jewish and Christian, they came from all over the United States. Interestingly, they never argued among themselves, no one was ever on the outs, and the spouses never fought. All of them had traveled before. Half had already been to China once and knew their way around Inner Mongolia. The rest were novices and called Mao 'Mayo,' and confused Thailand with Taiwan, and Fuji with Fiji. They were as tenacious and practical as the Chinese, and just as ethnocentric, but much funnier, and better at cards.

We boarded *Dong Fang Hong* ('The East is Red') – *Number 39* and were soon under way. Because of the construction of locks and a dam at Ichang, we would travel downriver in two ships: the M.S.

Kun Lun awaited us just below Ichang. Both *Number 39* and the *Kun Lun* were the same size, built to carry 900 people. But they had been specially chartered by the Lindblad Tour Company. There were, as I say, only thirty-three of us, and a crew of 102. No hardships for us, and it seemed at times, though we were traveling through the very heart of the country, that China was elsewhere.

My mind kept going back to my first impression of China, and my disbelief. We had left the frenzy, the scavengers, the free-for-all of Hong Kong and were heading toward the hills – so blurred and blue you might mistake them for clouds. China began there, on those bare hillsides. There were voices behind me.

'Look, Jack.'

'Yeah.'

'Lush vegetation.'

'Yeah.'

But for an hour, until the train reached the Chinese border at Lo Wu, it was not lush. It was still farming country, dusty fields and skinny crops, as far as my eye could see.

Mrs Ver Bryck was saying to me, 'I've been everywhere, more than once.' I took her to be well over seventy. In fact, she was just sixty-two. She chain-smoked. She had a shopping bag full of cartons of cigarettes. In another shopping bag she kept her supply of vodka. On this express to Canton, she told me how much she liked the Chinese. She loathed Italians – they controlled all the gambling in Nevada, she said. She despised the Japanese – they had charged her 410 dollars for a room in Tokyo a few days before. It was the royal suite, but she had not asked for it, and she had spent only twelve hours in it. That was thirty-four dollars an hour. She looked out the window at the cabbages, the lettuce, the beans, and at the culverts and ditches. 'Look how they work,' she said. 'I love the Chinese.'

Just before Lo Wu there was a fence – coils of barbed wire about twenty feet high – and then, as the train penetrated the People's Republic of China, billboards by the side of the trains advertising 'Ginseng Bee Secretion' and 'Tiensin Shoes and Slippers' and 'Marlboro Cigarettes'. And inside the train, on a television set that had been showing a Chinese travelogue about Guilin, there were commercials for Rainbow Brand television sets and Ricoh watches – men and women dancing sedately and all of them wearing Ricoh watches. It was all a flatter, duller version of Hong Kong commercialism, this communist parody of advertising; and it was a bit sad, because it was the imperfect mimicry of the Hong Kong vulgarity which was in turn an imitation of American crassness. It was saddest of all because it was unconvincing.

And it bore no relation at all to what was going on outside the train window. There in Guandong Province everyone was harvesting rice. The train tracks were surrounded by paddy fields. Some of the rice was already tied into bunches, and the rest was being gathered by hand or threshed. They threshed it the old way, by whipping the rice grains into a basket. The people worked in groups, never alone. In one field, about eighty people were threshing in the heat, and this was the beginning of my disbelief. I did not want to think how primitive this method was.

The land looked scraped – no trees, only tiny houses, or huts, and cultivation everywhere. In places there were small stands of scrub pine or tall weedy eucalyptus trees. But there was no shade. The people working in the dazzling dust had black cloth fringes sewn to their lampshade hats to keep off the sun. Some were yoked to huge watering cans, and they looked like miniature crucifixions in the mass of these bald hills.

That was the other strange thing. It was hot, even tropical, but the hills were naked, bald, scarred with plow-marks and paths. It was not lush. I saw an old man whipping a buffalo's wrinkled back with a stick to beat him out of a ditch.

The first town, an hour out of Lo Wu, was a railway junction named Tang t'ou-hsia. Outside it was a brickworks. Men and women were making bricks in the old way here, out of mud and straw, clumping them out of wooden molds and stacking them into a cathedral shape which they turned into a furnace. Sweltering, the brick-bakers stoked the fire. All the houses in this area were made of these liver-colored bricks.

'What do you think?' Mrs Ver Bryck asked.

'Rustic,' I said. 'Very nice.'

But it was mournfully backward: no cars, no tractors, no threshing machines, only farming by hand, and brickmaking. I saw no livestock – no pigs, no chickens. It was like all the pictures I had seen of old China: the same baggy smocks and sandals and straw hats, the same laborious agriculture, the same simplicity.

On the television set in the train a film of singing soldiers began to roll. They were well-dressed soldiers and as they sang a pretty girl in a red dress skipped through fields and past a waterfall. Outside the train, people were harvesting rice, sweating their guts out in the brickworks; and there were soldiers there, too, standing by the tracks in their flimsy uniforms, looking too small and meek to be soldiers.

Later, I could tell how important a person was by the way his blue suit fitted him. The 'Blue Danube' was playing on the ship's loudspeakers as *Number 39* swung between the sampans and the fishing smacks and the burdened ferries. The captain greeted us in the lounge and told us the current was moving at six and a half feet per second and added, 'As your captain, I am responsible for your safety, so please don't worry about it.'

Captain Liu was sixty. He had a narrow, flat-backed head and bristly hair and a seeping wound in his left eye and large spaces between his teeth. He had always worked on the river. His father had been a tracker on a junk, rowing and towing junks upstream. Captain Liu himself had started out as a steward, serving food on a Chinese riverboat, at the age of fifteen. 'I was the "boy" as they say in English, but I worked my way up to captain. I never went to school. You can't learn about this river in a school. You can only learn it by being on the bridge.'

This is true; and not much has been written about the Yangtze. But before I left London I had been given a list of twenty-eight landmarks on the Upper River, patiently typed by Captain A. R. Williamson, who spent nearly thirty years sailing up and down the river. Captain Williamson is ninety, living in vigorous retirement in Hove, and is one of the historians of the river. I was lucky in meeting him and lucky to have a detailed list of things to look out for – towns, skiffs, pagodas, rapids, and shrines. It was Captain Williamson's list that convinced me that, though a great deal has changed in China, the river today is essentially the river Captain Williamson traveled on in 1920, and Archibald Little sailed on in 1887, and the Abbé David botanized on in the 1860s, and Italian missionaries proselytized on in the seventeenth and eighteenth centuries. The river and the ways of many of the river dwellers are as old as China. There is a painting in the Shanghai Museum of junks and sampans on a river, by Zhang Zheduan. Those vessels have the same sails, mats, rigging, rudders, and oars as ones I saw on the Yangtze the other day. But it is a Sung dynasty painting, 1,000 years old.

A half-hour below Chongqing, Captain Williamson's notes said, was a large Buddha in a shrine at the top of a long flight of steps. The niche was there, and the steps; but the Buddha was gone. In

Captain Williamson's day, all upbound junks fired strings of fire-crackers on passing the Buddha, 'in gratitude for safe passage.' There were no firecrackers, though there were dozens of passing junks.

Mottled hills appeared in the mist on both sides of the river, and here, just above Chang Shou, the river narrowed to about seventy-five feet. The ship slowed to negotiate this rocky bottleneck and gave me time to study the hills. In the last century, Abbé David saw fortifica-tions on the tops of these hills. In his *Diaries* is a wonderful account of his Yangtze trip. 'These are refuges in times of trouble for the country people, where they can go with their possessions and be safe from the depredations of rebels and brigands.' Banditry was widespread on the Yangtze from the earliest times; the 1920s and 1930s were especially terrible, as warlords' armies fought their way toward Chongqing. Peace did not come to the river until 1949, when a brooding bureaucracy with parrot-squawk slogans took over.

Now, every inch of these hills was farmland: it is the agricultural overstrain of China. On the steepest slopes were terraces of vegetables. How was it possible to water the gardens on these cliff-faces? I looked closely and saw a man climbing up the hillside, carrying two buckets on a yoke. He tipped them into a ditch and, without pausing further, started down the hill. No one is idle on the Yangtze. In the loneliest bends of the river are solitary men breaking rocks and smashing them into gravel. You might think they would sit down and rest (who is watching?), or soak their feet in the shallows. It is killing work. But they go on hammering, and the sound I associate with these hidden stretches of the Upper River is the sound of hammers and chisels, a sound like the sweetest chimes.

In 1937 Captain Williamson saw only the city walls of Chang Shou from the river. Today there are no city walls, and Chang Shou (the name means 'Long Life') is one of the nightmare cities of the river. It burst through its old walls and sprawled across the banks, blackening three hillsides with chimneys and factories and blocks of workers' flats. 'Looks like Pittsburgh,' someone said. But Chongqing had looked like Pittsburgh, and so had six others downstream. Yellow froth streamed from pipes and posterns, and drained into the river with white muck and oil and the suds of treated sewage and beautifully colored poison. And on a bluff below the town, there was an old untroubled pagoda, still symmetrical, looking as if it had been carved from a piece of laundry soap. These pagodas have a purpose. They are always found near towns and cities and, even now in unspiritual China, serve a spiritual function, controlling the *feng shui* of a place: they balance the female influences of the Yin ('Darkness') and the male influence of the Yang ('Light'). The Chinese say they no longer believe in such superstitious malarkey, but the visible fact is that most pagodas survived the Cultural Revolution. Anything that a fanatical Red Guard left intact must be regarded as worthy, if not sacred. The pagodas on the Yangtze bluffs remain pretty much as they always were.

It was near Chang Shou, about noon on that first day, that I saw a sailing junk being steered to the bank; the sail was struck, and five men leaped onto the shore with tow-lines around their waists. They ran ahead, then jerked like dogs on a leash, and immediately began towing the junk against the current. These are trackers. They are mentioned by the earliest travelers on the Yangtze. They strain, leaning forward, and almost imperceptibly the sixty-foot junk begins to move upstream. There is no level towpath. The trackers are rock-climbers: they scamper from boulder to boulder, moving higher until the boulders give out, and then dropping down, pulling and climbing until there is a reach on the river where the junk can sail again. The only difference – but it is a fairly large one – between trackers long ago and trackers today is that they are no longer whipped. 'Often our men have to climb or jump like monkeys,' wrote a Yangtze traveler, in the middle of the last century, of his trackers, 'and their backs are lashed by the two chiefs, to urge them to work at critical moments. This new spectacle at first revolts and angers us, but when we see that the men do not complain about the lashings we realize that it is the custom of the country, justified by the exceptional difficulties along the route.' Captain Little saw a tracker chief strip his clothes off, jump into the river, then roll himself in sand until he looked half-human, like a gritty ape; then he did a demon dance, and howled, and whipped the trackers, who – scared out of their wits – willingly pulled a junk off a sandbank.

The trackers sing or chant. There are garbled versions of what they say. Some travelers have them grunting and groaning, others are more specific and report the trackers yelling, '*Chor! Chor!*' – slang for '*Shang-chia*' or 'Put your shoulder to it.' I asked a boatman what the trackers were chanting. He said that they cried out '*Hai tzo! Hai tzo!*' over and over again, which means 'Number! Number!' in Szechuanese, and is uttered by trackers and oarsmen alike.

'When we institute the Four Modernizations,' he added – this man was one of the minuscule number who are members of the Chinese Communist Party – 'there will be no more junks or trackers.'

One day I was standing at the ship's rail with Big Bob. We saw some trackers, six of them, pulling a junk. The men skipped from rock to rock, they climbed, they hauled the lines attached to the junk, and they struggled along the steep rocky towpath. They were barefoot.

Brantman winced. It was a wince of sagacity, of understanding: yes, it said, I now see what this is all about. Then he spoke, still wincing a little.

'The profound cultural difference between people!'

I looked at him. He was nodding at the trackers scampering among the rocks on the shore.

'They don't care about television,' he said.

I said, 'That's true.'

'Huh?' He was encouraged. He was smiling now. He said, 'I mean, they couldn't care less if the Rams are playing tomorrow.'

The Los Angeles Rams were Big Bob's favorite football team.

'Am I right, or not?'

'You're right, Bob,' I said. 'They don't care about television or the Rams.'

The junks and these trackers will be on the river for some time to come. Stare for five minutes at any point on the Yangtze and you will see a junk, sailing upstream with its ragged, ribbed sail; or being towed by yelling, tethered men; or slipping downstream with a skinny man clinging to its rudder. There are many new-fangled ships and boats on the river, but the Yangtze is a river of junks and sampans, fueled by human sweat. There is nothing lovelier than a junk with a following wind (the wind blows upstream, from east to west – a piece of great meteorological luck and a shaper of Chinese history), sailing so well that the clumsy vessel looks as light as a water bird paddling and foraging in the muddy current.

That image is welcome, because there is little bird life on the Yangtze – indeed, China itself is no place for an ornithologist. It is hard to say if the absence of trees is the reason for the scarceness of birds; or is it the use of powerful insecticides, or the plain hunger of the people, who seem to kill anything that moves? Apart from a few kites and hawks, and some feeble sparrows, the only wild ground-dwelling creature I saw in China was a rat, and in twenty-two trips on the Yangtze a Lindblad guide told me he had only seen one wild thing, a small snake. No wonder the Chinese stared at mink coats and alligator handbags! Abbé David saw very few birds on the Yangtze in the 1860s and, as a naturalist, he was looking hard for them. He put it down to the wilful destruction of animals by the Chinese, and his reflection on this has proved to be prophetic:

A selfish and blind preoccupation with material interests has caused us to reduce this cosmos, so marvelous to him with eyes to see it, to a hard matter-of-fact place. Soon the horse and the pig on the one hand and wheat and potatoes on the other will replace hundreds of thousands of animals and plants given us by God.

Down the Yangtze the awful prediction has been fulfilled. You expect this river trip to be an experience of the past – and it is. But it is also a glimpse of the future. In a hundred years or so, under a cold uncolonized moon, what we call the civilized world will all look like China, muddy and senile and old-fangled: no trees, no birds, and shortages of fuel and metal and meat; but plenty of pushcarts, cobblestones, ditch-diggers, and wooden inventions. Nine hundred million farmers splashing through puddles and the rest of the population growing weak and blind working the crashing looms in black factories.

Forget rocket-ships, super-technology, moving sidewalks, and all the rubbishy hope in science fiction. No one will ever go to Mars and live. A religion has evolved from the belief that we have a future in outer space; but it is a half-baked religion – it is a little like Mormonism or the Cargo Cult. Our future is the mildly poisoned earth and its smoky air. We are in for hunger and hard work, the highest stage of poverty – no starvation, but crudeness everywhere, political art, simple language, bad books, brutal laws, plain vegetables, and clothes of one color. It will be damp and dull, like this. It will be monochrome and crowded – how could it be different? There will be no star wars or galactic empires and no more money to waste on the loony nationalism in space programs. Our grandchildren will probably live in a version of China. On the dark-brown banks of the Yangtze the future has already arrived.

It struck me that many of the American passengers were sedentary types. One man said to me, 'Back home, my wife and I lead a very sedimentary life.' I knew what he meant. And this was a kind of sedentary travel. Nor did these armchair travelers read books. All their talk was about places they had been. Many of their sentences began, 'When we were in Kenya . . .' Or it might be Tierra del Fuego or Inner Mongolia: they were well traveled. For facts they seldom referred to anything but their travel. They had seen crime in Korea, or an election in Costa Rica, or poverty in Turkey. To me they said, 'You've got a big race problem.' It wasn't personal; they meant England – I lived there.

Most of them had discovered that if you had enough money and time you did not have to read. You could discover things for yourself – or, rather, be told about them by a national guide. In the corporate lives that they led they had become used to people telling them things, filling them in on a situation. In China we had 'briefings.' They loved 'briefings.' You sat there and someone with a briefcase gave you the low-down – facts, figures, a little history – and you interrogated him for ten minutes. Then it was over. It was so much easier than reading, so much more reassuring. But, of course, as travelers we were regarded as big and busy; in a sense the commune workers and the people in factories and the sailors in the Yangtze ships were working for us.

'I've known a lot of women like her,' a man told me. 'A hell of a lot of women. I've met them on trips like this. They go to Mongolia. They go to Pago-Pago. Peru. Sri Lanka. And they never do anything. We had one with us on the Galapagos trip. She never got off the ship! Can you imagine going to the Galapagos and not getting off the ship? It was a twenty-eight-day trip!'

'Why do you suppose she came here?' I asked.

'To drink. Haven't you seen her? She's having a grand time. She's got a whole box full of whiskey sours. She stays in the hotel and drinks while we're at the communes. The only thing is – she's got to drink them warm. She doesn't trust the ice. It's got germs!'

Later, he said, 'I'll make a prediction. I'll bet you she never gets off the boat on the Yangtze. She'll just sit there, drinking her whiskey sours.'

He was right. But sometimes I was grateful for this old woman's company – at night, in the lounge of the *Dong Fang Hong – Number 39*, after everyone had gone to bed. By half-past nine nearly everyone was in bed, except this woman and me, drinking and playing gin rummy.

One night she looked across the table and said, 'I was rotten spoiled,' and she smiled. 'My daughter was rotten spoiled. And I'm going to make goddamn sure that my granddaughter is rotten spoiled.'

Sixty-five miles below Chongqing, at Fuling, I was joined at the rail by one of the passengers, a stockbroker. We talked about the price of gold and the delinquent bullion market as, on the shore, small tent camps of Chinese sifted gravel and lugged it in buckets to waiting sampans. We passed gardens and talked about land deals and Washington real estate.

'Timber,' he said. 'This is a very good time to buy timber. Something like Weyerhauser. The slump in building has meant the stock's depressed. But you can't go wrong with timber. What you want is a well-managed company, with a good product and good record.'

There was a commune on the next hill: vegetables, a factory, chimney, huts, a brickworks. We watched it pass. He told me the American stock market was vastly underrated. Then the dinner gong rang.

We were soon at Feng Tu. Abbé David: 'Very pretty because of its pagodas, towers and the green hills around it.' Captain Williamson: 'One hill is said to be haunted.' Nothing had been torn down, but a certain amount had been added: it was a sullen agglomeration of scorched factories and workers' flats under a weeping corona of smog.

'It certainly looks haunted to me,' I said to the political commissar on our ship. The political commissar is the labor relations man. If there is slackness in the galley or the engine room on a Chinese ship, the political commissar reminds the workers of their duties. Ours was Comrade Sun; he had been working on the river since 1950 ('just after Liberation'), when he was seventeen. He knew the hills and temples of Feng Tu very well.

No, he said, it was not haunted.

'There are no ghosts,' says a Chinese pamphlet entitled *Stories about Not Being Afraid of Ghosts*. 'Belief in ghosts is a backward idea, a superstition and a sign of cowardice. This is a matter of common sense today among the people. But while there are no demons . . . there are many things which resemble them – imperialism, reactionaries, difficulties and obstacles in work, for example.' Comrade Sun was a member of the party; he agreed with this pamphlet.

We talked about river superstitions. It was not easy. He did not want to give me the idea that people today were silly enough to believe any of this stuff. But I pestered him for frights and beliefs.

'There was an old belief,' he said, 'that if a fish jumped out of the water onto the deck of a ship you could not eat it. Fish often jumped onto the junks. They still do, when they're swimming upstream. Such fish were regarded as demons.'

'Did they throw the fish back?' I asked.

'No. They had to take it ashore. Dig a hole. Then bury it.'

'What do they do now?'

'Eat them.'

I had read of another belief of the junk sailors, that when the wind died they stood on the deck and whistled, to call the wind, so that they would not have to go ashore and tow the boat. Whistling up a wind may once have been a practice among old British sailors – the idea occurs in *Macbeth*. It struck me as a weird and attractive superstition.

Comrade Sun said yes, long ago it was believed that if you whistled, the wind would rise. Then he smiled. 'I don't think it does any good at all.'

That evening, our ship, *Number 39*, anchored below the remote town of Shibao Block (Shih Pao Chai, or 'Precious Stone Castle'). This is one of the most unusual – and probably least spoiled – places in China. It is a perfect butte, 150 feet high, which once had a monastery on top and now has a bare temple. The way to the top is up a staircase in an eleven-story red pavilion built against the perpendicular side of the rock. Amazingly, it remains just as it was described by travelers 100 years ago. The view from the top is a reminder that there are towns in China with no factories, little mechanization, and only the oldest methods of plowing and planting. The town at the base of the rock is a labyrinth of slimy alleys and muddy streets, and cobblestone passageways that look like the 'wynds' of Edinburgh. And shops: carpenters, bakers, weavers of funeral wreaths, fruit sellers. Just outside the town an old man led a blind-folded buffalo trampling around in circles, to soften the mud for the making of bricks and roof tiles.

I had brought a snapshot to Shibao Block. It was one of Captain Williamson's and it showed the town through the simple eye of a box camera in 1927. The townsfolk were interested. They called the mayor, Comrade Lu, and examined the snapshot. They found it very odd. It was clearly their town, and yet one house was not where it should be. This snapshot was the past; they had never seen an old picture of the town. The mayor asked to be photographed holding the picture.

'Please take his picture,' the interpreter said. 'He is a big potato.'

He meant it as the highest praise.

Nearly the whole town of Shibao Block saw us off: silent faces staring at Howard Buhse's red golfer's cap and Ira Weinstein's foot-long telephoto lens and Lurabelle's mink and Jerry McCarthy's whirring movie camera and old Mr. Chase's tape recorder (he recorded everything, even the sound of the ship's engines) and the pinks and blues of the ladies' 350-dollar synthetic 'ultra-suede' dresses and my yellow suede shoes. We were bizarre. There was not a sound, not a murmur from the hundreds of people on the shore.

There were more watchers downstream at Wanxian, a city more nightmarish than Chongqing – mud, rain, black street, broken window, smoke, and every house-front wearing a film of soot. It was once a city of great beauty, famous for its perfectly poised *feng shui*. But the bluffs and hills that were praised are now covered with factories, the most shocking a silk-weaving plant where 1,300 women and girls were losing their health in the dim light, making silk thread from soaked cocoons. It was a sweat shop, all these women sacrificed to the manufacture of hideously patterned bolts of silk in garish colors. They worked quickly, silently, with ruined hands, to the racket of the jolting looms.

In the days that followed, we passed through the gorges. Many people come to the Yangtze for the gorges alone: they excite themselves on these marvels and skip the rest of the river. The gorges are wonderful, and it is almost impossible to exaggerate their splendor; but the river is long and complicated, and much greater than its gorges, just as the Thames is more than what lies between Westminster and Greenwich.

The great gorges lie below Bai De ('White King City'), the lesser gorges just above Ichang. Bai De was as poisonous-looking as any of the other cities, but as soon as we left it the mountains rose – enormous limestone cliffs on each side of the river that plunged straight into the water. They were formed at the dawn of the world, when the vast inland sea in western China began to drain east and wear the mountains away. But limestone is a curious substance. It occurs in blocks, it has cracks and corners; and so the flow zigzagged, controlled by the stone, and made right angles. You see no exit, only the end of what looks like a blind canyon.

From Captain Williamson's Notes

Pa Yang Hsia (Eight Cliffs Gorge): About twelve miles below Wanhsien, the river flows through plateaux of sandstone for about five miles. On the left bank, three Buddhas are carved in the cliff-face and when the river falls low enough the little figures are cleaned and repainted.

Yun Yang Hsien: This city is on the left bank about 145 miles above Ichang. Opposite the city is a picturesque temple which is said to contain a magic bell.

Bai De (White King City): Below this important city the scene changes dramatically, as the river hence to Ichang – 110 miles – winds its way through gorges in the mountainous regions which lie athwart its course.

Feng Hsiang Hsia (Wind Box Gorge): Below Bai De is one of the most picturesque of the gorges, four miles long, precipitous sides, 700–800 feet in places. At the upper entrance to this gorge, off the left bank, is the isolated Goose Tail Rock – the summit about 80–90 feet above the river at winter level. Below the Goose Tail, the square holes of 'Meng Liang's Ladder' can be seen zigzagging up the right-hand cliffs, on the right bank, while further down the gorge, in a niche high up on the left-bank cliffs, can be seen the ends of the 'wind boxes'.

Wu Shan Hsien: Below the Wind Box Gorge is an open ten-mile reach . . . end of the reach is Wu Shan Hsien, the easternmost city in Szechuan – a picturesque, romantic city, with its walls and drum towers – situated immediately above the entrance to the longest gorge of the river.

Wu Shan Hsia (Wu's Mountain Gorge): Wu (witch) was a legendary wizard who dwelt on the mountain at the first reach of this gorge and is credited with blowing a twenty-five-mile gap through the mountains to permit the river to pass.

Kuei Chou (now called Zi Gui): Picturesque small town on the left bank behind low prongs of projecting reefs.

Niu Kan Ma Fei Hsia (Ox Liver and Horse Lung Gorge): Situated below Kuei Chou, this gorge is four miles long on a bend in the river. It takes its name from a rocky outcrop on the cliff-face on the left bank.

Teng ying Hsia (Lampshine Gorge): This gorge is about eight miles long. At the end of the gorge the river turns abruptly left, into the Yellow Cat Gorge.

Huang Mao Hsia (Yellow Cat Gorge): In the bend is a large smooth round rock which, because of its appearance, is called the Sleeping Pig. This last of the gorges is about eight miles long, and at its lower end the river emerges into open country and reaches the port of Ichang.

After seeing the great gorges of the Upper Yangtze it is easy to believe in gods and demons and giants.

There are graffiti on the gorges. Some are political ('Mankind Unite to Smash Capitalism'), some are poetic ('Bamboos, flowers, and rain purify the traveler'), while other scribbled characters give the gorge's name or its history, or they indicate a notable feature in the gorge. 'Wind Box Gorge' is labeled on the limestone, and the wind boxes have painted captions. 'Meng-liang's Ladder,' it says, at the appropriate place. These are the zigzag holes that Captain Williamson mentioned in his notes; and they have a curious history. In the second century AD the Shu army was encamped on the heights of the gorge. The Hupeh general Meng-liang had set out to conquer this army, but they were faced with this vertical gorge wall, over 700 feet high. Meng-liang had his men cut the ladder holes in the stone, all the way to the top of the gorge, and his army ascended this way, and they surprised the enemy camp and overwhelmed them, ending the domination of Shu. (In 1887 Archibald Little wrote, 'The days are long past since the now effeminate Chinese were capable of such exertions . . .')

The wind blows fiercely through the gorges, as it does in New York between skyscrapers; and it is a good thing, too, because the junks can sail upstream – there is little room here for trackers. On the day I passed through, the sky was leaden, and the wind was tearing the clouds to pieces, and the river itself was yellow-brown or viscous and black, a kind of eel color. It is not only the height of the gorges, but the narrowness of the river – less than 300 feet sometimes – which makes it swift, 195 feet per second in the narrower places. The scale gives it this look of strangeness, and fills it with an atmosphere of harmonious splendor – the majestic cliffs, the 1,000-foot gorge walls, the dagger-like pinnacles, and the dark foaming river below, and the skinny boatmen on their vessels of splinters and rags.

Archibald Little wrote, 'I rejoiced that it had been my good fortune to visit the Yangtse Gorges before the coming stream of European tourists, with the inevitable introduction of Western innovation in their train, should have destroyed all their old world charm.' The cities, certainly, are black and horrific, but the gorges are changeless and completely unlike anything I had ever seen before. In other landscapes I have had a sense of deterioration – the Grand Canyon looks as if it is wearing away and being sluiced, stone by orange stone, down the Colorado River. But the gorges look powerful and permanent, and make every person and artifact look puny. They will be here long after Man has destroyed himself with bombs.

It is said that every rock and cliff has a name. 'The Seated Woman and the Pouncing Lion,' 'The Fairy Princess,' and – less lyrically – 'The Ox Liver and Horse Lung Gorge' (the organs and boulder formations, high on the cliff-face). The Yangtze is a river of precise nomenclature. Only simple, wild places, like the volcanic hills of south-west Uganda, are full of nameless topography; naming is one of the features of Chinese civilization and settlement. I asked the pilot of our ship if it was so that every rock in the Yangtze had a name. He said yes.

'What is the name of that one?' I asked, quickly pointing out of the window.

'That is Pearl Number Three. Over there is Pearl Number Two. We shall be coming to Pearl Number One in a few minutes.' He had not hesitated. And what was interesting was that these rocks looked rather insignificant to me.

One of the millionaires said, 'These gorges come up to expectations. Very few things do. The Taj Mahal did. The Pyramids didn't. But these gorges!'

We passed Wushan. There was a funeral procession making its way through the empty streets, beating drums and gongs, and at the front of the procession three people in white shrouds – white is the Chinese color of mourning – and others carrying round paper wreaths, like archery targets. And now we were in the longest gorge, twenty-five miles of cliffs and peaks, and beneath them rain-spattered junks battling the current.

At one time, this part of the Yangtze was filled with rapids. Captain Williamson's list of landmarks noted all of them. They were still in the river, breaking ships apart, in 1937. But the worst have been dynamited away. The most notorious was the Hsin Lung Tan, a low-level rapid caused by a terrific landslide in 1896. It was wild water, eighty feet wide, but blasting opened it to 400 feet, and deepened it. Thirty years ago, only the smallest boats could travel on the river during the winter months; now it is navigable by even the largest throughout the year.

Our ship drew in below Yellow Cat Gorge, at a place called Dou Shan Tuo ('Steep Hill Village'). We walked to the road and took a bus to the top of the hill. Looking across the river at the pinnacles called 'The Three Daggers,' and at the sun pouring honey into the deep cliffs, one of the passengers said with gusto, 'What a place for a condominium!'

The M.S. *Kun Lun* is by any standards a luxurious ship. She is popularly known as 'Mao's yacht' because in the 1950s and early 1960s she was used to take visiting dignitaries up and down the Yangtze. Any number of prominent Albanians can boast that they slept in one of the *Kun Lun*'s sumptuously carpeted suites and danced in the lounge or got stewed to the gills in the sixty-foot-wide club room. The idea for the fancy ship was Jiang Qing's – Chairman Mao's third wife and now the celebrated political criminal of the Gang of Four. She had the guts of a river ship torn out and she redecorated it in the style of Waldorf Astoria Ming – art deco and lotus blossoms – and did not stint on the curtains or the blue bathtubs. The Gregorys (Fred and Muriel) had a rat in their room, but never mind – Raymond Barre of France once slept in their suite.

The chief feature of this wilderness of antimacassars is space: wide passageways, large cabins, huge lounges, and sofas on which seven can sit comfortably and catch up on the *Peking Review* or listen to *News About Britain* on the World Service of the BBC – there are two gigantic Spring Thunder-brand short-wave radios on board. You hardly notice the grand piano, the bar is so big. For this reason, the *Kun Lun* was 'criticized' during the Cultural Revolution; she was turned over to the people and vandalized. Cots and bunks were crammed into the suites, and for four years the proletariat used her as an ordinary river ship. When the Lindblads found her a few years ago she was in mothballs. Mr Lindblad made a deal with the China Travel Service: he would fix her up, restore her to her original splendor, if he was allowed to use her for tours. The scheme was agreed upon, and now the *Kun Lun* is afloat once again, as great an anachronism, as large a contradiction, as could possibly be found in the People's Republic.

We transferred from *Number 39* to the *Kun Lun*. We were on the Middle River now, and there were no complaints. Or rather, not many. I did hear a shrill drunken voice moan one evening, 'I hate Chinese food. Once a month, maybe. Not more than that. But every damned day? I can't eat the stuff.'

And another night, Mrs Ver Bryck looked at me tipsily and said, unprovoked and unbidden, 'Of course I'm happier than you are. I've got more money.'

We stayed two days at Wuhan. The river had become wider, the banks lower and flatter; but the cities had grown more interesting. We watched a thyroidectomy at a hospital at Wuchang, the patient anesthetized by four acupuncture needles in her hands, and a little voltage. In the early morning I prowled the streets of Hankow and noticed that free markets had sprung up – until this year such improvisatory capitalism was forbidden. At six o'clock one morning I saw my first Chinese beggar, and on the next corner a trio of child acrobats balancing plates on their heads and doing handstands, and then passing the hat. New Hankow looked something like old Hankow.

At night in Hankow and Canton and other hot places where the windows were open I could hear people playing mah-jong, the sounds of the tiles clicking like castanets and the chatter of the players. It has not been outlawed, and the various types of Chinese chess – *xiang qi*, which has certain similarities to our own chess game, and *wei qi*, which is the same as the Japanese game *go* – are actually encouraged. In alleys, sitting on overturned crates, Chinese men can often be seen playing cards, the game they call Aiming High. In Hankow and Wuhan I saw gamblers throwing dice in the shadows, playing dominoes, and arguing over cards.

The suggestion that the Chinese might be gambling was always sharply denied. Gambling is seen as one of the worst things that a person could do, and there was such shock expressed when the subject came up that I was certain the urge to gamble was still strong.

'Games should be played just for fun,' Comrade Wu said. And he told me the story of the man who gambles away his money, his food, his radio, and is finally forced to use his wife to give value to a wager – and he loses the bet and his wife.

But there are all sorts of stakes. In Shanghai four men were squatting in an alleyway, playing cards. There was a bottle of home-made gin and a pile of clothes-pins near the men. Each time someone lost a hand of cards he had to put a clothes-pin on his ear and take a swig of gin. The drunkest of them had a cluster of clothes-pins on his ear, and looked a complete jackass, which was of course the point – the others were laughing at him.

Public humiliation was a sort of teaching technique. A gambler paid his debt by submitting to humiliation. But if the gamblers were caught by the authorities they would be punished with another form of humiliation.

'Oh, it is very bad,' he said. 'They pay a fine, some are even put into prison. We educate them!'

'Educate' is said with force. It is discipline, a humiliation, and I seldom heard the word 'education' in China without its sounding like a smack in the face.

At Suchow primary school the headmistress said that they never used corporal punishment. They 'educated' people who used corporal punishment, 'and if a teacher cannot learn to teach patiently, and resorts to hitting, he is criticized.'

She made 'criticized' sound like a whipping. It was another form of discipline, a refinement of humiliation. A person, one of the billion, was criticized by being singled out and exposed. He was severely questioned by the various members of his block or commune and made publicly to show his contrition.

This, in effect, was what the Gang of Four trial was all about: it was public humiliation. The trial was its own punishment – it did not need any sentences at the end. Dragging someone out of a mob, singling out an individual, demanding that a student stand up while the others remain seated – these are the worst things that can happen to someone who values his anonymity and sees himself as part of the powerful Chinese army of workers. Isolated, the person loses his power and is humiliated and weakened by the gaze of the mob. In the nineteenth century it was done with the 'cangue' – a heavy wooden collar that thieves were made to wear.

It is hard to disentangle education from discipline, since both are imposed and carry penalties. Education is learning English, but education is also learning your place. Education might be a discussion with neighbors following a misdemeanor – it is a telling-off, and the offender is given a few books of Mao or Lenin to read. Education might also be a 'struggle session' or something similar with the local committee – 'Change your ways or else' – and many books of Mao or Lenin to read. But education also means a pig farm in Inner Mongolia, a farm in Shenyang or Ganzu Province – long days slopping the hogs or planting trees, and studying communist texts at night. In China, the most extreme form of education is prison.

At Lu Shan, a hill station above the Yangtze port of Juijang, Harry

Laughlin pointed to one of the millionaires walking up a hill and said, 'He's captious – that's what we call his type.'

Harry, a millionaire too, sometimes described himself as an educator. He had taught psychology – never mind his two Mercedes (or Lurabelle's Rolls).

'He's insecure,' Harry said, as we walked along the stony path to the pagoda. 'Notice how he's always alone? He's trying to prove something. He always walks ahead, always apart from the group. See, he wants to show us his ass. Very interesting. He's making a statement there.'

I had thought that the odd man out was Mr. Clark, because he was almost eighty-two and kept stepping on his camera. Or he would look up and smile and say, 'I lost my pen. I had that pen for years.' He became friendly with Dr. Ringrose, and then I decided Dr. Ringrose – 'Ring-nose,' one of the New York ladies called him – was the odd man out. He was a cancer doctor from Calgary, but originally from Leeds. He had some Yorkshire traits – downrightness, unsmiling humor, practicality – but also a sense of grievance. He dressed like a camper. He was a bachelor; he was very intelligent; and he was a pedant. He boasted about his travels and his books. In that gray guest house at Lu Shan he said, 'I have 6,000 books. People in Calgary are amazed.'

Lu Shan was a quiet gloomy place, paradise for the Chinese who visit there. It was the opposite of every other Chinese city I had seen. It was cool, not crowded, nor elbow-bumping. The Chinese did not seem to notice Lu Shan's smell or its decrepitude. It was exotic – they made movies there, because the landscape – the piney backdrop, with cliffs and peaks and deep valleys – was the classical Chinese topography. The package tours from Shanghai and Nanjing to Lu Shan cost thirty to forty *yuan*, about a month's wage.

The Chinese went in groups marveling at the azaleas and dwarf cedars and the lone pines and waterfalls they recognized from scroll paintings. The rhododendrons were tall bushy trees. The architecture was very English-looking – stone bungalows and stone shops, and a large stone church. The Catholic church had been turned into a movie theater (a bust of Chairman Mao in the foyer) and that month they were showing *She*, a love story. On the hill paths there were little signs carved in Chinese characters in the gray stone. 'Share happiness, share difficulties' – the slogan of a Chinese general in the 1920s. Near a stone seat, the motto, 'Sitting here and dreaming here.'

In the early morning Lu Shan resembled every hill station I had ever seen, from Simla and Fraser's Hill, to the ones above Medan in Sumatra, and Surabaya. The people had rosy cheeks, the pine trees dripped, the stone bungalows were dark and damp-stained, and the low cloud and fog settled over the mission steeples and villa roofs until their outlines were faintly penciled in the mist. The gloom in the place was the same gloom I had noticed in other hill stations, perhaps because such places were entirely a European invention, always damp and hard to manage, the architecture English, requiring intensive upkeep, and the inheritors rather baffled by the layout. The Lu Shan Guest House had English virtues – fine banisters and light fittings and solid walls. But the rooms smelled of mildew, the lights did not work, and the whole place had lost its ornaments – no pictures, no plants. The previous occupants had moved out, the new occupants – being poor – could not furnish the house properly.

In Lu Shan I listened to our Comrade Tao question one of the millionaires' wives about life in America.

Mr Tao asked, 'Is rent very high in America?'

'I've never paid rent,' the American lady said.

This surprised Mr Tao. He said, 'What about food? You must spend ten or twenty dollars a week on food.'

'Twenty dollars is nothing,' the lady said.

In China it was almost a month's salary.

'Do you have a bicycle?' the Chinese man asked.

'Yes, I do, but I only use it for fun.'

'A bicycle for fun!' he said. 'What about a car – do you have one?'

'Yes.'

'What kind is it?'

This was a difficult question. The lady could not answer. She said, 'Actually, I have four cars.'

Comrade Tao seemed to swallow something very large, and he blinked and squinted at the lady, who had become self-conscious and was saying, 'There's a Chevy convertible, but I can't really use it in bad weather. I usually take one of the smaller ones – they're easier to park, and you save gas. And the others . . .'

Comrade Tao stared.

But the lady had seen her mistake and tactfully changed the subject to azaleas.

Near Lu Shan was a nursery and botanical garden. I asked what effect the Cultural Revolution had had on the operation of the botanical garden and the nursery. The director said, 'All my greenhouses were destroyed for being bourgeois.'

There were faint traces of huge 'big character' slogans on the façade of the Lu Shan Guest House. No one would translate them for me, and two Chinese men denied seeing them.

The millionaires on the Yangtze were always polite, always sociable, and always stayed off contentious topics. 'Don't talk to him about politics,' Jerry McCarthy said. 'No way! Don't mention the Equal Rights Amendment.' Occasionally I heard people issue warnings like this; it meant that a potential conflict had been discovered and was to be avoided in the future. In this way an atmosphere of harmony was maintained.

But when they played games they played to win. I played gin rummy with one of them and he spent the whole time badgering me, mocking me, telling me what I was doing wrong, predicting my discards. He was actually very angry at one point, and after about eight games, when it was clear that I had beaten him, he cursed and stomped away.

The next day he followed me around the deck saying, 'The shill ... the gin rummy expert ... the novice,' and he demanded that I play him again.

'This time we'll play for a dollar a point, just to keep up your concentration. What do you say, Paulie-boy? What about it? A rematch! Come on!'

He was not happy until he had beaten me three nights in a row, and then he refused to play me again on the pretext that it was a waste of his time. So I played gin rummy with the ladies from New York, who proved exhausting opponents.

I played Scrabble, and that was worse. I had never played such unenjoyable Scrabble in my life. And the fact was that most of the Scrabble players cheated, or tried to slip non-words by me. One lady insisted that adze was spelled 'adz'. There was no English dictionary on our ship, and she claimed that 'yo' was a word. When I challenged her, she said, 'Yo-ho-ho!'

They were also full of odd information. The paint on an airplane fuselage weighs between 150 and 400 pounds – there was a fuel economy in flying unpainted planes. I was told that by one of our millionaires while we were touring Nanjing. 'And did you know that Dustin Hoffman is a dwarf?' a lady said one day. 'No bicycle in

China has gears but every one of them has a lock,' an observant passenger said.

I discovered that the term for yogurt in Chinese was *suan niu nai* (home-made cheese does not exist in China). I ordered some and was eating it with pleasure, when Dr. Ringrose said, 'We put yogurt on certain forms of skin cancer.'

And they asked questions, sometimes the damnedest questions. Before we went ashore at Hankow a lady asked the Chinese tour leader, 'What shall I wear?' She meant what style of dress.

At the thermos bottle factory, Mr. Clark asked the American guide, 'How many pounds per square inch is the pressure on that glass-blowing apparatus?'

At the Wuhan Conservatory, Mr. Jones asked, 'What is the name of that instrument?' He was told it was a harp, but he wanted its Chinese name. The musician looked at him and said loudly, '*Zhong!*'

People asked how much water flowed through a particular spot on the Yangtze, and what the depth was, and the width, and the population here and there ('Four or 5 million' was a frequent answer to many different questions). I decided that demanding statistics was a way of getting their money's worth – why else would someone pay 10,000 dollars to sail through China?

At Hubei Medical College Hospital one of the millionaires gazed at an electrical transformer hooked up to some acupuncture needles that were inserted into a patient's wrists.

'How much voltage?' he asked.

He was told.

'Is that A C or D C?' he asked.

He was told, and, satisfied that it was D C, he walked away.

All over the river people were fishing, some with hooks and lines, others with circular weighted nets, or curtains of nets which they trailed behind their sampans, or the complicated tent-like nets in bamboo frames that Abbé David saw raised and lowered in Shashi. They caught tiny fish – sardine-sized – and they kept even the minnows. More modern methods might have emptied the Yangtze of all its fish, but Comrade Sun had told me that some men still fished with trained cormorants and otters.

The river had widened again: on this stretch I was seldom able to see the far bank, and we sailed to Juijang in a heavy mist, glad for the night at Lu Shan ('The road is very twisty,' Mr. Chen said, 'but we have a good driver and he will not go bananas'). In both Juijang and Lu Shan, people could be seen fighting for cinema tickets. The same films were playing in both places, *The Great Dictator* and *City Lights*, starring China's favorite actor, Cha-Li Zhuo Bi-lin.

On our way to Nanjing, I talked to the *Kun Lun*'s captain. Like Captain Liu of *Number 39*, he had worked his way up to captain, from steward, by on-the-job training, and had never gone to naval college. 'There is no reason for a man to remain a steward his whole life. I tell my men, "Work hard and there will be promotions for you."'

I asked him what the difficulties were in navigating on the Yangtze.

'Two main ones,' he said. 'From December to March, the water is very low and the channel is narrow. This makes things difficult, because there is so much other traffic on the river. The second is the weather. There is fog and mist from October to April, and sometimes it is impossible to see what lies ahead. Radar is often no help. To avoid getting into an accident, some nights we anchor until the weather clears.'

I said that it seemed that very little had changed on the Yangtze. People fished in the old way; they sailed and rowed and towed wooden junks; they watered their fields carrying buckets on yokes; and right back here in Juijang, women were washing clothes, clubbing bundles of laundry and thrashing it in the muddy water. They crossed the river in rusty ferries and still drowned by the score when the river was in flood.

The captain reminded me of the Four Modernizations and said that, with the smashing of the Gang of Four, things would improve. How ironic, I thought: the leader of the Gang of Four had probably sat in this very cabin; she was certainly responsible for its décor.

'Before Liberation, this river was different. The foreigners were very careless. They ran rampant. The Chinese people hated and feared them, because they had a reputation for not stopping for a junk or a sampan, or they might swamp a small boat in their wake. It made them unpopular. The gunboats were the worst of all. The foreigners were disliked for the way they used the river – Japanese, French, Italian, English, American. But things are different now.'

We went ashore at Nanjing. The Gang of Four trial had started. The China Travel Service guides encouraged us to watch it. This show trial reminded me of Hate Week in *1984*, and the defendants looked sick and crazy after four years in prison. I ended up playing gin rummy with Harry Laughlin, who said he was dying to get back to Pasadena.

Above Sun Yat-Sen's mausoleum in Nanjing, there was a slogan which was translated in my guidebook as, 'The world belongs to the people.'

I mentioned this to Mr. Gregory, one of the Connecticut millionaires. Mr. Gregory said President Carter was stupid. Mr. Gregory was also an authority on semi-precious stones, and he told me that he had owned more than twenty Cadillacs. He had the security and burglar alarm business and one day he told me, 'I think it's about time the world started to be afraid of America again.' He often said something at dinner and the whole table of ten went silent. Then someone would smile at a big bowl and say, 'Now what do you suppose *that* is?'

'The world belongs to the people,' Mr. Gregory said. Then he breathed hard. 'Well, that's not true.'

'Why not?'

'The world belongs to *some* people, but not *the* people.'

He was speaking of the world as it ought to be, not as it was.

'No, sir, not *the* people.'

Later I came across a different translation, without the loaded word 'people'. 'The world belongs to everyone,' it said.

I mentioned this to Mr. Gregory.

'That's better,' he said. 'That's true.'

He liked everyone, but he didn't think much of the people.

Slogans were often a problem. At the Xiao Ying Primary School in Nanjing, a slogan which had been painted on a wall at the time of the Cultural Revolution had read, 'Never Forget Class Struggle.' Half of it had been obliterated. It read, 'Never Forget.'

Then there were the Four Modernizations: National Defense, Science and Technology, Industry, and Agriculture. At school, children were taught the Five Loves: Love Work, Love People, Love Neighbors, Love Science, Love Public Property. In the mid-1970s the Eight Antis were to be supported, and it was patriotic and comradely to be Anti-Intellectual, Anti-Western, Anti-Bourgeois, Anti-Capitalist-Roader, Anti-Revisionist, Anti-Traditional, Anti-Confucian, and Anti-Imperialist.

It was important to remember that the Four News were different from the Four Modernizations, and that the Four Olds were especially pernicious. I never discovered what the Four Olds were.

Slogans of an abusive nature had been removed from the building façades in western China, but many of Chairman Mao's picturesque phrases still remained lettered on the walls of certain buildings, and it was one of the pleasures of China to hear these translated by our guides. 'Yes, it says, "Despicable American Imperialist and Their Running Dogs Must Never be Allowed . . ."'

The name of the oldest restaurant in Suchow, the Pine and Crane (perhaps 300 years old?), was thought to be too bourgeois during the Cultural Revolution, so it was changed to the East is Red Restaurant. Recently it has been changed back to the Pine and Crane. Heavenly Park, an ancient garden, was changed to Workers' Park, but it has also reverted to its original name.

Many slogans served only to intimidate the passerby or to deface a lovely wall. 'Love Public Property' might be scrawled on a fine building. Slogans were merely a form of public graffiti. In the Yangtze gorges some of the graffiti were very old, but I came across more recent stuff. I went to the formal garden in Suchow called the Garden of the Master of Nets. It had been laid out in the year 1140. In the Pavilion of the Accumulated Void (it is a Taoist concept), the rosewood walls are covered with graffiti – for example, 'Li Han Ming Came Here on His Travels 1980.'

We were often invited to admire buildings or objects by the Chinese. Look at this Catholic church! they would say. Look at this jade suit made for a nobleman! Look at these tombs! Their explanations were very brief – a date, an anecdote, a name; and then on to the next sight.

But there were always signs near these sights, and I discovered that the signs were usually different from the explanations we received. I asked the Chinese guides to translate these signs. They did so with great reluctance, but the experience was illuminating.

Caption under a photograph of a Catholic church in Canton, built in 1861: 'In order to build this church people were forced to move away. The citizens felt very angry. People were not allowed to build residences around this church. No person was allowed to look through the windows of this church.'

Caption under a photograph of a Catholic church in Nanjing, built in the 1850s:

American imperialism took preaching as its cover. All over China they erected churches like this and carried out destructive activities. In 1853, in Shanghai, the Small Sword Society echoed the Tai-Ping rebels. They occupied

Shanghai, country and city. The American missionaries joined up with the Ching dynasty troops and attacked troops and attacked the Small Sword Society troops, and the church acted as a stronghold. After the Ching troops lost, the American missionaries escorted them to safety at the American Embassy.

Sign next to the jade burial suit (Han dynasty, AD 25–220) in the Nanjing Museum:

The feudal rulers exploited the workers before birth, oppressed the laboring peoples, and even after death wanted to wear the blood and sweat of the laboring peoples, as represented by the jade suit. They planned to preserve their corpses. This reflects the tremendous waste of the feudal rulers and reveals the limitless exploitative nature of the feudal rulers.

Inscription on the Ming tombs outside Peking:

The real landlords of this fifteen square miles were the peasants. But after the Emperor selected this site, the imperial troops came in like mad animals. They destroyed the orchards and razed the villages. They used military might to expel the laboring peasants, who had been here for centuries, and they occupied the site.

The numerous peasant families remembered with malice. They took everything they owned and left behind their destroyed lives.

After the tombs were established, this area was labeled 'Off-Limits.' If one of the Masses came here he was caned 100 strokes; if he grabbed a handful of earth he was executed.

This is the background of the feudalistic ruling classes' oppression of the peasantry . . .

These explanations are for the Chinese. Foreigners were given different explanations, or none at all. At the churches, the jade suit, and the Ming tombs, there was always a Chinese to say, 'Isn't it pretty?'

At Suchow I took the Shanghai Express, the last part of my sail through China. There were policemen at Suchow station barking orders at the people streaming in. The policemen were rather nasty-looking. I had seen such men be very rough in China, at times manhandling cyclists and pedestrians. Now they were barking orders at the travelers, telling them which platform to go to, how to line up and look sharp.

Within a few minutes we were out of the ancient city of Suchow and had lost sight of the canals and the city moat. We traveled across the vegetable fields of Jiangsu. The last hills I had seen were south of Nanjing. Long ago, this plain through which the Shanghai Express was passing was part of the Pacific Ocean: the Yangtze had extended China's land mass and swelled its estuary into several new provinces, over millions of years.

The soil did not look fertile – Chinese soil seldom did. The gardens were oblongs, stretching to the horizons on both sides of the train. This was Chinese topography, the vegetable plot. When there were hills they had vegetables on them. When there was a riverbank it was a riverbank with vegetables. A valley, a plain, whatever – it always looked the same, slightly exhausted and orderly with cabbages.

Someone said, 'Look, a pig!'

Because there were so few animals to be seen, a pig or a goat caused great interest, and a dog – those rare cross-eyed mongrels – was a sensation. The Chinese did not grow flowers except in pots, in parks, and for special occasions. The Chinese were practical, unspiritual, materialistic, baffled, and hungry, and these qualities had brought a crudity and a terrible fatigue to their country. In order to stay alive they had to kill the imagination; the result was a vegetable economy and a monochrome culture.

Shanghai was commercial, but the advertising often puzzled me: 'Dragonfly Cotton shoes! They Are Stylish and Cheap!' 'Rado Watch! Styleproof, Scratchproof, Timeproof!' and 'Aero Tennis Racket – Indeformable!'

I decided to have a look at the Antique Exchange. On the way there I met a Chinese man who had worked for the US Navy during the war. He had a perfect American accent. He summed up for me the years since Liberation: 'The first ten years were bad, the next ten years were okay, but the past ten years have been terrible. I don't know how we got through them. It was the Cultural Revolution. Boy, that was terrible.'

I asked him whether he thought there would be another cultural revolution.

'Sure,' he said.

'Why?'

'Mao said so. Another one. And one after that. Just one after the other.'

The Antique Exchange is where the Chinese sell family treasures to the government, so that they can be resold in the government antique shops and Friendship Stores (which are full of valuable and pretty museum pieces).

On the high stool of a darkened room sits a skinny Chinese man, with yellow protruding teeth and wire-frame glasses. He is sitting cross-legged on the stool, and he wears a skullcap, and he puffs a cigarette by the light of a dim lamp. He points, raises a long fingernail, and beckons a man forward.

The man steps into the light, carrying a canvas bag. He wears a loose army uniform and slippers. He begins to take crockery out of the bag – rice bowls, plates, dishes.

'No, no, no –' The smoker waves this pretty stuff away.

The soldier takes out a stone lion.

'No –'

The soldier puts the lion away, and takes out more rice bowls.

'No –'

The soldier takes out a blue porcelain jar, about ten inches high, luminous and lovely even in this bad light.

The skinny man stops smoking. He sets the jar aside.

There is nothing else. The man shifts on his stool and writes a chit. There is no bargaining: the antique is assigned a price. The soldier puts the rejected stuff into his bag, takes his slip of paper, and collects some money.

'They buy things for ten bucks, they sell them for 100 bucks,' a Chinese man told me in Shanghai. Shanghai was full of English speakers, using slang from World War II.

What interested me was that this smoky, seedy interior was a government bureau. But it was the old China. Outside it, a sign in Chinese said, 'Sell Your Old Plates, Bronzes, and Carvings for Cash.' Of course, this is capitalism in the service of the state, buying up heirlooms to sell to tourists, but the old man, the back room, the shelves of cracked porcelain and the dusty bronzes, and the pitiful prices, the pawnshop gloom – it all looked as old as China.

The antique shop prices were very high, but most of the merchandise deserved to be in museums. How long, I wondered, would these treasures be available to tourists?

Not everyone saw these objects as treasures. There was a New York lady, Dorothy Hirshon, who would squint at an item on the shelf and say, 'That's the ugliest thing in China.'

One night after dinner, at about nine o'clock, I went for a walk down a dark street. I had been walking only about ten minutes when I was greeted ('Good evening, sir') by three young men, Comrade Ma, Comrade Lu, and Comrade Wee. They wanted to practice their English. I said that I had been reading the supernatural stories of Pu Sung-ling, his *Strange Tales of Liao-chai*. I asked them whether they believed in ghosts. They found this very funny.

'I don't believe in ghosts,' Comrade Ma said.

I asked him why not.

'I never see one.'

I said, 'So there are no ghosts in China?'

'No,' Comrade Lu said.

'What about your ancestors?' I asked.

Comrade Ma said, 'They are under the ground.'

I asked them whether they celebrated the Ching Ming Festival by exploding firecrackers in the graveyards.

They said they didn't celebrate it at all.

'Overseas Chinese do that.'

We were passing a railway embankment where, behind a row of trees, there were young people kissing. They embraced standing up, in the shadowy side of the tree trunks. I called attention to the couples.

Comrade Ma said, 'Since the Gang of Four were smashed there is now kissing. From 1949 until the Gang of Four there was no kissing. Now there is kissing. Even on television there is kissing.'

'Did the Gang of Four kiss?'

'Oh, yes. But inside their houses!' Comrade Ma said.

The others laughed. They regarded Ma as a great wit.

I asked whether they themselves kissed girls.

Comrade Ma said, 'Comrade Lu has a darling. He kisses. I have two darlings. I kiss them.'

I said, 'Indoors or outdoors?'

'Only married people can kiss indoors, in a room. We kiss over there. In the trees. Sometimes in the park. In the park, at night, you can put your hands around the girl – and other places. Ha-ha! Also other things. But it is very stony on the ground – too many rocks!'

'Mr. Paul,' Comrade Wee said, 'what is the proper way to kiss?'

He had told me earlier that he was a printer. This inspired me. I said that kissing was like printing. You printed your lips on the girl's lips – not too hard. They laughed and said, yes, that's what they thought it was like.

I asked them when they planned to get married. They said when they were about thirty-five or so. They were twenty-six and twenty-seven, and each earned fifty *yuan* (thirty dollars) a month.

The trial of the Gang of Four had recently started, so I asked, 'Are the Gang of Four guilty?'

'Oh, yes. Guilty.'

'But not Chairman Mao, eh?' I said. 'Chairman Mao was a great man, right?'

Comrade Ma smiled at me and said, 'Maybe.'

Comrade Wee said, 'Do you think so?'

'I don't know,' I said.

'You are very clever!'

We talked about the Yangtze. The people there, they said, had different clothes and different 'hairs.' This topic provoked Comrade Lu to tell me that his father lived in Surinam – in South America, of all places. But he hated it. 'Too many Negroes.' Hong Kong was better, Lu said.

Comrade Ma told me that he had a bicycle, a TV, and a radio. I said that he had everything, apparently.

'No. I want to go to Hong Kong.'

They all agreed: they all wanted to go to Hong Kong. But they had never been outside Shanghai. They lived with their parents, and would go on living with them until they married. I asked whether they regarded themselves as revolutionaries. No, they said, they were workers.

'I don't want to be a revolutionary,' Comrade Ma said.

Had they been in the army?

'There are too many people in the army,' Comrade Lu said. 'They like the army. It is better than farming. Harvesting rice is hard work. It is easier to be a soldier.'

They were cheery, candid fellows, and we continued walking the dark streets of Shanghai, talking about everything.

'What about sport?' I asked.

'Table tennis,' Comrade Ma said.

'Badminton,' Comrade Lu said.

'I take –' Comrade Wee glanced nervously at the others – 'I take cold showers.'

In Shanghai, as in other cities in China, the air was bad, it stank, it was dark brown. There were people in the streets, mobs of them, because their rooms were so small and crowded. The streets were free. There is little sign of money, no sign of wealth. Small ugly coins and filthy paper rags are money – it is worthless stuff. The people have clean faces and they observe a kind of ragged order. One can only compare this to the competing crowds and distress of India. Here there are scarcely any beggars; there is little apparent violence. Most people are dressed exactly the same. They all wear shoes.

There is a powerful silence in these streets, and the junkyard smell – dust and old rags – is not the smell of death but of illness. Motor traffic would make these cities uninhabitable, but in a crude way the people have made motors unnecessary. The people seldom talk – their silence, which looks enforced, is the most amazing thing.

Sometimes you can discern the future in the present, yet I could not tell what was in store for these people. Would it always be freezing in winter in cheap cotton clothes, walking through the muddy streets in slippers, carting the steel rods that are used for these awful buildings, saying nothing, masked against the air pollution that gives China the look of existing in a permanent sunset? China looked sad in its simplicity; it seemed to me that it would look hideous if it ever became prosperous.

POSTSCRIPT, 1999

My Yangtze trip was taken in November, 1980, when the hard-line Maoists were still in control of the Politburo and Hua Guofeng was Party Chairman. The reformers in the government, among them Deng Xiaoping, had not yet consolidated their power. China had hardly changed since the end of the Cultural Revolution in 1976. The Chinese still wore their revolutionary clothes, blue boiler suits and cloth slippers; their motto was 'Serve the People,' though they were already sick of saying it. China is a different country now.

Chinese Miracles

MEMORIES OF CHINA

Suddenly, in eastern Guangdong – all bulldozers and buffaloes – my driver, Mr. Li Zhong Ming, began driving on the wrong side of the road again. Was it the freshly dismembered human corpse, all its separate parts splashed Chinese red, scattered widely like a load of fresh pork off the back of a truck on our side of the highway – and the ensuing traffic jam – that made him do it? No. Mr. Li liked spinning the steering wheel and whipping over to face the oncoming traffic, racing to pass cars in front of us. He had hardly glanced at the mutilated body. 'This is quicker,' he said.

Of course the risks were enormous – trucks and buses bore down on us head-on – but he sped by everyone with an eat-my-dust expression on his face, his teeth ajar in aggression. He was so persistent I began to think of his driving on the wrong side (and the carnage on the right, one of the numerous auto accidents I saw in an average day) as a metaphor for modernized China – the so-called miracle you read about every time you open a magazine or newspaper. Seen from a distance the country does seem wondrous, but up close it is messier and more complicated. Like most economic miracles it is also an ecological disaster. And it has its victims – that disemboweled pedestrian, and millions of Chinese with their skinny shoulders to the wheel.

Not Mr. Li, though, booting our assembled-in-China Audi down the main road to Shantou (old Swatow), past red hills being shoveled apart and bulldozed to use for filling rice fields and to make room for tenements and factories. The entire landscape was being leveled for hundreds of miles and, when it began to rain, water coursed down the clawed, eroded hills, washing silt into the sewers and drains and flooding the roads, causing another traffic jam.

Into the wrong lane Mr. Li went again, playing chicken with oncoming dump trucks and tractors and bikes. He did not dodge them. He just blew his horn and surged forward against the flow of cock-eyed headlights.

Strengthening Mr. Li in his luck was a portrait of Mao Zedong on his dashboard. This gesture – wholly non-political – was a recent fetish for drivers in China. Just a year before, a taxi driver in Peking claimed in *People's Daily* that he had been spared in a car crash, in which there had been many fatalities, because he had kept a picture of the old man on his dashboard. Many Chinese drivers began using the picture for spiritual protection. They reminded me of the images of St. Christopher that I saw in cars when I was growing up in Massachusetts in the 1950s.

Mao kitsch is popular in China now. You can buy Mao badges and Mao portraits, and embroidered knickknacks of the great man in baggy pants. His speeches are back in print. I often thought of them, of one in particular, his 'Report on the Peasants in Hunan,' when, in 1922, he had traveled around the countryside, noting abuses and jotting down wisdom, and making suggestions. That was what I told myself I was doing – simply looking around, gathering impressions for my 'Report on the Factory Workers of Guangdong and Fujian in this Era of Chinese Prosperity.' Mao was on my mind, too.

High art comes and goes in China, but Chinese kitsch is indestructible. In a dusty shop of a small town in rural Guangdong I had bought some Mao playing cards and some Mao cassettes. *Memories of Mao* was playing on Mr. Li's tape deck, the tuneful '*Dong Fang Hong*'.

> The East is Red!
> The sun rises!
> China produces Mao Zedong!

We passed two men on a big red 350cc joint-venture WuYang Honda motorcycle, and the man on the rear seat was yakking wildly on a cellular phone – making a deal without a helmet at seventy miles an hour. Gunning his engine, Mr. Li was happy. And everywhere I looked I saw ruined hills and abandoned paddy fields and bamboo scaffolding where just months before there had been bamboo groves. There were no sights here, only freshly robbed graves, one of the more recent growth industries in rural China (burial artifacts to smuggle and sell for good prices in Hong Kong), and the odd forlorn pagoda seemingly flummoxed in its *feng shui*, and almost certainly doomed. But nothing ancient, nothing notable, no 'sights,' nothing but new brown crumbly buildings – factories and tenements – rising from the filled-in rice fields.

Mr. Li drove erratically, leaning on his horn, and only hunger made him slow down, which he did at a medium-sized town, by the shores of a stagnant lake. And as though guiding himself by his sense of smell he was soon parked in front of a hotel restaurant, where we were joined by Miss Ma, who was to escort us to a local factory.

'I did not order these *ji jao*,' I said when our dishes began arriving at the table. Two plates of deep-fried chicken feet were steaming in front of me.

'The driver likes them,' Miss Ma said, 'And, um –'

She hesitated, she had something more to say, she was trying to find words for it; at this stage we hardly knew each other. Then she risked her correction.

'They are not *ji jao*,' she said. 'We call them *feng jao*.'

'Phoenix feet?'

'It sounds nicer,' she said.

Mr. Li was tonguing chicken feet into his mouth and humming snatches of '*Dong Fang Hong*'. As I paid the bill, I was thinking, 'It's quicker this way!' 'The East is Red!' 'The driver likes them!' 'Phoenix feet!'

After snoozing for two hours in his car in the parking lot while I interrogated the factory workers, Mr. Li woke, wiped his mouth with the back of his hand, and glanced at his watch at the same time. Then he demanded 200 *yuan* (a month's salary for most factory workers). It was a tip, he said, yawning, for working overtime.

Not long ago it was Red China. For those of us who grew up in the 1950s, it was a forbidden place, like a throwback to the much older China of the Middle Kingdom, ruled by the Celestial Emperor, the Son of Heaven, who demanded the kowtowing of outsiders. These days we are colloquially termed *gweilos*, 'ghost men' (Mr. Li would have used that word when referring to me; 'foreign friend' is now just prissy bureaucratese). But in those other, darker days we were serious *gweilos*. In 1956, the now-forgotten American doctor Tom Dooley wrote with feeling from his little hospital in Laos, 'I am at the rim of Red Hell.' That just about summed up China's image as a nightmarish dictatorship, where persecution and torture and slave labor were commonplace. And Mao – arrogant, ruthless, serene – was the emperor. Mao's various campaigns of the 1950s and early

1960s – Religious Reform, Hundred Flowers (and its aftermath), Anti-Rightist, Great Leap Forward – were seen from the outside as nameless and indiscriminate witch-hunts.

To a great extent, witch-hunts is what they were, though it was only after the trauma of the Cultural Revolution that the Chinese bared their souls to the outer world. Now we have extensive proof (though with an inevitable bias) of the convulsions of their Maoist history. Until recently, Chinese life was not so much enigmatic as unknown. We did not have a clear perception of Chinese stubbornness, tenacity, or materialism; the Chinese lack of illusions; their strong sense of family; their powerful survival instinct; their hatred of complainers; their passion for secrecy. More than any people I have ever come across, the Chinese are obsessive about living in the present. They don't look back, because in the strange interplay of light and shadow, splendor and misery, of their history, there is too much to look back upon – and so it is fatal to be sentimental, they seem to say. Chinese life has a kind of peristalsis; it is both active and hesitant, like a creature being pursued, now in motion, now stopped and tremulous, never at rest, always alert.

The Chinese clock has a tick unlike any other on earth, sometimes fast, sometimes slow, contracting, expanding, with an alarm that might go off at any moment. We Americans expect tomorrow to be pretty much like today, and perhaps a little better. We find it strange that a people perpetually anticipate disasters. But then, 6,000 years of disasters have made the Chinese skeptical and somewhat untrusting. These days everyone speaks of the Chinese miracle, but when has the world taken much notice of Chinese catastrophes, of which the Japanese rape and plunder of China before and during World War II and the earthquake (8.2 on the Richter scale) which instantly killed a quarter of a million Chinese in 1976 are but two instances?

Undeluded by the hubris or presumption that burdens European nations or the Third World, the Chinese know that their destiny is in their hands alone. They cannot count on the future, since 'future' in Chinese terms might mean a brutal decree or sudden reversal enacted in the dark hours of tomorrow morning. There might be a tomorrow, but they don't bank on it, because what they are doing now was illegal yesterday, and might be proscribed once again. Understanding the uniqueness of the Chinese clock, you begin to get an inkling of Chinese hope, and the attentiveness of Chinese labor. Their sense of survival is not a racial but a political imperative.

Chinese life is full of instances of people who lingered and looked back and were lost, overwhelmed and buried by one avalanche or another in their unpredictable history. The Chinese take each day as it comes, and they hope for good times; but they always prepare for the worst. After what has happened to them, who can blame them?

We know that the turbulence of the mid-1960s, which began in the West as a celebration of peace and love, turned into a much uglier revolt a few years later. It is my own feeling that Mao's Great Proletarian Cultural Revolution, begun in 1966, had an enormous influence worldwide, particularly in Europe and the United States. Its anti-imperialism was a statement against Vietnam, and its assault on authority, which gave it its greatest ferocity, was a feeling that was shared outside China. The essence of the Cultural Revolution was outrage. All the canting about 'the generation gap' was also Red Guard guff, and it justified and put into words the anger and the sense of alienation many of us felt as despised student activists.

Many of the 1960s protesters in the United States and Western Europe naïvely identified with the Red Guards, and like those howling at 'the Five Black Categories' – Landlords, Capitalists, Revisionists, Counter-Revolutionaries, Criminals – the campus foot-soldiers and radicals were for the most part pimply students shrieking at our teachers and elders.

Mao raised the political consciousness of the world, by giving revolution simple slogans and a distinctive style. In East Africa, where I was living in the late 1960s, many politicians affected Mao jackets – not just the opposition leader Oginga Odinga of Kenya, but charismatic would-be statesmen such as Julius Nyerere of Tanzania and fairly respectable tyrants such as Milton Obote of Uganda. To a large extent, it was their way of taunting American officials and aid agencies and making them feel insecure.

(Later in the 1970s, the Chinese officially admitted that the Cultural Revolution had been a mistake. But what no one seems to have ascertained is what an unmitigated disaster it was for the African countries who bought it wholesale. Numerous countries in sub-Sahara Africa organized their party structure and their economies around the slogans 'Serve the people,' 'Political power grows out of the barrel of a gun,' 'Reactionaries are paper tigers,' and so forth. The Soviet Union always had more client states in Africa than China did, but China tended to get a stronger grip on those countries it patronized. Tanzania was one that went bankrupt, politically and economically, because it had become possessed by China at the time of the Cultural Revolution.)

I had to wait until 1980 to visit China, but that was an interesting time because of the power struggle going on, between Maoists, led by Hua Guofeng, and the reformers, led by Deng Xiaoping. Hua was in power and his portrait was displayed everywhere with that of his benefactor, Hua's cheek next to Mao's jowl. I went down the Yangtze and visited ten cities. China then was all struggle, people in blue suits and cloth slippers, riding bicycles down muddy streets, workers going blind in poorly lighted factories, waiters refusing tips and chanting, 'Serve the people!' The only bright colors were the ribbons the more daring women and girls wore in their hair.

Near Canton, I visited a Maoist model commune called Da Li. It was like a good-natured prison of reluctant sloganeers and suppressed ambitions – 71,000 people working the land (6,000 acres of rice fields) and making Whistling Cicada Brand firecrackers. It seemed at once appalling and wonderful for its unity and its innocence. Every job was carried out with crude tools and a great spirit. It was a society of intimidating and ingenious frugality where everything was mended – shoes, clothes, vehicles. The Chinese were poor but their ingenuity made them seem indestructible. I wrote in my notebook, 'This is the highest stage of poverty.'

I found it admirable, but also sad and strange, and that month in China killed my desire to see anything more. Meanwhile my brother Eugene, a Washington lawyer, was doing business in China, and the business deals were growing larger and less affected by ideology. In the mid-1970s, the Chinese had refused to make Muhammad Ali boxing gloves, because the boxer's signature and the company name smacked of (they used the word) imperialism. Nor would they make shoes with foreign labels. It was a matter of ideology as well as pride. Flying Pigeon Brand was all right, but not Wilson. Within a few years they had signed a joint venture agreement to make Reeboks, and soon were themselves wearing – not Reeboks, but (a sign of things to come) a knock-off variety of sports shoes. Blue cotton quilted jackets gave way to nylon parkas and sneakers. Appearances are important in China, especially when they assert individuality, and this new 1980s way of dressing – women had begun to wear skirts, some men wore ties – looked like defiance. My brother said that China was becoming prosperous. This I found hard to believe.

And so in the spring of 1986 I made another visit to China, taking the train from London through West and East Germany, socialist Poland, the Soviet Union, and the People's Republic of Mongolia – all of them gone now – and, astonished by the changes and by new attitudes, the communes either closed or changed – the charade over, the rice fields buried, the people turned loose to find employment at large – I decided to stay in China and write about it. Late in 1986 there were student demonstrations in most of the larger Chinese cities. Shanghai was shut down for two days. No one outside China took any notice. It is wonderful to travel in an unknown and changing land, even better to write about it. I managed this in my book *Riding the Iron Rooster*.

'We had no idea this was going to happen,' an American diplomat said to me in 1987. 'And so we have no idea of what is coming next.'

Greater prosperity came next, a looser economy, more free markets and foreign teachers and wider travel by Chinese, and then more demonstrations, peaceful ones in 1986, and finally the massacre in Tiananmen Square in 1989.

That was the end of student protest, and the death of public idealism or any altruism. Tiananmen was the last hoarse cry of 'Serve the people.' It was also the beginning of a sort of stubborn, intense but highly personal industry. Now it was every man for himself – everyone worked, either to save money and live better, or else to emigrate.

Considering another trip to China, to verify these changes, I spoke to a lawyer in Hong Kong.

'It's a feeding frenzy,' he said, with what seemed real emotion.

If so, it was something I did not want to miss, because I knew that it would be years before I would read about it in a book.

In my travels around the southern provinces of Guangdong and Fujian I saw that roads are being built so fast, in so many new directions, no maps are accurate. The guidebooks cannot keep up with the hotels and restaurants that have opened – every guidebook is out of date. So are telephone directories, and company listings. The Special Economic Zones have exploded – Shenzhen grew in ten years from a village of 3,000 people to a city of 3 million. But so have other towns exploded – little ones I saw in remote places, townships, and industrial areas, all of them under construction – kindly jump that ditch, watch that manhole, take your shoes off and wade to the sidewalk, ignore the film of dirt, pay no attention to those cruel policemen and that truckload of men being paraded around Guangzhou prior to their execution, turn your back on those choruses from *The Sound of Mucus* . . .

This process of change – unfinished China, grubby prosperity – makes it *terra incognita*, and there is no better place for a traveler than a land outside the ken of guidebooks, beyond the reach of maps, where only local knowledge matters, and word of mouth is everything.

The old cycle of Cathay is traditionally sixty years, but that is too generous a figure; in fact China seems to experience a serious and sudden convulsion every ten years or so, during which it reinvents itself. For the past fifty years, books have appeared with the words '*The New China*' in a title or subtitle. In fact, China is too vast, too changeable a world, to be summed up. It needs to be explored.

Hundreds of articles have been written about China's new prosperity. I have read some of them. But they were obsolete by the time they had been printed. This place simply did not exist before. Phenomenal is the perfect word for it.

THE MAN WHO CAME BACK FROM THE DEAD

In a simplified history, China's prosperity may be charted by the rise of Deng Xiaoping, who Mao had long ago sniffed out as a 'capitalist-roader.' Later, Deng was described with more elaborate scorn as 'an arch unrepentent capitalist-roader and harbinger of the right deviationist wind.'

Yet this early comrade-in-arms of Mao's is someone who, politically speaking, came back from the dead – and not once but three times. Born in Sichuan in 1904, the son of well-to-do landlords, Deng left school in 1920 and at a fairly tender age went to Paris. For the next six years he studied, debated the future of China, and made such important friends as Zhou Enlai, himself from a privileged background. This friendship lasted until Zhou's death. Returning to the chaotic China of warlords and factionalism of the 1920s, Deng joined the Communist Party and was a fellow sufferer with Mao and others on the Long March (1934–5). Deng's intellectual alliance with Zhou, who remained his apologist on the Politburo, distanced him from Mao, who held Deng and Zhou in the contempt he reserved for dilettantes or those he did not regard as red enough. In any case, China in the 1930s and 1940s needed mass organizers and military strategists, and so in the early stages of the Chinese revolution Mao was more inclined toward comrades such as Lin Biao, whose military tactics against the Japanese had proven ingenious and successful.

Yet there is a parallel, behind-the-scenes history of modern China in which the leader in the people's hearts is not Mao but Zhou Enlai. In this secret history, Deng and Liu Shaoqi are important subsidiary figures, conniving, while in the foreground Mao and Lin Biao and the people we know as the Gang of Four think of ways to get rid of them. Zhou put forward his idea of the Four Modernizations (National Defense, Science and Technology, Industry, Agriculture) in 1964, but this accomplished little except to alienate him from Mao. Distrusting Deng and Liu Shaoqi for their criticism of the various radical campaigns of the 1950s, Mao chose Lin Biao as his successor. It was Lin who compiled and published in the millions the *Little Red Book* of Mao sayings.

One of the many goals of the Cultural Revolution was to rusticate the bureaucrats and 'class traitors,' sweep aside such bourgeois notions as modernizing, and to take the starch out of the people who had become known as 'revisionists' and 'capitalist-roaders.' Deng was put under house arrest, Zhou too was in seclusion, Liu was imprisoned (and died under torture), while Liu's wife, Wang Guang-mei, was put on trial and 'struggled' by Red Guards (one of her crimes was putting on makeup and wearing a pretty dress). One of Deng's sons, Deng Pufeng, was 'airplaned' (held hand and foot and swung) and chucked out of a window (he is still in a wheelchair). Deng might have looked dead at the end of the Cultural Revolution, but he was only sleeping. He rose again.

After the death of Zhou Enlai in 1976, an event that provoked greater grief and more intense emotion in China than the death of Mao earlier that same year, Deng was purged by the Gang of Four. He was to have his revenge, for the Gang of Four were arrested (a month after Mao's death) for conspiracy. They were blamed for (among many other things) the excesses of the Cultural Revolution, and Deng was reinstated to the party and all his posts by the Eleventh Party Congress in 1977. In order to get his way, Deng had somehow to overcome the old 'leftists' and hard-line Maoists in the party. Deng first rehabilitated the victims of the Cultural Revolution – and one of the more celebrated ones was Liu Shaoqi. From the shadows (because he made a virtue of being invisible) Deng then dealt with Hua Guofeng, Mao's chosen successor. ('With you in command, I am at peace,' the old man is said to have written to Hua.) Deng eroded Hua's influence and promoted the program that Zhou had put forward in 1964 and 1975 of the Four Modernizations, at this point political shorthand for 'the Capitalist Road.' In 1979 and 1980 Deng consolidated his power, even as Hua's portrait was hanging all over China. Deng put his friends and like-minded associates and bridge partners and hatchet-men in key posts.

Any illusion that Deng was a high-minded Jeffersonian at odds with the forces of Marxist-Leninist darkness was shattered in 1980 when, for political convenience, he proposed deleting the Four Bigs from the 1978 constitution. These Four Freedoms were: Speaking Out Freely, Airing Views Fully, Holding Debates, and Writing Big Character Posters. This proposal of Deng's was endorsed in the fifth plenum. And so Tiananmen Square in 1989 was Deng at his most characteristic. Sun Tzu's *The Art of War* recommends hacking a disobedient soldier to pieces in front of his regiment to make a memorable point about discipline. The feebler the pretext, the sterner the lesson.

In other respects, 1980 was a banner year for Deng. Besides the trial of his old enemies, the Gang of Four, which went without a hitch, there were two Dengist ideas, both successes, which had far-reaching economic implications. These were the Statute of Joint Venture and the new Commission for Foreign Investment. Although business with the outside world had been going on since the Nixon visit in 1972, these two policy changes marked the beginning of recent Chinese prosperity. It meant that foreign companies could start factories in China with Chinese partners – making almost anything – and that capital and technology could be easily transferred, and perhaps most importantly that foreign loans (both government and private) could be negotiated. Just as crucial, it meant that business affairs were decentralized. Now foreign businessmen could negotiate directly with factories, bypassing the bureaucracy (and bribery) that was necessitated when every deal had had to be routed through the ministries in Beijing.

Along with this start of China's Open Door Policy was the ousting of Hua, the adoption of the official and greatly modified view of Mao, a break with the radicalism of the past, and some practical steps to develop China. One of these was the concept of Special Economic Zones. China is a world of compartments. Special money was created, not *renminbi* – people's money – but FEC, Foreign Exchange Certificates. The idea of Special Economic Zones was another compartment, and it was nothing new. Strictly speaking, that is what the city of Canton was in the 1950s and 1960s (and what Shamian Island in Canton was in the nineteenth century): a sealed zone where foreigners could transact business without stinking up the rest of the country with their decadent or subversive notions. So, just over the Hong Kong border station of Lo Wu, in a village on the railway line fringed by bamboo groves, at a place then known in its Cantonese form as Shumchun, a new city was planned.

This was hardly an overnight success. In 1983, the Rand Corp. Sinologist and National Security Advisor, Richard H. Solomon, published an article titled 'China's Uncertain Future.' Granted, any article on China in any given year could justify that title, but Professor Solomon's was a well-argued thesis that almost anything could happen next. Not much did happen. Stung by the ferocity of the Cultural Revolution, and receiving mixed signals from the right and the left of the party, the Chinese people were tentative in carrying out Deng's exhortations. His cry, 'To get rich is glorious!' remained little more than a yearning. What I saw in China in 1986 and 1987 was mainly confusion and tentative steps toward a free market, and official severity resulting from, and the usual Chinese horror of, crime and chaos (10,000 people were executed for various crimes between 1983 and 1986). I believe that the comparatively mild government response to the student demonstrations of late 1986 inspired a greater boldness, which resulted in the demo and hunger strike during Gorbachev's visit (with many junketing journalists) to Beijing in 1989, and the subsequent massacre. After that, it appeared that China was in the economic doldrums. This was an illusion, of course. As we now know, no businessman is likely to be deterred by a little thing like a massacre. The Japanese government did not even condemn the killings.

Deng was unrepentant about the Tiananmen Square massacre. 'Pragmatic' is the word most often applied to him. He is no fund of ideology, but plain-spoken and full of down-to-earth saws and maxims. ('It doesn't matter what sort of cat you have, so long as it catches mice,' etc.) He strikes me as soulless, unspiritual, a skeptic, unsentimental: the embodiment of the tough, risk-taking side of the Chinese character. He is a card-player, rather mocking of art or literature or artistic expression. A survivor to his nicotine-stained fingertips, he is all business.

Mao had a sort of monstrous style, in contrast to Deng's absence of style. Idealizing peasants and the virtues of toil and learning-through-doing, Mao tried to be a man of the people. But his ego was on a much grander scale, and he was a romantic, a poet, almost Byronic, and yet someone who rather enjoyed his reputation as a demon manipulator. He was happy to hand power to the Red Guards and turn the country upside down for ten years just to see what would happen.

While both Zhou and Deng had been affected by their years in France, Mao enjoyed belittling European countries as imperialists or running dogs of the Americans. Asked what his view was of the effect on France of the French Revolution, Mao said loftily, 'It is too early to say.'

Mao welcomed (and trained) African and Latin American guerrilla fighters and discussed with them his theories of protracted war. It is hard to imagine Deng writing a poem or caring very deeply about exploited African workers and peasants. While Mao was happiest debating the hypothetical African siege of Johannesburg, Deng might exult in selling the South Africans steel or Christmas ornaments. His outlook is quite different from the internationalism of the previous Chinese leadership. He is without charisma – doesn't have it, doesn't want it. No cult of personality has grown up around him, nor will it. His briskness and frankness is a reaction to the time-wasting and secrecy of the past. Mao was an emperor whose image was iconographic, Deng is a sort of CEO and is almost faceless. Deng's main dictum of reform is 'Tighten on the inside, loosen on the outside.'

It is hard to imagine, but in these years of Chinese miracles Deng's initiatives were not an instant success. In the first half of 1990, China experienced almost zero growth, and finished the year about 3 percent ahead; compared to its more recent annual growth of around 10 percent and the incredible heating of its economy. How to explain this swift infusion of cash? I think there are many reasons. The collapse of Eastern Europe and the fragmentation of the Soviet Union created new markets and diverted investment to China. The world recession inspired manufacturers to look for cheaper labor and more consumers – China, these businessmen discovered, can not only make electronics and Ninja Turtles and costume jewelry at a fraction of the cost elsewhere, but also can supply hundreds of millions of potential customers. Traditional cheap labor centers such as Taiwan and Korea and Hong Kong were being undercut by the even smaller wages in China.

Confidence in China (and Deng) is the key thing, and it seems to be limitless at the moment. China is a good credit risk. China is a serious market as well as manufacturer. The handing-over of Hong Kong is an important factor, too. Suddenly, China is no longer a seedy sprawling monolithic gerontocracy of enigmatic ideologists, but rather an enormous, orderly, businesslike place that inspires confidence and comes up with the goods very cheaply. It now seems almost laughable that a company would contemplate setting up a plant in Britain or Ireland or Poland or Italy, when for a fraction of the cost and the prospect of no labor unions at all the same company could be set up in China. That is precisely what is happening. As a result, China, with whom the USA has an 18-billion-dollar trade deficit, is its largest trading partner after Japan, the hottest economy in the world, and south China is 'The Gold Coast.' High-tech aircraft parts are being made in Fujian Province, a place known for 6,000 years only for its cork paintings and its oolong tea. In their dealing with Britain over Hong Kong, China seems to have realized that it is negotiating from a position of much greater strength. This is evident in the way China intentionally humiliates the British diplomats (creating delays, refusing to greet them or else not meeting their planes, making them wait, and occasionally issuing contemptuous statements). Chinese machismo these days is unmistakable, and businessmen are lining up to arrange joint-ventures for anything from jet planes to Barbie dolls. China has moved quickly from being twentieth, to eleventh, to the third largest economy in the world. The USA is greatly in their debt.

Mao's legacy is all those communes and collective farms that have been reconstituted as go-ahead villages, or else plowed under, their people dispersed to struggle to find their niche in the labor market. Deng's creation is Shenzhen. I went there several times – took a train from Hong Kong (less than an hour from downtown Kowloon), and went by road from the nether parts of Guangdong Province.

A billboard in Shenzhen showed the eighty-nine-year-old Deng looking ghostly and cadaverous. A life-long chain-smoker who has carried an oxygen bottle for the past eight years, his emphysema apparent in his sucked-in cheeks and popping eyes, he is making an admonishing gesture with his fingers:

> If you don't adhere to the socialist road
> If you don't follow the reforms
> If you don't develop the economy
> If you don't improve your livelihood,
> Then the only way for you is death.

It was part of the speech he had made on his Southern Tour when he had visited Shenzhen earlier in 1993.

The growth of Shenzhen has been prodigious. Formerly it was no more than a railway platform. In 1971, the Harvard Sinologist Ross Terrill stopped here, when it was still spelled Shumchun and a township, and he wrote, 'The traveler enters a building which is combined railroad station, customs house, and hotel.' Nine years later, I stopped and described it in my diary as a wilderness of barricades and barbed wire; it had just been designated a Special Economic Zone. Now Shenzhen is vast, with a railroad station as large as Grand Central, and scores of hotels. It is a city nearly the size of Hong Kong in population, and sprawling in all directions. It is as famous for its prosperity, and its buoyant stock market, as it is notorious for its massage parlors and prostitutes, and with organized (and approved) gambling – its own racetrack – its bustling streets and busy factories brilliantly lit by its own blinking signs. Deng had said famously, 'I like this.'

But Deng also made statements about corruption, and the local party official, Mo Huashu, specified 'red tape, embezzlement, dereliction of duties, abusing power for personal gains, and party members and officials visiting prostitutes.'

Mr. Mo quoted Deng as saying, 'If the society decays, what is the point in achieving economic success?'

THE FORTUNE COOKIE

There are no fortune cookies in China – the things are unknown, people laugh when you explain them, and even the name they find absurd and meaningless. Yet, inspired by the effusion of Chinese enterprise, two Chinese men are attempting to register their patent of a fortune cookie, though they don't call it that. *Qian yu bing* is their phrase, 'words-written-on-paper cake.'

Last December the *People's Republic of China Patent Gazette* contained a description of design #92303321.1, their 'cake' – the novelty is in the unique folds in the dough, though the finished article looks little different from other fortune cookies (or other tortellini, for that matter). Having been gazetted it could well be approved, and owning the patent, Mr. Bei Xian and Mr. Zhiang Ren Li, of Qingdao, Shandong Province, would become China's next millionaires. All they have to do is find a way of collecting revenue from such fortune cookie users as 'The China Moon' in Stoneham, Massachusetts, or 'Woodland's Potstickers Restaurant' in Honolulu, and numerous other infringers of their patent.

The Chinese are themselves masters of the art of copyright infringement and have found it an effective way to generate business, make enormous profits, and earn hard currency. They are closely monitored in Hong Kong by people acting for the brands and labels that are assiduously pirated. Even so, the infringers get away with murder.

'Take running shoes,' a Hong Kong lawyer told me. 'It is a billion-dollar business. I am not exaggerating when I say a billion. They make the shoes and label them "Nike" or "Puma," they put them in boxes printed "Made in Korea" and they ship them all over the world.'

The Chinese purloin trademarks and labels and logos willy-nilly. You don't have to be in China very long to see the rip-offs. Mickey Mouse is gallivanting all over China without a license – on every conceivable consumer item – and sometimes Mickey has a curiously almond-eyed expression. The Playboy bunny appears on any number of products, without the approval of Hugh Hefner. Knock-off Swiss Army knives are fairly common. Lux soap has been popular in China for so long there are a dozen pirate versions, the same-colored wrapper, often the same name or a similar one – 'Lid,' 'Lix,' 'Lud,' 'Lus.' They are exported to Africa and South East Asia, where they may be found stacked near 'Goldgate Toothpaste' and 'Rodigate Toothpaste' (the same Colgate colors, no relation), 'Pepsi-Cola Biscuits,' or fake and almost unchewable Chiclets.

False labeling – especially the label of origin – extends to clothing exported worldwide, but especially to the United States, where China is limited to certain quotas. It is known that China's production far exceeds its quotas, and so many Chinese products are given labels such as 'Made in Haiti,' or 'Made in Mongolia,' and transhipped through those places, the third country connection, where a fax machine in a dusty office may be the only apparent chinoiserie. 'Made in Mongolia' has been very popular on Chinese labels, because little is manufactured in that country of grasslands and yaks and nomads. A Hong Kong trading company was raided recently and found to have sold 2 million dollars' worth of falsely labeled Chinese goods. That was only one case. The value of Chinese textiles passing through Hong Kong with false labels rose 150 percent in 1992 to 24 million dollars.

The United States is the world's largest purchaser of Chinese clothes, 4.5 billion dollars in 1992. I wanted to visit some textile factories, especially ones that produced designer labels – Ralph Lauren, for example. This would be a problem, I was told.

'Ralph Lauren and the others are very uptight about giving the locations of the plants they source from,' I was told by a China expert in Hong Kong. 'It is bad PR for customers to know that their suit costing hundreds of dollars is made for peanuts in China. And cheap competitors want to source from the same factories so that they can pass their producers off as "just as good as Polo" – or buy the surplus production.'

Long before Mr. Li and I were humming Mao hymns and dodging carnage on the Shantou road, I visited a wholly owned American enterprise outside a major Chinese city – I promised my informant I would be circumspect. I was met by a fresh-faced American manager, who asked me why I happened to be interested in his company's product.

'I'm planning to write an article,' I said, 'about change in south China. And your part in it.'

'Wait a minute,' he said, becoming officious. 'I don't want to be in your article. I don't want to be quoted. I don't want my name on it. Everything I say has to be off the record. If you want information you can talk to our PR people in Hong Kong.'

'It won't be much of an article if I use public relations brochures,' I said, and I thought that it was precisely the sort of unhelpful attitude I had met among old commies and hacks in the older, Marxist-Leninist China.

'I'm sorry, I can't help you.'

'I was just curious about your experience in China. I promise to respect your wish to be anonymous.'

The Nameless American Factory Manager in the Nameless American Factory considered this and finally said, 'We're doing very well. We're on schedule. Everything's going ahead. We have a great team.'

He set his face at me as though defying me to find anything wrong with what he had just said. I found a great deal wrong. He was unhelpful and probably untruthful. It was the sort of thing you would hear from the cadre of the Revolutionary Red Star Work Unit during the height of the Cultural Revolution.

'How many people do you employ?'

'Eighty-five.'

'So it's not very labor-intensive?'

I had been told by a factory manager that if an industry was not labor-intensive there was almost no point in setting it up in China, since low wages and high productivity were the key to Chinese success. On the other hand, if you wanted to sell something to the Chinese the best position was to be wholly owned and to saturate the market, as this company obviously wanted to do.

'We have a lot of machines,' the Nameless American said.

'What do you pay people?'

'See?' he fumed. 'That's the wrong question! Why don't you ask whether they get transportation? What about cafeteria privileges, holidays, overtime, all the rest of the benefits?'

'I was coming to that,' I said (and he might have added haircuts and showers, two mother joint-venture perks for Chinese workers). But seeing that I had stung him I persisted with my wage question.

'About 500 a month – maybe less.'

Call it 450 *yuan*. That is eighty dollars a month at the official rate of exchange. It was slightly above the going rate by Chinese standards. The clothing factories, run mainly by Taiwanese and Hong Kong businessmen, pay 200 *yuan* or less a month. If you are wearing a garment marked 'Made in China' the chances are very good that the person who cut and stitched it earned a little more than five dollars a week. Your Chinese-made umbrella? Your children's toys? The angels on your Christmas tree? This easily made stuff was probably made by Chinese earning less than five dollars a week.

'That's a very good salary here,' the man said, and it is very likely that he was earning 250 times that amount.

'What if your workers didn't think it was adequate and decided to go on strike?'

'They'd have a problem. We're a non-union operation in the States. We don't deal with unions – we deal with individuals. My door is always open to anyone who's got a complaint.'

I doubted that anyone would risk it. Even in our brief conversation this Nameless American seemed to me to be a rather forbidding person.

He told me that he had been living in a hotel in the nearby city for almost seven months. A manager of a US plant in one of the western states of America, he had never lived in China before.

'How do you like it here?'

'It's an incredible place.'

'I think Guandong is horrendous.'

'I've seen fewer beggars here than in Santa Cruz.'

'Have you been to the railway station? Every third person is bumming money.'

'Maybe you're right. I wasn't counting that. But there's no hippies. In Santa Cruz you find hippies everywhere. Guys with long hair, just living off the government. I've got a personal pet peeve against graffiti. Santa Cruz is full of it. You don't see that here. And even if a person lives in a humble house they're still neat and clean. I like that.'

Very soon after, he signaled that this interview was at an end and that it was time for me to leave the building. He did not offer to show me the plant. What I thought about afterwards was that in the course of the conversation he had without realizing it more or less parroted *The Thoughts of Chairman Mao*. He believed in obedience, respect for property, cleanliness, thrift, learning by doing, and hard work; he wanted each worker to be the 'rustless screw' of the Chinese ideology. He was opposed to the sort of organized mass dissent that a trade union represented. He would not go on the record with me, and obviously did not care enough about press freedom to realize that a free press depends on truthful sources. I was sure he had voted for George Bush and was a staunch Republican, but that was only further proof that in his heart he was a Maoist.

I had the distinct sense that most American businessmen in China were Maoists in the same sense – not dreamers like the old man, but resembling the monopolistic-minded bureaucrats who followed him, the Hard-Liners (*Qiang ying pai*) or Extreme Leftists (*Ji zhou pai*). But a 'leftist' in China is actually very repressive and right-wing, and to their delight many foreign businessmen find they have a great deal in common with their own enthusiasms, prejudices, and obsessions.

The more commercial-minded Chinese, like the Japanese before them, have created ways of circumventing the rules. They seem to be able to make anything, and to sell it anywhere, in whatever quantity they wish. They sell rockets to the Iraqis. They sell semi-automatic rifles to anyone with – dollars per unit. It might be true to say that the indestructible AK series, sold by North Industries Corp. (NORINCO) in Beijing, have made war all over the world cheap, deadly, and endless. NORINCO has been described (by a US Treasury Official) as 'the K-Mart of arms manufacturers.'

'No other rifle design has shown the rugged dependability of the series AK,' the NORINCO catalog states. 'Through harsh climatic conditions ranging from rain to dust to snow the series AK has proven itself available.'

The Chinese sell tin pots in African countries and baseball caps in America and, ever since the pit closures in Britain, might well be shipping coal to Newcastle. There is hardly a gift shop in America that is not stocked from top to bottom with candles and carvings and baskets and nameless knickknacks from the many kitsch-producing provinces in China. Those pretty masks and doormats and mailboxes and Santa Clauses and almost-Hummels and classic cars that are so sensibly priced in any number of branches of Olde Worlde Gyfte Shoppe? They're from China. Those old English pub signs? *The Regatta Inn – Imported Wines – A Selection of Beers – Delicious Food. The Red Lion. The Cricketers. The Horse and Groom.* They are carved in a factory in Liaoning and bought by the quarter-container load for about a dollar each.

Except for the rockets, rifles, and tanks, which are sold at the annual Chinese Arms and Armaments Fair, much of this stuff is bought at the Chinese Export Commodities Fair in Guangzhou, often called the Canton Trade Fair. The first fair was held in 1920. I went to this year's, the seventy-third, describing myself on my application as 'in publishing.'

A frenetic ten-day bazaar, the fair fills one of the largest buildings in Guangzhou. Before Deng's reforms, the Trade Fair was the only way foreign businessmen could do business in China, since they were forbidden to pass beyond the Canton (Guangzhou) threshold into China. These days foreigners travel to factories around China to place their orders, and yet the Trade Fair is the main focus of Chinese commerce and a wonderful way to window-shop. In past years the fair's areas have been demarcated by varieties of merchandise – carpets here, electrical appliances there, hairpieces and bikes over here, and so forth. But this year, for the first time (and perhaps the last – it proved very chaotic), the fair was divided into provinces: Jiangsi here,

Shandong there, Inner Mongolia right down the stairs. It costs about ten dollars to register as a delegate and have your picture inserted into an ID badge, and the rest is easy, like a long vulgar trek browsing through the biggest gift shop on earth.

In the lobby is a musical fountain, with responsive lights flashing to the piano of Richard Clayderman, playing 'Don't Cry for Me, Argentina.' The buyers, bused in from their hotels, are mainly huge sweating men and feverish-looking women from all over the world, squinting and poker-faced like most bargain hunters.

'Zis bench grinder – tell him I want two sousand pieces,' a Frenchman is saying to his interpreter.

'When these shirts arrive Lebanon?' a Levantine woman is saying.

A man is buying an orange lifeboat, another haggling over cotton baseball caps made in Shanghai, which cost seven dollars a dozen, at 1,000 dozen per color, minimum order.

A German is ordering sleeping bags, made in Tianjin in a factory that employs 2,400 workers. Two million are exported, a great number to Germany. The wholesale price for these well-designed ones – warm, light, easily compressible – is 11.80 dollars a bag.

I drifted over to a stall where a sign read 'Foshon Hardware & Plastic Factory', and in this one small space I saw fishing rods (eight sizes), mortise door locks, hammocks, pipe joints, cups, plastic flowers, brake shoes, welding electrodes, hinges, washers, faucets, windshield wipers, spoons, small toy dogs that jumped and yapped, and an assortment of cigarette lighters – fifty or more – one of which was a panther whose eyes lit up as its mouth expelled a jet of fire.

In other stalls you could get a floor-length raccoon coat for 418 dollars (including delivery to the West Coast). A 'Chinalight New Magnetic Massage Cushion' (fourteen dollars). Black Dragon Brand in-line skates made in the remote northern province of Heilongjiang (13.60 dollars a pair, delivered) – the skateboards were cheaper. A wig made of Chinese human hair, dyed blonde, Shirley Temple style (Code HW 400) for 10.25 dollars. A mountain bike was fifty dollars, cashmere scarves were eight dollars, herbal remedies and surgical tools were all reasonably priced, and a XingFu 250cc motorcycle was 663 dollars. The WuYang I had seen on the road where the man riding pillion had been yakking on a cellular phone was 2,000 dollars wholesale. There was every machine tool known to Man. There was drilling equipment. There were inflatable toys. There were more

Virgin Marys and plaster saints and crucifixes than you would see in a whole year's pilgrimage in Italy.

'We're raiding a stall tomorrow,' a man in Guangzhou had told me. He worked for a law firm representing a company that made the sort of peculiarly repellent-looking porcelain animal in which the Chinese seem to specialize. A company was copying this ugly creature, and I was being given a chance to witness the bust. A team of lawyers and heavies were going to approach the stall-holder, tap him on the shoulder, and tell him to stop pirating this thing or else face the music.

In the end, the copyright infringement raid was canceled, because no one really knew what to do if the infringer made a fuss.

I spent two days at the fair, taking a kind of disgusted pleasure at the profusion of stuff and making a solemn vow never again to buy a basket or a candle or anything else at a gift shop in the US. They were all bought by the pound here and they cost next to nothing.

My most productive time was spent at the tea stalls, where all the varieties of tea in China are displayed. It was an industry thousands of years old, even if tea-drinking had only started (according to the French historian Fernand Braudel) in the eighteenth century. My preferred type of tea is Long Ching (Dragon Well) tea, from Hangzhou. It is green tea, and its flat smooth leaves resemble the needles of a fir tree.

'Why is this tea so expensive?' I asked the man from Zhejiang, Mr. Jin.

Mr. Jin said, 'This tea is picked in a small area. The best is found on just one hill. There are not many trees, the season is short, only two tons a months of the best quality are picked in the harvest season.'

I discovered it on my first visit to China in 1980 and have drunk it ever since, buying it in Friendship Stores or else in New York, where the best quality sells for fifty-five dollars a pound. But 'expensive' is an impression you get only if you buy it outside China. This same tea at the Trade Fair can be bought for roughly two dollars a box (868.20 dollars a carton, 450 boxes per carton, two cans per box) from the China Tuhsu Zhejiang Tea Import-Export Corp.

Walking through the exhibition hall I came across a provincial stall selling herbal remedies, which included ginseng, royal jelly, anti-cancer pills (made of 'myrrh, muschus, mastix, and calculus bovis'), and my eye was caught by something called LOVE SOLUTION. As if mountain bikes and rollerblades were not proof enough, this was also one in the eye for anybody who has criticized the Chinese for having poor market research, probably one of the most up-to-date potions at the fair. It was concerned with health and sex and claimed on its box that with it '100% of AIDS virus and chlamydia can be killed within two minutes.' There was a spray version for men, a plunger for women.

This product has the function to kill off the Diplococcus gonorrhea, staphy-coccus aureaus, chlamydia and AIDS virus rapidly with no toxicity and no irritation to the human body. It is specially used for the prevention of bacterial and viral infection of womans pudenda. It also has the function of prevention and cure [of] vaginitis.

Usage: Plunge the tube into the vagina and spray once a night or before sexual intercourse.

Ingredients: Germicide No. 1, [etc.]

Many of the products at the fair are lovely and finely made – the carpets, the embroideries, the lace, the silks. The tools, even hammers and screwdrivers and socket wrenches, are among the cheapest and finest in the world, and have put many American tool companies out of business. But if there is one business which the Chinese now monopolize worldwide it is Christmas decoration. There is hardly a Santa or a hanging ball on earth that is not produced in the People's Republic, and even the Christmas lights that were formerly made in Taiwan are now made in China, many of them in joint ventures with Taiwanese partners, as wages have risen back home.

'Are they any good?' I asked an Italian, Mario from Modena – here in Guangzhou for no other reason than to buy Christmas lights to sell in Italy.

'They are very good,' he said. 'They conform to Italian standards. They are cheap. It's perfect.' And he smiled. 'But this place –' and he made an Italianate gesture, his hands and face simultaneously expressive, to take in not only the fair, but Guangzhou, and perhaps the whole of China – 'is 'orrible, eh?'

Yet it was Mario who summed up the fair and perhaps Chinese business generally. We were talking about how China made everything and shipped it everywhere.

'China,' he said, 'is the manufacturer for the world.'

Hearing of a model factory, I went by road through east-central Guangdong to the once-sleepy town of Huizhou.

There were now four expatriates in Huizhou but four years ago there had been only one, Mel Dickinson. He was sent to the town by the Austrian family firm of Swarowski, purveyors of crystal to every duty-free shop on the planet. Mel's orders were to sort out an almost bankrupt jewelry factory. This too was like an outpost in old China, the *gweilo* stuck in a factory in a riverbank town in rural Guangdong, hating its snakes, consoling himself with his pint of Tsingtao beer at night, dreaming of his dog and his last fishing holiday back in Britain while he labored with his workers to produce costume jewelry by the ton. The heat, the rubble, the stink, the terrible town, the melancholy – it was like a portrait out of Maugham's *On a Chinese Screen*, or the much earlier narratives of American or European expatriates in China, summed up in the genial British expression 'wog-bashers.'

Mel considered my comparison, and then said, 'It is the same except for that difference. People like me came in the nineteenth century, and they lived the way I do. But they exploited the natives. We don't.'

This proved true in Mel's case. He was a kind and funny and hard-working man, clearly liked by his workers. His factory, Huisi Fashion Jewellry and Crafts Co. Ltd., had won a top award in the province, Number One for Light Industry in Guangdong, for being the best run, the most productive. Another prize had been awarded for environmental reasons – Mel had his own waste-water treatment plant in the factory.

Mel was forty-eight, a chemist by training, a salmon fisherman and former rugby player, Welsh by birth, resident in Ireland, childless, dog-owning. His wife, Fred (Freda), had come with him and ('to keep myself sane') also worked full-time at the factory. They had come to Huizhou in January, 1989, 'and almost walked straight out. The factory was filthy and silent. All I saw were workers having naps amidst orange peels and peanut shells. But I decided to stay. I liked the town. It was quiet and very safe.'

Four months later, production was in full swing.

'We had a ceremony – a box of swan pins. The Swarowski logo. We had a man hand-carry the box to Hong Kong to present to the office there.'

Soon after that, the students occupied Tiananmen Square in Beijing.

'Not a peep here in Huizhou,' Mel said. 'It was business as usual. There were some tanks in Guangzhou.'

Within four years many things changed in Huizhou. Prices tripled. The small town became a very large town – a city by American standards. More factories opened, rice growers whose fields had been filled in and built on by developers flocked from the surrounding countryside, and unable to find jobs they slept rough and made the place unsafe with their crimes. Highway robbers frequently went through a hijacked bus emptying passengers' pockets. Murders, burglaries, muggings, fights. The day before payday when the Huisi safe was full of cash, one of the factory workers broke in. Mel and some other men caught the man before he opened the safe. The man received a four-year sentence for the break-in. If he had managed to get the safe open he would have been executed.

'This is the Wild West now,' Mel said. 'The authorities try hard but it's not enough. Go downtown and you'll see masses of policemen. But after five o'clock there won't be any. They'll all have gone home.'

He lived in a small apartment above the factory courtyard, behind the spiked factory gates, liking the seclusion and the safety of the two night-watchmen. He worked all day and at night sipped beer on his verandah and tied salmon flies.

He was modest and humorous in his self-effacing Welsh way, but he was clearly proud of his factory, pleased with its awards and its profits. In this slack period he employed 220 people, but soon the Christmas orders would be coming in and 350 people would be working to turn out the bracelets, pins, necklaces, and pendants. His people earned between 350 and 400 *yuan* a month (sixty–seventy dollars), their hours were eight to five, with an hour for lunch. The cafeteria had also won a prize, for cleanliness and the quality of the food.

Huisi Jewellry had been intended as an export effort, the gold-plated jewelry that was sold in American department stores (forty-dollar earrings, sixty-dollar pendants), the sort of sparkly things that made some women say, 'These are fun.' But they had caught on locally and were now being snapped up all over China, and the Chinese were now buying more than half his output of affordable jewelry.

His factory seemed a happy place, most of it air-conditioned, all of it well-lighted. What impressed me about the operation was the amount of technical training the workers received, as designers and model-makers, creating the baubles. Three of them were being sent to Thailand to study another Swarowski operation. Everything was made on the spot, the wooden models, the rubber molds, and even the metal was bought in China, which made Chinese sales of the jewelry sensible, the *renminbi* convenient for buying the tin alloy.

We passed through a room where men and women were polishing earrings and pins.

'Polishing is the expensive part of the operation. See that gold mushroom?'

It was a gold vegetable, curvaceous and gleaming, about two inches high.

'A polisher can only do five an hour. That's why you cannot afford to polish in Europe.'

He told me that a worker in Ireland would get fifteen Irish *punts* an hour, perhaps twenty-five dollars. A polisher in China was paid fifty cents and did the job just as well. Anyone wondering why world manufacturing had moved to China might consider this simple example.

'This is the heart of the factory,' Mel said in the electroplating shop. 'This is where we make a silk purse out of a sow's ear.'

The alloy, plated with a layer of copper and then nickel, was gilded in a solution of potassium gold cyanide, which Mel bought in large quantities (about 4,500 dollars a pound) from Hong Kong.

Being in this well-run and apparently happy factory made me reflect on the sweatshops that existed in this part of China. They were mostly in villages, and damnably hard to find. I had tried hard to visit one, but the owners kept them hidden and off-limits, not wanting their exploitation to be observed, particularly by a foreigner. I knew from various informants that the classic sweatshop was a textile or umbrella-making operation, or simple electronics, owned by a Taiwanese or Hong Kong businessman, and typically it was an anonymous building in a rural village in which all the employees had been brought from one of the poorer provinces – Sichuan or Gansu.

Back in the courtyard after our tour, I asked Mel whether he had seen very bad working conditions.

'Oh, yes. I've seen many. Even joint-ventures. They were so awful they would have made Charles Dickens throw up.'

'What about sweatshops?'

'They're all over the place but you'll never get in. My secretary's brother worked in one, though.'

Mel's workers were his window on China. If you mentioned theft, Mel said, 'Richard was robbed last week on the bus to Shenzhen.' If you mentioned corruption, Mel said, 'Betty was asked for a bribe last month.' If you mentioned carnage on the roads, he said, 'Mary saw a torso yesterday. David saw a leg last week, just lying by the side of the road.'

I talked to Mel's secretary about sweatshops. In her late twenties, formerly a school teacher, her name was Linda. Her English was excellent. She had been born in Huizhou, and she lamented the rising crime. She too had been robbed.

'My brother works in one of those places. At first he was making ovens, now he is making telephones. He works until ten or eleven at night. Most weeks he works seven days, but now and then he gets a day off. His boss is from Taiwan.'

For this he was paid 200 *yuan*, or thirty-five dollars a month. This was not exceptional – in fact, many of the rural people who had come to Huizhou would have settled for that sort of job.

'See that man?' Mel said to me as I was leaving.

It was a dapper Chinese man in a well-cut suit, his hair fashionably permed, picking his way across the cobbles of the courtyard with his narrow shiny shoes. He was in his thirties, the sort of man I imagined I would be seeing in large numbers when I set off for China, the new executive – little man, big Rolex. Since traveling around I had seen enough of them to realize I had lost interest in such people, because they were the exception. I was more interested in daily life as it was being borne by the majority of people, workers, gardeners, market-traders, and the changing configurations of the landscape.

Still this man was unavoidable. He was a client from Shanghai and had come to sign a contract for an order. When the man was out of earshot, on his tour of the factory, Mel whispered to me, 'He has a check in his pocket for me, made out for a million *renminbi*. That's the down-payment. His order is two and a half million.'

There was another man in the courtyard, a cripple, and his body was so twisted and misshapen he could move only by occasionally touching the ground with his free hand, straining with his serious face. But he was tidy, his clothes were clean. He made his way crabwise through the gate to the porcelain factory next door.

'When I think the world's against me and I'm feeling sorry for myself I look at him and I realize I don't have it so bad,' Mel said. 'I've been looking at him for four years. I have never heard him complain.'

THE CORRECT HANDLING OF CONTRADICTION
AMONG THE PEOPLE

I happened to be present when an American manager in his company's plant in Guandong innocently asked an old China hand, 'So how do they choose their leaders in China, anyway?'

'You are used to leaders being chosen from the outside and below,' was the reply. 'In China they choose them from the inside, from above.'

'Oh, I see,' the American manager said, and went back to work.

But he did not see anything. A kind of moral blindness afflicts many people who do business with the Chinese, since – along with everything else – China is still a dictatorship of pitiful wages, fairly miserable living conditions, and a brutal legal system, and still practicing such quaint customs as convict labor, child labor, and mass (and often public) executions. Most people engaged in trade with the Chinese are so besotted by their profits that they could not care less about this. When the British pharmaceutical firm Glaxo perceived a need for anti-asthma medicine they set up a 10-million-dollar factory in a joint-venture, choosing an appropriate city, Chongqing, where the air quality is eight times worse than normal. Glaxo produces the world's leading anti-asthma medicine, Ventolin, which they sell in a pressurized inhaler. This is entirely for the Chinese domestic market.

'With 30 million asthmatics in China, Chongqing Glaxo will have ready customers for a long while,' a company employee explained when I asked why that particular product was being manufactured. In less than two years, the Chinese Glaxo operation has grown larger than the one in Hong Kong.

China is about as far from a democracy as it is possible to be. There are people who contend that China's authoritarianism is the reason for its success and its current wave of prosperity. In other words, that the Chinese government has a firm grip on things. But Chinese authority is a loose and baggy monster. It is more likely that an absence of government control has been crucial to Chinese success. Chinese workers and entrepreneurs did not need political guidance, they needed permission and – after such a turbulent recent history – especially needed a firm assurance that they would not be accused of being traitors, class enemies, capitalist-roaders, and spies if they made deals with foreign companies. Prosperity was a sure thing

(Chinese sources told me) when it became politically safe to transact business.

Even as recently as the mid-1970s, manufacturing foreign merchandise was the moral equivalent of sleeping with the enemy. After all, Mao had envisaged a self-sufficient China with a vast population, a classless society in which money was irrelevant. Ultimately, the whole world would be revolutionized in this way, and from time to time purges would be necessary. These would be very violent for, as the old man was fond of saying, 'A revolution is not a dinner party.' In all this, the hard thing for the Chinese has been in knowing when to stop.

China has evolved quite differently from anything that Mao (or anyone else) envisaged. When Mao's widow Jiang Qing was on trial she was apoplectic in denouncing the power structure and the direction China had taken. She was given a death sentence but with true Chinese ambiguity it was changed to life imprisonment. She never stopped howling about betrayal throughout her incarceration and eventually she died in prison.

Although China accounts for one-fourth of the world's population – many voices, you might say – public opinion hardly exists. From 1949 until the present all the political changes have come about by internal wrangling. No Chinese leader has deliberately tried to please the people, although there are many instances of famine-through-blunders, natural disasters, and political abuse.

As Americans we are used to our government caring about us, and responding to our frustrations, but the Chinese people are happiest when they are ignored. Left to their own devices, they manage quite well, and of course they are now in the unique position of having every businessman and his brother wooing them. They were watched and manipulated socially and politically engineered from Liberation onward. They may have needed a degree of unity, but they did not need a life-long course in Maoist doctrine. Yet even the thorough indoctrination they received did not dehumanize them or make them less fond of their families or less reverent toward their ancestors.

In China all appearances are deceptive.

One of Mao's most interesting essays is called 'On the Correct Handling of Contradiction Among the People.' It deals with unity and harmony. He writes, 'As for the imperialistic countries, we should unite with their peoples and strive to coexist peacefully with those countries, do business with them, and prevent any possible war, but under no circumstances should we harbor any unrealistic notions about them.' A few pages later, he goes on, 'We must learn to look at problems all-sidedly, seeing the reverse as well as the obverse side of things. In given conditions, a bad thing can lead to good results, and a good thing to bad results.'

The wealthy people are not those spivs yakking on cellular phones or sporting designer clothes. The millionaires are invisible. If anything, the cities look much worse than they ever did – more crowded and chaotic and far less comfortable than ten or fifteen years ago. The gardens and parks are a mess, people's manners generally are aggressive and their attitudes insufferable. The physical fabric of China (in what one presumes is this transitional stage) is in tatters. Strangely, this is progress.

Ever since arriving back in the People's Republic I had had a sense of this new prosperous, overcrowded, and in-your-face China as being much more like old China than the period dominated by Mao's selfless mottoes of anti-capitalism. 'Serve the people' had penetrated daily life so completely that waiters were offended by tips and doors were never locked. In those days people liked wearing old clothes, I was told. There was a fetish for old duds, for blue boiler suits and work clothes, and patches were like badges of honor. That had lasted roughly thirty years, from Liberation until Deng Xiaoping's last comeback when he declared his Open Policy.

Old China in my mental stereotype was an ugly landscape of factories and farms, expatriates and competing crowds, back lanes ringing with the hammers of tinsmiths, and vast cities of tycoons, prostitutes, beggars, hawkers, hustlers, and peasants – furious activity, everything for sale, crowded lanes and markets piled high with produce, and an intensely competitive commercial life. Factories turning out crystal goblets and sweatshops making shirts. Except for the occasional intrusion of police, life went on, and politics was a novelty and a nuisance that no one liked but everyone tolerated. Old China was not a tourist destination. And yet what looked at a distance like the chaos and anarchy of sweatshops, missionaries, compradors, deals, and dirt, was, close up, meticulous order.

I had that impression in many places in south China, the ones that had grown in four or five years from being landing stages on tributaries of the Pearl River, like the East River (Dong Jiang) to the size of proper towns. These settlements were like ones in the old, big, and bustling China. That was their appearance, but it was contradicted by a tougher reality. *Why be sentimental?* seemed to be the Chinese attitude now. Why trust another leader? This was a pushing and shoving China that had learned its Maoist lesson of self-reliance and survival, and rejected the rest of the Maoist altruism. Because of the hardships and unpredictable events of the Maoist years, people had developed sharp elbows and an instinct to snatch what they could while the time was right.

Four years ago, the demonstrators in Tiananmen Square had demanded the removal of Premier Li Peng. But it was the demonstrators who were removed. Li Peng remains a sloganeer, and the best translation of his exhortation, '*Zhua zhu shi!*' ('Grasp the time and the chance!') at the National People's Congress in Beijing (March, 1993) is 'Seize the day!'

Now he is preaching to the converted. Mao had wanted to create a population of revolutionaries. But his campaigns and purges were more like aversion therapy. What emerged from the Age of Mao was a vast army of reactionaries and opportunists. Mao's greatest success – though he may not have realized it – was in turning his people into single-minded materialists. Ideologically speaking, the Long March has taken a right turn down the capitalist road.

Does it matter financially whether China continues to be accorded Most Favored Nation status by the Clinton administration? Not in the short term. What the Chinese especially crave – something that is bestowed by MFN status – is an appearance of respectability, because the Chinese hierarchy is eager to host the next Olympic Games. To this end, the Chinese have performed political and ideological somersaults by (among other comic turns) exchanging ambassadors with Israel, a country it vilified until it discovered a mutually beneficial interest in the international arms trade. It is of no consequence to the Chinese that the Olympics is largely a pantomime world war of nationalistic athletes; the games are worth money in the marketing of TV rights – and the games have more to do with business than with sports. They also encourage investment. And in a profound sense any country hosting the Olympics can claim to be upholding the lofty Olympic ideals. The Chinese will do almost anything, it seems, for the sake of respectability, except tolerate dissenters. In this they have the connivance of everyone in the world, because every country on earth buys Chinese.

There is a high price for the current wave of prosperity in China. It has both human and environmental implications. The growth in industrial output factory pollution in China is horrendous, with the sludgiest rivers and in some cities the worst air quality to be found on earth. Beijing has an annual water crisis. Flooding is commonplace in south China, and with the building boom and the destruction of paddy fields and deforestation, it is much worse now, in 1991, than ever before. Some ecologists have singled out China for its insensitivity in killing and cooking various rare animals. When the *Endangered Species Cookbook* is published it will have Chinese authors. Certainly, killing tigers for the rejuvenating powers of their blood and bones, slaughtering elephants for their ivory, rhinos for their horns, and stuffing themselves with owls, turtles, herons, snakes, and the celebrated Heilongjiang dish of bear's paw seem diabolical in this green age. These habits have less to do with prosperity than with a tradition which holds that food is pharmacopoeia, and this insensitive gobbling will be modified by – if nothing else – the disappearance of these species. The floods, the droughts, the cutting of old-growth forests, the pollution – these are in the long run more destructive than the eating of monkey brains and moose noses.

Crime – another price the Chinese are paying for their new wealth – is unprecedented. Explicating Chinese punishment, even the paltry statistics that are officially published, reveals that Chinese crime is pervasive and takes all forms.

Seeing no policemen on duty after five o'clock in the town of Huizhou (as Mel Dickinson had foretold), I asked various people about the crime-rate. They all said yes, it's terrible, it's these outsiders, young boys mostly, no respect. I asked elsewhere. No one cared to elaborate. No one liked discussing this subject with a *da bidze* (big nose), and who could blame them? Two interesting points emerged, though. The people said that many of the thieves carried weapons. That was alarming. Armed robbery was always a capital offense in China. And everyone I spoke to was in favor of the death penalty – for murder, for robbery, for arson, for pimping, you name it. But this was not a topic for idle conversation. With the growth in prosperity and reform, there were more executions than ever, and in some cities crime was out of control, the public security often accused of being in cahoots with the criminals.

I had had death-penalty conversations many times before in China. The Chinese response was still unanimous. Give the criminal a bullet in the head. Let the victim's family watch the death throes, and make the criminal's family pay for the bullet.

One argument for the death penalty is that it deters crime. I happen to think this is a specious argument, and it is manifestly not the case in China, where the numbers of executions have risen – and so has the crime rate. Amnesty International's *Index* (May, 1993), reported, 'Estimates from unofficial sources for the number of executions in 1991 range from 5,000 to 20,000. The escalating use of the death penalty in China since 1989 is apparently continuing: in the month of January, 1992, Amnesty International recorded 334 death sentences including over 200 executions.'

When I challenged a more forthcoming Chinese man named Liu, he told me that people stole – and murdered – in spite of the death penalty 'because they don't know the law.'

'But the government publicizes the executions. They drive the condemned men around town in the back of a truck, with signs around their neck. They put the dead people's pictures up at the railway station. How could they not know?'

'They are ignorant.'

'But everyone in China knows that they will be executed for committing certain crimes,' I said.

Mr. Liu said, 'Some people feel it won't apply to them – that they will get off with a prison sentence.'

Some time later, Miss Ma said to me, 'Many people in China do not value their lives. They don't regard their lives as precious, and therefore they're willing to take risks.'

Hearing us talking, Mr. Sun, the driver, said, 'People must die if they break the law' – an odd sentiment from someone who spent most of his driving time on the wrong side of the road.

They scoffed at the argument that executions ought to reduce crime. It was a good thing if that happened but that was not the purpose.

'Not as a deterrent,' Miss Ma said. 'As a punishment. If you kill someone you have no right to live.'

'What about the large numbers?' I asked, was it a matter of the Chinese adage, 'In order to correct a wrong, it is necessary to exceed the limits' (*Jiao wong bi xu quo zheng*)?

'Perhaps.'

Iran, China, and the United States were the countries most wedded to the idea of capital punishment, I said, and they had the highest body count. Also a case could be made for the death penalty making a country more savage, increasing the number of violent crimes.

The next day Mr. Sun, who had clearly been thinking about this during the night, said, 'You asked me why people go on committing crimes in China in spite of the death penalty.'

'Yes, I don't get it.'

'Tell me then,' he said, smirking, 'why do Americans go on getting AIDS in spite of knowing that it will kill them?'

We were on the road to Shenzhen. Was it true, as I had heard – I asked Mr. Sun – that the Yellow Trade (prostitutes, gambling, porno) flourished in Dongguan?

Mr. Sun's answer was perfect: 'All developed countries have such things.'

I went to the market in Shenzhen with a friend of a friend, Mr. Lu, who told me, 'I would much rather live here than in Hong Kong. I have a larger apartment here than I would have in Hong Kong. Shenzhen is cleaner and better organized.'

Mr. Lu was interesting. When I asked him about his family he said, 'They were very red' – they had had power but no money, had never been landowners, and were party members. That obviously meant that their credentials were perfect during the Cultural Revolution. Mr. Lu said this was so. I asked him whether he had been active himself – he was forty-eight, just the right age. He said yes. Had he been a Red Guard? He said yes.

'What was your unit?'

'Revolutionary Revolt – the reddest,' he said, and smiled, as though having been a member of this fanatical ultra-leftist unit had been a youthful indiscretion.

Mr. Lu had been teaching English in 1966, but after being subjected to intense self-criticism (essays, confessions, recitations), he had become a Red Guard. His unit fought regularly with other units, mostly chair throwing. The dispute: which unit was the truest guardian of Mao's thought. In 1969, Mr. Lu was chosen as a model Red Guard, having worked for a year at a milling machine – a lathe making parts for machine tools – in a factory in the countryside. Machine tools during the day, Marxist-Leninist study at night. He was selected to be a propagandist, traveling the country, galvanizing Red Guard units, and leading political pep rallies from Mongolia to Shanghai.

In his spare time he studied revolutions around the world. Then, when foreign visitors began arriving, Mr. Lu, whose English was now an asset, was appointed to take them around. Many were well known. John Kenneth Galbraith was one. That was in 1973. Time passed. Mao died in 1976, 'of disappointment,' Mr. Lu said, 'because he had been betrayed by Lin Biao.' Just after Deng took control, Mr. Lu was sent to study in the United States and Canada, and that experience, the sight of prosperity, transformed him. 'It was the way people lived,' he said. 'I wanted that for us.' Mr. Lu became a passionate reformer. In June, 1989, he was at the barricades in Tiananmen Square.

'It was too bad that some students died,' he said, obviously chastened by the violence. 'But that is the past. We have to be optimistic.'

I asked him about the man whose speeches had incited the students, Professor Fang Lizhe, now a teacher in the United States.

'The great number of Chinese people don't care about his ideas. He is better off in America, anyway – he is more American than Chinese.'

He seemed the perfect person to walk around Shenzhen with. He was small and slight of build but he said that having been through the Cultural Revolution he was not daunted by any adversity, whether it was walking a long distance or carrying a heavy load.

Passing the railway station I mentioned that we could nip through the turnstiles, hop on a train at Lo Wu, and be drinking a beer in Kowloon in less than an hour. I had made the trip myself from the other direction one rainy morning, catching the subway train outside the Sheraton Hong Kong, changed trains in Kowloon Tong, and was at the border before I had finished reading the *South China Morning Post*. I had gotten back to Hong Kong Central in time for lunch. 'I would like to go to China,' the poet Philip Larkin had said, 'if I could come back the same day.' That was now possible.

'I don't like Hong Kong,' Mr. Lu said. 'It's too crowded.'

'Is it too full of *gweilos*?'

Mr. Lu laughed politely. There were no *gweilos* here. No tourists at all. Why would they come here? I had seen no tourists in Guangzhou. None in the provincial towns. None in Huizhou, none in Dongguan. There was a park in Shenzhen but it was not for foreigners, it was for Chinese, a China theme park with replicas of every 'sight' in China – a Great Wall section, a temple, a pagoda, a group of terracotta warriors, a portion that looked like Guilin (limestone mountains), and so forth. Tourists are an irrelevance in these economic zones, there is no place for them, everything moves too quickly for them, and really there is nothing to see. Only lives being lived, people working and undramatically raising families. There is not even a pretense of these places as tourist destinations. Tourists would be in the way. Although it is only just over the border from Hong Kong's New Territories, there is no sense of non-Chinese here – no big noses at all. One might as well be in the middle of China.

One night in Shenzhen with Mr. Lu we were in a restaurant which at ten o'clock was abruptly turned into a disco. There we were, Mr. Lu and I, talking about the future of Hong Kong over our shrimp and bamboo shoots, and the lights dimmed and young men began setting out sound equipment and tuning their guitars.

'Hong Kong will be handed over. China will give no assurances. These people in Hong Kong who are asking for elections and referendums are wasting their time,' Mr. Lu was saying.

Then the lights were dimmed, the youths appeared, and the music started – so loud we could not hear each other.

The guitarists wore silver jogging suits, the lead singer was in blue. I recognized one or two of the songs – Michael Jackson was obviously popular here. Then the singer started hectoring the audience, and waving green slips of paper.

'What's he saying?'

'He's asking for requests.'

The idea was that you would write down your request and hand it over to him.

I took a slip of paper. 'I have a request. I want him to sing *Dong Fang Hong*.'

Mr. Lu, delighted, copied down the Chinese characters and we passed it to the singer, who glanced at it and called out to his musicians. And without batting an eyelash, he began marching in step and singing,

> *Dong fang hong!*
> *Tai yang shang . . .*

> The East is Red!
> The sun rises!
> China produces Mao Zedong!
> He works for the happiness of the people,

He is the savior of the Chinese people,
The East is Red!

When he was finished, he went back to singing rock songs.

CHINA NOW

A book just published in China is called *A Modern Rich Man's History of Getting Rich (Xian Di Da Heng Fa Zhia Shi)*. It is full of Horatio Alger stories of people starting businesses, filling a need, buying low and selling high, making something out of nothing, lead into gold, turning scrap into millions. In one story, a man who was sent to the countryside during the Cultural Revolution spent his nights reading Mao and his days learning to assess antiques; he began buying objects in Free Markets during the Reforms, and reselling them to tourists until he had the price of a down-payment on an antique store. He got rich in three years.

But as soon as you get to China you hear the success stories. Everyone tells them, affirming the Chinese miracle.

The eight-dollar-a-week driver for the company in Shanghai who spent his nights at the Free Market flogging defective shirts with designer labels used the profit to get involved in a joint-venture and is now making 60,000 dollars a year, and is the owner of a house in Australia, having paid in cash by sending his cousin to Sydney with the purchase price in a brown paper bag.

The man who recognized a need for cycle helmets. His were very cheap, because his were very unsafe – just a plastic shell, but never mind, you could have one for ten *yuan*! This entrepreneur became a multimillionaire and he prospered until he died in what was described to me as 'a bizarre fishing accident.'

Foreigners tell these stories even more than the Chinese, and always in a tone of admiration and amazement, because anyone who was in China ten or more years ago knows that this bountiful place exploded from a colorless country of boiler suits and gruel, a scrimping, saving, mend-and-make-do society of reluctant sloganeers. These days the stories are of decadence and wealth.

'Last year ten new Rolls-Royces were imported into Guandong by Chinese businessmen.'

'The most popular dish in Canton these days is lobster sashimi.'

'There is a Chinese businessman in Zhuhai who buys ten bottles at a time of Louis XIII brandy, and it costs thousands of dollars a bottle.'

'There's a massage parlor in Shenzhen staffed entirely by Russian girls.'

Foreigners are surprised not so much by the extent of the development but that it happened at all. The Chinese are less amazed.

'We knew it would happen eventually,' a Chinese woman told me.

It is not a cultural enigma but a political necessity that the Chinese keep their dreams and their fears to themselves.

There is a quaint Chinese expression for turning capitalist or starting a business. '*Xia lai*,' a person might say, meaning 'Down ocean!' *Into the sea*, or *Take the plunge*. An American friend of mine was at a dinner with a high-level Chinese diplomat, and they were chatting about their next assignments, when the diplomat said enthusiastically, '*Xia lai!*' He was about to leave the PRC Foreign Ministry, where the pay is poor and prospects dim, even for an ambassador, and he was entering into a joint-venture with a foreign partner. What makes the story especially interesting is that in June, 1989, he made his name by denouncing students. Never mind! Take the plunge! Everyone else is doing it – or trying to.

I penetrated farther into Guangdong, beyond the red hills and paddy fields and the stands of bamboos, the muddy ditches and hot boulders, the haunts of snakes and eels and lizards and frogs, popular in the restaurants in those parts.

In spite of all the new wealth, some things in China never change. The small side roads made by hand, squatting people pounding the asphalt flat with mallets. The rice-growing process – women scooping water into the terraces using large wooden ladles, others bent double planting the rice shoots, the men plowing with buffaloes, up to their knees in water. Cyclists transporting squealing pigs or lengths of steel reinforcing rods on their bike racks. The edge-of-town dump pickers, usually a man and a boy, studiously sorting junk into piles – glass, metal, rags, paper. The barefoot men kneeling by the side of the road welding metal without masks or eye protection, sparks flying. On the highest and most ambitious building, men erecting a scaffolding of poles and tying them together with string or split cane strands instead of using metal clips. The gardeners lugging heavy buckets on yokes and watering their beautiful vegetable gardens. The men fishing for tiddlers in canals. 'The principle of diligence and frugality should be observed in everything,' Mao said, though it hardly needed saying.

We came to a town. What was its name?

'I don't know,' the driver said.

We asked. It was Bou Lou.

'It was just a small place last year.'

It would be a city next year.

The strangest place I saw was like a movie set, all bamboo scaffolding and rising buildings, another city-in-the-making in the middle of nowhere, with an archway lettered 'Welcome to Zhang Mou Tou.'

'So this Zhang Mou Tou,' I said as we drove through the flying dust, in this city of unfinished buildings. 'It's not on the map.'

'It is new.'

Last year it existed as a mud-and-buffalo rice-growing village of ten huts. The rice fields have been filled in, the buildings are rising, and to fill in the rice fields they have had to pull down all the surrounding hills – an amazing sight, just like the Maoist fable, quoted in the *Little Red Book*, of 'The Foolish Old Man Who Removed the Mountains.'

It was on the way to Dongguan that I had a vision of the new strangeness of China. Perhaps it was the late afternoon light, perhaps it was the dust, or the detour. Whatever, it was the apparition of a city-in-the-making. I had been seeing them for days, but they were additions, enlargements, new subdivisions and districts. This was something else, the sort of thing the stranger sees in horror movies rising from wisps of fog – a vision of the weird city, weirdly lit.

It was skeletal, unfinished, all of it brown with blown dust and dried mud. Everything was being built at once – the roads, the pedestrian bridges, the apartment houses, the factories, the stores. The buildings were thirty or forty stories high, and still clad in spindly scaffolding. Because of the time of day – twilight – no one was working; and only workers were involved in this. No one lived here. Except for the detour arrows, there were no signs. There was no color. Nothing alert or alive.

I had never seen anything like it in China, or the world, a whole city under construction, and what made it strangest of all was that no heavy machinery was in evidence – no bulldozers, no cranes, just the odd wheelbarrow or ladder, and the stitched-together scaffolding covering every structure and making the city seem fragile.

We drove through looking for someone to ask about it – perhaps its name? But there was no one around. Then it was behind us. But this was south China. In a short time – months maybe – it would be inhabited and brightly lit.

Dongguan could not have started very differently from this nameless place. Dongguan had been little more than a village when it declared itself an Economic Development Zone. It was not on any railway line. Now it was full of factories producing the sort of light industrial products I had seen at the Trade Fair. It had eight large hotels and many restaurants and it was the only place in the province where I saw large numbers of infants and small children.

Barbie lived in Dongguan and so did Ken – they were produced in vast quantities in the Mattel plant there. K-Mart imported Batman electronic games from Dongguan, too. There were Mattel plants outside Guangzhou, as well, but in a profound sense Dongguan was toyland, and I knew that later I would not be able to see a Barbie doll or a Batman item and not think of the muddy streets and dreary tenements of Dongguan.

The morning news from the BBC (I was listening on my short-wave radio) reported that inflation in China in the first quarter of 1993 had risen to 15.7 percent. I had so far spent my time in factories and shops. I decided in Dongguan, and again in Shenzhen, to look at the food markets and ask people about inflation.

All the shoppers agreed that the quality of fruit and vegetables in the markets was much higher than before the reforms, because now the farmers were growing what they wanted, in their own way. There was a greater selection, and this competition had resulted in better food items.

Chinese in the south subsist on bowel-shriveling meals of oily greens and boiled rice and sticky portions of sinister-looking meat.

At a spinach stall, I asked a woman, 'How long have you been running this business?'

'Five years.'

'How much did greens cost five years ago?'

'How am I supposed to remember that?'

The market at Shenzhen was fifty miles away, across a bridle path, through a ten-mile-wide building site, down a race track, behind a checkpoint. You needed an official pass, a sort of internal visa, to be admitted to this Special Economic Zone.

This was another aspect of old China, the high walls surrounding the city that gave each city a forbidding and fortress-like look. There are remnants of walls in Beijing and Xian and some other cities, though most of the walls were torn down during the Mao era and the bricks recycled. It made little difference that the crenelated walls and battlements were now chain-link fences, and the archers and spear carriers now members of public security. It came to the same thing. There was even a district in Shenzhen with the name Dong Men – East Gate – which was a resonant name if ever there was one. Certain cities were sealed, off-limits to outsiders. The proof of it was the woman in tears, being physically pushed through the turnstile, because her papers were not in order.

The Shenzhen market covered six acres or more and was on two levels – vegetables, meat, fish, clothes, crockery. At the butchers' stalls the cheapest meat was chicken or beef, seven *yuan* a catty (eighteen ounces), pork was eight, dog was ten, and snake was fifty. The dog meat section of the market was no different from any of the others – a series of long stone slabs, smeared with blood, and blood-flecked Chinese working their cleavers through stringy bone joints. The creatures themselves were either gutted and strung up on hooks or else piled in cuts, and even headless they were recognizable as dogs, from their long narrow muscles and their lean haunches.

Looking for an antique shop, we wandered through the Shenzhen Small Commodities Market: leather goods, electronics, video games, clothes, and knock-offs. The antique shop displayed crockery and lacquerware and jade along with old Rolex watches and battered Kodak Brownie cameras.

Mr. Lu also told me that as a result of Guangdong's huge commercial success, it had become stylish in other parts of China to use Cantonese expressions. It was fairly common for people to say, '*Mo men tai!*' ('No problem!'), or '*Ho sai ye*' ('He's got class') or to call for their check in a restaurant by calling out, '*Mai dan*' ('I'm buying').

As I drifted around the city with him, it was clear that Mr. Lu had put his Red Guard past behind him. He was proud of this proliferation of factories and housing blocks. It was undoubtedly the best-organized city in China. The authorities tried to keep crime to a minimum. Eighty-two men in Shenzhen had recently been stripped of their party membership for being 'prostitution patrons' (and a 'half-year reeducation' was also part of their punishment). But still women quietly solicited in many bars – they wore the current Chinese hooker fashion of very short shorts, once known in America by the evocative name 'hot pants.' The girls were pretty. There were brothels, too, many of them using the cover of barber shops ('I got suspicious when my husband needed a haircut every day,' a wife said in a current Shenzhen joke).

They did not bother Mr. Lu. He called them 'flies.'

'If you open a window, you get some flies,' he said, and he might have been quoting one of Deng's speeches.

Whenever we saw something decadent or jarring in Shenzhen – I would have been happy for more, I found the big city fairly tame – Mr. Lu said, with the Chinese love of euphemism, 'More flies.'

It was obvious that the ancient places and new places in developing China seemed interchangeable. It was an effect of the building boom – frugal, hastily erected structures did not age well, and looked elderly and renovated as soon as they were finished. The Chinese miracle has not so far encompassed graceful or even sturdy architecture, though China has a knack for being able to bury its history in shallow graves. Old Whampoa on a tributary of the Pearl River was now a sprawling industrial estate. Shenzhen, in under ten years, was not only bursting with a commercial intensity, but had also quickly mellowed, looking venerable, with the patina of Hong Kong, as though defying anyone to date it. The old port of Shekou in the Pearl River delta had been redeveloped, its go-downs and shop-houses buried under office blocks.

The Chinese have a genius for putting up buildings that are instantly seedy and almost ruinous. The dust clings, the cracks appear as soon as the ribbon is cut. Every building acquires a mid-nineteenth-century look almost overnight.

And Zhuhai, a one-hour ferry ride across the wide tea-colored river mouth of the Pearl, was a Special Economic Zone just a few years away from being a village resort, but looked as old and citified as Macau, founded in 1557. Walking from the Gong Bei district of Zhuhai to Macau – it took me an hour, including passing through two sets of immigration officers – is like a stroll from one side to the other of the same city.

I had gone to Zhuhai because I had heard there had been a labor dispute at the Canon camera factory there. There had been eighteen strikes in Guangdong in 1993, but they had been small affairs. This was a strike with a difference, because the workers were reasonably well paid, the company was immensely profitable (a 70-million-dollar turnover in 1992), and because some of the strikers were administrative staff.

The ferry from Shekou to Zhuhai, the *Hai Shan*, had 400 seats – and, this being China, every seat was taken. Each one was numbered and reserved. You would have thought, since everyone had his or her own seat, that boarding the ferry would be a relaxed business. This was not the case. It was a physical struggle up the gangway. Whenever a signal is given in China, people jump. It is as though there is a deep racial memory of individuals having gone hungry or got lost or left behind because they hesitated or weren't aggressive enough. Learned from periods of extreme poverty, the habit has now become a Chinese reflex, the instinct to push toward any door, any vehicle, any ticket window; shoving is the only way forward. And so China is an experience of elbows, now more than ever.

This get-it-now instinct has been officially sanctioned, and one of the features of society that these old *gweilos* lament is the absence of politeness – real or pretended. I was on half a dozen airplane flights and each time the plane began to descend, people threw off their seat belts and jumped up and staggered down the aisle, to be first off the plane. Flight attendants howl and the passengers retreat, but when the flight attendants' backs are turned the people are up again, gathering their bags, moving unsteadily down the aisle of the still-taxiing plane. Even traffic in Chinese cities or on congested roads can be seen to push and compete in the same way, beeping and queue-jumping, darting into any available space.

There was still a stand-off at the Canon factory. After a three-day stoppage (this was in early April), the 800 striking workers were back on the job while talks continued. But the workers know it is a losing battle, because there will always be Chinese lining up for jobs at low wages. The Chinese government has made it very nearly a duty for its nationals to work uncomplainingly. And foreign companies will continue to bring manufacturing to China.

Yet Zhuhai, on its breezy bay, was one of the pleasanter places I saw. It had beaches, and parks, and a main drag. In every restaurant and lobby bar there were Chinese yakking on cellular phones, and on one occasion at each of six tables around me there was someone talking on a cellular phone. Five years ago it was almost impossible to make a call from the best hotel. The boom in telecommunications is part of the Chinese miracle, and even prostitutes wear beepers.

'The Yellow Trade' – the euphemism for vice in China – was brisk in Zhuhai. The city's fairly steamy reputation no doubt derived from its proximity to Macau, as Shenzhen's derived from Hong Kong. But the present concern with manufacturing and the downplaying of tourism has meant that the Yellow Trade is mainly for locals or visiting provincials. A foreign industry would have produced much larger numbers of massage parlors and call girls, more vicious practices, much higher prices. The narrow lanes in Gong Bei were the haunt of skinny hookers in shorts and high heels, and they circulated among the outdoor restaurants and sidewalk cafés and the men selling live snakes – *xiao long*, little dragons – out of baskets (500 *yuan* each, for the thick ones they called 'Cross Mountain Blacks'). Fengboshan Park was popular among transients and seniors, and in a vice raid while I was in Zhuhai ten men were arrested, the eldest seventy-two. After the madam blabbed, her rates were published. Full sexual intercourse cost up to sixty *yuan*, bosom-touching was ten *yuan*, and 'nude peeks' were five *yuan*. As in other parts of China, barber shops and hairdressers were the cover for 'relaxation services' – masturbation at fifty *yuan*.

In Zhuhai I was able to verify the rumor about expensive brandy. I found some likely bottles at the Zhuhai Merchandise Fair and asked to examine them. They were crystal decanters of Rémy Martin 'Louis XIII Grande Champagne Cognac,' and at 85,800 *yuan* that was more than 1,000 dollars a bottle.

'Do you sell many of these?' I asked.

'About four a month.'

'Any to *gweilos*?'

'No. All to Chinese.'

Later that day I was marveling about this to a Chinese woman, who said to me, 'When Americans first came to China we thought they were rich. Now we are rich.'

This remark developed into a discussion about envy among a number of Chinese. Several of them maintained that there was very little envy in the new prosperous China.

'If a person gets rich the attitude is "good luck to him,"' one said. 'If I work hard I'll get rich too.'

'You don't burn a man's house down because he has a better one than you,' another Chinese said. 'There is even a sense that the rich man might help you.'

Just as confidently, this view was contradicted by a man who described *Hong Yen Bing*, or 'Red Eye Disease,' a chronic condition in China whereby the envious person stared greedily at anyone who had more than he did.

Most of the speakers agreed that the wealthiest people in China were hidden. They were not the ones talking on cellular phones or buying expensive brandy and wearing Rolexes. They were perhaps living as they always had, except that they were squirreling their money away, preferably in hard currency (the currency dealers thronged every sidewalk in these economic zones, pestering and offering twice the bank rate for Hong Kong dollars). People with disposable income bought gold, TVs, appliances. Some bought land. Many invested in the Shenzhen stock market. The 1,000-dollar-a-bottle brandy story was colorful but misleading. Many people saved to send their children abroad (there are now 80,000 Chinese studying in the US, the largest number from any single foreign nation).

Meanwhile, there were posters and radio lectures listing the Four Adheres:

> Adhere to Marxist Leninism.
> Adhere to the Socialist Road.
> Adhere to Proletarian Dictatorship.
> Adhere to Party Leadership.

'Do people repeat these things?' I asked a man in Xiamen.

I liked his answer: 'Yes. Like the Bible.'

I thought, *Exactly*, because that clearly reminded me of all the cant and hypocrisy that goes under the name of Christianity. And it was no different for the Chinese, who were able to parrot party slogans while at the same time hustling on the black market or trying (as one man did) to run me down in his BMW while he talked on his cellular phone.

Xiamen was the third of the three Special Economic Zones and in its way the prettiest, the least ruined, with more space than the others. Modernity elsewhere in China had seemed slightly ridiculous and imitative, looking out of place and foolish. But much of Xiamen was unmodernized, and consequently retained its dignity; it had old shop-houses, and hawkers, beggars, hookers, Buddhist nuns, rickshaws, and general confusion, as well as chugging ferries in the harbor. The old town remained – I had thought of it when I went there the first time as being one of the most interesting in China, with a busy harbor and a lovely island, Gulangyu, just offshore, where old mansions of returned Chinese had been preserved and cars were forbidden. The island was marred only by its billboards (for Coca-Cola, Marlboro cigarettes and eighteen other products). These days even Chinese flocked to see it, to take the ferry to Gulangyu and to climb its ancient hill.

Xiamen was now five times bigger – both in area and population – than it had been five years ago, when I had first passed through. It had a McDonald's now (a Big Mac was eight and a half *yuan*, a burger three and a half, fries five), and while this fast food place and 'Hamburger City' were just across the road from the traditional Fujianese restuarants that had menageries out front (live snakes, lizards, eels, frogs, and rabbits trapped in cages and waiting for diners to single them out to have their throats cut before they were skinned and cooked), the dull fact was that the mass of people did not eat either snakes or Big Macs. They went to bun and dumpling shops, to noodle stalls, they stuffed themselves with cheap candy and boiled rice and crackers; they slurped stewed vegetables at home, with their elbows on wobbly wood tables.

I had been told that the large town of Shishi ('Stone Lion') in the hinterland was the center of the Fujianese Yellow Trade – not only prostitutes but contraband. I spent a whole day getting there, and it did seem odd for this large prosperous place to be in the middle of nowhere. That was the point: Shishi flourished because it was off the map. You could buy anything in Shishi's markets, and its bars were far more louche than their counterparts in Xiamen. But what I remembered afterwards was the long drive there, the pretty preserved town of Jimei with its handsome buildings, the brand-new walled-in eighteen-hole golf-course surrounded by rice fields and vegetable gardens and barefoot peasants. Every five miles or so there was a school or college. And then perhaps fifty miles into the countryside the strange junk villages, one village piled high with glass bottles, another with scrap iron, another with paper, another with rubber tires, a whole province of scrap, awaiting recycling. Then Shishi, and the realization that Shishi simply had not existed a few years ago, except as a wide place in the road.

Outside Xiamen I found my first sweatshop, 'The Rubber and Plastic Shoes Making Factory,' a nightmare of squatting women and toxic fumes and bad light, where no one earned more than 200 *yuan* a month. I failed in my attempt to find convict labor or child labor, but people swore they existed and did not see much wrong with employing ten-year-olds or convicted criminals.

The Hui Industrial Zone was one of many outside Xiamen, where joint-ventures flourished. One factory produced cigarettes. It was a huge success, an R. J. Reynolds partnership, with work for 1,110, an annual profit of 33 million dollars, making Camels as well as 'Youyi' and 'Haima Peppermint Type Filtertip.' Other factories were Pirelli Tires, Golden Dragon Auto Body Co., United Clothing. This zone comprised about six square miles of factories, with two luxury hotels, on a grid of streets. Every factory was booming. Dynasty Optical, for example, contracted to make designer frames and sunglasses under license. The workers got the standard 400 *yuan* a month, and the frames were shipped to America and Europe, where they retailed (because of the quality and the famous label) for hundreds of dollars. I kept thinking of the Italian man at the Trade Fair: China is the manufacturer for the world. How had it happened that the Chinese had taken over? Simple, perhaps. Foreign investment was invited. Factories got built. The Chinese workers showed up on time. They accepted the lowest wages in the world. They didn't fight. They were not religious. Because of their peculiar political indoctrination they were totally materialistic.

China now looks the childhood cityscape of so many middle-aged Americans. It reminded me of my childhood, just as busy, just as fully employed and go-ahead, just as ugly and confusing. There had been a time when all American cityscapes looked like Xiamen's industrial zones – street after street of factory buildings. They are lighted working versions of the mills in Massachusetts that fell into dereliction after World War II. Fall River had them, so did New Bedford, Lawrence, and Brockton; they still have them – the structures have been revived now as 'factory outlets,' selling designer-label Chinese-made goods. South China's would be familiar to anyone who has lived in an urban area in Europe or America, where the factories are now empty and the machines are stopped. Not just Boston and Chicago, but Bradford and Manchester, and Derry in Northern Ireland, and so many others. China is doing it now, for everyone.

In the 1950s Raytheon was the great patron and employer of high school graduates in Boston and its suburbs. They manufactured electronics equipment. I often heard it said approvingly, of people I knew, 'He's got a job at Raytheon – he's pulling down good money – he'll be all right.' In Xiamen, in Hull Industrial Estate, one of the booming factories bore the sign 'Raytheon'.

China has succeeded because China is at work. The world has put it to work and has invested in it, and the world has received a return on its investment. Most people reading this are wearing a Chinese-made shirt, or sweater, or trousers, or pair of shoes. Traditional Nantucket baskets are Chinese. Carved Christmas decorations are Chinese. Our do-it-yourself tools are Chinese. Our children's toys are Chinese. Our bikes. High-fashion beaded dresses are Chinese. Ninja Turtles are Chinese. The tires on our cars are Chinese. Many of our Japanese electronic goods are assembled in China.

As Michael Lind wrote in *The National Interest* (Winter, 1993):

In the nineteenth century, corporations in European lands of settlement would actually import coolie labor from China and India by the thousands to compete with home-country nationals for jobs, driving down wage rates. In the twenty-first century, corporations may take the jobs to the coolies as it were, rather than bringing the coolies to the jobs. The result is the same – the lowering of developed-country wage costs towards Third World levels – only the rhetoric is new.

What will happen next? is never asked in China, but outside China the question is on everyone's lips. That the answer is unknowable does not stop people from speculating. I am one of those speculators.

When countries modernize these days they become Americanized, and often lose their cultural identity. China is exceptional. The more China develops the more it seems to be turning back into the old China, just as regional and unequal and busily self-sufficient and hard to read as ancient Chung Guo. As it modernizes it reveals a greater complexity and a deeper Chineseness. The difference is that while in the past there had been an ethical sense – Confucianism or else patches of Christianity – it seems now totally materialistic, cannier, wiser, even selfish. The provinces of Guangdong and Fujian may have the oily muddy look of old China, but except for filial piety they have few of China's old reverences, the Confucian virtues of refinement, gentleness, decency, and good order.

And there are the throwbacks which show in something as simple as tipping. In Maoist times it was not done. Then with the tourists and businessmen of the 1980s some tips were given. Now in the 1990s a tip is expected when a transaction takes place or service is given. There can be a real ugliness when a tip is not offered, and there is a new permutation – for many services the tip comes before any act is performed. In a very short time in China tipping has turned into bribery. Or is it bribery? After all, this is the East. Perhaps a tip has become what it has been in this hemisphere for thousands of years – baksheesh; not a reward, but grease.

The pressure to get things done quickly has bred crime. With bad roads and slow services and backed-up deliveries, grease helps. Many people I spoke to in China, foreign and Chinese alike, said that grease was an absolute necessity for a smooth business operation. Their view was that prosperity without crime is almost unthinkable. Obviously, corruption is not new in China, but it has become pervasive, and China's biggest single social problem will continue to be crime. The triads, crime syndicates and secret societies that flourished in China for centuries and seemed to be stamped out, have returned – many from Hong Kong and Taiwan, where these ritualistic brotherhoods and protection rackets were reconstituted. And the highwaymen and cat burglars are back. As recently as seven or eight years ago you could with confidence have sent your eighteen-year-old daughter traipsing all over China alone. No longer. China has become unsafe; I feel it will become even less safe. But then, for thousands of years it was a country famous for its perimeters – behind the Great Wall were more walls, walled compounds and fortified cities. These days, look at any new housing development of condominiums or apartments or single-family dwellings and you will see high perimeter walls.

Outside these walls there are the poor, some of them predatory, most of them simply pathetic. There are the rural poor of subsistence farmers in neglected provinces that have never known prosperity in the whole of Chinese history. It is doubtful that life will change for them. In the cities, the struggle will go on, but such extreme class divisions will obviously recreate even more of the old China – of more conspicuous wealth and ownership and a deeper oppression, of which the client and his prostitute is just one version, and the factory owner and his sweatshop is another.

No one owned gold in Maoist China, there was none to buy, but before Liberation the Chinese had always been great buyers of gold and jewelry. The habit is back. It is not greed, it is another technique of survival, a Chinese way of concentrating wealth. In the past, whenever times were bad, periods of famine or war or repression, the Chinese – the most portable of people – picked up a small bundle of their belongings and fled for their safety and well-being. Not all Chinese have gold in their little bundles, but some do. The others pay it in advance to men who smuggle them out of China and into other countries. As recent events have shown, the United States is a prime destination for Chinese illegal aliens. At the moment US Immigration officials estimate that 100,000 undocumented Chinese are arriving each year, and the number is rising.

With crime and class and immigration linked, it is not hard to envision the future of Chinese tensions. Already China is corrupt and its provinces unequally rewarded. Although the Tibetans are oppressed and occasionally volatile, and there are discontented Muslims in Xinjiang, it is hard to imagine any change in their status. China does not thrive on chaos, because the Chinese are not blame-shifters, not confrontational, nor litigious. These days the Chinese who are aggrieved or ambitious can travel throughout China in search of work. Many yearn to emigrate, the perennial solution to Chinese misery. This fact, of many millions of people out of sympathy with the destiny of their country and eager to come to America, seems to me to be of overwhelming significance. But if emigration becomes impossible in a climate of economic confusion and rising or thwarted expectations, then I believe there will be real chaos in China. It will be hell for them. It will be hell for the whole world.

Ghost Stories: A Letter from Hong Kong on the Eve of the Hand-Over

I

'Here comes the ghost man,' someone muttered in Dr. Gwai the herbalist's waiting room on Sugar Street, Causeway Bay, Hong Kong island, as I limped in, foot swollen, toe joints inflamed. Piled high with trays containing bark and twigs and leaves, the office smelled like a hamster cage. The mutter went around the room, '*Go gor gweilo lay lai*.'

The word *gweilo* is usually translated as 'foreign devil.' The non-Cantonese speaker thinks of a little red monster with horns and a pitchfork, but no, *gwei* is ghost (a *gwei gwu* is a ghost story). The ghost can be malevolent or benign. It is invisible. And now that Hong Kong has begun to seem haunted, and foreigners (especially the British) have become more and more invisible, the word *gweilo* has acquired an aptness and a novelty, and ever more suitably describes the white folk on these last imperial days, before the 234 offshore islands (Hong Kong island is one, some others are mere rocks) and the parts of the mainland known as Kowloon and the New Territories cease to be British Hong Kong and would become (as specified in the 1984 Joint Declaration – the Anglo-Chinese hand-over agreement) a Hong Kong Special Administrative Region. After that, the *gweilos* will definitely be ghosts.

'People here have used the word *gweilo* more freely since the signing of the Joint Declaration,' a Hong Kong woman told me, as she explained the meaning. 'It used to be our secret word for white people, but now it is used in a sort of friendly way.'

Like 'Chinky-chonk,' *gweilo* is offensively affectionate.

The white people (for whom a politer term is *sai-yahn*, 'Western persons') number around 124,000. Hong Kong's population is 6.2 million, spread over 413 square miles, nearly all of the people Cantonese-speaking ethnic Chinese. The present paradox is that in almost every case, these people – or their parents, or grandparents – came to the colony to escape the political convulsions of the People's Republic, from the late 1940s, just before China's independence, to the subsequent reigns of terror – the Campaign for Religious Reform, the Anti-Rightist Campaign, the Hundred Flowers Campaign, and others. The Great Leap Forward (1958–62), recently chronicled by Jasper Becker in *Hungry Ghosts*, produced pure horror: wide-scale famine, murder, and even cannibalism. Hundreds of thousands of Chinese at a time rushed to Hong Kong, as they were to do some years later during and after the Cultural Revolution. Typically, when people flee China they head first for Hong Kong. They are still, even now, sneaking over the border – almost every day an illegal immigrant ('eye-eye' in local parlance) is captured in Hong Kong.

This makes the hand-over on July 1 this year like an Oriental version of An Appointment in Samarra, in which the escaped Chinese find themselves in the wrong place, entangled after all with the very government they had sought to avoid.

Some of these refugees comprised the long line of the walking wounded ahead of me at the herbalist's and, like them, to kill time, I read the papers. We were not the only ailing people. It was mid-February and the *South China Morning Post* was reporting the deteriorating health of Deng Xiaoping. There were subtle hints that it was serious. The previous day the Chinese authorities did not say Deng was well, which meant he was ill. 'No big change' today meant a definite change. Share prices fell with 'Leaders Gather Amid Fears for Deng.'

No one in the waiting room seemed to care very much that Deng was sick. Hong Kong newspapers are among the freest in the world, distinguished by vigorous political, business, and investigative reporting. But it is the crime stories that rivet the readers in the herbalist's waiting room. Serious crime is low in Hong Kong; the streets are generally safe; there is hardly any graffiti. But when a crime is committed it is nearly always bizarre.

That morning it was 'Worker with Criminal Face.' A man, Mak King-man, a harmless computer worker with 'a criminal-like face,' had run amok after years of persecution by police, who had constantly picked him up on suspicion, because of his 'sinister looks.' He was now being tried for running through a housing block 'setting fire to umbrellas.' In the previous days I read, 'Shouting Woman Hacked to Death' (slashed forty times for yelling); '"Voices" Drove Father to Chop Baby Girl,' 'Man Rapes Step-Daughter on Toilet,' and 'Boiling Oil Victim' (angry wife deep-fries husband); 'Teenager Had Sex with Sister' ('because they were curious about sex'); and 'Toilet Charge' (buggery in a toilet cubicle in Taikoo Shing).

Dr. Gwai, the herbalist, took my pulse and diagnosed *tung fung* (gout), put me on a radical vegetarian diet, and gave me three pounds of mulch in paper bags which the Ritz-Carlton Room Service (Dial 3) obligingly boiled up for me, one pound a day. I drank the foul result, a bowl of black twiggy-tasting water, which looked like essence of mud puddle.

I made more visits to the herbalist and it was as though in treating my *tung fung* I was engaged in an intense process of Hong Kong acculturation – making friends, reading the papers, chin-wagging, and learning things. The herbalist's waiting room was a good cross-section of Hong Kong society – tycoons and paupers, young and old, traditional and modern, most with cellular phones, lots with pagers and beepers. The new 'Society' issue of *Hong Kong Tatler*, listing the billionaires and playboys, lay in Dr. Gwai's stack of magazines. Sample entry: '*Brenda Chau*. With her husband Kai-Bong, Chau is a party lover with a penchant for glitz. She favours bright colours, especially pink, and has a gold mansion . . .'

At just about the time I recovered my former nimble footwork, Deng Xiaoping died.

'You're lucky!' people said, regarding this act of God as auspicious. I was here to write about Hong Kong and Deng does me the favor of dropping dead.

A death-watch was exactly how I had envisaged any visit to Hong Kong in these latter days – 'Contemplating the mysteries of death,' was how Jan Morris had described her own view of the place in her valedictory book on Hong Kong. But there was no crash with Deng's demise. There was hardly a murmur in the stock market. Hong Kong's Hang Seng Index, which had been havering with his illness, rose 317 points as soon as Deng was confirmed cold on February 20, and another thirty-three points the next day. 'Sell on rumor, buy on news,' is a Hang Seng rule. Some flags were flown at half-mast afterwards, all Union Jacks stayed at the top of their poles.

In the days following, many Hong Kongers lined up to sign the visitors' book at Xinhua, the New China News Agency, China's unofficial consulate in Hong Kong. At ten a.m. on the day of Deng's cremation the cross-habor Star Ferries blew their whistles and some buses of the China Bus Company fleet were decorated with black bunting. But it was a working day like all days in Hong Kong.

The minute of silence in Hong Kong out of respect for Deng on February 26 was an utter failure in the screeching city of pile drivers and traffic and pop songs and human voices in crowds speaking plonkingly in Cantonese on cellular phones.

Some members of Hong Kong's small but vocal pro-China faction implored Deng's relatives to release a few spoonfuls of the paramount leader's ashes to sprinkle in Hong Kong harbor. It was Deng's wish to be present for the hand-over of Hong Kong to China at midnight on June 30 this year, and a portion of his ashes dissolved in the SAR harbor could stand for him in a sort of watery way, as Tincture of Liquefied Leader on a State Visit.

In the event, the plea was ignored, and Deng's ashes were scattered secretly by his family on an unidentified stretch of China's coast.

It had seemed to me a matter of urgency that I see the British governor, Christopher Patten, 'the last colonial oppressor,' as he self-mockingly styles himself. This being tiny Hong Kong, Government House was just a few minutes' ride on a twenty-five-cent tram, Causeway Bay to Central, from the herbalist's fourth-floor walk-up to one of Hong Kong's most venerable buildings, finished in 1855, and dwarfed by the skyscrapers around it.

The gate on Upper Albert Road had been flung open for me. I was greeted by the police and I was shown to a waiting room. On the wall were rows of portraits, beginning with Captain Charles Elliott, who had annexed Hong Kong but on such poor terms he was recalled and discredited; the rest were all the past governors since 1843, beginning with the first, Pottinger, and onward through Bonham, Sir Hercules Robinson, Bowring, Pope Hennessy, DeVoeux – all of them looking like swashbucklers. The later governors look duller, meaner, more politically sinuous: Young, Grantham, Black, MacLehose, Youde, Wilson, with the smugness of company directors who could be summed up in the pitiless word 'suits.'

Patten, the last of this lot, was not pictured and will perhaps never be pictured, for it is hard to imagine the Chinese taking the trouble to hoist the portrait of someone they so thoroughly despise and have vilified over the past five years. He is known universally as Chris. He is fifty-three, witty and well educated, from a modest background, and he rose through the ranks of the Conservative Party (researcher, speech-writer, MP for Bath) to be a member of Thatcher's cabinet, and it was while serving in her cabinet that he urged Mrs. Thatcher to walk the plank, which she reluctantly did. John Major is said to be a mate of Patten's. Major has spoken of Patten as being the next leader of the Tory Party, though when I asked Patten about this he said, 'I've heard that rumor too. I wish they would say something to me!'

'Hello,' he said, stepping briskly into the room, like a country doctor seeing his next patient. 'Let's go to my office. Nice to see you again.'

That 'again' was an excellent touch, considering it had been about twelve years since I had seen him. It was easy for me to remember, because he had been a member of the British Parliament and he had said complimentary things about my supposedly anglophobic books. Patten has aged significantly since he came to Hong Kong. Five years in as governor have made him look unconvincingly older, like a young actor in makeup, whose complexion is just a touch too florid, who put on weight and got his hair dusted white for the part of a statesman and potential stroke victim. After all, this is not an old croak, but an animated and highly intelligent fellow of fifty-three in suede loafers, and you have the feeling that in a different job, in a different place – prime minister, perhaps – he will look physically different, younger and not so full of dim sum.

We went to his office, followed by his private secretary, Mr. Llewellyn, who had already started scribbling notes of our conversation. I was talking and listening, yet I was distracted. The *feng shui* in Government House is famously bad. Hong Kong is one of the last repositories of Chinese myth and tradition (dragon legends, cricket fights, card games, big families), and no Chinese superstition is more assiduously studied – by Hong Kong businessmen especially – than *feng shui*. This so-called 'wind-water' determines the mood and fortunes of a site. The classical Five Elements of Wood, Water, Fire, Iron, Earth must be harmoniously balanced in all buildings, offices and residences alike, or disorder will occur. Patten's office seemed to bear out the bad tidings of the geomancers. The gray walls, the few windows, and the poor light – no fire, no water – were all obstacles to a free flow of *feng shui* energy called *ch'i*. The governor sat under a large photograph of one of his daughters, and the only crucifix I have ever seen in a government office in my entire life.

It is impossible not to like someone whom the Chinese have called 'a liar,' 'a clown,' 'a serpent,' and 'a strutting prostitute,' who has been snubbed at the highest levels. Patten had arrived in Hong Kong in July, 1992, and very soon afterwards he announced various democratic reforms, some of which called for free elections, and has since battled on. Many people have wondered out loud and in print why Patten has spoken so vigorously of reform so late in the day. I asked him that.

'What have I done? I've responded to social and political developments,' he said to me. 'If we hadn't responded – if we'd done much less – we might have had a quiet time with China, but we would have had a bloody awful time with the people here.'

The Chinese still hate him for his insolence in attempting these late reforms, the pro-China factions in Hong Kong hate him out of sycophancy to China. The pro-democracy people in Hong Kong say he has not been democratic enough and that he has not set up, as he said he would, the Court of Final Appeal, Hong Kong's equivalent to the United States Supreme Court. Yet the out-going governor's approval ratings are significantly higher than those of his successor, Mr. Tung Chee-hwa, China's choice.

Patten obviously relishes the irony of being the people's choice. He approached the job shrewdly, giving many speeches and press interviews, making himself visible, going on walkabouts in the urban throng and giving himself such a Hong Kong-friendly persona of hard worker and trencherman that he had a heart attack in the year after he arrived. His ratings soared. Nothing like infarction and angioplasty to endear yourself to fellow workaholics.

'I feel – forgive me for sounding sanctimonious – that I have been living out a Victorian hymn, doing well by doing the right thing.'

Patten is perhaps aware that he is the Hong Kong governor people will remember, and though this job could have been a wilderness for him it has raised his profile as he has made it a platform for his views on political philosophy. Several times he introduced a subject by saying, 'I'm just enough of a Marxist to believe –' but he spoke at such speed that I got the first half of the tantalizing sentence but not the last.

'What is astonishing is how moderate and responsible people are politically,' he was saying.

Patten, as always, was praising Hong Kong people in the most trusting and likable way. This praise and his friendliness are rarities, for all the Chinese leaders have ever said is how subversive and untrustworthy the Hong Kong people could be, and if you give them too much leeway they will overthrow the Chinese government. In

1987, Deng had said, 'We cannot accept people who want to use democracy to turn Hong Kong into an anti-Chinese base.'

But the current legislature in Hong Kong, a third of it having gained seats in free elections, has proven its integrity.

'It is only a slight exaggeration to say that this is perhaps the only legislature where people don't debate by punching each other on the nose,' Patten said. 'I find what is most encouraging is the way people here have reacted in the last few months to the curtailment of their freedom. It disproves what outsiders say about people in Hong Kong, "No one gives a toss about human rights," "All they care about is money."'

It seemed to me, as it did to many people in Hong Kong, that human rights and prosperity were linked. The clear-sighted Hong Kongers cared about both freedom and money; using their lunch hour to demonstrate on each anniversary of the Tiananmen Square massacre was an illustration of that balance of priorities. Hong Kong, with its dress codes and its class structure, is a notoriously philistine and trend-spotting place, but perhaps no more so than any other important financial center. And it is distinctly Hong Kong. Full of lawyers and bankers and accountants and businessmen, it has good bookstores but is not at all bookish. All these careerists in a hurry and on the make are natural supporters of the unsubtle and the highly visible, the lively arts, for a musical or a dance performance can be turned into a social occasion. The most surprising thing is that there are any boat-rockers and big mouths in Hong Kong, and yet there are a fair number, and some have paid a high price for it. A few years ago, the Hong Kong entrepreneur and publisher Jimmy Lai wrote an open letter to the Chinese Premier Li Peng, after Li boasted of killing students in Tiananmen Square. Mr. Lai called Li 'a turtle's egg' – quaint-sounding in English but a crude term of abuse in Chinese – and his stores were closed all over China.

Patten sees the Hong Kong opposition as constructive, far-sighted, and hardly radical. Firebrands are in short supply.

'What do we have? A couple of dozen Trots. What else? Martin Lee. Nobody could conceive of Martin Lee as a radical threat. We've had 139 demonstrations in front of the New China News Agency – and only one arrest!'

As the question, *So what's the problem?* passed through my mind, Patten was saying, *The Chinese have three problems.*

'Firstly, the Chinese see everything we do here through the prism of their reaction to the imperialist aggression of the nineteenth century. For example, we are constantly being lectured about the opium trade. Every time we send someone to Beijing they're shown a propaganda film about this. As if it's news to us!'

The Opium Wars seem like an antique phrase buried in an old history book, but it is vivid in Chinese demonology, and it is usually a mistake to underestimate the depth of the national memory, whether to illustrate a genuine slight or to use as a wicked pretext. British gunboats shelling Chinese ports and defeating them in these battles in order to sell them British East India Company opium for Chinese silver has never been forgotten, precisely because it ended with the British gaining Hong Kong.

Dismissing this, Patten added, 'Secondly, there are questions in their mind. Will we make off with the reserves? Will we fuck things up before we go?'

Smiling, as I was writing, *Will we fuck things up* . . . Patten said, 'And thirdly there have been genuine problems of comprehension in knowing how a free society ticks – understanding the movement of goods and ideas.'

Expanding on this last point, he said, 'Can you really expect an old Chinese cadre to understand the rule of law? Since Tiananmen, the Chinese have been seriously worried about control. Those old gentlemen saw over a million people demonstrating in a Chinese city. I think that made some Chinese officials jolly anxious.'

It became obvious to me that a great deal of what he was saying was in reaction to all the smelly little orthodoxies he has had to endure in the past five years. In particular, the term 'Asian values' seemed to rankle. It was nonsense, he said. What were Asian values? Who embodied them? One had to study the views of Lee Kwan Yew and Prince Sihanouk and Aung San Suu Kyi and the prime ministers of Taiwan and Japan to see the range of opinion in Asia.

But values were something else. 'I think values are universal. I don't think freedom of speech, of assembly, or habeas corpus, are looked at differently in Asia than in the West. It's insulting to suggest it.'

The intensity of Hong Kong's last days, this unlikely but inevitable ending, which to some minds is like a fatal illness, had made Patten more a philosopher – with a philosopher's smiling and pedantic pugnacity – and less of a politician. He was now interested mainly in the bigger questions, and this mood had made him impatient with the utterances of the Chinese leadership and their mouthpieces.

Leaving Government House, walking under the porte-cochère and the flower beds to the gateway, to hail a taxi on Upper Albert Road, I marveled at the strangeness of turning Hong Kong, this furious engine of capitalism and free speech – and this very mansion, with its flower beds and portraits – over to China. Such a hand-over has never happened so peacefully in the history of the world.

2

Hong Kong has existed since the reign of the mythical Yellow Emperor, when Chinese history began.

'It was a barren rock,' the more tendentious historians say of Hong Kong, quoting Lord Palmerston, but for 6,000 years Hong Kong was China and Chinese people lived there. They were the ancestors of the villagers and fishing folk whom the British confronted when they used the Pearl River delta as an anchorage for their blockading gunboats and drug-running ships in the Opium Wars. This period is an amazing story, which starts with the craze for tea drinking in Britain in the eighteenth century. The tea was imported from China in such large quantities that it tilted the balance of trade, and Britain, having nothing to sell the Chinese, had to pay for the tea in silver. When Britain desperately tried to interest the Chinese in British woollens and trinkets, the emperor laughed and demanded silver and obedience. Meanwhile, the British had taken over the opium trade from the Portuguese (who had been selling opium to the Chinese for hundreds of years); the number of Chinese opium smokers had also increased markedly by the early nineteenth century. Britain, owning India, owned the largest supply of opium in the world, and with a monopoly of the drug business solved the balance of trade problem by shipping tons of the stuff illegally through the East India Company. It went up the Pearl River; it was smuggled through scores of coastal towns; it created a subculture of bribery in China. A chest of opium weighed 140 pounds. Shipments in the hundreds of chests in the late eighteenth century rose to thousands in the nineteenth. Between 1835 and 1839, many thousands of tons of opium went into China, demoralizing the country. It was India's largest export – it was the making of the Raj; it was China's ruin, a loss of money, prestige and – with so many addicts – manpower.

The crisis occurred in the late 1830s when the Imperial Commissioner in Canton confiscated 20,000 chests of British opium, and banned opium's importation and sale. The British exploded, howling that it was a violation of free trade (a new doctrine at the time) and sent gunboats to Canton to carry out a short vicious war. The idea was not only to force the opium down Chinese throats, and get money for it, but also to humble Imperial China and forcibly open China, allowing foreigners to sell goods to the enormous Chinese market. This has great resonance today. Britain's victory in the First Opium War meant the creation of treaty ports for trade, but it also allowed Britain to demand a large cash indemnity from China, as well as a trophy, the island of Hong Kong 'in perpetuity.' A strip of the mainland Kowloon coast was ceded in 1860.

Although there were ceaseless protests, the British opium trade remained unregulated until 1905, and opium production and sale continued in British colonies until World War II. It is the most emotive single subject, where Anglo-Chinese relations are concerned. China felt ganged up on by the industrial world at the time. There was an American connection, too, because Americans benefited by the creation of treaty ports. It was with great glee that China observed the drug-taking by American soldiers during the Vietnam War; these addicts were seen and spoken about as a just retribution for this, *gweilos* brought low at last by Asian poppies. The humiliation by the British, the blockades, the siege and capture of Chinese, the forced sale of opium, have never been forgotten. Don't ask what's wrong with the Chinese; instead, ask American Southerners why they still grizzle about the Civil War and fly the Confederate flag. Both defeats happened just as long ago.

But there is more to Hong Kong than the island. Most of what we know as Hong Kong, the greater part of it, inland Kowloon and the large expanses of the New Territories – a whole notch of Chinese mainland – was gotten on a ninety-nine-year lease in 1898. Britain simply wanted more space, and China was too weak to resist. But the land had a use-by date stamped on it and from the moment the lease was signed, the clock has been ticking. The People's Republic never recognized any of the treaties and never ceases to repeat that they were 'unequal' and 'signed under duress' by the mandarin, Li Hung-chang. One of Deng Xiaoping's sayings was that in dealing with the British he would never behave like this despicable mandarin, who had handed over a part of the Motherland. Instead of snatching Hong Kong, China has let the clock run down.

The class system, the unsubtle sense of racial superiority that underpins the fear and resentment in all colonialism, was present in Hong Kong from the beginning. The injustice became law when in 1918 the British decreed that no Chinese could live on the Peak or at Repulse Bay, the two most salubrious parts of Hong Kong island. This law creating 'white areas' stayed on the books until World War II. Hong Kong was 'a mini-South Africa,' the Professor of History at Hong Kong University, Chan Ming, wrote recently. It was not until the 1960s that the Chinese were emboldened to build residences in any number on the Peak, and relations between the British and the Chinese, though outwardly cordial, are fairly frosty. An Englishman who came to Hong Kong in the early 1970s told me, 'If a British civil servant married a local woman, it was very unlikely that he would ever get a promotion.' The period he was speaking of was less than twenty years ago.

Hong Kong, always anomalous – Britain's colony, China's exit route – was a sweatshop into the 1970s, and it was politically backward too. Free elections did not exist, the vote was unknown, the governor was like a sultan, and his divan was the Executive Council. Composed of comprador-like Chinese and the mostly Scottish *tai-pans* of the great British-owned companies like Jardines or the Swire Group, the Executive Council was an advisory body penetrated with conflict of interest. The Hong Kong government has always been in the land business: real estate, the issuing of commercial leases, is one of its greatest sources of revenue. The Legislative Council was appointed. Democracy was an utterly foreign concept. It has been a foreign concept until just a few years ago.

Yet Hong Kong remained, quintessentially, even self-consciously, colonial. The word 'colony' is savored by the sort of backward-looking twit I heard a few months ago braying across a bar, in the Hong Kong Club, greeting a florid-faced man with the line, 'Ah, jolly good! So you decided to bring some joy to the colony!' That is of course fatuous. And technically it stopped being called a colony in 1976. Though anyone can see that the Territory of Hong Kong is an ant-hill of scramblers, hustlers, refugees, exiles, dissidents, white collar criminals and over-achievers, in a narrow sense it is an imperial time-warp. It is the site of the Noon Day Gun of Noël Coward's 'Mad Dogs and

Englishmen;' the setting of Maugham's *The Painted Veil*; the sleazy port of flesh-pots in *The World of Suzy Wong*. Hong Kong has been jeered at for its class-consciousness and its money-grubbing. W. H. Auden had anticipated much of this jeering in 1939, in his poem 'Hong Kong,' part of which goes,

> Here in the East the bankers have erected
> A worthy temple to the Comic muse.

Gateway to Red China, Hong Kong was inevitably a vantage point for China-watchers and often in the news. The rioting inspired by the Cultural Revolution's Red Guards in 1967 frightened businessmen and created a panic in the stock market. China merely watched impassively, and even at the height of the Cultural Revolution did not demand the return of the colony. At some point in every discussion of the Hong Kong character the words 'refugee' and 'refugee mentality' come up, and no one disputes them. Temporariness seems to be the human condition here, but it is an illusion, for the longer you stay the less Chinese, the more a 'vivid, sterile hybrid' it seems.

As a British colony, Hong Kong could have faced a far different future. After all, Kenya and Malaya and India and even little Nyasaland were granted their independence. What prevented this from happening? A little-noted event – indeed, it was secret at the time – took place in 1972, when under pressure from China, which had just joined the United Nations, Britain quietly dropped Hong Kong from a UN list of places scheduled for decolonization. 'Independence for Hong Kong is not practical politics,' a British official told me. 'It could only have been effected with the cooperation of the Chinese.'

'No, no,' a Hong Kong lawyer told me, referring to the independence question. 'China objected, Britain caved in.'

'What should have happened?' I asked.

'The Hong Kong people should have been consulted,' he said.

After Edward Heath became Britain's Prime Minister in 1970, he set up a clandestine committee to examine the status of Hong Kong. 'The existence of the committee has never before been revealed, and its findings are still secret,' writes Mark Roberti in *The Fall of Hong Kong*, which anatomizes in close detail the events which have led to the hand-over.

'The British delayed giving us democratic institutions,' a distinguished Hong Kong journalist told me. He was at school at about the time Heath was Prime Minister. 'When I was a schoolboy we argued for the free election of people to municipal councils, district boards, urban councils. It wasn't asking for much. But the government made excuses.'

Prime Minister Edward Heath – or any of his predecessors – could have put Hong Kong on the road toward democracy years ago; could have held free elections; could have established a truly representative Legislative Council and made universal suffrage a fact. But there was no talk of democracy until Hong Kong was a goner and it was clear that China was definitely asserting its sovereignty.

'Look at the past here,' Jonathan Grant, a history lecturer at Hong Kong University said to me one day at the faculty lounge in Pok Fu Lam. 'In 1948 they put in a new code here – the Hong Kong government could fire or deregister any teacher who was too pro-China or national-istic.' The British also had a policy of discouraging democratic ideas. 'There was a Special Branch in education, that was linked to the police Special Branch. It eliminated from the textbooks the terms "democracy," "representative government," and "civic responsibil-ity." The attitude was, "We don't want you to know about your own government." It was only in 1986 that "civics" was rewritten. Instead of the Confucianism that had been there before, it was stressed that people had rights and obligations.'

Until about ten years ago the British did not consider a democratic solution in Hong Kong but only versions of imperialism, and they wanted it both ways. They regretted the terms of the ninety-nine-year lease; they wanted to stay on. Since democracy was not an option, the expressed aim from early on was to fudge the dates – to obtain China's permission to go on administering Hong Kong while still acknowledging China's sovereignty. This unworkable idea, which was meant to give comfort to the business community and to extend the commercial leases beyond 1997, took little note of China's sense of shame and fury over the Hong Kong treaties, or China's repeated demands for 'unification' – a Chinese Motherland which included Xinjiang, Tibet, Inner Mongolia, as well as Taiwan and the Spratly Islands, and perhaps bits of India too.

Governor Murray MacLehose sprang the idea of a continued British administration on Deng Xiaoping in 1978, and Deng instantly rebuffed him. At the same time Deng tried to reassure Hong Kong businessmen by telling them, 'Put your hearts at ease,' and he repeated this to the next governor, Edward Youde. At the same time he contrived in a famous phrase the Hong Kong solution, which was to be 'One country, two systems.' This was his formula for China continuing to be a socialist paradise, while Hong Kong was maintained as a capitalist tool; and it was also a promise (eventually broken) not to meddle in Hong Kong's affairs.

Sometime later, after more uncertainty, Britain's panicky response was to hurry the Nationality Bill through Parliament. This was meant to exclude the 3 million Hong Kong people who qualified from becoming resident in Britain. There was yet another rebuff when Margaret Thatcher, who had succeeded Heath as Prime Minister, visited Beijing for discussions in September, 1982. She was still preening herself on having seen off the Argentines in the Falklands War. But Hong Kong was quite a different sort of island. As Hugo Young wrote in his Thatcher biography, *One of Us*, '"Our People" in Hong Kong were perforce to be treated rather differently from "our people" in the South Atlantic.'

Throughout her 'abrasive' exchange with Deng, the Chinese leader chain-smoked and hoicked into a spittoon at his feet, a life-long habit. Thatcher raised the question of Hong Kong's continuing to be administered by the British after 1997. Spitting at intervals, Deng lectured her on Chinese sovereignty and repeated that it was not negotiable. And looking ahead fifteen years, Deng specified a date for the hand-over: July 1, 1997. Subsequently he never wavered. The recovery of Hong Kong he saw as his personal mission and in the end it remains one of his principal victories.

You would have to have a heart of stone not to find comedy in what happened next. On leaving the Great Hall of the People and this audience with the intransigent Deng, Mrs. Thatcher lost her footing on the stairs and fell clattering to her hands and knees. Bobbling her handbag, her pearls swinging, and with her ass in the air and her face flushed with fear, the prime minister of Great Britain appeared to be kowtowing to Mao in his nearby mausoleum. From this moment on, the climate of negotiation became frostier, even glacial.

After a period of deadlock in which China gloated over having all the cards, Thatcher conceded the sovereignty issue and the Hong Kong stock market dropped further. It was soon on the brink of collapse. When Britain began talks to discuss details of the hand-over, the word 'treaty' was avoided, since China did not recognize any of the treaties. The term for the agreement would be 'the Joint Declaration.' Thatcher said she was demanding 'guarantees' in it, but in the Asiatic complexity of British politics, that was little more than face-saving.

The fate of the colony was argued over for almost two years in twenty-two rounds of talks. At last, the Joint Declaration was signed by Mrs. Thatcher in December, 1984. In it she agreed to hand over the 6 million people in Hong Kong to one of the most repressive governments in the world, with a long history of political wickedness and social injustice. This was the hand-over agreement. What would replace the British legal system, the judges in wigs, the Privy Council?

In order to eliminate the uncertainty over legal provisions in a China-governed Hong Kong, it was further agreed that a legal code known as the Basic Law, derived from clauses in the Joint Declaration, would be written. The Basic Law was to be a guarantee that the rights and freedoms of people in Hong Kong would be protected, along with the more practical details of the new Special Administration Region. It would even specify what the SAR flag would look like, for example ('. . . a red flag with a bauhinia highlighted by five star-tipped stamens' would be prescribed in Article 10 of the Basic Law; the bauhinia, 'a vivid, sterile hybrid,' is Hong Kong's flower). Many people saw hope in the drafting of this document, but in the course of discussions there were deep divisions among the various drafters – some wanting democratic elections, others opting for limited elections, and a pro-China faction seeing no pressing need for any free elections.

All this time, Britain was at pains not to upset the Chinese by introducing reforms, and in April, 1987, Deng warned that democracy was not a good idea in Hong Kong. 'The people who will rule Hong Kong [after 1997] must love the motherland and love Hong Kong. Can universal suffrage definitely produce such persons?'

Riding the Iron Rooster all over China, for my book, I spent a great deal of time in Hong Kong refueling, and I thought the answer to Deng's question (though it was rhetorical) was yes. In China in the winter of 1986–7 there were many student demonstrations demanding greater reforms.

It was acknowledged that China would be taking over Hong Kong. People, *gweilos* and locals alike, asked me what I thought they would do when they were in power.

'Kick ass,' I remember saying. It was what I had seen them doing all over China.

At one of those mid-1980s Hong Kong dinner parties an American businessman said with memorable succinctness, summing up 6,000 years of Chinese culture, 'The Chinese are pretty much giving you the finger the whole time.'

There was still, even then, quite a lot of innocence in Hong Kong regarding its future. Only a small number of people spoke up in favor of free elections, and those that did were accused of 'stirring up fear.'

The events in Tiananmen Square changed everything. Deng's orders to shoot the demonstrators made pro-democracy activists seem prescient and gave them some moral authority. In the aftermath of June 4, people in Hong Kong had a new perspective on the British, on the Chinese, and on their own fate; and there was more unity among the worriers. The speeches and demonstrations of sympathy in Hong Kong gave way to large-scale emigration – to Canada, Australia, and the United States. There was also a brisk trade in foreign passports – for those who could afford them – from such places as Tonga, Belize, Panama, and Gambia.

In that Tiananmen year of 1989, Hong Kong's Basic Law was published. Some of its articles seemed to guarantee important freedoms of thought and assembly, while other articles were vague, and still others contradictory. Article 23 forbade 'subversion' and it was apparent that the application of these ambiguous strictures would mean that a Hong Kong citizen would have to tread very carefully. Anyone who wonders how strictly Hong Kong will be governed in the future ought to read the terms of Article 23 of the Basic Law:

The Hong Kong Special Administration Region shall enact laws on its own to prohibit any act of treason, secession, sedition, subversion against the Central People's Government, or theft of state secrets, to prohibit foreign political organizations or bodies from conducting political activities in the Region, and to prohibit political organizations or bodies of the Region from establishing ties with foreign political organizations or bodies.

The implications of this paragraph became ominous when Wang Dan was sentenced to eleven years in Beijing for treason after he wrote an Op-Ed piece for the *New York Times*. And recently when Xi Yang, a reporter in Beijing for the Hong Kong paper *Ming Pao*, scooped other papers by quoting a leaked speech of Jiang Zemin, he was convicted of 'theft of state secrets' and given twelve years in prison.

Into the volatile and fraught atmosphere that surrounded the publication of the Basic Law came the new and ultimate governor, Christopher Patten. He saw his role as Hong Kong's last British proconsul in Hong Kong to try and rectify many of the old inequities and to introduce reforms. He was opposed by the mainland Chinese, who saw him as a sanctimonious opportunist. But Patten, undeterred, managed to raise people's awareness of the more sensitive political issues. This infuriated China and, though it won many people to his side, Patten has been largely unsuccessful in introducing any far-reaching reforms.

The most important questions remain unresolved – in particular the Court of Final Appeal and the definition of Acts of State. As a colony, Hong Kong's version of the Supreme Court is the Privy Council in London, but it was to be left to China to appoint judges to the Court of Final Appeal. In an attempt to be in a position to resolve these questions and amend the Basic Law, the Hong Kong Legislative Council, some of whose members had by then been democratically elected, passed an election reform bill. Annoyed by this end-run, China announced that on July 1, 1997, it would dissolve Hong Kong's Legislative Council and form a Provisional Legislature. Going further, in January, 1996, China appointed a Preparatory Committee of 150 people who were obviously chosen for their loyalty to China, and these poodles – or perhaps Pekinese? – chose the 400-member Selection Committee.

The Court of Final Appeal has yet to be constituted. Patten had said he would form it before midnight, June 30, but he has not done so. Some people think it is a good thing that he has left it, because by appointing judges himself he would effectively be marking them out as targets for the Chinese.

'The Court of Final Appeal will be implemented,' Patten said, when I asked him about this matter. 'I hope that my successor will appoint good open-minded judges.'

He spoke in such a considered and thoughtful way, I was sure that the answer was well rehearsed and that he had given it many times. When he found himself slightly on the defensive, he sounded most like a history tutor.

'Secondly,' he said, in that tutorial manner, 'I hope that the Court of Final Appeal is able to deal satisfactorily with the inevitable tensions with the Basic Law. The definitions of Acts of State will be potentially awkward. If Hong Kong appears to be losing – if the rule of law is undermined – it will have an effect on the way of life and on business confidence.'

3

Where do they come from? people say when a powerful figure emerges in China. When I asked people in Hong Kong to speculate on Deng's successor, the most intelligent ones said that only fools speculated on Chinese leadership struggles. The only certainty was that the leader would in the long run probably not be Jiang Zemin – anointed leaders in China have a habit of falling by the wayside – and that he would emerge from nowhere and take control.

This has become the case in Hong Kong. Just months ago, on December 11, 1996, the Chinese-appointed 400-man Selection Committee chose Chris Patten's successor, C. H. Tung, to be chief executive designate of the Hong Kong Special Administrative Region. 'Now we are finally masters of our own house,' he said when he was chosen, yet a day later, sounding anything but masterly, he indicated that he supported China's hard-line policies, which included scrapping all levels of elected government. A month after that he said he was in favor of repealing laws protecting various freedoms, using Chinese anti-demonstration logic that 'social order' took precedence over 'individual rights.'

He has been known to the Chinese for years, but he is such an obscure figure that he is not mentioned in any of the many books which describe the recent history, and look into the near future, of Hong Kong. His name is not to be found in *Hong Kong: China's Challenge* by Michael Yahuda, or *Beating Retreat*, by Tim Heald, or *Red Flag Over Hong Kong*, by Bruce Buena de Mesquita, David Newman and Alvin Rabushka, or *The End of Hong Kong* by Robert Cottrell, or Mark Roberti's *The Fall of Hong Kong*.

Tung is another example of how in the Chinese orbit a person may flourish in obscurity. A billionaire, he seemingly emerged from the shadows. He was born in Shanghai in 1937; his family were typical escapees, but with strong links to Taiwan. Tung studied in England, worked in the United States (he lists 'American sports' as his pastimes), and joined the family shipping business, Orient Overseas (International) Ltd., in 1969. Ten years ago a well-documented two-part article in the *Asian Wall Street Journal* described how in 1985, when Tung's company was insolvent with debts of 2.5 billion Hong Kong dollars, he borrowed 120 million US dollars from PRC's state-owned China Ocean Shipping Company. To avoid upsetting the Taiwanese, the Chinese passed this loan secretly through an intermediary, one Henry Y. T. Fok, a Hong Kong businessman with ties to China. Tung became viable once again, but of course ever since has been deeply indebted to the People's Republic.

Tung was the personal choice of Deng Xiaoping. Tung is said to have approved of Deng's action in Tiananmen Square – certainly he has been entirely uncritical of the Chinese, and more and more testy, and even abusive, toward journalists and pro-democracy people.

Tung's role model is Lee Kwan Yew of Singapore. If he has his wish, Tung will turn Hong Kong into a version of orderly, repressive Singapore, 'Disneyland with the death penalty,' in the words of a recent BBC correspondent. In Hong Kong everyone mentions Tung's fascination with Lee Kwan Yew, and they wonder what he is really like. As a member of the University of Singapore English department (1968–71), I can perhaps help here. Lee loathed our department and singled out our department head, poet and critic Professor D. J. Enright, for his more corrosive scorn. He believed we were subversive. He thought the teaching of English literature was a waste of time.

I was privileged to witness at first hand Lee's intolerance of students and strikers in the late 1960s. A paranoid and manipulative man, whose strange career oddly parallels North Korea's Kim Il-Sung even to his dynastic ambitions (his own son Lee Hsien-loong is his successor), Lee Kwan Yew was one of the stoutest defenders of Deng's massacre in Tiananmen Square. On Deng's death he wrote in the *South China Morning Post*, 'Deng has regularly been criticized by the Western media as the man who ordered the killings at Tiananmen Square in 1989. But if he had not dispersed them, and the demonstrators had their way, China would be in a worse mess than the Soviet Union.'

I like that word 'dispersed.' Singapore's old traditions of hanging and flogging are as stoutly maintained by Lee Kwan Yew as they had been by Stamford Raffles in the 1820s. Apart from this monstrous barbarism, Lee Kwan Yew also has robustly stated beliefs about men's haircuts and gum-chewing. Singapore's gagged and pusillanimous press has kept it a paranoid and barren place, without any debate, without one word of dissent. If this is to be Hong Kong's fate, God help it.

Soon after Tung was nominated as Patten's successor, he was asked to speak at the Hong Kong General Chamber of Commerce. It was important because it was his first post-nomination speech.

'It wasn't much,' a Hong Kong businessman told me. 'It was lengthy and long-winded, and it was empty, but –'

Something took place there, he said, that had never before happened on such an occasion in Hong Kong. At the question and answer session after the speech, each time Mr. Tung gave an answer, there was applause. And clapping followed each of Mr. Tung's replies.

'That is just the sort of thing that happens on the mainland,' the businessman said. 'It is totally alien to Hong Kong.'

The last question was, 'Mr. Tung, you have an important audience gathered here, and many of us are journalists. What would you advise the press regarding press freedom?'

Tung said, 'All of you should be fair and accurate, especially the foreign press.'

And there was more applause.

That answer ('definitely a premeditated reply,' my informant said) has become typical of Tung. When fears were expressed in February by the British Foreign Secretary about the future of the judiciary in Hong Kong, Tung took it as a personal slight, and said, 'I have a set of values and beliefs which I hold onto very much.' I was not put out that Tung refused to see me; he has never given an interview to any journalist. But his reclusiveness encourages hearsay. One friend of mine reported Tung saying to her, 'If there had been democracy in Hong Kong the MTR [the mass transit railway] would never have been built.' Another person quoted Tung saying, 'No one ever lost money betting on Hong Kong.'

'Tung wants to be a patriarch,' Martin Lee has said. 'He would make a good village elder. I am not so sure he is the man to lead Hong Kong.'

What Hong Kong needed was not a spokesman for China – 'Hong Kong has enough of those already,' Lee wrote in a newspaper piece. 'We need a leader who will defend Hong Kong when Chinese leaders insist on meddling.'

In a very revealing moment, when he was moving to a new office, Tung retaliated to the taunts of Martin Lee by accusing the campaigner for democracy of 'bad-mouthing Hong Kong.' Lee had raised concerns about civil rights in speaking engagements on a recent European trip.

'This proves that the Chinese are controlling everything that Tung says,' a Hong Kong writer told me. 'Tung believes in *feng shui*. He won't move a chair without consulting his *ken yu* [geomancer]. Even the seating arrangement of his council is determined by *feng shui*.'

Amazing that the man chosen to lead Hong Kong should be obsessive in the matter of cosmic forces and the apportionment of the Five Elements, but it happens to be true. We have Tung's own word on it. He himself has said, '*Feng shui* is something you cannot refuse to believe in.'

'Normally he would never have said that against Martin Lee, because it was the day Mr. Tung moved to a new office, and when you move to a new place – house or office – *feng shui* determines that you must be very peaceful. He would never have spoken those words willingly. I am sure he was asked to say it by Lu Ping [Director of China's Hong Kong-Macau Affairs Office], otherwise he would not have said anything.'

Tung believes that Government House has bad *feng shui*, because so many geomancers have said so. The fact that it has been the residence of *gweilo* governors for 142 years might also have contributed to its malevolent aspect. One geomancer said that the problem was its being 'surrounded by tall buildings which blocked its spirit.' It is the wrong shape, it is wrongly place and the new buildings have cursed it. 'Look at the side of the Bank of China – it is sharp like an ax, and it seems to be cutting it,' a *feng shui* enthusiast told me. Ten years ago the then governor, Wilson, was urged to plant a willow tree to improve the flow of *ch'i*. Yet Government House is still seen as a place of ill omen, and Wilson's very governorship came about as a result (so it is said) of bad *feng shui*.

One morning, earlier in 1986, Governor Edward Youde, a healthy man on a diplomatic visit to Beijing, was found dead in his room at the British residence there. It was an apparent heart attack. But the death also had a *feng shui* dimension relating to Hong Kong.

'There was a feeling at Government House that the bad *feng shui* was the reason,' a British civil servant told me.

He was on my list. There were particular people who seemed to form a chorus for the hand-over: a civil servant, a party hack, a local journalist, a China-watcher, a shop assistant, a Hong Kong University lecturer, and the ubiquitous Martin Lee, QC. Richard Hoare, OBE, a British civil servant who would be resigning on the day of the hand-over, was someone I had made a point of seeing. Mr. Hoare, who looks even younger than his age, which is forty-eight, is about to retire and be pensioned off from Her Majesty's Overseas Civil Service. He was twenty-three when he joined as a junior civil servant in 1972. And now, *Go gor gweilo zhao la*, 'the ghost man is leaving' – and he was not the only one.

Of the 539 members of Her Majesty's Overseas Civil Service, just about half (255) are leaving by June 30. They include members of the judiciary and administrative officers. One hundred and fifty *gweilo* police are leaving, 126 are staying on – and it will be interesting for them, for Deng has insisted that in addition to the police he will station 4,000 members of the People's Liberation Army in Hong Kong, and these soldiers will function as a security force.

But Richard Hoare was telling me about the *feng shui*: 'The previous summer a fountain had been put in – it was felt that a water feature was needed. For some reason it was built rectangular. It was supposed to have been circular. The rectangle was seen – after the fact – as coffin-shaped. A very bad omen. It was dug up and made circular.'

An assistant to Governor Youde, Mr. Hoare had accompanied him to Beijing and had found the governor's corpse the morning they were to fly back to Hong Kong. Director of Administration ('a meaningless title,' he told me), Mr. Hoare was in every sense a mandarin – bureaucrat, go-between, underboss.

'I'm boss of the guy who runs the records office,' he said, explaining his title. 'I mainly do jobs that no one else wants to do. Supervise legal aid. Supervise the ombudsman. I'm boss of the Director of Protocol. Deal with natural disasters.'

Mr. Hoare went on to tell me in his tidy, even austere, office in the Government Secretariat, 'My decision to leave is purely personal. I could stay if I wanted. Under the Joint Declaration all senior civil servants can stay. But it would mean that I could never get promoted. I'm at director level. I would stagnate.' He reflected a moment: retirement at such an age is inevitably a leap in the dark. 'I would feel a little out of things.'

So instead of retiring in the year 2004 at the age of fifty-five, he is making a traditionally English move, from an office job to a village in the South Downs, near Chichester.

'I have shelves of books I want to read. I'd like to educate myself in art, music and wine. I'd like to get some exercise, lose some weight.'

I asked him what his fears were for the future of Hong Kong and he gave me a nice mandarinesque response. 'What is written in the sacred texts is all good,' he said, referring to the Joint Declaration and the Basic Law. 'People are imagining the worst. But I think that it will be easier to have the Hong Kong equivalent of a family discussion after July 1. Then no one can be accused of being pro-British.'

It was Richard Hoare who told me, as Patten had done, of the fears the Chinese had about the British making off with the reserves before July 1. 'We have tremendous financial reserves,' Mr. Hoare said. They are estimated at 60 billion dollars. 'But no, we haven't removed any. We've gone on building and maintaining Hong Kong. We are building the airport without any British help. Apart from a percentage of the defense budget, the British taxpayer has never had to pay for anything in Hong Kong.'

And, he said, in his twenty-five years of looking at accounts, Hong Kong had never once received the sort of foreign aid that was habitual in countries throughout the world.

There was a poignancy about his departure. But he modestly insisted that he had to go, and he made it seem like a symbolic act, even an act of sacrifice, in which his future (with a substantial pay cut) was extremely nebulous.

'I feel the colonial era is over,' he said. 'I'm in the wrong place, at the wrong time.'

The next one on my list was the party man, not so much a capitalist-roader as a consummate opportunist. As hardly middle-aged Richard Hoare was ending his career, David Chu Yu-lin was beginning to soar.

'You are talking with the most colorful and physical person in Hong Kong,' he told me on the forty-ninth floor of the Exchange Square Tower Two, all of Kowloon spread out before us across the harbor. 'I do amazing things.'

One of the things this Shanghai-born naturalized US citizen had done was flamboyantly renounce his US nationality, and he placed his discarded and voided American passport in a time capsule that was publicly buried this past February.

He had driven to see me on his motorcycle, he told me. He owned three Harleys. He had just ordered the fastest motorcycle in the world, a Honda 'Blackbird' 1100, which could do 180 m.p.h. It was very expensive. Mr. Chu was very rich. He had paraglided from Hong Kong to the Great Wall of China. He held three paragliding records. He was a spelunker. His exploits took him beyond mere spelunking to cave diving. He made a solo descent in Silver Fox Cave in Fung San, down 650 feet, then into the water and down another seventy.

He almost died. 'I was trapped! The ultimate challenge! Stuck in a conical hole! Under water!'

'Sounds like a nightmare, Mr. Chu.'

'Nightmare!' Then he smiled. 'Fortunately I have a tendency to go around in circles. I have an uneven kick – that is my normal swimming tendency. I go in widening circles, and that is how I saved myself.'

On another occasion in the Wu Yu Mountains he had gone down a river of rapids, alone, wearing a helmet, a wet suit and a snorkel, flippers and mask; just tumbled from top to bottom, a vertical drop of 6,500 feet. It had taken eight hours. He had been bruised but otherwise unscathed, and it was worth it: 'I was the first man in the history of China to do it. My picture was in magazines!'

He was a marksman. He had a custom-made .45, made in Texas, an Eagle ST. He had shot grizzly bears, elk, mule deer, a red stag in Scotland, a moose.

'But a moose is a lovely trusting thing as big as a house,' I said. 'Why is that such a trophy?'

'A moose is hard to find!' he said, and continued to tell me of his exploits. Now he was in Montana, then riding with the Harley Club down Nathan Road in Kowloon, and then up the Zambezi.

The hand-over was his opportunity for political advancement. In the time I spent in Hong Kong I was to meet many people who cursed the British and hailed the coming of the Chinese, but none wagged their tails so briskly as Mr. Chu. Except for his cowboy boots, to which he called my attention, he did not look like Action Man. He was podgy and pale and middle-aged, an unlikely member of the Hong Kong Harley Club.

I would have thought that Sweetwater Avenue in Bedford, Massachusetts, in the 1950s could aptly be described as the wrong place and the wrong time for a Chinese boy from Shanghai. That was David Chu's neighborhood after his parents emigrated. But David was ambitious, he went to Cambridge Latin High School, graduated in 1960, went to Northeastern, got a job, and then his company sent him to Hong Kong in 1977. He had stayed and prospered. He had been elected a member of the Legislative Council, and had been selected by the Chinese to be a member of the Preparatory Committee. He had been chosen to be a member of the Provisional Legislature, the parliament that China had contrived to enact legislation after June 30.

He was said to be one of the most pro-China legislators. I tested him by asking him about the recent death of Deng Xiaoping.

Mr. Chu gave me the Deng-inspired eulogy he had written. The three-page piece compared the departed Chinese leader to Alexander the Great, Napoleon, Peter the Great, George Washington, Abraham Lincoln, Dr. Sun Yat-sen, Theodore Roosevelt, Winston Churchill and Zhou Enlai.

I asked him whether he had any anxieties about the hand-over.

'The hand-over of Hong Kong is the beginning of the new China and the renaissance of Chinese civilization.'

What about the subversion clause and press freedom?

'Our freedom is appropriate to our culture and current stage of development.'

What about Mr. Patten's attempt at reforms?

'Ha! It's easy to be a nice guy when you're leaving – when you're giving away the future.'

Surely, I said, people in Hong Kong came here to get away from the Chinese.

'Yes, but things have changed and in reality now China is not communist. It is modified socialism.'

I wondered whether he had any feelings about the events in Tiananmen Square in 1989.

'Demonstrations have a special meaning in China,' he said. 'China is having a difficult time controlling minority groups. And we don't want the US rocking the boat. Current US policy is wrong. US interference put Wang Dan in jail. They promoted him to a hero.'

What about right of assembly?

'The average education in China is low. A man can wave a banner and start trouble.'

Just one man is no more than a pest, surely?

'The pest is a threat to stability. Listen, I can start a riot in China very easily. If the government didn't stop me, I could take over China.'

It was so interesting to talk to a hack who, having no hesitation in speaking his mind, perhaps said more than he meant to. It had seemed to me one of the oddest aspects of the hand-over that, despite the slogan 'One country, two systems,' a Chinese political structure and ethic were being imposed. For one thing, he himself was in a legislature that had not been freely elected.

'I was elected by a 400-man committee.'

But the committee was hand-picked by the Chinese. And they said nothing was going to change for fifty years.

'"No change for fifty years" means capitalism – not law, not government, not politics.' And the marksman, biker, diver, paraglider, spelunker, and traveler smiled and added, 'They are evolving.'

Almost everything he said was a crock. And I had been warned. 'David Chu is a stuntsman,' a pro-democracy activist told me, and said that I should not take him seriously. But really he seemed to be just the sort of person the Chinese would need in Hong Kong if they were to get their way. He was loony and self-promoting, of course, but he also seemed to me – as perhaps he seemed to himself – a Hong Kong man of the future. But there were still annoyances, outside his control, and no sign that they would go away. Mr. Chu had complained to me that he had applied to join the Hong Kong Club and after seven years he had still not been admitted. I told him that he should consider himself lucky to be able to apply – women could not join, women could not eat in the main dining room, indeed they could only show their faces in selected rooms. He took no comfort from this.

'Hong Kong is very Orwellian at the moment,' an American said to me, and when I spoke to politicians and diplomats this struck a chord. 'People here are conscious that what they say is scrutinized by the Chinese.'

That was undoubtedly true, but an interview, far from being a conversation, is usually a monologue and it is often self-serving. Interviewing was not to my taste. Anyway, apart from my sitting at the size fourteen feet of the King of Tonga in his wooden palace in Nukualofa, when in travel had I ever interviewed anyone? The way to the truth was the humbler route of anonymity, faceless me striking up conversations with strangers. The Hong Kongers were worried, they giggled with apprehension, thinking out loud in the most un-Chinese way.

The people I spoke to in an interviewing manner could become animated and bare their souls, but after a spell of these high spirits they would become self-conscious and say, 'Don't use my name.' One of the straightest-talkers I met in Hong Kong was a reporter for a Cantonese-language newspaper. Seeing him meant traveling to the far end of an MTR line, and past the middle-class tower blocks of new housing estates (handsome and roomy by Hong Kong standards), to his office at the paper. He was young, hardly in his mid-thirties – though with the Chinese you could easily err by fifteen years; he was small and attentive and unusually frank.

'If I said I had no anxiety about the future I would be lying. But, for example, I felt no pressure covering the Deng death story – and we mentioned Tiananmen Square. The press in China would never touch that.'

I asked my customary question about press freedom being guaranteed in the Basic Law.

'The Chinese constitution guarantees the same things – freedom of press, freedom of assembly, all those things. Promises on paper are one thing, practice is another.'

At this point he urged me not to use his name, but that was all right; many other people in Hong Kong had requested the same thing.

Then he said, 'You know, newspapers here have had problems with the British, too.'

It was hypocritical for the British to be warning people of the erosion of press freedom, he said, when in fact the Hong Kong government had prosecuted local journalists. He was not trying to ingratiate himself with the Chinese; he was merely trying to be fair. He told me of a case in which a Hong Kong newspaper, *Ming Pao*, had published a detailed story about a scam at a real estate auction. Hong Kong's Independent Commission Against Corruption (the ICAC) asked for details of the newspaper's investigation. The paper did not cooperate – indeed, it turned around and published a story about the ICAC's interest, of their asking the paper to reveal their sources. And *Ming Pao* published the name of the investigator. The newspaper was then taken to court by the ICAC, for leaking the identity of the official. The newspaper won the case in the magistrate's court. The ICAC appealed in the high court, and won. The case – by now it was costing millions of Hong Kong dollars – then went to the Privy Council in London, and *Ming Pao* won.

'So you see, even under the so-called democratic law of Hong Kong under the British a newspaper is prosecuted for what it writes. But no matter which government is in power we are still watchdogs. The only question is, do we have the guts to go on doing it?'

For many years Hong Kong has been one of the best vantage points for China-watchers, who are unwelcome in China; a base for Chinese dissidents, and the key place for the dissemination of unbiased news about China. And this place, rife with skepticism, with anti-communism at its core, will soon be a region of China.

Lee Yee came to Hong Kong in 1970 to run a China-watching magazine, which he called *The Seventies*. Taking its title from the decade, it is now called *The Nineties*. Supported by 1,000 shareholders and with a circulation of 40,000 (but a readership four times that figure), it is as independent as a magazine can be. Mr. Lee had contributed a tough article on the future of Hong Kong to the *Hong Kong Goes Back* issue of Index on Censorship (January, 1997). Among other things he had said that in Hong Kong 'an intellectual can speak his mind on subjects forbidden in China without endangering his personal safety.' His forthrightness made me eager to speak with him.

I had agreed to meet Lee Yee at the China Club, the center of transitional Hong Kong, which was founded by the entrepreneur David Tang. 'Cigar-smoking,' 'stylish,' 'socialite,' are the descriptions usually applied to this flamboyant and funny man, who keeps his scholarly side well hidden. Tang is a book collector, an omnivorous reader, and an art connoisseur who has single-handedly created a market for modern Chinese painting. I know him also to be an accomplished pianist, for on another occasion he played the piano transcription – sight-reading – of Elgar's 'Enigma Variations' for me at his villa in the New Territories near Sai Kung.

Speaking of the hand-over, David Tang had told me that he was an optimist. 'I have to be, because if I become pessimistic I won't act.' Anyway, he went on, China was the biggest foreign investor in Hong Kong – not Britain, by far. Out of pride, China would not let Hong Kong perform worse in the next five years than it had in the last five years.

And that was probably true. The Bank of China holds a quarter of all the money on deposit in Hong Kong and continues to invest in Hong Kong at an enormous rate, accounting for a fifth of the trade and a quarter of the cargo. Almost all Hong Kong's food comes from China.

'Want to check the truth of what you write about Hong Kong after 1997?' Tang said before he left. 'Whenever you write a sentence about the Chinese, substitute the word "communist" for "Chinese." Then re-read it. If it still reads well it's true.'

I had expected Lee Yee to be a firebrand. He looked instead, in his gray suit and tie, like a paid-up member of that ancient class in China, the scholar gentry. He was a gray-haired soul of about sixty – benign, even a bit phlegmatic, yet friendly.

He reiterated something he had said in his essay 'Stick to the Facts,' in *Hong Kong Goes Back*, that the most sensible thing the business community could do is encourage the free flow of ideas. That in the absence of freedom commerce would falter, as it has done in so many countries. 'Freedom of speech is essential to Hong Kong's role as an international financial center. If there is no free flow of information, how can you make decisions? Singapore cannot be a financial center because there is no press freedom.'

It rankled, he said, that the Joint Declaration had been a document put together by Britain and China, that the Hong Kong people were not consulted. Both China and Britain were afraid of free elections, for when given a chance to vote the vast majority of Hong Kong people voted for pro-democracy candidates rather than for China's Pekinese.

'As for the future, I have two big worries,' he said, 'corruption and press freedom.'

Another meeting, another ethical debate, but at the margins of my consciousness I was tantalized by decadent music and pretty perfume and the lisping silk of women's dresses. A combination of vegetarianism and Dr. Gwai's potions had cured my gout, and I was walking again. It is a city of pedestrians. So many people thrown together in such a small area makes Hong Kong a profoundly physical experience, in which one is always in the presence of material goods and money.

Of the cost of apartments locals said, 'You get nothing for a million US.' Not just cameras and binoculars (objects so common these days that the duty free shops at Hong Kong's airport no longer stock them), but designer fashions of every kind, hung in your face the way the food in Hong Kong restaurants appears in the windows – plump ducklings varnished with sauce like pieces of mahogany, slaughtered hogs still bleeding, and pigs' trotters, and trays of fish lips, and dishes piled high with chicken feet, 'phoenix feet.' Always the reminders of the sheer expensiveness of life. Hong Kong prostitutes enjoy the same lexical ambiguity, sometimes called chickens and sometimes phoenixes. Self-employed Hong Kong prostitutes are legal under a law known as *Yet lau, yet feng*, 'One room, one phoenix.'

Hurrying to an appointment to discuss a political or legal issue in the middle of Kowloon, I would see an announcement by a door, four Chinese characters on a scroll, *sun dou bak mui*, 'New Girl from North,' a phoenix just arrived from China. The karaoke bars varied from place to place, and ranged from jolly lounges where customers sang drunkenly and out of tune to brothels, for which 'karaoke bar' is a synonym in Kowloon's Mong Kok and Jordan, areas of sleazy vitality.

In Jordan one day, I saw Jeremy Irons leaving 'Lucky Sauna,' a *gai dao* or 'chicken house,' famous for its cheap rates for buccal coition. He was wearing a green Barbour jacket and make-up, and, towering over the tiny hurrying Hong Kongers, was taking stock of the district in much the same way I was, making notes.

The Chinese actress Gong Li and the director Wayne Wang were not far away, for this disreputable spot was a location for the film *Chinese Box.* I myself had been here just a year ago, working on this same film, and so it was not really an accident that I had run into Jeremy Irons.

'Party tonight,' he said. 'Ruben Blades is leaving for the States tomorrow.'

His suite at the Peninsula faced the harbor, and Hong Kong island, and the Peak, dotted with long strings of lights that gave its upper slopes the look of a ski resort. The Peninsula's guests are mainly Japanese, who stay for the nostalgic reason that the Japanese Commandant was quartered there after the siege, rape and occupation of Hong Kong which began the day Pearl Habor was attacked.

In contrast to the parts he plays ('mainly weirdos,' he says), Irons is an affable person, with the English actor's knack for doing funny accents, clever in conversation, and musical. After Ruben Blades had sung several boleros, Irons took the guitar and sang 'St. Louis Woman.' Sushi and smoked salmon was passed around, and champagne, and then coffee. Following Dr. Gwai's diet, I had a banana offered by Irons's wife, the actress Sinead Cusack.

'Hong Kong is a superb place,' Irons said. Sinead agreed. So did the rest of the cast. They had been there a month, they had a month more of shooting.

But their Hong Kong was not my Hong Kong. They were shooting in knocking shops and atmospheric apartments. In this intensely social place of tit shows and race tracks, noodle shops, five star hotels, Rolls-Royces, superstition, the streets aromatic with Chinese herbs and joss sticks, I spent most of my time debating issues of law and morality with policy wonks and passionate dissidents.

'I've got to go,' I said. 'I've got an early interview tomorrow.'

'What are you doing in Hong Kong?'

'Playing a journalist.'

'Me too,' he said. 'As you know.'

The next morning, while Irons was doing a love scene with Gong Li, I was meeting her namesake, the defiant Martin Lee, whose father, Li Yinwo, had been a general in the Nationalist army. In *The Fall of*

Hong Kong, Mark Roberti writes that though Martin Lee was born in Hong Kong in 1938, while his mother was on vacation, the 'intensely patriotic General Lee did not want his son to be British and prohibited his wife from registering the birth.' And also this interesting fact about Martin Lee's father: 'Li disliked the communists because they rejected the family as the basic unit of society.' This is perhaps the reason Martin Lee has the reputation for being a family man. He is known to be stubborn, incorruptible, and insistent that the people of Hong Kong be guaranteed justice in a Chinese court.

Fearless and (uncharacteristic for a Chinese) confrontational, Lee has the intense and solemn gaze of a Jesuit. This demeanor changes completely when he laughs, which is often. His chosen path could lead to martyrdom, though when I asked him directly he said, 'I don't think it's likely that I will be thrown into prison, because I am known. But what of the people who are not known? The possibility is there.'

Mr. Lee, who has recently been to Washington and met President Clinton, as well as members of Congress, had at that time just returned from a triumphant speaking tour of European capitals. It is a measure of the respect that people have for his courage that he is usually received as though he is a senior statesman. While on his European tour he had continued to write and publish articles. In one he summed up the Hong Kong situation, saying that the Joint Declaration 'promised that Hong Kong's people would have their own elected legislature, an executive accountable to that legislature, an independent judiciary, and a "high degree of autonomy." Over a decade later this agreement is in tatters.'

Because he is articulate and open-minded, hospitable to journalists, kindly and charismatic and highly intelligent, he is welcome everywhere. When C. H. Tung criticized Lee for 'bad-mouthing Hong Kong,' it was Tung who was put on the defensive for this crude remark, for it is well known that Martin Lee's concerns are for the rights of Hong Kong citizens.

In his law office in Admiralty, he explained to me how, by refusing to define terms such as 'acts of state' or key provisions of the Basic Law, China would be able to manipulate the human rights. 'There's a big hole in the common law now,' he said. Theoretically China had agreed to the articles in the Basic Law that insured an independent judiciary. But while it was expressly stated in Article 82, for example, that 'judges from other common law jurisdictions' would sit on the highest court, the Court of Final Appeal, there was no sign that China intended to abide by this. Indeed, as July 1 approaches, there is no court of final adjudication for the people of Hong Kong, who know that in China justice is swift, and a frequent punishment for wrongdoing is a bullet in the neck. Amnesty International reports this as the fate of thousands in China every year. The executions, sometimes five or ten at a time, often take place in provincial sports stadiums. The more pessimistic Hong Kongers wonder whether the racecourse at Happy Valley, with its vast TV screens, will serve this function in years to come.

And Martin Lee is also gloomy on this point. He told me, 'When you see clear provisions of the Basic Law and Joint Declaration being violated, how can you guarantee any of the other clauses will not be violated?'

Speaking of the non-elected Provisional Legislature, which has been appointed by China's obedient and carefully chosen Selection Committee, Mr. Lee said, 'How would Americans like an appointed Congress, with the promise of elections some time in the future?'

He then said, 'Britain adopted a policy of appeasement.' He calls the United States' policy on China, 'single-faceted – just trade.' People in Hong Kong who demanded the rule of law were regarded by American businessmen and diplomats as 'just a nuisance.' As for China's concerns with rights and freedoms, 'There is only one right in China – the right to be fed. It's the sort of right all dogs and cats enjoy.'

Governor Patten has voiced his concerns about these issues, and in a celebrated policy address late last year he emphasized that Britain will continue to monitor human rights in Hong Kong. This is a noble sentiment, but given Britain's indifference to Hong Kong's aspirations in the past it is little reassurance. Anyway, Patten will go. The foreign businessmen are free to go. Even many wealthy Hong Kong businessmen have foreign passports and a ticket out. But Martin Lee, in identifying himself with the humblest and most vulnerable people, seemed to me the conscience of Hong Kong; the man to watch, the man to listen to. His nature is uncompromising, and so there was little of the politician in him, but quite a lot of the moralist.

'What are your fears?' I asked him.

'My fear is the loss of freedom generally and loss of the rule of law.'

The great news was that Martin Lee had no plans for relaxing his vigil. Since arriving in Hong Kong I had heard him praised and abused

– mostly praised; but it is not admirable in traditional Chinese society to stick your neck out. For some dim folk he was an embarrassment, a bit of a nuisance, yet just the sort of person they would flock to were they not so terrified of the coming commissar culture. In the end, Martin Lee will be hailed as a hero, though it may take the equivalent of the twenty-six years that it took Mandela to achieve his goal – and for all those years you hardly heard a good word about him from any of the businessmen or politicians who are presently kissing Mandela's bum.

'I'm hoping for the best,' Mr. Lee told me as we parted.

He was the single most impressive person I met in Hong Kong and the one I intend to listen to, whenever something significant happens.

Nothing will change for fifty years, was China's cry. It was meant to build morale among the Hong Kong businessmen. It has succeeded in that to a certain extent.

But now, months before the hand-over, there is uncertainty and quite a lot of change. It is not just the new flag; or the disappearing trash barrels that had colonial emblems on them, now replaced by plum-colored bins showing the Special Administration Region bauhinia, presently a familiar logo; or the rubbed-out word 'royal' that once appeared in so many club names that has vanished even from police station façades. There is a self-consciousness about Cantonese-speaking and a definite apprehension about the official language of China, Mandarin or *Putonghua*, which few people in Hong Kong speak or understand. Residency requirements are changing, so are the details of work permits. The vast numbers of Filipinos, mostly women doing menial jobs, are anxious; on Sundays in Statue Square they squat in their thousands and chatter and make the whole of Hong Kong Central sound like a rookery. And though China had said there would be only 2,000, there will now be 4,000 soldiers of the People's Liberation Army based at Stanley, as soon as the last of the British Gurkhas leave.

At Hong Kong University most of the political science lecturers have left. The department will probably close. The Chinese do not recognize political science as a subject. Other lecturers are worried about the retirement fund. What if it is taxed? What if restrictions are placed on its remittance to another country? What if it is paid in Chinese money, *renminbi*?

The Chinese have their own notion of world history, which was why I sought out a history lecturer at Hong Kong University. I was lucky in finding Jonathan Grant, an American about my own age, who had been in Hong Kong teaching history for twenty years. His special field was post-war Hong Kong history, and so he could recite a whole litany of colonial wickedness and hypocrisy. He knew the Chinese, too.

'On an academic level, the fear here is that the Chinese will do in Hong Kong what they do in Chinese universities,' he said. 'Put in political academics. They came in with the Cultural Revolution. They're the eyes and ears of the party.'

'You mean spying?'

'China takes knowledge seriously, unlike the West. So they feel it has to be controlled,' he said. 'People on the Preparatory Committee have made pronouncements, saying that Hong Kong will have to know its history. Hong Kong history will have to be rewritten in terms of a national history. But all national history is skewed. I didn't know about Indian massacres. China will put their own spin on Hong Kong history. It will be "those fucking opium drug-dealers." The history that China will write will describe foreigners on the China coast, and the British drinking in the Long Bar, while the Chinese worked. That will please the Hong Kong Chinese.'

One day I was with a *gweilo* friend in the Hong Kong Club. He was a successful businessman who had lived in Hong Kong for more than thirty years. I knew a number of such people, *gweilos* all, sardonic, funny, but when the subject of politics came up they were implacable.

'What do you think will happen?' I asked.

'We'll probably be all right,' he said. 'Not to worry.'

That was another thing. They were Americans who had picked up English colloquialisms.

'What if the shit hits the fan?'

'If Hong Kong folds, there's always Shanghai. The *gweilos* will head there. Shanghai's doing fine.'

I laughed at this paradigm of Hong Kong's lateral thinking.

'But you're an American,' I said.

'Not any more. I renounced my citizenship.'

And he disclosed to me his new nationality, and watched my eyes widen as he named a tiny, mostly illiterate equatorial country.

'So aren't you apprehensive about the hand-over?'

He pursed his lips and, sipping, seemed to kiss the rim of his schooner of sherry. 'A non-event,' he said.

Part Five

The Pacific

Hawaii

THE OTHER OAHU

Writing is hell, especially in Hawaii, where it tends to turn paradise into purgatory. So on the sunniest days I try to finish my writing before lunch, then I load my kayak on the roof rack of my car, hurry to India Bazaar for a vegetarian curry, and afterwards I go paddling out of Ala Wai harbor (easy parking), looking for green sea turtles and listening to NPR on my waterproof Walkman. I return to the shore at sunset, have a shower nearby at Ala Manoa Beach Park, and on the way home stop for a beer in Manoa marketplace and discuss skiing and nothingness with my carpenter friend who is on his way to Vail.

A perfect day: I have written something, I have exercised, I have seen perhaps three green sea turtles, and probably some dolphins, and always a brown booby roosting on the marker buoy a mile out of the harbor. All this has taken place near Waikiki, yet I have not seen a tourist.

The fact that I have been oblivious of tourists all day – none at the restaurant, none at the harbor, none at that particular beach, nor at that bar – is not so remarkable, even in a place that hosts 6 million visitors a year. Tourists always labor under a time constraint and are the unwilling victims of cost efficiency; so they stay together, they travel within a narrow compass, and they tend to stay put, once they have arrived. This is the result of both accident and design; it is a favor and it is also a conspiracy. Tourists are contained, partly for their own benefit, partly for the benefit of locals. By being kept in one place, there is no risk of their interrupting the flow of local life.

So there is a sort of voluntary apartheid that keeps tourists and locals separate. It seems odd to me that this should be so, because locals know where the best fun is to be had and how to avoid being overcharged. Perhaps the oddest aspect of being resident in a tourist paradise is the way in which you seem to lead parallel lives.

All my adult life I have lived in places regarded as prime tourist destinations, in Africa, in South East Asia, in England, and now Hawaii; yet for the whole of that time I have never had much to do with tourists – hardly saw these birds of passage. They never visited my bush school in Malawi – they were getting bug-bitten and sunburned 200 miles away on the stony beaches at Lake Malawi. (In Africa only tourists sunbathe; everyone else – nationals and Peace Corps Volunteers – stay in the shade.) In Uganda, while I was teaching at Makerere University, tourists were bumping in Land Rovers through the game parks, in a fruitless search for endangered species. Tourists in Singapore shopped, while we residents enjoyed the hilarious club life of the island state. I lived in south London for eighteen years, but tourists seldom percolated south of the Thames, to savor its seedy charm and glorious parks. They were hot-footing it to *Phantom of the Opera* or the Crown Jewels; I never saw them, never felt the need to.

For my past four years or so on the island of Oahu the story has been the same, visitors and locals enjoying separate pleasures. They are not hated; if anything they are patronized and pitied by the locals, because they seem so innocent, inhabiting a tiny corner of the island in a timid toehold. Hawaii is a culture of genial mockery, yet no one pokes fun at tourists; there are local Filipino jokes, and Samoan jokes, but you seldom hear anyone say, 'Did you hear the one about the tourist?' Most local residents are silently grateful for the revenue. The tourists stick pretty much to Waikiki, and for them Oahu is the glitter of that mile of streets, its wall-to-wall hotels, T-shirt shops, and (with some notable exceptions) indifferent restaurants, meretricious entertainment, and lovable Polynesian kitsch.

But there is another Oahu, where real people live modestly, go to work, and to church, and to high school reunions; they go swimming and on picnics and seldom see tourists. They eat local food in local restaurants, they go to local movie houses, they have a private language and distinctly local rhythms and intonations in their speech. One version of local is a sludgy plate-lunch meal at Zippy's and then fishing off the jetty at Magic Island and that night *Wayne's World II* at Pearl Ridge. The middle-class alternative might be spending the day in Manoa. Or you could spend your life in Manoa. ('I am not leaving this zip code,' a Manoa resident said to me, and he never does.) You could stroll around the university, visit Hamilton Library, walk the streets of Manoa valley, its cemetery, its several pleasant restaurants, have a beer at Danny's or a cup of exotic coffee at Manoa Coffee, and then catch a play that night at the Manoa Valley Theater. Locals go pig-hunting in the interior, locals play polo. Late every Friday afternoon locals who own sailboats engage in a race to a buoy and back, starting from the Honolulu Yacht Club. This race marks the end of the work week, but is hardly invisible to the tourist, who would probably regard it as a rowdy regatta of crapulous sailors and their friends; it is of course that, but – celebratory and skillful – it is more.

One of the more interesting aspects of life on Oahu is its sense of locality. There are people who never leave the suburb of Hawaii Kai, who don't stir from Waianae, who stay put on the North Shore. Some people who have grown up in Honolulu regard Haleiwa as 'the country' and simply don't go there. This is not strange; the island is only 112 miles in circumference, but the relatively small size of Oahu (608 square miles), makes it – like all small islands – not simpler but more complex. The micro-climates that exist because of the steep volcanic mountain ranges and the precipitous valleys make it even more complex: very wet in Manoa, very dry in Nanakuli, usually pleasant in Honolulu, the wind in your face in Laie. The weather at Waikiki, which was once swampy ground, with a royal residence, is usually gorgeous.

The weather is variable elsewhere on the island, but the other Oahu is first its people – most have roots as deep as any found on the mainland; indeed the native Hawaiians can trace their first migration to the island to about AD 600. Many other ethnic groups can claim many generations of residence, to the point where they have been thoroughly deracinated. Local Chinese seldom speak Chinese, local Japanese tend not to be Nipponized. One of the few cultural facts associated with the large community of local Portuguese is that the ukelele and sausages were brought from their homeland. The Spam-eating and hymn-singing islanders from the rest of Polynesia have become local – in some cases aggressively so, claiming parts of the island as their own. I sometimes have the feeling that a Tongan visa is required in certain parts of Honolulu, and Tagalog and Ilocano are widely spoken in the service industry.

Local people have their own haunts. They eat in their own restaurants, go to their own neighborhood movie houses, take walks, go to church, swim at beaches some distance from Waikiki. They are charitable with a strong spirit of community fascinated by sports – high school teams are followed as assiduously as national teams. They surf, go fishing, they play golf. Because of the island habit of frugality they are – typically – not spenders. Because of their curious history they are America-firsters. They are proud to live in Hawaii and tend to be sensitive to criticism because they are themselves easygoing and somewhat in awe of the mainland.

Beyond the suburbs of Oahu is a hinterland that is seldom visited – because it is vertical, or wave-lashed, or inaccessible. The highest mountain on Oahu is over 4,000 feet high. Some of the hinterland is military, and therefore off-limits; much of it is inconvenient. This is true of the Pacific generally, for people on small islands travel in ever-decreasing circles, and tend to preserve their notions of remoteness. There are tourist-related places where locals never go, because they feel overexposed and overcharged in them. Ironically, local people avoid *luaus*, except when they are family affairs.

Technically speaking, Hawaii is not a wilderness, yet a good deal of it is wild enough, and seeing it fully requires taking a calculated risk. In any given week, people in Hawaii – both visitors and locals – are drowned, or rescued from drowning; are airlifted to safety from hikes, or else lost forever; suffer heatstroke, or fatigue, or trauma. Two or three times a year there are shark attacks, nearly always on surfers or boogie-boarders. These are salutary indications of how frail human beings really are when confronted by the overwhelming forces of nature, even on a pretty little island. That is how it ought to be. During one week in January this year an average of ten people a day were rescued by the lifeguards on the beach at Waimea Bay. 'The surf was up,' a lifeguard told me, 'and they didn't know about the Waimea Express' – the swift undertow and rip tide that drags swimmers offshore.

The other Oahu is, inevitably, dangerous. That should not be an excuse to avoid it; rather, it ought to be a reason to forearm yourself with more information. I love paddling; nothing is more liberating. Visitors to the island seldom paddle, yet some enterprising companies and outfitters rent boats and give lessons. The best view of the island is from a mile or so at sea: off Honolulu you have a sight of the hotels on Waikiki, and the bungalows on the slopes behind them, the mansions of the ridges, a mist in the deep valleys of Manoa and Pauoa, and above the rainbows the somber ridge of old volcanoes, the black ridges and dark green peaks. From the sea the North Shore is first a narrow beach, and an escarpment of pineapple and sugar cane fields and then an enormous expanse of forest. You can usually depend on sheltered paddling at Waikiki and Ala Moana, because this is leeward Oahu. The surf can be diabolical on the North Shore, yet some days in winter the sea is like a millpond. I set out from Shark's Cove at Pupukea on a January morning, and immediately saw three large green sea turtles. Paddling onward I saw some locals hoisting crab nets from their anchored boat. They told me they had just seen some dolphins, and the day before they had seen two whales. I put into Waimea Bay, where the lifeguard gave me the details of their rescues, and then, keeping outside the surf zone, went on about six miles to Haleiwa, where the channel and harbor are often free of heavy surf. The name Haleiwa means 'Home of the Frigate Bird' and, coincidentally, I saw one of these soaring kite-like creatures high in the sky. That night, star-gazing, I saw a pueo, a Hawaiian owl, which is a subspecies of the short-eared owl.

You have to be lucky to paddle the North Shore in winter, because the conditions that are favored by surfers are hell for kayakers. But if paddling is out of the question, you can hike – up the slope to Puu O Mahuka (Hill of Refuge) Heiau, where, in 1792, three English sailors who had wandered from Vancouver's supply ship *Daedalus* (anchored in Waimea Bay) were captured by Hawaiians and murdered. This *heiau* (shrine) is still regarded as sacred, as having *mana* (mystical power). Offerings of flowers and piled stones and ti-leaves are still left in a solemn propitiatory gesture.

Another good hike begins where the tar road ends at Mokuleia Beach. This is a six-mile round trip, below the high sheer cliffs that descend to Kaena Point, where there is a lighthouse and nearby rockpools and lagoons and the fiercest waves and the most inhospitable shore on the island: two ocean currents meet here. But few people ever come here. Mountain-bikers can round the point and continue down the Waianae coast on the path that was once a railroad bed. Built in 1899 and closed in the 1940s, the track was finally dealt a death blow by a storm in 1988. From December until late March there is always a chance of seeing whales spouting and occasionally broaching, smacking their tails, a few miles from shore. I saw six whales the sunny winter afternoon I hiked to Kaena Point. The dramatic cliffs of the Kaena *pali* rise to well over 2,000 feet. At the foot of them are the native plants – the *ohai*, which is said to grow there and nowhere else; the *naupaka* and *ilima*, treasured by Hawaiians for their mythic or royal associations.

Because of the various localized climates on the island, there are always outdoor options on one part of Oahu, even if other parts are racked by wind or rain. Some of these are more demanding than others. Pupukea Road on the North Shore zigzags to about 800 feet, where it becomes a narrow path, open on weekends to hikers and cyclists (the US military commandeers the path on weekdays). The ironwoods and eucalyptus give way to dense woods and in places koa, one of the world's most beautiful hardwoods. There is abundant bird life in these heights, as well as smaller game – wild pigs and mongooses. On the opposite part of the island is the easy walk to Makapuu lighthouse. A good half-day's hike on the knife-edge ridge above Manoa is only a fifteen-minute drive from Waikiki, to St. Louis Heights and then down Ruth Place to the entrance to Waahila State Park. Local workers – repairmen and delivery people – often take their lunch to this high-altitude park, a pleasant shady spot sweetened by a breeze. A prospective hiker need only follow the arrows. After a few hundred feet the path contracts from a gentle stroll to a teetering hike along several miles of a windy knife edge, fringed by native trees, and one of the best views of Honolulu. Similarly, if the wind and surf are terrible on the North Shore, they will probably be gentle elsewhere. Local paddlers have a specific route off Waikiki, making for the large buoy that lies about a mile from Diamond Head; they race to this marker from Ala Wai Boat Basin in the late afternoon, unseen by tourists – men in kayaks, in outriggers, or paddling surfboards. In a strong wind it is very hard paddling, and there is a strong current that runs just beyond the buoy. The reward of that trip is the sight of the pale shapely lighthouse on an outcrop of rocks just below the leonine cliffs of Diamond Head.

In good weather it is not difficult even for a novice with a little instruction to paddle from Kailua Beach to the islands called the Mokuluas. Small and steep, on the windward side of Oahu, they are both bird sanctuaries, where shearwaters nest on protected ground. The islands are also connected to a reef that extends from just off Kailua Beach, and the snorkeling offers wonderful vistas of fish and coral. If I am in the mood for snorkeling I tie an eight-foot line from my waist to the bow loop of the boat and tow the boat as I snorkel ahead. Another accessible offshore island is Goat Island, near Malaikahana Beach Park, where there is also some good snorkeling and a sense of being away from the crowds. But in general, the snorkeling off Oahu is adequate rather than brilliant: the reefs are either gummed up (as at Hanauma Bay) or hard to get at – too deep, too far offshore, or else broken apart.

Off-road biking is underrated on Oahu, but the touring kind – pedaling along a paved road – is so dangerous (Oahu drivers are oblivious of bike etiquette) that I think cyclists ought realistically to regard themselves as potential organ-donors rather than adventurers.

When I first moved to Oahu I was thrilled by the softness and fragrance of the air, the steepness of the surrounding mountains, the profusion of flowers, the sense that I was suspended between air and water. But I was appalled by the traffic, and by the density of Honolulu. It seemed to me a city of suburbs and bungalows, rather forbidding in its coziness, as though the whole population had closed ranks against the visitors. But this was mostly paranoia on my part. Until recently there was no city, only the town of Honolulu, and it is still a small town, Polynesian in complexion, American in its essence.

Any city where beeping your horn is considered the height of bad manners is worth living in. Still, why not head for the hills, on foot or on a bicycle, or paddle offshore, or find its wilder shores? It is no exaggeration (but it is none the less amazing) to declare that some of the greatest beaches in the Pacific are on Oahu.

In many respects, the best way of visiting Honolulu is to leave it – not simply to understand it from this new vantage point, but to enjoy the sort of life that up to now has mainly been a local secret.

IN MOLOKAI

The forecast for all islands said that the strong Trade Winds would drop, to be replaced by light breezes: perfect weather for paddling out of Molokai's usually dangerous Halawa Bay. Many places on the Hawaiian islands are named Halawa – it means 'curved.' This Halawa was Hawaii's earliest documented settlement and even fifty years ago – before a tsunami hit – there were Hawaiians living in the valley, growing taro. (Taro is a staple food, the roots pounded into pasty poi, and eaten with fish and fruit.)

When I arrived at Halawa with my folding kayak and my camping equipment all I saw were enormous dumping surf and a turbulent white sea with the wind-blown foam flying from the peaks of the waves. The wind was blowing faster than I could paddle and such a rough sea was unsafe on this rocky coast. So I bided my time.

I met a man on Molokai soon after this. He said he had lived there for nineteen years. He had come as a surfer from California. I asked him how the island had changed.

He said, 'It hasn't changed at all.'

In almost two decades? He said no, sir. It seemed to me that I had never been to a place where I had heard such an answer to that question, and so I insisted to him that it must have changed somehow and I asked him for details.

'Oh, a few buildings have gone up.' He equivocated. 'One hotel has been built. Some buildings have fallen down. The agriculture's over. No more pineapples. There's no work here. Many of the people are on welfare. It's poorer than it was. There are fewer people. And not many tourists come here.'

It is true that Molokai attracts few visitors. Of the millions of tourists who come to Hawaii each year, fewer than 100,000 visit Molokai. Although nicknamed 'The Friendly Isle,' Molokai is in Hawaiian terms the poor relation, with a reputation for clannishness, local feuding, and xenophobia. In the distant past it was known as a place of refuge and tradition. Lozenge-shaped, only thirty-eight miles long and ten wide, it is an isolated place. Isolation breeds suspicion, even paranoia. But the positive result of isolation is that traditions are kept, the culture is maintained, and families become extended and interlinked. Molokai, once famous for its sorcerers, is still noted for what Hawaiians call *mana* – spiritual power.

There are about 7,000 people on this island. About 100 of them are lepers, living in the almost inaccessible Kalaupapa peninsula. Molokai has a grim history of being the dumping ground of lepers in the nineteenth century. Father Damien de Veuster came from Belgium to tend them and his effort in organizing the leprosarium of Kalaupapa put Molokai on the map and made Father Damien a candidate for sainthood. Jack London wrote about Kalaupapa, Robert Louis Stevenson, who was briefly resident in Hawaii, also wrote of the island in a famously eloquent defense of Father Damien in his open letter to the odious Reverend Hyde.

On Molokai's north coast, there are sea cliffs that extend from Halawa Valley on the eastern tip of the island to Moomomi Bay in the west. This gothic wall, as soaring and complex as a green cathedral, is the most beautiful I have seen in Oceania. The Na Pali coast of the island of Kauai is praised, so are the high islands of the Marquesas, and the smoldering volcanoes of Vanuatu and the glorious mossy and ferny cones of Tahiti and Moorea. But nothing can compare with this thirty miles of green cliffs – the highest, the most majestic in the entire Pacific.

The question is how to see them.

'Be very careful,' I was told by the resident of nineteen years. 'They call this the Friendly Isle. But don't be fooled. It's not friendly. It was never friendly.'

Yet which island in the world is friendly? By their very nature, islands have a fortress mentality – the configuration of an island landscape is fortress-like; indeed, the high volcanic islands of the Pacific actually look like medieval castles. In order to survive, islanders develop an innate suspicion of outsiders. They have the intuitive skills of seamen, and they need them, for if the volcanic islands of the Pacific appear castellated, then the low coral atolls are like ships, and their inhabitants are like sailors. 'Friendly' is just a tourist-industry sobriquet. In my experience, the friendliest people on Pacific islands are those who have the greatest assurance that you are going to leave soon.

The high winds and heavy seas continued. Even on the South Shore there was an irregular sea of vicious waves all the way to Maui on the east and Lanai on the south. I had planned a solitary trip along the north coast, from Halawa to Kalaupapa, but this was not paddling weather. Kept onshore, I found myself falling into conversations with local people. Some of them frankly and cheerfully warned me that if I camped anywhere near Halawa my gear would be stolen. Another man warned me of the aggression of local boys. It was mostly bad news.

Near Honouliwai Bay on the South Shore I met a young woman named Puna (it means 'Spring,' in the sense of water). She was about twenty, mixed Hawaiian-Portuguese.

She said, 'I could not live anywhere but Molokai. It is lovely, it is quiet. I hate Honolulu.'

'Have you been to the mainland?'

'To New Mexico,' she said, and she laughed. 'People spoke to me in Spanish – they thought I was a Mexican!'

My back-up plan was to camp at Honouliwai Bay. In many ways the strange fate of Molokai is illustrated in this little bay. Once it was the site of taro growing and traditional fishponds. But hardly any taro is grown in the valley now, and the fishing is poor, the fish stocks depleted. The valley stream is clogged in places with a run-off of silt from the hills, which have been overgrazed by cattle or nibbled by wild goats, and worst of all was a sign near where I was going to camp: 'Warning: Leptospirosis Health Hazard – Fresh Water Stream and Mud Possibly Polluted with Bacteria – Swim at Your Own Risk.'

More bad news – leptospirosis (a problem in some European streams) is caused by rat urine. And on the eastern, rocky end of the island there were many fences which had been put up by private ranches. My impression of Molokai so far was an island of restrictions and barriers: warnings and 'No Trespassing' signs and whispered suspicions and fences.

But the ocean is free, is it not? Making an island to the east my objective, I set up my kayak and paddled into the wind. The hump-backed island, called Moku Hooniki, is a bare black cinder cone from Hawaii's period of vulcanism – in effect the birth of the islands. *Written permission must be given before anyone can land on the island*, I had read in my guidebook. It has been designated a sea-bird sanctuary. But I was not planning to land – only to paddle around it.

The ferocity of the wind and waves here made me wary of attempting a North Shore trip. Yet as with all kayaking in the Pacific, I gained a new perspective on the island of Molokai itself. It was one of the emptiest islands I had seen in the Pacific – a place of great scarred bluffs and volcanic ridges which lay below the rugged heights of Molokai's highest peak, Kamakou (4,961 feet). There were ancient ruins that were visible from offshore, old altars and abandoned house platforms made of black boulders and the sacred places they called *heiau*. Enormous rock formations dwarfed the sparse stands of trees, and although there were coconut palms and mangroves at the shore-line, the tiny houses were hidden, giving an impression of being an island without people – rather ghostly and stark, its *mana* almost visible.

I did not make it to the island – the sea was just too rough. After I came ashore I looked for a camping place. I had not sought permission in advance – my idea was to use a secluded stretch of beach, under the palms. But I found nothing but 'Keep Out' signs and angry guard dogs and more fences. The place had been designed to repel any casual visitor. Campers were not wanted, and so I found an inexpensive hotel and stayed there, making forays to Halawa Valley to contemplate the wind and waves.

'It's the wrong time of year,' a surfer named Harry told me. He was watching the waves breaking from the sandy beach at the Halawa's shore. 'This is pretty bad even for surfing – all that wind is awful.'

'Junk waves,' as they are known – because they are bad for surfing – were slapping into the bay; beyond them was a rough sea, torn by the strong north-east wind.

But there were other ways of seeing the lovely sea cliffs of the north coast. If I could not paddle I would hike over the top and down to the leper settlement at Kalaupapa.

More permission was needed – written permission from an official who controlled Kalawao County. Amazing! Here, in one of the emptiest and least-visited islands I had ever seen, it seemed impossible to roam freely. Of course there was a connection. The island did not want casual visitors. They welcomed short-timers, day-trippers, golfers – people who would obey regulations. Since I had come to the Pacific to get away from regulations, this was obviously a problem.

Yet the contradiction interested me. The island's xenophobia and maddening restrictions had kept it underdeveloped. There were no traffic, no stop-lights, no big buildings; an island without elevators. A little paradise, you might say – wonderful, yet a paradise in which you are not really welcome. If people came in large numbers it would cease to be what it is. It is the only Hawaiian island which is less prosperous than it was twenty years ago, where employment and income are on the decline. That would be fine if there was a traditional lifestyle of fishing and agriculture, but that is not the case. Many of those people flying the Hawaiian flag and living in charming huts and sitting under the palm trees are welfare recipients who buy their fish and poi in the supermarket.

Nowhere on the island is this sense of isolation more profound than on the Kalaupapa peninsula, the old leper settlement, where I hoped to paddle. Small planes can land on the airstrip, but the usual way that people visit is on horseback, down a two-and-a-half-mile trail that zigzags from the top of the cliff to sea level. Only organized tours are allowed. Although the beach at the foot of the cliff is spectacular, swimming is not allowed. In the early nineteenth century lepers were dumped here. It was like a prison camp, and noted for death and suffering; an extreme example of Molokai itself, perhaps

– a refuge, a place apart; and so it has remained, isolated and beautiful.

Rejecting the horse-back ride, I secured written permission to hike to the bottom of the cliff. The county official warned me that I was not allowed to camp, not allowed to use the beach, not allowed to enter even the outskirts of the leper settlement. And he closed by saying, 'The hiking trail is very strenuous and steep. If I were you, I would not do it.'

Determined to defy him, I set off early, before the party of horse-back riders entered the trail. The official had not exaggerated: the trail was more difficult than I had imagined, but it was also vastly more beautiful. Though the horses' hooves had worn a deep groove in it, the trail had been carefully secured against erosion by boulders and steps, and so in the cool sparkling morning, with some birds twittering and long-tailed tropic-birds making their harsh cry, and the brilliant green cliffs towering over the furious sea, scored blue and white, like a world of marble, I made the hour-and-a-half descent down the miles of staircase to the foot of the Kukuiohapuu cliffs.

I walked to the edge of the Kalaupapa settlement and peered at it: small, neat houses, a church, a dispensary, many graveyards. It was a tiny village surrounded by gravestones.

A pick-up truck drove toward me, a woman at the wheel. She said, 'Are you looking for the bus?'

She said that I was not allowed to walk around the leper settlement but that a bus was waiting for the horse riders. She offered to take me to it.

'I married a patient,' she said, explaining how it was that such a healthy sixty-year-old happened to be driving a truck around a leper colony on this lovely morning.

'What's it like, living here?'

She laughed out loud. 'It's different!'

That was all she said, but it was enough: the simple word was full of meaning.

The tour was led by Henry Nalaielua. He told us about the history of the place, the effort of Father Damien, of Sister Marianne, of Brother Dutton, who, speaking about good intentions, said significantly, 'It is the same one place as another. One's Molokai can be anywhere.' We saw the original settlement that dated from 1866. The memorials. St. Philomena's Church. The sacred groves of the old Hawaiian villages. In the past, the prevailing mood of Kalaupapa had been

'Abandon all hope, ye who enter here,' and one of the Hawaiian sayings was, 'In Kalaupapa there is no justice.'

Henry said all this with a smile. He was a pleasant man with a kindly manner. He was also a leper. After being diagnosed with leprosy he had been sent from the Hamakua coast of the Big Island to Kalaupapa in 1941, at the age of fifteen. Except for ten years in a leprosarium in Louisiana (the only one in mainland USA), he had spent his whole time here.

'When I came here, it was a place of many deaths. People were dying before I could say my last name. There were three deaths the day I arrived. It was a place of suffering, and the people here had memories of great suffering. I myself have suffered – the nerves in my body so painful that I couldn't sleep. See the graves over there, and there. Thousands of them –'

But beyond the toppling graves, and the memorial to Damien, and the wooden houses of Kalaupapa, were the vertiginous heights of sea cliffs, the rounded fluted folds of their walls, the deep dark-green recesses of the valleys. I stood on aching legs, and sore feet, bewitched by these soaring cliffs, and the mists of the wave-pounded shores.

This forbidden place of lepers and illness and abandonment had become, because of its very isolation, a place of magic, surrounded by outstanding natural beauty. That is probably the way of the world: a place is preserved as wilderness because it is inaccessible – too far, too hidden, maddening to visit, with a rocky coast, buffeted by wild weather. It is also the conundrum of Molokai, beautiful and impossible.

Connected in Palau

As someone who prides himself on traveling light, it seemed odd to be flying across the Pacific, to an uninhabited island in the Republic of Palau, with five bags, seriously overweight.

'What's in these?' the customs inspector demanded at Antonio D. Won Pat airport in Guam, where I was spending the night.

The smallest bag held my clothes (not many – Palau is warm). Another held camping equipment (tent, sleeping bag, lamp, stove, mask, snorkel, fins); several were filled with electronic devices (night-vision goggles, a camcorder, a Newton Message Pad, and so forth). The heaviest bag contained a fifty-pound Navcom Satellite Magna-Phone with its own power supply (a nicad battery slab), and built-in antenna dish – a 'secure uplink,' Steven Seagal called this phone in *Under Siege*, though his was an older, heavier model.

'A satellite telephone, a computer, a CD player –'

Bored by my power-user litany, the customs man interrupted me and asked, 'You got fruit?'

'No fruit.'

'Pass.'

I had with regret left another portable phone, an Alden Satphone, in Honolulu; it was a user-friendly device, very light and affordable, with fax capability, but I had not been able to solve the power supply problem (a car battery as additional hand luggage). And beyond Agana, Guam (specifically Wet Willie's Bar in Tumon Bay, where they were a conversation piece), my pager and my Virtual Vision TV Goggles were no use. Heavily laden, a tech-weenie traveler, I was headed for Koror, the capital of Palau.

There I intended to hire a boat to take me to the small Ngemelis group at the western edge of the reef of the Rock Islands. My chosen island was nameless but when I say that its position was Lat. 7° 07' 25.1" N., Long. 134° 14' 24.7" E it will be obvious that I also had with me a Trimbal Global Positioning System. The idea was that I would set up camp on this desert island and in spite of my remoteness I would be in touch and well connected. 'Hold on, Mrs. Crusoe, your son Robinson is on the line . . .'

Palau, so far away, so pretty, seemed the perfect place to test communications equipment. In the Caroline Islands, in the western Pacific, just north of New Guinea and east of the Philippines, Palau is one of the last great island wildernesses of the world; another constellation of islands in the galaxy known as Micronesia. From Honolulu it is a seven-and-a-half-hour flight westward to Guam, a large ruined island of fast-food outlets and shopping malls and bungaloid subdivisions. And then a two-hour flight south-west to the main island of Babeldaop and the town of Koror, which is the capital of Palau (Belau in its revised spelling).

I arrived and set up camp under the palms of deserted Omekang, one of the many Rock Islands. In the middle of the night, I crawled out of my tent and was uplifted. In my entire life I have never felt a sense of such serenity in the open air. I had the strong impression of the physical world as a peaceful room. Perhaps because it was midnight, and I had just woken up, the specific image that came to me was an enormous bedroom. The night was dead still, and the full moon lighted the beach with a glow that was lovelier for its mild fluorescence. In the mass of bright stars the Southern Cross was distinct. I stood stark naked and marveled at my luck.

There was no wind – not even the slightest movement of air. The temperature was about eighty, or a bit more. There was complete silence: the birds were asleep, the insects were still. The sea was flat – not only no waves, but no sound of water lapping at the shoreline. No flies buzzed. There were – this still amazes me – no mosquitoes.

There are hazards in Palau: sea snakes, stinging jellyfish, venomous cone shells, poisonous lion fish, crown of thorns starfish, stone fish, fire coral, crocodiles (*C. porosus*, the saltwater croc), sea urchins, sharks. There are drunks and bad drivers too. There are harmless but sinister-looking creatures of which fruit bats and spotted eagle rays and huge eels are just three. Yet if certain precautions are observed, it is possible to live more or less unscathed in this archipelago.

But electronic equipment on a tropical island is another story. This stuff was expensive and all of it was on loan. I worried constantly about the dampness, which ranged from Micronesian moisture to torrential downpours; and I kept every item in a plastic bag, many of them in layers of them, fearful of sand penetrating and fouling them. I watched most of *Top Gun* on my Sony camcorder. I kept my MPR Satfind 406 Pocket PLB (emergency rescue device) near to hand. (Essential on a desert island experience, but I did not use it. You switch it on and it emits a signal and they find you.)

Then I began making notes about this on my Newton Message Pad, but as soon as I wrote them down they were turned into gibberish. Or was it? I wrote, 'Paul.' It printed 'tense.' I wrote, 'This trip.' It translated 'the test.' It seemed to be a sort of sibylline oracle which translated scribbles into gnomic utterances. Then the Newton complained of low memory, and hefting it in my hand was like holding an expensive, rather moronic and temperamental paving stone. I stowed it with the Sport Vision Goggles and the pager, and after that kept my diary in a small notebook with a ballpoint pen.

My Palauan friend Benna took me farther west in his boat, to the edge of the Rock Islands, and as this was the typhoon season Michael Gilbeaux, from Athens, Georgia, came along to help me. Michael, twenty-five, runs the Sea Turtle Research and Conservation Program in Palau, which is basically a running battle with turtle poachers. Most of the Rock Islands, several hundred of them, great and small, are themselves turtle-shaped, low and humpy limestone islands. They are the pitted remains of old coral reefs that were thrust out of the sea long ago by the forces of undersea vulcanism.

Covered with pandanus and palms, the Rock Islands are known in the local language as Ellebacheb, which is also a synonym for small uninhabited islands of rocks and trees. They are very green, rounded, all sizes, from small green lumps in the ocean, to long rounded ridges. Their sides are vertical and unclimbable. Some have white sand beaches. Birds nest in their hollows. One of the pleasures of paddling there is being able to listen to the sounds of these birds, the swifts, the finches, the swallows, the Palau fruit dove, the black Nicobar pigeon, the screech of the greater sulphur-crested cockatoo, the white-tailed tropic-bird that swoops and glides and makes a clicking chatter among the heights of the islands and never seems to come to rest. Benna dropped Michael and me with my bags and electronic equipment and some water and a sea kayak on the beach of a tiny island in the Ngemelis cluster. This was at dusk. After we unloaded, one of Benna's crewmen stood in the bow and grunted and threw his arms apart in a gesture of crucifixion.

'Shark!' he called out. 'This big!'

'But sharks only feed at this hour on an incoming tide,' Benna said, to reassure me, 'seldom on an outgoing tide.'

Palau is notorious for sharks. I saw my first shark in the Rock Islands on my first swim, while snorkeling at the edge of a reef called Blue Corner. It was a black-tipped shark cruising along the coral wall about twenty feet below me, intent and preoccupied. It looked wicked and sleek, like a live torpedo, and its unhurried air made it seem more confident and more lethal. We were both swimming in the same direction. I was so alarmed by the shark that I hardly noticed its size. Only later I estimated that it was seven or eight feet long. I changed course, trying not to make much fuss, and swam away from it. And then I saw my second shark. This one was nearer, but similarly uninterested in me. I kept on, making for my kayak and saw my third, fourth and fifth sharks. These were resting, motionless on a flat ledge of coral, close enough for me to see the coarse texture of their skin. At last I was back at the boat.

Later – after the placid sharks, the calm air, the sunshine, the tropical heat, the birds, the fish, the bats – in my happy high-tech camp, on the green island at the edge of the reef, I stood under the moon and heard the intrusive noise of rustling. It was a familiar sound, like a person kicking angrily through dry fallen leaves. This grew to a commotion. I got my flashlight from my tent and turned it in the direction of the sound and saw ten or more rats, fat and black, with glittering eyes and raw pink tails, and twitching whiskers, not at all deterred by my bright light, a whole verminous parade traipsing boldly through a mass of dead palm fronds.

So instead of sleeping on the beach I zipped myself into my tent and reflected that no place is perfect but that Palau certainly came close. The Rock Islands were as near as I have ever been to the Peaceable Kingdom of the natural world, in which there was complete harmony. I'll make my phone calls tomorrow, I thought.

Waking in the night, I played the short-wave radio. This Sony twelve-band receiver was digital, with a scanner, and was technically better than my own knob-twirling radio; but I found the scanner a disadvantage here. I could not see what I was tuning, and the scanner skipped stations that were faint. Turning a knob is a more reliable way to find short-wave stations in the darkness of a tent on a tropical island. Nevertheless, I located the BBC World Service and Voice of America and learned (June 22, 1994, on my Micronesian island, June 21 in the USA) that the dollar had dropped to 99.9 Japanese yen (lowest exchange rate ever), and was weakening against the pound sterling; that a hospital had been shelled in Rwanda; that Haitians fleeing their country had been picked up in the ocean and were being processed; and that O. J. Simpson had just been arrested in connection with the murder of his wife and been denied bail.

Michael Gilbeaux was the cameraman. We made the video, then watched it and, watching it, were warned that the battery was low, almost dead, and that our camcorder watching and filming were at an end.

I called my folks on Cape Cod again. The line was busy again. The satellite phone told me that the battery was weak. On my last roll of the dice, I got through and spoke to my mother long enough to hear that she was well and to say that I was in Palau ('It's south-west of Guam!' I shouted, standing on the beach, feeling absurd). Then, having made contact – phone calls, a video, caught a news program on the radio, discovered that you can perhaps teach a Newton to recognize your handwriting – did exercises; we paddled to Eiul Malk Island and climbed to the center of it, to Jellyfish Lake, and went snorkeling.

There are a number of these marine lakes in the Rock Islands. This one lies in a limestone bowl at the center of the island. Some are connected by caves to the sea, others are sealed. They are strange, with high sides and muddy brackish water and mangroves. We swam through the brackish water where a mass of jellyfish lived and shimmered – millions of them perhaps. There was no question that the Jellyfish Lake was a wonder of nature; in a previous incarnation these jellyfish were poisonous. Here they had evolved into a harmless species, and there was not one, but two – the first (a species of *Mastigias*) like a large soft polyp, orangy-pink, the second (*Aurelia aurita*) white and rounded and delicate, almost lacy, and when it filled to propel itself it resembled a white mobcap or a billowing hanky. They were so thick in the water that they softly crowded me and slid against my face and arms – my whole body. I was suspended in a gelatinous mass so dense I could hardly move my arms.

Palau is famous for its quarter-ton giant clams (*Tridacnid gigas*), but its undersea beauty is in its coral. There are sixty-nine species of hard corals in the Caribbean. There are 400 varieties of hard corals in Palau. In addition there are 200 species of soft corals; the merest glance into Palau's lagoons is a vision of abundance.

Some corals look like flowers, but with more extravagant blossoms than ever seen on land; and under the sea they have the effect of a great embankment or bower, flowers clustered together in glorious profusion. Some corals look like miniature hot air balloons, others like polyps, or grotesque millipedes or spiders. Still more look like the gorgon Medusa. Others like human organs, red and pulsing. These and hundreds more exist in the waters of Palau. I was especially struck by a gray and elongated type of coral which looked like a bundle of bones, the youngest varieties looking like ribs, the oldest like a cluster of femurs, a whole clutch of leg bones. The action of storms, or perhaps anchors thrown casually over the side of dive boats, had broken many of these corals, and I began to think of this particular spot as the boneyard.

Eventually, Benna's boat came and took us to Koror, where I charged the batteries, and then we returned to the Rock Islands. We carried our kayaks on the deck of this power boat, which I thought of as the mother ship. We went to Mkumer, a large, beautifully formed island on the outer reef; on one of its beaches the Micronesian megapode birds lay their eggs and leave, letting the eggs incubate and hatch in the heat generated by rotting palm litter. As a tenacious coconut crab attacked one of my gear bags, Michael photographed it, hoping to get his picture in the Patagonia catalogue.

'I am looking for a deep dark cave,' I said to the boatman.

He said he knew one, a burial cave, where there were bats. It was to be the ultimate test of the night-vision binoculars. We moored alongside and I swam to the rocky shore, holding the binoculars out of the water, keenly aware of their dollar value (2,400) as I carefully backstroked to shore, holding them aloft. And then I climbed to the mouth of the cave and walked into it, looking for sea snakes (none) and bats (many). As for the burials that had taken place here, all old coral has the appearance of shattered human bones. When I removed my binoculars I could not see my hand in front of my face. With them, I was able to walk out, all the while seeing green bats flapping erratically along the green walls in the green air.

One of the most beautiful island clusters in the Rock Islands lies in the south-west, and is called Ngerukewid and often referred to as 'The Seventy Islands.' In fact there are forty-six islands – very green and rounded and close together, and so strangely shaped that paddling among them in the limpid green water is as disorienting as paddling in a maze, among misleading shapes and bays and openings. The foliage is thick and consequently the bird life more various and vibrant: noddies, terns, swallows, kingfishers. A variety of swiftlet that is endangered elsewhere in the Pacific is prospering here.

It was the lowest tide of the year – inches deep in some shoaly places – but we were able to make our way to a cave entrance and paddle as far as an interior corner. We had kayaks here in Ngerukewid. We drew our boats up on a narrow shelf of coral and climbed into the cave, where we found a log platform, a rusted transformer, and an old moldering radio. Without question this was an outpost of World War II, but whether the haunt of a Japanese soldier looking for Americans or vice versa it was impossible to tell. Certainly no one else had left a mark there. It gave the impression of a gravesite, or more properly a burial chamber, another mausoleum of the war.

Scott Davis, who was also a member of the Turtle Project, joined us. He showed me a turtle nest that had been raided by poachers, many of the eggs gobbled on the spot by a Palauan or two who were helping to assure the extinction of the hawksbill turtle in these islands. Turtles may lay eighty to ninety eggs, but only one or two hatchlings survive to maturity.

'Palauans can be strange,' Scott said. 'I was camping with a woman friend on an island and at two in the morning we were awakened by a Palauan. He might have been drunk. He said, "I'm going to fuck your girlfriend and kill you." He had a gun, too, one of those rifles they hunt pigeons and bats with.'

It was to me a terrifying story. How had he calmed the Palauan?

'I said, "Hey, listen, I'm real tired right now. Why don't you come back and kill me tomorrow?"'

Amazingly, this logic had worked.

We snorkeled and fished in the morning, snoozed under trees in the heat of the day, and set off again in mid-afternoon, looking for a camp around five or six o'clock. The coral was only one of the wonders of the Palau depths. The profusion of fish was another – and it was not their numbers, the schools of grouper and tuna and surgeon fish and barracuda; it was also their size. Thirty- and forty-pound groupers were not unusual, and the wrasse were the size of big dark pigs. Seeing some fish jumping beyond the western edge of the reef, we headed out and saw a school of about two dozen dolphins surrounding a school of tuna, which themselves had been feeding on smaller fish; a churning example of the food chain.

* *

We were camped on one of the low islands, where there was a sandy beach and easy access for our kayaks. We had left our mother ship anchored in a pretty bay, and we returned to this bay in our kayaks and made camp, choosing a spot well away from the tidemark. As we made camp, the fruit bats were jostling in the high trees, and taking off, leaving the islands to feed – then they were in the sky, great flights of these fat creatures beating across the channel to find food.

The phone battery was dead again (it had been good for thirty minutes of transmission time), the camcorder battery was flat, too; I had given up on the Newton. The radio was working well, and so were the night-vision binoculars. But almost everything, even the compass with its light, needed batteries. In time almost all this stuff would become useless. I began to think that the next frontier is not more sophisticated communications equipment but a quantum leap in power supplies. It seemed odd for the vitality of such wonderful and subtle electronics to be supplied by such clumsy, feeble batteries.

And so, in a matter of days, as the battery life drained away, my uplink was as useless as the gold and doubloons that Robinson Crusoe ironizes about on his island: 'I smiled to myself at the sight of this money. "O drug!" said I aloud, "what art thou good for? . . . one of those knives is worth all this heap . . ."' Indeed, my little lamp with its stump of candle, my jack-knife, and kayak paddle were of more use to me now than the phone, the camcorder, the radio, the Newton, all dead weight. A single fish-hook was of far greater value than my global positioning device or my pager, and in the fullness of time would have been the difference between life and death in these islands. My high-tech camp went quiet.

It is rare to find silence anywhere in a natural landscape. There is always the wind, at least. The rustle of trees, of grass, the dronc of insects, the squawk of birds, the whistle of bats. By the sea, silence – true silence – is almost unknown. But on my last day here in the Rock Islands there was no lap of water. The air was motionless. I could hear no insects, nor any birds. The fruit bats flew high, beating their wings in absolute silence. It seemed a perfect place: the world as an enormous room.

Tasting the Pacific

My outlook changed radically, and I was inspired to write my novel *Millroy the Magician* one day a few years ago when I happened to be camping on a beach on Kaileuna, one of the smaller of the Trobriand Islands. This delightful place, off the coast of New Guinea, is about as far off the map as it is possible to be. But it is plagued by tropical diseases, which was another reason for my astonishment that day, when I found myself thinking, *Every person in this village has beautiful teeth.*

Most Trobrianders I had seen had terrible teeth, from their habit of chewing the mildly narcotic betel nut, and mixing the nut with lime from a coral reef. This stained their teeth bright red and then destroyed the enamel which resulted in rotten stumps. My villagers with the lovely white teeth were exceptional, and were also unusually energetic and muscular.

Later in the week, we were out diving and spear-fishing from an outrigger canoe, when I discovered the reasons for this good health. A shark nosed toward us as we were harrying some fish, and then another – much larger – shark took an interest. These great pale creatures moved effortlessly through the greeny depths. I surfaced, and after what seemed a long time the rest of the divers hoisted themselves into the canoe. I asked Zechariah, one of the young spear-fishermen, whether he had seen the sharks. Yes, he had seen three sharks.

'I shout at them, "Hoop! Hoop! Hoop!" That scared them away. They are stupid fish.'

Howling underwater is reckoned in coastal New Guinea to be a good method for sending a shark on its way.

'Why didn't you kill it?' I said.

'Because we don't eat sharks,' he said.

It is inconceivable that someone in the Trobriands would kill something that is not eaten afterwards.

'We are Seventh-day Adventists,' he said, and soon after was quoting me the food prohibitions in the Mosaic Law set out in Leviticus 11, specifically regarding fish without scales – shark, tuna, ray.

Also, no smoking, no betel chewing, no pig eating, no manner of fat, and so on, even unto Deuteronomy 14. Religious piety explained the villagers' white teeth, sturdiness, energy and absence of excess body fat. It was not their fault that their life expectancy was less than fifty – severe malaria and bacterial infections were common on the islands, and so was TB and leprosy. Under the circumstances, they were doing well.

Their diet – a sort of Pritikin Diet, enhanced by Holy Scripture – of fish and fresh vegetables, with almost no seasoning, made them excellent physical specimens. Contemplating those villagers, I began imagining a novel in which spiritual regeneration was accompanied by enormous physical vitality, the entire American package derived between the covers of the Bible. And it made me think that so many of our habits are written on our bodies. This is not a new idea – anyone in 1850, reading Dickens's description of Uriah Heep in *David Copperfield*, would instantly have grasped that Heep's pallor and red eyes indicated that he was an ardent onanist. In many cultures (Italy is just one) a man's big nose indicates that he is virile. Sitter's Butt and Drinker's Nose are familiar to most people, but I began to see Druggie's Eyes, Sweet-Eater's Fatigue, Carnivore's Gut, Smoker's Face.

It was a happy accident, this discovery. I needed regeneration – most writers do. In contrast to the life of a Pacific islander, the routine of a writer is extremely unhealthy. All serious writers work long hours, and inevitably feel trapped.

I had gone on that trip through the Pacific because writing a book at home is like imprisonment for the reason I have always been a traveler. I grow sick of being indoors, alone all day, for several years, needing isolation and at the same time hating the hostage-like atmosphere of alienation. I am sure some writers love this monkish inactivity, but a long spell of it drives me nuts. I think it is also physically unhealthy to be incarcerated like this.

That cue from the Trobrianders suggested to me that even a writer who is trapped in his room writing a book ought to be able to find some harmony in his life. My villagers were Seventh-day Adventists, but with the added restrictions of living on a remote island. They had the simplest diet imaginable. In great contrast, I saw that islanders in Samoa and Tonga loved Spam, corned beef, and soft drinks. This careless diet turned them sullen and sleepy and mountainous. The piety of the Trobrianders seemed to explain their good health; the obesity of other islanders seemed like a logical consequence of their wayward Spam-eating junk-gobbling hymn-singing hypocrisy. I visited fifty-one islands and started writing my travel book *The Happy Isles of Oceania*.

In order to understand Pacific islanders' syncretic cosmology – their spiritual salad of beliefs, mixing Christianity and Polynesian animism – I read the Holy Bible. Besides the Seventh-day Adventists clinging to Leviticus (which reads like a tract in defense of endangered species), there were Jehovah's Witnesses, who frequently invoke their horror of eating 'the blood of strangled animals;' the Christian Scientists, inspired by Mrs. Eddy's *Science and Health* urging spiritual self-help; and the Mormons – the most American of any religion, ubiquitous in the Pacific because of its hordes of proselytizers.

I profess no religion and so I read the Bible with an open mind. I discovered what many people know already, that the Good Book is full of food, full of meals, and there are plenty of recipes, some implied, others set out as systematically as in a cookbook. Of course there are the well-known mentions of loaves and fishes, and milk and honey, but obscurer references to apricots and vetches (fitches), herbs, grains, pulses, beans, and various vintages of wine. Daniel cannot work magic unless he reverts to his old diet of lentils (Daniel 1 : 1–21); Ezekiel (4 : 9) provides a precise recipe for nourishing high-fiber bread. Nearly all Bible food is nutritious, bulky, beany, energy-inducing, low in fat and sugar.

I began to dabble in food myself. After all, I was stuck in a room, with only writing to occupy me. And what began as idle dietary speculation became more serious experimentation. At first I regarded my body as my hobby, and then it became my chief preoccupation. If you are home all day it is very easy to turn your house into a laboratory where you are the guinea pig. I had been a casual vegetarian, but Bible reading – and writing my book in seclusion – made me more tenacious. There is a certain amount of meat-eating in the Old Testament – so much roasted lamb that it is hard to read certain prophets and not think continually of mint sauce. Yet hardly anyone is carnivorous in the New Testament. Christ usually arrives at meal time, but the expression 'they sat down to meat' is often merely a Jacobean way of saying, 'they ate.' There is a good example of this in 1 Kings 19 : 8 – the Gideon Bible describes Elijah the Tishbite eating, and uses the word 'meat,' while a better translation in the Revised English Bible gives 'food.'

People in the Bible eat remarkably well. 'Your bowels shall sing like a harp,' Isaiah says, and it is easy to see why. Only one person (Eglon in Judges) is described as being 'a very fat man.' Inevitably biblical people live a very long time. This could be an ancient method of reckoning years; yet, a little arithmetic shows 200 to be a typical life-span. That is not an unreasonable goal. The idea of living a long time becomes increasingly attractive as I grow older. Time matters more to me now. And it has been shrewdly observed that an obsession with longevity is a characteristic of the very rich. The German physician and literary critic A. L. Vischer described the consequences of this phenomenon when discussing Tolstoy's fictional character Ivan Ilych:

Simple uncomplicated souls who do not attach such great importance to their own life are able to accept their fate; life and heart have done their work, time for them to go. By contrast, successful and self-assured people are usually at a complete loss when faced by the reality of a physical collapse.

By the time I had finished *The Happy Isles of Oceania* I had assembled the elements of some key scriptural doctrines related to diet; chapter and verse of the Bible's health-giving verses. I was not a prophet, but wasn't it possible to be a sort of messenger? A novel is a perfect vehicle for such speculation. I began my novel *Millroy the Magician* and I continued to experiment. I baked Ezekiel's bread. I made Jacob's pottage and Daniel's lentils. I ate loaves and fishes. I drank a little wine for my digestion. I comforted myself with apples, with milk and honey; I cooked with bitter herbs. I gave up meat entirely. I wrote all day and late in the afternoon I exercised – used a rowing machine or went paddling in my kayak. I weighed myself morning and evening, and I watched TV, taking special notice of the beefy evangelists who looked as though they might profit from a diet of Ezekiel's bread or lentils. I felt wonderful.

I became convinced that a new sect could be founded in America. It would offer complete salvation, on earth and in the hereafter. It would advocate Bible food – all of it healthy eating; it would promise longevity – biblical life-spans; it would purify, it would be uplifting, and strengthening. This reaction against reading junk and eating junk was not a frivolous speculation. I had the evidence that it actually worked. I had been restored to health. Anyone else could do the same. The proof was a person's physical health, and since this was Bible food, that strength would also be an index of your spiritual health.

That was Millroy's message, and I suppose it helped the writing of my book that I believed it too. Nearly every American novel about an evangelist (*Elmer Gantry* is the classic) is denunciatory in tone and mainly about hypocrisy and scandal. My Millroy is scandalous but he is not a hypocrite. How could he be? Writing this book restored me to health. So Millroy must be right. Eating this holy food was a form of piety, even prayer; and following the Bible diet you would become pure in body and soul, destined for heaven, immensely long-lived, with buns of steel.

Palawan: Up and Down the Creek

I liked the look of Palawan on a map – the sausagy shape of it, the way it linked Indonesia to the Philippines, its great distance, its apparent insignificance, only one town-dot of any size, its fringe of 1,000 scattered islands, some in the Sula Sea, the rest in the South China Sea, and it was nearer to Borneo than its own mainland. All this stirred me: it had just the right profile to be a great place for kayaking.

My ideal in travel is you just show up and head for the bush, because most big cities are snake-pits. In the bush there is always somewhere to pitch your tent.

But I knew nothing about Palawan and even the guidebooks were pretty unhelpful. All my ignorance made me want to travel there and hop those islands. Then, whenever I talked about it, people said, 'Don't go,' because the very mention of the Philippines brings to the narrow mind the images of dog-eaters and cockfights, urban blight and rural poverty; and Mrs Marcos's ridiculous collection of shoes; where the visitor industry consisted mainly of sex tours and money launderers and decaying old white men looking for doe-eyed Filipinas to marry, or else willing catamites in Manila, and of course the furtive visits of European branches of Pédophiles sans Frontières.

The Philippines general election loomed. Campaigning – so I was told – involved high-caliber crossfire, the supporters of one candidate raking the opposition in a bloody enfilade of horrific gunplay. It was a country of ferry disasters and kiddie porn and government thievery on a grand scale. In other respects it was what Ireland had been in the nineteenth century, a producer of menial workers for the world. Name almost any country and there were Filipinos in it, minding its children and mopping its floors. The Philippines was a place that people fled; so why would anyone want to go there?

Some of this was incontestable, yet I remained curious. Palawan looked like what it had obviously once been, a land bridge, and I could just imagine the fauna and flora that had tumbled across it. With three weeks free I wanted to disappear and go paddling my folding kayak somewhere I had never been.

It did not concern me much that in Hawaii toothy comedians made whole careers out of mimicking the Filipino accent and the funny names and the dog-stew business. Oddly enough almost the first person I met in Manila was a man named Booby. 'An Australian said to me that my name means "poolish," but my farents give me this name!'

Booby had a dog recipe. Everyone had one. Just for the record, Dog Stew: 'Don't get a Dalmatian! Too expensive! Find an "*aso kalye*" – street dog – chop him up and morrinate in Seven-Up. If you can't find Seven-Up use Sprite. It takes the smell off. Then drain. Morrinate again in soy sauce and calamansi leemon for one hour. Drain again. Fry the drained *aso* in garlic, onion and pootato. Add tomato sauce and pineapple shunks. Stew for one hour or more. Oh, and before removing it add sheesh and wait until it is meelted. Serve with rum or strong olcohool, and a pockage of crockers.'

But the stereotypes seemed to slip away after Manila and – to skip ahead a bit – I had a wonderful time, I camped on empty islands and went up rivers and saw snakes in trees and had my tent butted by monitor lizards, and in seaside villages everyone complimented me on my tattoos, and I had several proposals of marriage. I teamed up with a man named Acong – Acong was his *palayaw*, or nickname, as Booby was Eduardo's; Filipino friendliness is often expressed in this way, for a nickname makes you approachable.

Acong told me, 'I am a native. I am a Tag Banua. When I was a small child there were only natives here.' He also said, 'There were so many fish in the lagoons that we killed them by standing and shooting arrows.' And: 'The rivers were deep when I was a boy but they started to cut trees and the mud came. And now it is shallow.' And: 'Most of these people you see in Palawan are not natives. They come from Visaya and Luzon.'

He ate dogs, he ate monkeys and monitor lizards, he ate snakes. He loved wild pigs because they tasted so much better than village pigs. He was forty and looked sixty. He knew why. 'My face is old because my life is hard.' Also his wife had run off three years before and left him to look after his four-year-old. He did not call her a perfidious bitch. He just shrugged and said, 'I don't know where she is.' He lived in a coastal village. He lamented the changes in Palawan:

the loggers, the illegal fishers, the loss of trees and fish. 'When I was a small boy,' he would begin. It was only thirty-odd years ago but Palawan was an Eden then, so he said.

I was camped on a little island in the middle of Pagdanan Bay, about six or seven miles out of Port Barton, and met Acong almost every day for a week. We paddled along the coast and up the hot airless rivers, he in his *banca* with the double outrigger and I in my kayak. We looked for beehives and monitor lizards and monkeys and snakes, of which there were many, coiled in tree branches. Every now and then Acong would call out, 'So, what do you think of my place?'

He meant this coast of Palawan, the whole of it.

I said truthfully that it was one of the best places I had ever been.

All that was ahead of me, the pleasure of island-hopping and camping and congratulating myself that I had come.

The shape of Palawan had fascinated the Spaniards too: it was so long and slender they had called it La Paragua, because it was shaped like a rolled umbrella. There are various etymologies of the word Palawan, which is also the name of one of the indigenous peoples. It is pronounced Pah Lawan; in Malay this means 'heroic warrior,' suggesting an obscure mythology. A mountain spine runs down the middle. 'Few paved roads.' That was promising. 'Thinly populated.' Even better. 'Thousands of uninhabited offshore islands.' That was what did it for me. I set off with some hot-weather clothes, camping equipment, snorkeling gear, and my folding kayak.

I happened to be in Hawaii. It is an eleven-hour flight from there to Manila. I stopped for the night in Manila – snake-pit – and flew the next day to Puerto Princesa, capital of Palawan, a town on one long street of pawnshops and grocery stores and sign painters and offices; the town was dusty and full of election posters. The gunplay (twenty-nine voters dead) was in Mindanao. In Palawan as far as I could see an election meant flapping posters and free T-shirts with slogans printed on them.

The prettily named Puerto Princesa was surprisingly tidy. Instead of cars there were motorized tricycles, part-motorbike part-rickshaw; twenty cents a ride. The market was vast and dark and full of dried cuttlefish and wild honey and the cashews which with rice and bananas were one of the island's cash crops. I had arrived on a Friday – men were praying at the mosque and a mixed crowd at the cathedral were listening to a priest holding a bilingual service, reading from John, the miracle of the loaves and fishes. The large youthful congregation looked hungrily hopeful. I walked on and saw a small neglected marker printed, 'A grim reminder of the realities of war.' It went on to say that in December, 1944, just in front of the cathedral, soldiers of the Japanese Imperial Army forced 154 American prisoners of war into a tunnel and poured gasoline on them and set them alight: 143 died, eleven escaped. The survivors' names and home towns were listed on the plaque.

That massacre and much else in Palawan – its dusty simplicity, its empty mountains, its inaccessible villages, and its indigenous creation myths about 'the Weaver of the World' – made it seem a ghostly place. But I had not been there long before I began thinking that there was nowhere else I would rather be, and its air of being haunted only added to my pleasure.

The hauntedness was not merely an aspect of its ambiguous past, its being on the old Spanish and Chinese trade route, the refuge of pirates and wartime cruelty. Because it had been off the map and rich in resources, it was the site of a great deal of plundering. Palawan was famous for its splendid hardwood forests of mahogany, *ipil*, *narra* and *camagong* – prized for furniture. The waters were full of fish, and many pods of dugong, known locally as sea-cows.

In the 1930s, British loggers began clear-cutting the west coast and giving English names to bays and harbors and islands – names which still stand: facing west at Port Barton (a corruption of 'Burton'), almost every island and headland you see has an English name. After the Spanish-American War (1898), American administrators and missionaries settled in Palawan. One of the enduring American legacies is the large rural prison at Iwahig, about twenty miles west of Puerto Princesa. Several buildings, put up in the 1920s, still stand, including an elegant recreation hall. I spent a day there marveling at what enlightened prison management can achieve. Prisoners mix with visitors. I was shown around by Luis, who was serving seven years on a drug-smuggling charge. 'A whole jeepney full!' He introduced me to his fellow inmates, all of them heavily tattooed.

'"To Trust a Woman is Death",' I read on one man's arm. 'You think that's true, Amado?'

'In my life, yes, Joe.'

'Sputnik' was tattooed on Amado's belly. Sputnik was a prison protection mob Amado himself had started twenty-nine years ago, when he was imprisoned for murder.

Iwahig, with its 1,500 inmates (known as 'colonists'), is completely self-sufficient in food; some revenue is earned by inmates making souvenirs – carvings, walking sticks, picture frames, furniture – that are sold in Puerto Princesa. Many of the prisoners are lifers or long-termers – multiple murderers, armed robbers, drug dealers; and some of these, thirty at least, live with their families, their children playing on the parade ground while their inmate fathers work in the fields. The inmates have not lost their sense of humor. When I passed one work gang on my motorcycle, they called out, 'Daddy! Daddy!' and laughed.

After the war swept through Palawan, and the Japanese, and chaos, many more loggers came, most of them illegal, denuding the mountain slopes and driving the indigenous people deeper into the forest. Drought and misery and over-fishing in the rest of the Philippines meant an influx of Filipino migrants. I saw these people up and down the coast and at the edges of many islands. 'Officially these villages do not exist,' a Dutch geographer told me. 'They are not on any census.' They were people from the populous and desperate parts of the Philippines, where marine stocks had been depleted.

'They say, "When the fish are gone we will leave and go where the fish are,"' said Yasmin Arquiza, an eco-journalist and editor in chief of the environmental magazine *Bandillo ng Palawan*. 'They always assume there will be another place to go.'

When times are tough, some hard-pressed villagers pass the hat and people stump up an airfare, and one of the young, strong unmarried girls of the village is chosen to go abroad – to Hong Kong, Japan, Singapore, or wherever there is work – and she will send a large proportion of her salary back to her sponsoring village.

Yasmin herself was from Mindanao. Ed Hagedorn, the mayor of Puerto Princesa, who was just about to be reelected for his third three-year term, was born in Paranaque in Luzon. The people with status, or power or money in Palawan all seemed to come from somewhere else. For her investigative journalism, Yasmin had been the object of the mayor's scorn, and he had attacked her in an open letter to the local newspaper. This mayor was a self-confessed crook and was known to have boasted of his shady past; so I sought him out while he was campaigning.

'Do you know Fernando Poe?' he asked me.

'In West Africa?' I said, thinking he said Fernando Poo. 'Never been there.'

'Fernando Poe the actor,' the mayor said. 'He starred in my life story a couple of years ago.'

This movie, *Hagedorn*, dramatized the colorful life of the reformed gun-toting gambling lord. Poe is the Bruce Willis of Filipino cinema, though physically unlike Mr. Hagedorn, a small, solid man with a chattering laugh, whose head seemed much too large for his body. He talked fast in the growly voice of a chain-smoker.

'I was a bad boy,' he laughed. 'I was a mother's worst fear. I grew up with guns. I hadn't even reformed when I got married!'

He admitted to gunplay and gambling and confrontations with the military – 'Because they crossed my path. Some people died. I never ran away from trouble – but I changed!' He said he had never been involved in illegal logging, or illegal fishing, or the slaughter of sea-cows; but he knew a great deal about these activities. Anyway he had a conversion (the high point of the biopic) and the story was that he used his criminally acquired fortune as the controller of an island-wide lotto game called *jueding* to finance his mayoral campaign. He was the classic example of a poacher who had become a game-keeper. He was as voluble describing his love of guns as he was in telling me of his new career as a greenie.

'When I took over as mayor there was no law or order,' he told me. 'Palawan was a microcosm of the Philippines – economic grief and environmental grief. Illegal logging, gambling, fishing, squatting.'

Sea-cows were being killed for their oil and their meat, the forests were being chainsawed into oblivion, and the fish were vanishing from the coastal waters. Villages of migrants were appearing all over Palawan.

In his telling, it was Mayor Hagedorn who single-handedly turned this situation around. With his violent past in mind he said, 'I was not afraid to tackle it. Take the illegal fishermen. We had 2,000 apprehensions in the first year alone.' Others have a different story to tell and say that Hagedorn is reaping the credit for many people's efforts, including the charismatic Governor Socrates (who has also just been reelected); but the fact is that a place that was going to eco-hell had begun to improve.

You hear the word 'illegal fishing' and you think of nets with small interstices; or the snatching of protected species; or the encroachment on preserves. You don't think of cyanide or dynamite or ship-loads of abused boys living in an atmosphere of semi-slavery, hundreds of them, spending every waking hour in the water, smashing the Palawan coral reefs with scrap metal attached to rubber tubes and heavy poles to drive fish into nets. This fish-collection technique is called *muro-ami*, a Japanese word. Ms. Arquiza's magazine reported cases of *muro-ami* fishing, where the divers (ranging in age from twelve to seventeen) escaped – not because of the brutal method of fishing but because they were physically assaulted by the captain of the vessel.

Then there is the poison. Diners-out in Hong Kong enjoy choosing their main course by pointing out a fat fish gliding through a restaurant aquarium. Until the recent ban on the export of live fish, most of these creatures came from the Philippines. But catching fish alive requires a dubious technique involving cyanide. The fishermen squirt the cyanide mixture on the coral reef. The dazed fish float to the surface and are scooped up, revived, and shipped out in barrels, still gasping. Meanwhile, the cyanide soaks into the reef and kills it.

Another fishing method is the use of air-freshener and so-called urinal candy. This toxic stuff is dumped into creeks all over the Philippines to knock fish unconscious. Then the immobilized fish are gathered.

Dynamite has also been popular in driving fishing to the surface. I saw the crime scene. For a chance to paddle my boat and go camping while I was in Puerto Princesa I took a rickshaw piled high with my equipment about ten miles north to Lourdes Pier, the boat dock at Honda Bay, and there I found a boatman who took me to Pandan Island, where there is a tiny village. I stayed for a few days in my tent, set up my boat, and went snorkeling there and off several other bay islands. And every reef showed signs of serious wreckage – massive collapsed coral walls, the litter of broken antlers and blasted-open brain coral. A broken reef has the look of a boneyard. Some chunks had been smashed by dynamite and other coral shelves had been killed with poison.

The 'Baywatch' program had been set up by Mayor Hagedorn for monitoring illegal fishing. One of the sentry posts was on Honda Bay's Snake Island, but with so many miles of unpoliced coast, it was impossible to eliminate the use of dynamite or sticks or poison entirely.

'Palawan is underdeveloped – ironically, that's why it's so nice,' Yasmin Arquiza told me. One of Yasmin's fears was that Palawan would, as she put it, 'become a playground for the rich.' Part of it already has, with the Amanpulo Resort – one of these trophy hotels that is half obscenity, half joke – on Pamalican Island, one of the northern outlying islands. The 1,200 dollars a night is more than most Filipinos earn in a year and the clientele are the usual assortment of timid millionaires. An oversized and unpromising resort is being built on the Honda Bay island of Arrecife. I went there in an outrigger pump boat, bluffed my way through security by calling myself 'Dr. Theroux,' and made notes on the ridiculous overdevelopment. Tourism is not the answer to Palawan's problems, yet it has an upside: it was partly to attract tourism that the Palawan politicians became environmentally minded. And their efforts have resulted in various well-deserved awards from the UN, which the mayor fondly listed for me.

Mayor Hagedorn took credit for the logging ban, and so did Cory Aquino. It is almost unimaginable that a country with old-growth forests and a small manufacturing base and limited resources would agree to stop logging for the sake of the environment. This is something that far more prosperous – and forested – countries (the United States, Canada, Brazil, the Congo) would not even consider. China is just now eliminating its last forests in the north-east province of Heilungjiang. To people who say, 'But they are planting trees too,' my reply is, 'Yes, and creating a monoculture!'

Actually, it was a far-sighted senator named Orlando Mercado who inserted the logging-ban clause for Palawan in the Philippines Strategic Economic Plan that was passed in 1992. Three major timber concessions were given a year to wrap up their business. The largest one was not far from Acong's village, at the town of San Vicente, north of Port Barton. The silted-up estuaries remain but the essential habitat has been preserved, and it is possible to see monkeys and pigs and the bearcats and the Palawan pheasant and the many birds – the red-headed tree babbler, the white-throated bulbul, the shama, the fly-catchers – among the tall trees.

My route from Puerto Princesa had taken me through the mountain passes of Palawan's mountain range – it is continuous for 270 miles along the spine of the island – to the little harbor of Sabang. This is not the most direct way from one side of the island to the other, but because boats are available at Sabang it is the best way to Port Barton, or almost anywhere on the western coast. The roads on Palawan range from bumpy to execrable, but there are boatmen at most of the coastal settlements who make regular runs from one little harbor to another. I chose the west coast over the touristy northern port of El Nido, or the pirate-ridden southern islands.

Sabang is well known as the point of departure for the nearby cave system called the Underground River. Some people visit Palawan specifically to travel a mile or so into this five-mile-deep cave system in a paddle boat. I was not allowed to take my kayak in, so I went in one of the outriggers. Pitch black, damp, and dripping, it is inhabited by tens of thousands of tiny bats, and you travel in the gurgling boat by the glow of a twenty-watt flashlight, among the orangy stalacmites in a stink of bat shit through the echoey chambers. These caves lie beneath one of Palawan's most beautiful mountains, St. Paul's Mount; this strangely rounded mass, like a fertility goddess tipped onto her back, is visible eighty miles away, on the other side of the island. Some of the ceilings in the cave system are hundreds of feet high, others scrape your head as you squeeze past.

An elderly Australian sat just behind me in the boat. He was wife-hunting in the Philippines. He had found a likely prospect in Mindanao, twenty-something, a nurse, eager to get married.

'She's not really a Filipina,' he said in the darkness, as though reassuring himself. 'She's more a sort of Spanish, and a little Chinese. See, she's almost white.'

After one night in Sabang, and another night a few miles away at a friendly place called Panaguman, I took an outrigger about thirty miles up the coast to Port Barton. The settlement at Port Barton is small, but there are half a dozen inexpensive places to stay and some grocery stores for provisions. Pagdanan Bay is large enough to contain twenty islands and islets, and to the north-west one of them – Boayan – is huge, with a number of empty beaches to camp on. Many of the islands are deserted, some are privately owned ('No Trespassing'), and others have been settled by migrants from other parts of the Philippines.

One of the advantages of camping in the hot season in Palawan – it was April, it had not rained since December – was that mosquitoes were almost non-existent except up the rivers. But the heat was terrific – in the high nineties most days, in the high eighties at night. I estimated that I needed four or more litres of water on paddling days and as no fresh water was available on the empty islands I had to go ashore or return to Port Barton every few days for water.

In the yellow-pink of the tropical dawn the still air was thick with gnats and the mirror of the sea showed a flawless reflection of the deep green mainland and the high outer islands and the rocky islets that had no names. There was hardly any wind until mid-morning and I paddled on a sea so smooth and air so silent that the only sound was the chuckle of the bow wave and the rattle of the passing kingfishers. In my first week the winds were predictable, freshening through the morning and blowing hard in the afternoon, usually offshore. By mid-afternoon I was supine in the shade of a palm grove, reading *Eminent Victorians*, about the death of General Gordon, and studying the chart for tomorrow's destination.

The shock of my second week of paddling was the sight of ink-black clouds looming in the north-west, the first of the monsoon – this was early May. There was a spatter of wind-blown rain and a very stiff wind from unexpected directions. One day it veered from west to east; another day I was caught in it and had to surf my kayak through three- and four-foot waves to the nearest island. When I didn't see any fishermen I took it as a sign to stay ashore.

The sun was the strongest I have ever known over a sea, invariably burning down from a clear sky, dazzling on the water and shriveling every leaf in sight; like a weight on my head and shoulders, it made me calculate my island crossings in liters per mile. Anyone who is not careful in such circumstances risks dehydration.

The reward for thrashing my kayak through the water on these hot clear days was the sight of a green sea turtle craning its neck or the flight of a dozen flying fish strafing my bow. Now and then I would see the swift shadow of a ray flashing through the water, startling the fish.

One day I paddled about ten miles south-west to a headland and then caught sight of an island that had been hidden from where I had been camping. I paddled out three or four miles to this hump of rock and found a sandy beach and some huts. A Germanic-looking man in a green bathing suit stood on the beach to welcome me. He said 'Hi' and grabbed my bow line and helped pull my boat to shore.

'Nice kayak,' he said. It was salt-smeared and wet from the long haul from the headland. 'Isn't that the kind of boat Paul Theroux paddled in his travels around the Pacific?'

Being cautious, I said, 'You read that book?'

'Oh, yeah. Great book.'

This happens now and then – more often in a remote place like Palawan than in places closer to home.

'I wrote it.'

'Cut the shit.'

Pretty soon we were sitting under a palm tree, swapping traveler's tales. He was Charlie Kregle, who had left a good job in Chicago three years before to ramble around the world. In that three years, such was the state of the stock market that even when he was traveling third class on an Indonesian ferry or an overcrowded jeepney in Mindanao, he had been earning steadily.

Like many independent travelers I had met, his stories were vastly more colorful and complex than most stories I had read. He had traveled in Brazil and South East Asia. He had crossed Africa, walking a large part of the way. His life had been on the line many times, and he had experienced the worst of travel, which is not danger but delay, weeks of it, the sort of extreme inconvenience the solo traveler endures in remote places. I liked his judgments on places, epitomized by his summary of Equatorial Guinea: 'Great place. Anarchic, though. Not ready for prime time.' He traveled on a shoe-string and from time to time, when he was in a place that sold newspapers, he checked the stock market quotes and saw that he was worth much more than the last time he had looked.

He laughed when I told him I knew nothing about the stock market and had no investments.

'What about your 401-Ks?'

'Nothing.'

'Why?' he said. 'Are you planning to die soon?'

This investment sarcasm seemed odd coming from a young man in a bathing suit who was living in a hut on a small island off Palawan, whose entire earthly goods fitted into a modest-sized rucksack. A little while later I asked him to tell me the most amazing thing that had happened to him in the Philippines and he looked at me and my boat and said, 'This!'

Around mid-afternoon I paddled back to my camp, but an offshore wind had sprung up and the journey took me almost four hours. Next morning, I saw a woman holding a yellow umbrella seated in a canoe being paddled by three men. The canoe glided onto what I thought of as my beach, and the woman got out, her umbrella upright, and she walked in a stately way down the beach. That was how I discovered that I shared this island with a small hidden village.

Later that day, looking for a new island, I ran across Acong. He was fishing on the reef, and with his shirt wrapped and folded neatly around his head against the heat he looked like an Egyptian sitting cross-legged in his canoe. He had learned English at school but had dropped out 'in elementary.' His boat was too small to use for taking people out to the islands. He used it for fishing and for transporting the rattan and coconuts he collected to use as currency.

'Those people are from Visaya,' he said of the village at the far end of the little island on which I had been camped.

He said it with a trace of bitterness, because it is non-regulated immigration. Many people in Palawan told me that such squatting was the cause of many land disputes. Yasmin Arquiza had said, 'Tribal people here had no homestead patents.' To protect them, the Philippine government instituted a 'Certificate of Ancestral Domain Claim.' This was not a land title but it gave them priority when the government handed out concessions for rattan and *almasiga*, a resin (sometimes called 'copal') used in varnish. The indigenous people had rights to the concession and could profit from it.

I told Acong that I was looking for a new camp site on an empty island. He suggested one that turned out to be perfect – a hidden cove, a sandy beach, a coral reef that had not been dynamited or poisoned. Acong's outrigger was small enough to negotiate shallow water and silted-up rivers and the remote parts of the great bay where there were jutting coral heads. I followed him to these places in my kayak. The largest river that emptied into the bay is the Darapiton. We traveled up to a narrow tributary, the Togdunan. The rivers were muddy, narrow, humid, buggy, and the deeper we went the more shadowy they became, overhung with a tunnel of boughs. The inconvenience of such branches is minor, but coiled on many of these branches were snakes, the thick yellow and black five-footers Acong called *binturan*; and strung across other branches there were spider's webs with hairy deep-green claw-shaped spiders clinging at the edge, at the level of my face.

'The snakes will not trouble you if you do not trouble them,' Acong said.

After a few miles on the tributary we came to an obstruction – a tree lying across the river. Acong was surprised and worried: it was not the custom for the people here to block the rivers. It was well known that the Tag Banua and the Palawan and Batak peoples had no traditional concept of land ownership. So this barrier was a grotesque novelty which had been brought about by all the encroachment and the new settlers.

'We could slide our boats over the log,' I said. But I was just needling him, to see what he would say.

'No. We stop here.'

Even though these people were of his own language group, he felt it was a bad idea to go farther. We might be misunderstood.

The Tag Banua were not territorial in any modern sense. Like many indigenous people they did not buy or sell land, because they could not separate themselves from the land: it would be perverse to sell it, something like an amputation.

On the way back he told me about the loggers, and how ships from Japan had been moored for years just offshore to pick up the big *apitung* logs, and how the logging coincided with the mud slides, and the rivers and river mouths were not deep any more.

The word 'Banua' interested me, because it seemed so similar to the Fijian word *'vanua'* or land (as in Vanua Levu, the name of the second-largest island). Acong said that *'banua'* meant land, and Tag Banua, People of the Land. I had made it a habit to compile word lists whenever I was in a remote place in Oceania, to assess the linguistic relationships among islanders who had dispersed the Austronesian language over thousands of nautical miles and thousands of years. There are a basic fifty words that are useful to compare. Wallace lists many of them in an appendix to *The Malay Archipelago*. I asked Acong the words for various numbers and for big, small, dog, fish, eye, canoe, house, day, sun, moon, water, and so forth; and I discovered that many Tag Banua words were cognate with ones from the Celebes, and others were straight from Malay – *ikan*, for fish, and *lima* for five, and *mata* for eye (as in Mata Hari – 'Eye of the Day'). *Mata* in Hawaiian is *maka*. Captain Cook, also a compiler of Polynesian word lists, was the first person to observe that Oceania is one world linguistically.

Some days, when it was too hot to go paddling – the tropical *aldow* dazzled in a cloudless sky – there was little else to do except sit under a palm tree and interrogate Acong, and his extended family. These people were settled, but some Tag Banua in the north were nomadic.

The other indigenous people of Palawan lived in the interior – the Batak, who are related to Negritos, on the slopes of the central mountain chain, the Pa'lawan people farther south. One guidebook reports, 'The Tau't Batu in the south of Palawan were only discovered in 1978.' This story of the Stone People (*batu* for stone is another Malay cognate) is not quite true. These people keep to themselves and use blow-guns and poison darts for hunting, and live in a bowl-shaped valley on the slopes of Palawan's highest peak, Mount Mantalingahan (10,075 feet), and move nearer the coast in the dry season. But this recent First Contact was one of several hoaxes perpetrated by a minister in the Marcos regime, one 'Manda' Elizalde, who tried to gain international prominence by pretending to discover hidden ('Stone Age') peoples in the Philippine hinterland. The Tasaday People near Lake Sebu in south Mindanao were another of his preposterous discoveries. This can be put down to a Filipino variation of Munchausen's Syndrome – attention-seeking by the retailing of tall stories.

Many indigenous people in Palawan none the less still subsist using traditional means – hunting wild pigs with spears and blow-guns, feasting on monkeys and snaring fish in lovely woven traps. And they lament the day that Palawan's resources began to be stripped away by non-Palawans, its fish to the Japanese factory ships and the canneries and the Hong Kong restaurant aquariums, its trees turned into chairs and chopsticks.

Palawan had been on the brink of devastation. Its fall had been arrested. Much of the island was still wild – I prayed that it would remain so. In the course of ten days' paddling I made a circuit of a dozen Pagdanan islands and camped on three of them, island-hopping north-west to the largest island, Boayan. On my return, one very hot night, on the uninhabited Double Island, I found myself lying in my mosquito-net tent, the moon bathing the island and the tree-tops in a lunar fluorescence. There was no wind. I had achieved the ultimate in fresh-air fiendishness. I was flat on my back. Fulfilled, content, stark naked, alone, happy, I thought, *I am a monkey.*

Christmas Island: Bombs and Birds

Ambo Keebwa, an I-Kiribati, was twenty-two and living in Tarawa in 1957 when he heard that able-bodied men were needed to work for the British on Christmas Island. The place-name transfixed him. 'I like "Christmas" so much! I think, "There must be many nice things there."' Imagining the bounty of a year-round, non-stop Yuletide, Ambo signed a three-year contract and traveled hopefully to this magic-sounding place, 2,013 miles away. A few months after he arrived on the arid, empty, coral-crunchy shore, the British exploded an H-bomb over the island and shattered Ambo's eardrums. After that he just worried and cowered under the coconut trees and prayed for deliverance.

On that early morning, this, the largest atoll in the Pacific, trembled like a meringue, the earth and sea quaked, and millions of seabirds, the feathered glory of Christmas Island, were instantly blinded and scorched. The birds flopped and screamed piteously, and the whole lot of them starved to death under the horrified eyes of the several hundred islanders and the thousands of British soldiers. When a second bomb was announced, Ambo and his fellow islanders begged to be sent back to Tarawa.

'We put a complaint to the big man. We wanted to go home. We were afraid. We were praying to God to help us be safe. The Air Vice-Marshal said, "We will look after you. Don't be afraid."'

The night before the second H-Bomb the Kiribati (pronounced 'Kiribass') men were taken to a ship that was anchored offshore and shown cowboy movies, cartoons and British films, one after the other, from seven in the evening until four-thirty the next morning, when suddenly the same searing ear-pain returned ('much worse than when you are in an airplane'), and the ship shuddered so violently that rust flaked from the ceiling and walls of the cramped cabin in which the 140 islanders sat goggling at the cowboy movies. The men went up on deck and saw again the aftermath of the thermonuclear explosion.

'Like a big flower opening,' Ambo thought, 'the color of clouds, with flames inside.'

Millions more birds died. Parts of the island were closed. But it was nowhere near the end. In the succeeding four years, there were thirty-two additional explosions, the latter series co-sponsored by the USA. Some of the bombs were the most powerful ever detonated on the planet – up to twenty-five megatons: quite a lot for a coral atoll sitting at sea level. By then the authorities had become so blasé they simply handed out blankets to the Christmas Islanders and told them to gather at the tennis courts in town and sit under these blankets.

'They said, "Turn away from the blast,"' a man named Tonga Fou told me. 'But even so, we saw the light through the blanket and got the pain in our ears and felt the heat on our back.'

I asked each man, 'What would you say if someone came today and said they wanted to test a bomb?'

'Now I would say, "No! Get off!"' Tonga said.

Ambo agreed.

'Did anyone die from the effects of the blast?'

Tonga said, 'No one examined us. People died. We don't know why. No doctors have ever looked at our bodies.'

A few years after the tests, Henry Kissinger said, regarding radioactivity and Pacific islanders, 'There are only 90,000 people out there. Who gives a damn?'

Merry Christmas, suckers!

I had stopped by Tabakea Village to see Ambo and Tonga on one of my paddling trips through the lagoon. Tabakea was halfway to London, the settlement where most of the island's roughly 3,500 people live. The other villages of any size were Banana and Poland. Paris, across the channel from London, was just a ruin. Most of these places were named by a whimsical French priest who started a 600,000-coconut-tree plantation. The priest was Father Rougier, the first entrepreneur, a wily French clergyman who abandoned preaching in favor of being Coconut King. He lived in Paris, on the south-west horn of the atoll. He earned a reputation as a slave-driver, Mistah Kurtz in a dog collar. His workers were mainly Chinese and Tahitian. Having made a fortune on the copra, Rougier retired to Tahiti, another colorful rascal in paradise.

By the late 1930s the island, part of the Gilbert and Ellice group, was again run by a British trading company, and after the war reverted to being a copra plantation. Christmas had been occasionally visited by whalers and castaways and perhaps in an earlier epoch by Polynesian voyagers who had been driven off-course. To the ancient Kiribati it was known as Abakiroro, 'Distant Land.' But it had never qualified as an inhabited island, and until the early twentieth century the island was as barren and unpopulated as it had been around Christmas, 1777, when Captain Cook first anchored near the lagoon entrance and named it. It became Kiribati, a corruption of Gilberts, when Britain granted independence in 1972. It is still not much more than a copra plantation, run by the Kiribati government, though the National Space Development Agency of Japan has just been given permission to develop a 'spaceport' (missile recovery station, hotel, communications, landing strip) on the southerly portion. No one on the island has any idea when this will happen, or whether it will happen at all.

I had taken the once-a-week three-hour flight from Honolulu – Christmas is Hawaii's nearest neighbor of any size. After I got my bearings, I headed for the empty interior. I camped alone at the eastern side of the lagoon, among the low salt bush. This shrub, a feebler cousin of the mangrove, covers the island but offers no shade. Neither is there much fresh water either – persistent droughts are one of the reasons the island remained uninhabited for so long.

Perhaps it should have remained uninhabited. It is a dazzling place, an arid Eden that even H-bombs could not destroy, a giant bracelet of coral, dappled with the hardiest shrubs and a million coconut trees; a lagoon that is not only shaped like a palette, but a palette splashed with every shade of green and blue; and the most fearless and friendly birds I have ever seen. Much of the island is still empty – just screeching terns and the wind in the salt bush. But the heresy that occurred to me again and again is that it is hard for such a place, blessed with birds and fish and balmy air, to be shared with humans. There are areas in the world that are perfect for their peculiar fauna and flora, but because of their remoteness or hermetic ecosystem are unsuited to our intrusions, to people and their pussycats, their bad habits, and their toilets.

In the island's interior, the sameness of the salt bush and absence of palm-groves, or any landmarks, makes it easy for a traveler to become disoriented. I got seriously lost twice and found that on the idlest jaunt away from my tent I was constantly using my compass. Two of Captain Cook's men lost their bearings the moment they stepped ashore. They groped for twenty-four hours, and survived only by drinking a turtle's blood. Many of the islanders I spoke to had a personal experience of befuddlement. I had been proud of my sense of direction until I began wandering around the maze-like shores and inner lagoons of Christmas Island. Even temporary disorientation acquainted me with a suffocating breathlessness; the bone in the throat, a rising sense of panic; the wavering compass needle. All the while curious birds squawked overhead – boobies, frigate birds, tropic-birds, terns in their thousands. Absolutely unafraid, many of them flew near my head and nipped at my paddle blade when I raised it.

My camp was near a sanctuary for red-tailed tropic-birds, on the water. I had to tie my tent down with guy lines, and in paddling I always seemed to be fighting the wind, even in the recesses of the inner ponds. But it was impossible to peregrinate the lagoon and not feel haunted by the nuclear events. One of the bombs was detonated by mistake at a lower level than planned, and it flattened the whole south-east end of the island: the damage is still obvious.

Being old-timers, Ambo and Tonga were among the few people on the island who lived on their own land, in the village of Tabakea (Tabwakeaua), on the narrow edge of the north part of the island between the lagoon and the sea. The rest of the island is owned by the Kiribati government and is run as a coconut plantation, though a heavily subsidized one, because the copra price is so low. Apart from picking coconuts and fishing, there is little else on the island to keep the 3,500 inhabitants busy. Farming is limited to a handful of breadfruit trees and some bananas, but there is no soil to speak of, and even the greenest thumb would not produce much in the crushed coral.

'Anyway, they are not cultivators,' the local priest, Father Gratien Bermond, told me.

A native of an alpine village in Haute Savoie, he had lived in Kiribati for thirty-seven years. Father Bermond was fluent in the language and knowledgeable about the myths and customs. He encouraged traditional dancing and drumming and singing in his church meeting hall.

'They are people of the sea.'

It's true. They are good fishermen and canoe builders, and as for down-time, many engage in traditional Kiribati dancing and singing, while others like nothing better than firing up the VCR, cracking open a beer, ripping the lid off a can of Ox and Palm Prime Luncheon Beef and watching American videos until they are too drunk to see straight. Drunkenness is a serious problem – everyone says so. Littering seems habitual. Where there are no people, there are masses of birds and wind-scoured beauty and wind-driven waves lashing the emptiest beaches imaginable. But the settlements and villages and picnic spots are sensationally littered with beer cans, and the Spam and corned beef cans that pose a particular hazard to the unshod foot. To be fair, the blight of these cans is small compared to the reckless detonation of the British and American nuclear devices; and as for trash piles, few junk heaps can compare to the vehicle graveyards that the military left behind. There are whole five-acre motor pools decaying in the coconut groves. In the remotest recesses of the atoll are collapsed drums and rusty paraphernalia, dating from the tests, mercifully decomposing into dust.

Some of the islanders are expert fishing guides, eagerly showing up at the airport for the weekly flight from Honolulu, to scope-out clients. In the last fifteen years, Christmas Island has been justifiably regarded as possessing the greatest opportunities for bonefishing in the world. Much has been written in praise of the quality of the fishing in the lagoon flats – not only bonefish, but milkfish, goatfish, and trevally. World records are set on Christmas Island and there is hardly a wall at the Captain Cook Hotel, one of the island's two hotels, which does not exhibit a photograph of an 'i-matang' – stranger – pop-eyed under the weight of a pot-bellied, scaly, slack-jawed trophy: the mirror-image of its captor. No, I am not a fisherman.

I had gone to Christmas Island to find some solitude, go bird-watching, and paddle my kayak. The wildlife warden in London sold me a five-dollar permit to enter a closed area – where visits are regulated because of the many nesting birds. He said I could camp for a night. I was intentionally vague about the number of days I would be out, and he was much more worried about the bird poachers. He was a scowling man named Utimawa who, like so many others on the island, had come to Christmas in the 1980s from distant Tarawa. Compared to overcrowded and unsanitary and drought-stricken Tarawa – with one of the highest population densities in the world – this was heaven. Here, you just reached out and there was food. The trouble was, the reaching out was regarded as poaching.

Bird catching was easy, because the birds were so numerous and so innocent. (Utimawa: 'You will not need binoculars.') It was a serious problem, Utimawa said. 'We have one or two incidents a week. We find corpses of tropic-birds and boobies. They also get the eggs – they eat them on the spot or take them home.'

I asked him why and he delivered what I consider to be the epitaph for many endangered species. 'Because they taste good.'

A red-tailed tropic-bird was plump enough to feed two people. The decorous tail was also prized by the islanders. And they breed only once a year.

Some islanders were caught and fined 200 dollars for poaching, but poaching was still said to be brisk. It was a hungry island. A can of corned beef or Spam was expensive. Never mind that world-class sashimi, or the choicest cuts of tuna were easily available to any of the fishermen. Boobies were tastier. 'All you do is put a red rag on a stick,' an islander told me. 'Boobies are attracted to the color. You wave the stick and when the booby swoops down you whack it.'

Ambo said, 'When we first arrived on the island, we ate the birds all the time. I like the *tei-tei* – frigate bird. It's very easy to catch. Offer it fish with your left hand, and when it comes down to take it, you grab the bird's neck with your right hand and twist it.'

Many terns nested on the ground. Their eggs were snatched. Tropic-bird chicks huddling in the brush under the salt scrub were just plucked, and their necks wrung.

'I like crabs,' a man named Tabai said. 'No – don't need a trap. Just pick them up with your hand.'

That was the trouble with the Peaceable Kingdom, all these serene creatures were there for the picking; the island was full of sitting ducks.

I asked Ambo, 'Why does the government stop you eating the birds?'

He said, 'Because people come from overseas and want to see the birds. *I-matang* like birds.'

This word was interesting. *I-matang* was generally used to mean foreigner (there are four such people on Christmas Island), but etymologically it was 'The Person from Matang.' In his celebrated book about old days in the Gilberts, *A Pattern of Islands*, Arthur Grimble explained that Matang was the ancestral home of the I-Kiribati, the original fatherland, a place of fair-skinned people, so the word implied kinship. And by the way, it is an actual place, Madang, on the northern coast of New Guinea, conjectured by historians to be the origin of these Micronesian people.

Terns strafed my camp; boobies followed me when I was paddling – sometimes large numbers of them, thirty or forty big brown birds, always shadowed by the larger frigate birds, which seemed, in spite of their thieving ways, angelic guardians. The sky was always filled with birds; and ghost crabs scuttled and crunched across the smithereens of infertile whitish-gray coral that passed for earth; and large fish were constantly thrashing the shallow lagoon – I could see them: bonefish and milkfish; and yard-long black-tipped sharks, moving like torpedoes.

I could not remember ever having camped in a place so blindingly bright, where there was so little shade. In the heat of the day I crouched under my flapping tent fly and read Celine – *Journey to the End of the Night*, in which the main character, Bardamu, in Africa speaks of a man with 'ten thousand kilos of sunshine on his head,' or again, 'If you don't want the sun to burn your brains through your eyes, you have to blink like a rat.'

Those descriptions resonated at the back of Christmas Island's lagoon, where it was dark at six-twenty, and then everything went black: too ambitious a walk or a paddle meant my having to grope back to camp in moon-shadow. For four days I saw no other people, and would have stayed longer in the bush but for running low on drinking water. Even so, an old-timer told me that I was only the second person who had ever gone camping on the island.

When I had first arrived I had looked at London, the small sleepy beat-up town, the cheery people in its cheerless shops selling identical canned goods, its littered main street, its defunct businesses, like the Atoll Seaweed Company, a victim of El Niño. The island had so few motor vehicles that mongrels slept contentedly on the main street, and only the foraging piglets were active. In one of the tiny shops, a young girl in a T-shirt leaned on a counter, murmuring as she read a foreign magazine she had borrowed from the library: ' "One of the very nicest treats arising from an English summer is to be able to have afternoon tea in the garden. It is even more delightful because of the infrequency of exactly the right weather . . . elderly retainers tottering under the weight of silver trays groaning with plates of thinly-cut cucumber sandwiches, tall silver teapots and the best china. Superior cakes, madeleines, sandcakes, meringues and Sachertorte" '

– at which point she said to me (I was buying beer), 'Mister, what is this word?'

After that, from the shore, where junked trucks were rusting, I could see the two surf breaks – one just off London, the other near Cook Island, where in season there were great rideable waves and surfers on them. London was obviously hard up but it had a blessed serenity and a palpable sense of peace.

That changed overnight. I returned to London on the day a cruise ship, the *Crown Princess*, fresh from Maui, was anchored offshore. Boat day! The whole somnolent place had come alive – though the cruise passengers, many hundreds of them, squinted in skepticism at the low tin-roofed buildings of the improvised town and tried to avoid stepping on the torn-open corned beef cans. But the most surprising thing was that the children I had seen a week earlier frolicking in the schoolyard or at Father Bermond's church hall, were now circulating among the cruise passengers begging like lepers. 'Give me money!' And the little girls were no longer in school uniforms, but were dressed in tremulous grass skirts and seductive makeup, with shell necklaces and flowers plaited in their hair; they sidled up to the visitors and winked and had their pictures taken – Christmas Island coquettes – and they asked for money too.

Islanders hawked shell bowls and shell necklaces, palm-leaf hats and shark jaws, postcards, sea urchins, and giant clams. The post office in town had closed for the day and become another stall at the boat dock, where Kiribati stamps depicting birds and butterflies were being sold for twice their value. Big brown people were dancing the explosive Wantarawa, the comic travesty of what was originally a war-dance. A semi-circle of hunkered-down men were harmonizing. Each group of performers flourished a plastic bucket, soliciting donations.

'There was no begging before the cruise ships,' Kim Andersen told me. He is the island's only American and runs a well-equipped dive and offshore-fishing outfit, Dive Kiribati. Having operated dive operations off the Turks and Caicos, as well as Panama and Mexico, Kim said that diving off Christmas Island is world-class.

The island's pioneer European, a Kiribati-speaking Scotsman named John Bryden, said, 'The cruise ship visits are important to the island. They definitely inject money into the economy and they get people busy.'

Few of the visiting passengers got farther than the edge of town. I heard one woman say to her companion, 'I don't think there's much on the island to see.'

Their hour on shore was up. They headed back to the ship. You couldn't blame them. But it was a pity, for even in the half-day they had they could have gone fifteen miles or so past the town line, where habitation ends and the richness of the island begins, the wild birds, the lagoon fringe, the 1 million coconut palms, the great windy emptiness, and the storm-free weather and silky air, the serene epitome of nature so safe and unthreatening that birds such as the golden plover and ruddy turnstone flew thousands of miles from Alaska to winter here; a place so perfect in its way, so isolated, a kind of Eden, which had hardly known humans – it was even spared the Pacific war – that British and American scientists, and ambitious soldiers, were encouraged to come here and deliver the ultimate Christmas present by exploding thirty-four nuclear bombs.

It says something for the tenacity of nature that even after this massive insult, the island's larger unpeopled portion is still thriving in its eccentric way.

Part Six

Books of Travel

My Own

THE EDGE OF THE GREAT RIFT — THREE AFRICAN NOVELS

'There is a crack in the earth which extends from the Sea of Galilee to the coast of Mozambique, and I am living on the edge of it, in Nyasaland.' I was writing in blue ink on a sheet of school foolscap, in my little house in the bush near Soche Hill. It thrilled me to be so far from home, and to be able to make a statement like that. It was the hot season, known locally as 'the suicide month,' because of the suffocating and depressing heat. But that was a settler expression, and most of the white settlers had bolted from the country when the Africans took power.

'The crack is the Great Rift Valley,' I went on. 'It seems to be swallowing most of East Africa. In Nyasaland it is replacing the fishing villages, the flowers, and the anthills with a nearly bottomless lake, and it shows itself in rough escarpments and troughs up and down this huge continent. It is thought that this valley was torn amid great volcanic activity. The period of vulcanism has not ended in Africa. It shows not only in the Great Rift Valley itself, but in the people, burning, the lava of masses, the turbulence of the humans themselves who live in the Great Rift.'

I went on writing, describing my school, my students, the villages nearby. It was a letter from a distant place where I felt I had arrived, and I knew I was happy. When I published this 'Letter from Africa' in an American newspaper I had a distinct sense that I had fully embarked on a writing career.

At the age of twenty-two, hoping to avoid being drafted into the US army, but also wishing to see the world, I joined the Peace Corps. When I went to Malawi in 1963 it was called the Nyasaland Protectorate and was administered by Britain. In rural areas, women and children dropped to their knees, out of respect, when a white person went by in a Land-Rover. African men merely bowed. The country became independent in July, 1964, and four months later there was an attempted coup d'état – sackings, shootings, resignations. People were arrested for repeating rumors, charged with 'creating alarm and despondency' – how I loved that expression. The President-for-Life, Dr. Banda, had spent much of his working life in Britain and did not speak any African language well enough to give speeches in anything but English. He wore three-piece pinstriped suits and a homburg hat and had an interpreter for talking to his people. It was, for some months anyway, very cold in the country. Many Africans I met were pious members of the Church of Scotland, but they also believed in ghosts and witches. There were stubborn mustached English settlers who said they would never leave Africa; and nuns, lepers, guerrillas, and runaways. Malawi had a once-a-week news-paper and a terrible railway station and steam locomotives. It was a country of constant rumors. In the deep south of the country the Africans often went stark naked; in the north they wore English flannels. This was not the Africa I had expected. I think my contemplating its oddness from my isolation at the edge of the Great Rift helped make me a writer.

I remember a particular day in Mozambique, in a terrible little country town, getting a haircut from a Portuguese barber. He had come to the African bush from rural Portugal to be a barber. It went without saying that he would only cut the hair of white people. Mozambique had been a colony for hundreds of years – the first Portuguese claimed it in 1489. This barber did not speak English, I did not speak Portuguese, yet when I addressed his African servant in Chinyanja, his own language, the Portuguese man said, in Portuguese, 'Ask the *bwana* what his Africans are like.' And that was how we held a conversation – the barber speaking Portuguese to the African, who translated it into Chinyanja for me; and I replied in Chinyanja, which the African translated into Portuguese for the barber. The barber kept saying – and the African kept translating – things like, 'I can't stand the blacks – they're so stupid and bad-tempered. But there's no work for me in Portugal.' It was grotesque, it was outrageous, it was the shabbiest, darkest kind of imperialism. I could not believe my good luck. In many parts of Africa in the early 1960s it was the nineteenth century, and I was filled with the urgency to write about it.

After my two years in Malawi, I went to Uganda and signed a four-year contract to teach at Makerere University, at the time considered to be one of the best universities in Africa. Uganda was a green wilderness of great beauty. I was self-sufficient, and I had fallen in love with the English woman whom I was to marry. I felt different from everyone I knew, and yet I had found a place for myself in Uganda. In this mood, I began writing about the Chinese man who ran the grocery store around the corner from where I lived in Wandegeya. This neighborhood was famous for the thousands of bats which hung in the branches of the trees, and took off in a black cloud at sunset to hunt for insects. The Chinese man, his grocery store, his Indian competitors, his African customers – these were my characters in *Fong and the Indians*. I had written two novels before this, but *Fong* was the first piece of fiction which satisfied me.

My future wife taught at a girls' school in Kenya. While I was writing this novel, I courted her by driving hundreds of miles on rutted roads, from Kampala to her bush school north of Nairobi. Kenya had been heavily colonized by unsubtle and presumptuous white people with sharp elbows; so the atmosphere – so different from Uganda – interested me, and a girls' school seemed to contain all the contradictions and snobberies and class distinctions of imperialism. My writing method, then as now, was to write a book in notebooks (first draft); and copy it out in longhand on sheets of lined paper (second draft); then type it myself (third draft), before correcting it and turning it over to be retyped by someone else (fourth draft). I was typing *Fong*, when I began to write the first chapters of *Girls at Play*.

It became clear to me that I was privileged to be living in an African world that had not been written about. This was not the Africa of Conrad, or Karen Blixen, or Hemingway, or even Laurens van der Post. No one had written about this particular Africa. That, I think, was my good luck. It was for me to describe this unknown time and place. There was a colonial hangover, and Africans were now being uncomfortably accommodated in the white clubs; but I was not a member of any club, I did not go on safari. I came to be fascinated by this Africa of hilarious dance halls and village feasts, and bush schools. There were crazed politicians ranting all over the countryside, and yet there was a power vacuum in which most Africans, rather enjoying the anarchy, felt free. In a cheerful scribbling and self-deluded frame of mind, in this in-between period that occurred after colonialism and before politics and soldiers put the screws on, I felt safe.

Jungle Lovers was the result of my departure from Africa. In 1968, after five years in Malawi and Uganda, my wife and I were attacked by rioting students in Kampala. After that, I lost my will to teach in Africa; my confidence was gone. I said to my African colleagues, *You do it. I have no business here.* I decided to leave for good and took a job teaching in Singapore. The Singapore authorities had got wind of the fact that I was a published author and, taking the philistine view that writers were troublemakers, they insisted that I sign a paper saying that I would not write or publish anything about Singapore while I was under contract. They also put me on the lowest salary scale. I wondered what they were trying to hide.

I discovered: nothing – or very little. Singapore was a small humid island-city that called itself a republic. It was dominated by puritanical overseas Chinese who were growing rich on the Vietnam War. My students said they wanted to emigrate to Australia. I taught courses in Jacobean literature. I questioned whether I was cut out to be a teacher in the tropics. Of course, I wasn't, and I saw writing as liberation.

Forbidden to write about Singapore, I wrote about Africa – *Jungle Lovers*. The weather was very hot. I could work only at night or on weekends, I kept my writing secret from my employers, and in the middle of writing this novel I contracted dengue fever. It took more than two years to write the novel. When at last I finished it and sent it off, I left Singapore (and teaching) to write my Singapore novel, *Saint Jack*. I never took another salaried job.

That was in 1971. Now, rereading *Jungle Lovers*, I am struck by its peculiar humor and violence. Some of it is farce and some tragedy. I suppose the insurance man and the revolutionary were the two opposing sides of my own personality. I had gone to Africa believing that political freedom would create social change. Five years did not change much, and now more than twenty-five years later this novel of futility and failed hopes seems truer than ever. That was my mood on leaving Africa. I was younger then. Now I should say that it takes a long time for change to come about, and change ought always to come from within. Outsiders, even the most well intentioned in Africa, are nearly always meddlers.

Nowadays, people my age are asked, *Where were you in the sixties?* Americans went various ways. They clung to universities, or dropped out and became part of the counter-culture; or they were sent to Vietnam. Some, like me, spent the 1960s in the Third World – it was a way of virtuously dropping out and delicately circumventing

Vietnam. I was in my twenties in the 1960s, and I think my African novels are very much of their time. Many African countries had just become independent; colonialists were going home; volunteer teachers – and insurance agents and revolutionaries – were arriving and wondering what would happen next. No one realized that the darkness they found was the long shadow of Africa's past.

The Black House

When I left the tropics after working for almost nine years in hot countries I came to England and experienced a great shock. It seemed to me one of the strangest places I had ever been (and I had lived in Uganda and traveled in the Congo and in upper Burma). This was Dorset. I was just about to write, 'Hardy does not prepare you for Dorset.' But of course he does. His work is very truthful to that county. I found the place dark and deeply rural; it was extremely beautiful and often inexplicable. People did not seem so much to live there as to be holed up there. There was an uncertainty and a tribal mistrust of outsiders. An outsider was not necessarily an American. It might be someone from Yeovil or Salisbury. Everything I had expected to find in Africa I found on the edge of Marshwood Vale. I was fascinated but I was also a little frightened. These are the emotions that produce fiction.

This was in the winter of 1971–2. Because of the miners' strike there were power cuts. Some nights the whole of west Dorset was lit by candles and oil lamps, and the landlord at the Gollop Arms wore a miner's hat with a light in front when he served drinks in the darkened bar. It was the time they discovered oil in the North Sea – and they found oil in Dorset, too, a great controversy. It was the time of Bloody Sunday. The papers were full of Ulster violence – dead Catholics, ambushed soldiers, and a picture that is still printed on my mind, of an Irish girl who had been tarred and feathered and tied to a lamppost for fraternizing with a British soldier.

There was the church and the pub, and it was a mile to the nearest shop. You needed the experience of Africa to survive here, I felt. And I should say that I was feeling insecure, because I had given up teaching and I had no regular income. I was working on a novel – *Saint Jack* – and doing book reviews. There was no money in book reviews; not much in novels either. My advance on *Saint Jack* was 250 pounds. It did not seem quite enough for six months' work. I always intended to go for walks in the afternoon, but before I could get my boots on darkness had fallen, and the wind tore through the oaks and made a moan in the chimney. My young children found the house confining, my wife began to inquire how much longer my novel might take.

I had the impression the house was haunted, and one day returning from a walk I saw a woman in a blue dress at an upstairs window, looking down at me. My wife was in the kitchen. She said, 'There's no one upstairs.'

I had never felt more alien or more uncomprehending in a place. I said I wanted to stay through the summer, but I was secretly pleased when my wife got a job with the BBC and we moved to London. In London I would be able to think hard about Dorset, and the house we lived in, which I thought of as the Black House.

When I wrote my novel, it seemed to come from the deepest part of my unconscious mind. I was often very surprised, and I was sometimes frightened. It seemed to be about fear and desire, death and love. I always believed it was a ghost story. It is also oddly comic and contains an episode that greatly pleases me – of a visit by an African to a Dorset village. His host, Alfred Munday, the central character, is an anthropologist.

I did not question the narrative. I needed to go on writing to discover what it was about. It amazed me. It remains a favorite of mine. And it changed my life. When I was done my publisher told me it would do immense harm to my reputation. I said, 'I have no reputation!' He said he would publish it if I twisted his arm. I told him he was making a big mistake and I went to a new publisher, where I have been ever since. The day I delivered the final manuscript of *The Black House* I set off for Istanbul, intending to make my way by train to Tokyo. I would have preferred to write another novel, but I couldn't for the moment – there was no money in it. I wondered whether there would be any in a travel book called *The Great Railway Bazaar*.

The Great Railway Bazaar

I had been traveling for more than ten years – in Europe, Asia, and Africa – and it had not occurred to me to write a travel book. I had always somewhat disliked travel books: they seemed self-indulgent, unfunny, and rather selective. I had the idea that the travel writer left a great deal out of his book and put all the wrong things in. I hated sightseeing, and yet that was what constituted much of the travel writer's material: the pyramids, the Taj Mahal, the Vatican, the paintings here, the mosaics there. In an age of mass tourism, everyone set off to see the same things, and that was what travel writing seemed to be about. I am speaking of the 1960s and the early 1970s.

The travel book was a bore. A bore wrote it and bores read it. It annoyed me that a traveler would suppress his or her moments of desperation or fear or lust. Or the time he or she screamed at the taxi driver, or mocked the oily tycoon. And what did they eat, what books did they read to kill time, and what were the toilets like? I had done enough traveling to know that half of travel was delay or nuisance – buses breaking down and hotel clerks being rude and market traders being rapacious. The truth of travel was interesting and off key, and few people ever wrote about it.

Now and then one would meet it in a book – Evelyn Waugh being mistaken for his brother Alec in *Labels*, or the good intentions and bad temper in parts of Naipaul's *An Area of Darkness* – a superbly structured book, both deeply personal, and imaginative and informative; or in a fragment like this from Anthony Trollope's *The West Indies and the Spanish Main*:

I was in a shoemakers' shop at St Thomas [Jamaica], buying a pair of boots, when a negro entered quickly and in a loud voice said he wanted a pair of pumps. He was a labouring man fresh from his labour. He had on an old hat – what in Ireland men would call a caubeen; he was in his shirt-sleeves, and was barefooted. As the only shopman was looking for my boots, he was not attended to at the moment.

'Want a pair of pumps – directerly,' he roared out in a very dictatorial voice.

'Sit down for a moment,' said the shopman, 'and I will attend to you.'

He did sit down, but did so in the oddest fashion. He dropped himself into a chair, and at the same moment rapidly raised his legs from the ground; and as he did so fastened his hands across them just below his knees, so as to keep his feet suspended from his arms. This he contrived to do in such a manner that the moment his body reached the chair his feet left the ground. I looked on in amazement, thinking he was mad.

'Give I a bit of carpet,' he screamed out; still holding up his feet, but with much difficulty.

'Yes, yes,' said the shopman, still searching for the boots.

'Give I a bit of carpet directerly,' he again exclaimed. The seat of the chair was very narrow, and the back was straight, and the position was not easy, as my reader will ascertain if he attempt it. He was half choked with anger and discomfort.

The shopman gave him the bit of carpet. Most men and women will remember that such bits of carpet are common in shoemakers' shops. They are supplied, I believe, in order that they who are delicate should not soil their stockings on the floor.

The gentleman in search of the pumps had seen that people of dignity were supplied with such luxuries, and resolved to have his value for his money; but as he had on neither shoes nor stockings, the little bit of carpet was hardly necessary for his material comfort.

Something human had happened, and Trollope saw it and recorded it; that, it seemed to me, was the point of travel writing.

The trip – the itinerary – was another essential, and so many travel books I read had grown out of a traveler chasing around a city or a little country – *Discovering Portugal*, that kind of thing. It was not like travel at all, but rather a form of extended residence that I knew well from having myself lived in Malawi and Uganda and Singapore. I had come to rest in those places, I was working, I had a driver's license, I went shopping every Saturday. It had never occurred to me to write a travel book about any of it. Travel had to do with movement and truth: with trying everything, offering yourself to experience and then reporting on it.

Choosing the right itinerary – the best route, the correct mode of travel – was the surest way, I felt, of gaining experience. It had to be total immersion, a long deliberate trip through the hinterland rather than flying from one big city to another, which didn't seem to me to be travel at all. The travel books I liked were oddities – not simply Trollope and Naipaul, but Henry Miller's *The Air-Conditioned Nightmare* (America, coast to coast, by car), or Mark Twain's *Following the Equator* (a lecture tour around the world). I wanted my book to be a series of long train journeys, but where to?

All this speculation took place in the autumn of 1972, when I was teaching for a semester at the University of Virginia. I was working on *The Black House*, and awaiting the publication of *Saint Jack*. In those days I began a new book as soon as I finished the one I was working on. My wife was in London with our two children, and she was working – indeed, earning a good living; but I still felt I was the breadwinner and that I was not earning enough. My advance for *Saint Jack* was small, and I assumed I would not get much more for *The Black House*. Money is rather a clumsy subject, but it was a crucial factor in my decision to write my first travel book – simply, I needed the money. And when I mentioned the possibility of such a book to my American editor, she was delighted. She said, 'We'll give you an advance for it.' I had never before received an advance. Normally, I wrote a book and submitted it and then was paid; I had never been given money on an unwritten book.

Often you begin to think clearly about your intentions only when someone asks you very specific questions. The travel book I vaguely contemplated had something to do with trains, but I had no idea where I wanted to go – only that it should be a long trip. I saw an equally long book with lots of people and lots of dialogue and no sightseeing. But my editor's questioning prodded me, and I thought *Trains Through Asia*. I could start in London on the Orient Express. When I looked at this route I saw that I could continue through Turkey, into Iran, into Baluchistan, and after a short bus ride I could catch a train in Zahedan, go into Pakistan and more or less chug through Asia. My idea was to go to Vietnam, take the train to Hanoi and then continue through China, Mongolia, and the Soviet Union. Much of this travel proved impractical or impossible. The Chinese Embassy in 1972 simply hung up when I said I wanted a visa to take trains through China (I had to wait fourteen years before I was able to take the trip I described in *Riding the Iron Rooster: By Train Through China*). There was a war in Baluchistan – I rerouted myself through Afghanistan. I decided to include Japan and the whole of the Trans-Siberian. I didn't mind where I went as long as it was in Asia and had a railway system and visas were available. I saw myself puffing along from country to country, simply changing trains.

Meanwhile I was finishing my novel *The Black House*. It was set in rural England and it was rather ghostly and solemn. I wanted my next to be a sunny book. I had just about decided on my travel itinerary when I delivered my novel to my British publisher. He suggested we have lunch. Almost before we had started eating he told me he disliked *The Black House*. 'It will hurt your reputation,' was how he put it.

That was why I went to a new publisher in Britain and it gave me a greater reason for having to publish this travel book: I was having grave doubts about my ability ever to earn a living writing fiction.

I think of the circumstances surrounding *The Great Railway Bazaar* rather than the trip itself. I hated leaving my family behind in London; I had never taken such a deliberate trip before; I felt encumbered by an advance on royalties – modest as it was. My writer friends generally mocked the idea. I never got around to worrying about the trip itself, though I was beset by an obscure ache that was both mental and physical – the lingering anxiety that I was going to die. I had always felt that my exit would be made via An Appointment in Samarra, and that I would go a great distance and endure enormous discomfort in order to meet my death. If I chose to sit at home and eat and drink it would never happen. I imagined it would be a silly accident, like that of the monk and mystic Thomas Merton at last leaving his monastery in Kentucky after twenty-seven years and accidentally electrocuting himself on the frayed wires of a fan in Bangkok a week later.

I left London on September 19, 1973. It was a gray day. I had a bad cold. My wife waved me goodbye. Almost immediately I felt I had made an absurd mistake. I hadn't the slightest idea what I was doing. I became very gloomy and to cheer myself up and give myself the illusion that this was work I began to take voluminous notes. From the time I left until the moment I arrived back in England four months later – homesick most of the time – I filled one notebook after another. I wrote everything down – conversations, descriptions of people and places, details of trains, interesting trivia, even criticism of the novels I happened to be reading. I still have some of those books, and on the blank back pages of the paperbacks of Joyce's *Exiles*, Chekhov's stories, Endo's *Silence*, and others I had scribbled small insectile notes, which I amplified when I transferred them to my large notebooks. I always wrote in the past tense.

In the manuscript I submitted to my publishers, there was a chapter about Afghanistan which I was advised to leave out ('There are no trains in that chapter,' my editor said), but I have since printed it in a collection of pieces, *Sunrise with Seamonsters*. My problem in writing the book was finding a form for it – a structure; I decided I would do it as a series of train journeys, and simply plunged in. I had never read a book quite like the one I was writing. This worried me as well as made me hopeful. The writing of the book took the same amount of time as the trip itself, four months.

That was 1974. The book is still in print and still sells well. Some people think it is the only book I have ever written, which annoys me, because I think the writing in *The Old Patagonian Express* is more fluent, and *Riding the Iron Rooster* is better informed. For example, in *The Great Railway Bazaar* my train passed through Nis in Yugoslavia. I mentioned this, but I never bothered to find out anything about Nis. I have just consulted *The Blue Guide* and found that Nis was the birthplace of the Emperor Constantine. Then I read on in the *Guide*, 'Though not a pleasant place in itself, Nis has several interesting monuments,' and I am reminded why I lingered in Nis. More recently, during the war in Kosovo, Nis was flattened by NATO bombs and discovered to be the scene of mass graves.

It was a satisfaction to me that my *Railway Bazaar* (I got the title from a street-name in India) fared well. I did not know when I wrote it that every trip is unique. My travel book is about my trip, not yours or anyone else's. Even if someone had come with me and written a book about the trip it would have been a different book. Another thing I did not know at the time was that every trip has an historical dimension. Not long after I traveled through these countries they underwent political changes. The Shah was exiled and Iran became very dangerous for the foreign traveler; Afghanistan went to war with itself – the USSR helping out; India and Pakistan restored their rail link. Laos shut its borders to foreigners and did away with its monarchy. Vietnam repaired its railway, so now it is possible to travel by train from Ho Chi Minh City (Saigon) to Hanoi. Many of the individual trains I rode were taken out of service, most notably the Orient Express. The train that plies from London to Venice under that name is for wealthy comfort-seeking people who have selfish sumptuous fantasies about travel, bearing no relation to the real thing. However awful my old Orient Express was, at least I can say that many people took it – rich and poor, old and young, rattling back and forth from Europe to Asia. It was cheap and friendly, and like all great trains it was a world on wheels.

When I wrote the book I was groping in the dark – although I was careful to disguise this; my self-assurance in the narrative was bravado, simply a way of whistling to keep my spirits up. I knew that I had taken over a venerable form, the travel book, and was writing it my own way, to suit myself, and my peculiar trip and temperament. It was not at all like a novel: fiction required inspiration and intense imagining and a long period alone in a room. A travel book, I had discovered, was a deliberate act – like the act of travel itself. It took health and strength and confidence; optimism and deep curiosity. When I finished a novel I never knew whether I would be able to write another one. But I knew when I finished this first travel book that I would be able to do it again.

The Old Patagonian Express

Some people say that the travel book is a type of novel, that it has elements of fiction in it, that it comes out of the imagination and is a sort of strange beast, half the prosy little animal of non-fiction and half the fabulous monster of fiction, and there it stands, snorting and pawing the ground, challenging us to give it a name. There are, no doubt, books that fit this description – little trips that writers have worked up into epics and odysseys. You want to write a novel, but you have no subject, no characters, no landscape; so you take a trip – a couple of months, not very expensive, not too dangerous – and you write it up, making it fairly harrowing and mocking, and dramatizing yourself, because you are the hero of this – what? Quest, perhaps, but full of liberties.

This is not my line of work at all. And when I read such a book and I spot the fakery, the invention, the embroidery, I can read no further. Self-dramatization is inevitable in any travel book – most travelers, however dreary and plonkingly pedestrian – see themselves as solitary and rather heroic adventurers. And the odd thing is that the real heroes of travel seldom write about their journeys. But I have just received a thick book detailing the travels of a young man through metropolitan France: 'essential reading for Francophiles, Francophobes, gourmets, gourmands and any curious traveler in truly modern Gaul.' It is as though this oversupplied, luxurious, and hackneyed place is some sort of *terra incognita*. Oh, I know, there's a great deal still to discover in this seemingly familiar old ingrate of a country, that sweet enemy, et cetera; but I for one would rather read of an adventure.

I was seeking an adventure when I took the trip that became *The Old Patagonian Express*. I wanted to leave my front door in Medford, Massachusetts, and head for Patagonia, and to do so without leaving the ground. I wished to travel from this cozy homely place where I was born, to the distant and outlandish – so I thought – area in the southern part of South America by degrees. I wanted to make a connection between the known and yet still remain in the western hemisphere. It would not be the circular journey that I described in *The Great Railway Bazaar*, but rather a linear trip, from Here to Way Over There.

It had always bothered me, when reading of an expedition, that the preliminaries were dispensed with. I describe this toward the beginning of *The Old Patagonian Express*, in the chapter that starts, 'Travel is a vanishing act, a solitary trip down a pinched line of geography to oblivion.' In my first travel book I had simply gone away – launched myself into the East; in this book I felt I was consciously experimenting with space and time. My object was to take the train that everyone took to work, and then to keep going, changing trains, to the end of the line – and this I took to be a tiny station, called Esquel, in the middle of Patagonia.

I was altogether more deliberate with this travel book than I had been with my first. For one thing, I was determined to speak the language. Not speaking Hindi, Japanese, Farsi, or Urdu – among others – had made my first book somewhat facetious, I thought; it was so easy, so cheap, to mock. I did not want to be that ignorant again. So I listened to Spanish-language tapes. I wanted to understand what was going on. One of the popular notions of travel books is that they are usually about the traveler; I wanted to get beyond this petty egoism and to try to understand the places I was passing through. I knew something of the politics but very little about the geographical features of these countries. One of my aims was to characterize each place, so that afterwards anyone who read the book would have a clear idea of El Salvador or Costa Rica or Peru; so that they would not be merely a formless and indistinguishable heap of banana republics.

I was not aiming to turn this book into a novel. I was just finishing my novel *Picture Palace* as I planned the trip. This was the summer of 1977. I set off, one freezing February afternoon in 1978, leaving my old home in Medford, taking the train to Boston, and then another train from Boston to Chicago, and so on. The skies were almost black, full of the storm clouds that were shortly to dump one of the worst blizzards in living memory upon the north-east. I read about this snow in steamy Mexico. How easy it had been to get there; and I continued to rattle south on progressively more geriatric trains.

Having written a previous travel book, and knowing some of my strengths and weaknesses, I had a general idea of the sort of travel I wished to do. More than anything, I wanted to meet unusual people, and I wanted to give them life – for the book to be a series of portraits, of landscapes and faces. I have always regarded the best writing as visual and in *Picture Palace* I had deliberately written about a photographer: most of her pronouncements on photography were my own views on writing. I wanted this book to be full of faces and voices, with a distinct foreground and background.

I was lucky in the people I met. The Panama Canal was in the news: President Carter had convened a conference to hand the canal back to the Panamanians. The Zonians – delightful name – were furious at what they took to be Carter's treachery. And I found a reasonable man to discuss these matters and more – Mr. Reiss, the head mortician in the Gorgas Mortuary. And there were others: the woman in Vera Cruz looking for her lover, Mr. Thornberry in Costa Rica, the Irish priest who had started a little family in Ecuador, Jorge Luis Borges in Buenos Aires. And I tried to make portraits of the towns and cities, as well. Borges told me that he was working on a story about a man called 'Thorpe.' Years later I found that character in the Borges story 'Shakespeare's Memory.' That can be seen, I think, in – for example – the description that begins, 'Guatemala City, an extremely horizontal place, is like a city on its back,' and then the business about the earthquakes. I looked closely, I listened hard, I sniffed and wrote everything down.

My friend Bruce Chatwin had told me that he wrote *In Patagonia* after he read *The Great Railway Bazaar*. I had always wondered how he had traveled to Patagonia – he had left that out. He had written about being there, but I wanted to write about getting there. This thought was always in my mind, and it made me meticulous about my own trip. I knew that as soon as I got to Patagonia I would simply look around and then go home. Mine was to be the ultimate book about getting there.

In spite of myself, I was distracted by what I saw. I am a novelist. I could not ignore the possibilities that were being offered to me in the form of suggestive characters and dramatic landscapes, and yet I knew I had to put them in my travel book; when they were there they were fixed forever – I could not haul them out again and give them fictional form.

What struck me was how dense the jungle was, so near the United States. A few days ago I had been in wintry New England, and now – just a few weeks later – I was in a place that looked like a ragged version of paradise – no roads, no factories, no houses, no missionaries even. A person could come here and start all over again – build his own town, make his own world. I had this feeling strongly in Costa Rica.

We were at the shore and traveling alongside a palmy beach. This was the Mosquito Coast, which extends from Puerto Barrios in Guatemala to Colon in Panama. It is wild and looks the perfect setting for the story of castaways. What few villages and ports lie along it are derelict; they declined when shipping did, and returned to jungle. Massive waves were rolling towards us, the white foam vivid in the twilight; they broke just below the coconut palms near the track. At this time of day, nightfall, the sea is the last thing to darken; it seems to hold the light that is slipping from the sky; and the trees are black. So in the light of this luminous sea and the pale still-blue eastern sky, and to the splashings of the breakers, the train racketed on towards Limon.

I imagined these castaways to be a family fleeing the United States, and I associated them with various missionaries and priests that I kept meeting. The defrocked priest in Ecuador (Chapter 15) was perfect – a sort of spiritual castaway, living a secret life, far from home. But I had vowed that I would be truthful in my travel book, and include everything and everyone who was interesting; and once I wrote about the priest I knew I could not return to him and recreate him in fiction. And yet I knew that when I had finished this travel book I would begin to think seriously about this novel of castaways on the Mosquito Coast.

I got to Patagonia. I returned to London. I wrote the book. My regret was that I did not visit Nicaragua – I was advised not to, because of the guerrilla war that had overwhelmed the country; I regretted that I had to fly from Panama to Baranquilla and from Guayaquil to Lima. I dislike planes, and whenever I am in one – suffering the deafening drone and the chilly airlessness that are peculiar to planes – I always suspect that the land we are overflying is rich and wonderful and that I am missing it all. Plane travel is very simple and annoying and a cause of anxiety; it is like being at the dentist's, even the chairs are like dentist's chairs. Overland travel is a great deal more trouble, and very slow, but it is uncomfortable in a way that is completely human and often reassuring. I also regretted missing out on Brazil. That is another book.

The mood of this book, which is at times somber, was the result of my knowing Spanish. It was easy for me to be light-hearted when I traveled to write the *Railway Bazaar*. I had little idea of what people were saying in Japanese and Hindi. But speaking to people in their own language, hearing their timid turns of phrase, or the violence of their anger, or the idioms of their hopelessness – this could be distressing. I was to have a similar experience eight years later, traveling in China, and hearing people worrying in Chinese.

A book like this – or any book I have written – is not a problem for a reader to study and annotate. It is something I wrote to give pleasure, it is something to enjoy. You should be able to see these people and places, to hear them and smell them. Of course, some of it is painful, but travel – its very motion – ought to suggest hope. Despair is the armchair; it is indifference and glazed incurious eyes. I think travelers are essentially optimists, or else they would never go anywhere; and a travel book ought to reflect that same general optimism.

When I was done with this book I began making notes for my next novel, *The Mosquito Coast*, but before I began I returned to Central America. I traveled through the hinterland of Honduras. I made notes, but I carefully avoided using them in an article or a story. They became a repository of everything I knew about that distant shore of Mosquitia – the landscape of my novel – and writing that book was not glorified reportage but an almost indescribable transformation, which is what fiction is.

Making *The Mosquito Coast*

When I began my novel *The Mosquito Coast* I thought it was about the son, Charlie Fox, who is the narrator and sufferer of his father's adventure. But after a while – and like Charlie – I became possessed by the father, Allie, who was always yapping, bursting with ideas, the greatest of which was to create a brilliant ice-making society in the Honduran jungle. He was a good inspiration. I often heard him thinking out loud. I knew his opinions, his reactions to most things. He was the sort of Yankee I had known my whole life, someone who says, 'If you can't find it on the beach and it's not in the Sears catalogue you probably don't need it.' I wrote the book in an Allie Fox mood. After he died the story was over. I had planned more – a long voyage of the remaining members of the family in Part Five. But it was not possible with the man gone. Part Five is only two pages long.

Readers still write to me to say that Allie was like their father or uncle – or especially husband. I have received hundreds of husband letters – always from ex-wives who last saw the crazy bastard swinging an ax in a wilderness. He was whacko, he had this thing about fresh air, he wouldn't stop talking; there were times when I wanted to kill him, but you had to admire the guy.

When I picked this novel up afterward I felt somewhat detached from it. It was an affectionate detachment: a book goes its own way, and if it is a good book it is indestructible. A movie is a simple version of it, provoking different expectations. No movie can be very faithful to the meandering complexities of a long novel, and so it must be good in its own terms – a movie has to be true to itself.

The effect that *The Mosquito Coast* had on me when I was writing it seemed to be repeated with most people who were involved with it in other ways. What one might call the 'Allie Factor' is strong among those who are supporters of the book. Just the other day a local man asked me about my new novel, *O-Zone*, and said, 'Is it as good as *The Mosquito Coast*?' I thought, *What a question to ask me!* And then he started talking admiringly about Allie Fox and sort of bullying me in an Allie-like way. It was another reminder that as soon as the book appeared it ceased to belong to me.

The film rights were sold shortly after the book was published in the United States in 1982; and this Allie Factor became evident again. It was not an option or a development deal but rather an outright sale, Jerome Hellman putting all his money down the way Allie bought Jeronimo. Hellman (producer of *Midnight Cowboy* and *Coming Home*) begin to exhibit Allie characteristics: he raved a little, he became very stubborn and embattled. When it was suggested by a studio that the movie might be made in Mexico or Jamaica, Hellman insisted that it had to be shot, no matter what the cost, on the Mosquito Coast, which actually exists, running more or less from Belize to Nicaragua. Off his own bat, Hellman hired Paul Schrader to write the script. It was the most faithful script I had ever read and I thought that was its weakness. When I made a few suggestions, but insisted that I did not want to influence him, Schrader said in an Allie-like way, 'I'm not influenceable.'

I said, 'Isn't the whole point about a good movie that it takes liberties?'

Peter Weir – who was then hired as director – agreed with me, and he rewrote the script, indefatigably tinkering. That was one of his

Allie qualities. He assumed others. He was inventive, he was very certain, and in the quietest sort of way his hot-eyed concentration indicated that he had fire in his belly. I had let go of the book, but it kept reappearing; it stiffened the resolve of these people and it was constantly being quoted at me. Peter Weir's copy of the novel was so heavily annotated you would have thought he was preparing the Norton Lectures at Harvard.

Meanwhile, the Allie Factor was animating Jerry Hellman. He flew from country to country, raising money. He kept saying, 'We're going to do it right. We're going to make this picture without cutting any corners.' He went to Belize and found the right spot in the jungle, and observers saw him bushwhacking and gesturing hopefully. Several deals collapsed at the eleventh hour, forcing him to look elsewhere for money and allowing Peter Weir to make *Witness*. But they kept *The Mosquito Coast* alive, and there was never any question of their abandoning it. When backers promised millions for them to turn Allie into a kind of Doctor Dolittle they laughed and walked away. To change Allie into someone, shall we say, less Promethean, was not merely bad judgment, it was to them a personal insult.

Two and a half years passed. I continued to speak to Hellman and Weir, sometimes to clarify lines, sometimes to listen to their interpretations. I had moved on to other things, another novel, a script for Nicholas Roeg. For me, Allie was gone. But they had a very firm grasp of *The Mosquito Coast*; they had Allie's single-mindedness. They often reminded me of things I had forgotten. 'But Allie says here.' Hellman had hired a graduate student to anthologize the observations and opinions of Allie, and this resulted in a fifty-two-page pamphlet of 'The Selected Thoughts': what Allie thought of God, America, inventions, sleep, junk food, war, ice, jungles, and so forth.

'How much money are you looking for?' I asked Hellman one day.

'Not that much. Listen, the average car-chase picture costs 20 million! Isn't that disgusting? Doesn't that turn your stomach?'

I kept myself from saying, Yes, Allie.

When the 1985 Oscars were awarded, and *Amadeus* won eight of them, the producer, Saul Zaentz, began exhibiting Allie Fox symptoms. He too became a man with a mission. He said he would bankroll the movie and make it soon. Many actors had been mentioned for the part, notably Jack Nicholson and Robert DeNiro. It was Zaentz's idea to cast Harrison Ford as Allie. It was not merely that Ford had proven himself in *Witness* to be a fine and subtle actor; it was also the fact that to play Allie in the jungles of Belize would take physical and emotional strength. Harrison Ford had it all – even the quietly smoldering gaze and the serious grin. Notably, he had started life as a carpenter and builder ('Carpenter to the Stars' had been the slogan on his business card: he remodeled houses in Hollywood). He could chamfer an edge or rabbet a joint if the occasion called for it. If things slackened on the set he could while away his time counter-sinking screws. He was Allie to his fingertips.

Belize was hot, buggy, poverty-stricken, and down on its luck: perfect, as Allie would say.

Peter Weir and Harrison Ford had gone down to look at the jungle, and Ford had ended up clearing a piece of land with a huge machete, leading a work-gang of Belizeans. It was a good start, and everyone connected with the film was enthusiastic about Belize. But when I saw it I found it hard to believe that anyone unused to jungle conditions would willingly live there for the six or seven months it would take to make the movie. Everything that made it perfect for the setting also made it impractical.

And then it seemed to me that you had to become the man Allie himself in order to make the movie.

Hellman had been first; then Schrader and Weir; and then Saul Zaentz. Harrison Ford was the latest incarnation. But the crew also had a spirited and visionary look. It was a movie set without any tensions. From the point of view of handiwork it was more like imperialism, Allie Fox-style, than movie-making. The construction crew built roads and bridges, they built houses and then a pair of villages, they had boats, they had their own water supply. It seemed that the movie had swallowed the country and become its sole industry. What the burnouse is to a Bedouin, the T-shirt is to a Belizean, and every T-shirt in Belize was lettered *Mosquito Coast*.

'What you doing in Belize?' the customs man said at the airport outside of Belize City.

'Mosquito Coast,' I began.

'The magic words,' the man said, and waved me through.

The fictional Jeronimo had become a real place, an entire settlement in which there were crops and houses and water-wheels, and all the necessities of life. People lived there; it had been built to last. After the picture was finished some of these buildings became community centers and others were taken over by homeless people.

For the traveler who thinks he has seen everything, I would suggest a season in Belize, where the bumper stickers say 'You Better Belize It!' Most of Belize City is seven feet off the ground, on stilts, because of tidal waves and regular swamping; over the years hurricanes have come close to wiping it out (which is why the capital, Belmopan, is inland). It is a small wooden town of tall tottering houses and lame-looking shacks and a few solid villas. There are vultures in the sky and slavering dogs in the streets and hawksbill turtles in the river that runs through town. The population is multicolored. There is no Belize face. There are Indians and mestizos, and undiluted Chinese and freckly-faced brown people; there are purplish blacks who wear woolen bags on their heads, and yellow women and Rastas and barefoot kids with hair like Velcro. You get the impression that everyone sings a great deal, though times have been hard, not to say desperate. The sugar price collapsed four years ago. People started growing marijuana and planes began arriving with such regularity on the long straight roads, the government put up iron pylons on the roadside every few hundred yards to frustrate landings. And yet it is said that Belize is still the second largest grower of dope in the western hemisphere – after the Guajira in Colombia, which is legendary. Before writing my novel I traveled in Honduras, but now Honduras has been penetrated by American troops and vindictive Contras, and the landscape of the novel more closely resembles that in Belize.

'I came down here and looked around,' Harrison said. 'Looked at the houses and looked at the hotels. Jesus, those hotels. They said, "Where do you want to stay?" And I said, "Get a cargo plane –"'

Without any apparent effort he had turned into Allie Fox: the beady cap, the flapping shirt, the pushed-back hair, the I-know-best eyes, and the gently maniacal voice explaining his brilliant plan.

'"One of these C-130s," I told them. "A big mother. Fill it up with a prefab house in lots of sections, all the plumbing, all the wires, maybe a helicopter, too. Drop the whole thing into Belize in one package and bolt it together. That's where I'll live."'

I asked him why he didn't do it.

'Because I had a better idea. I didn't have to live in Belize City – didn't have to live in Belize at all!'

This again was pure Allie. He decided to hire a venerable 126-foot air-conditioned yacht – mahogany and brass and awnings and etched glass; a gourmet cook and a crew of five. He anchored this magnificent boat offshore and commuted to the set by speedboat, returning to his yacht every evening. His wife, the screenwriter (*ET*, *The Black Stallion*) Melissa Matheson, remained on board, working on a script about General Custer.

Harrison is a brilliant mimic; he is funny and physical and full of ideas, a kind of embodiment of Allie, chinning himself over the taff-rail as he talked.

One night we were talking about anxiety attacks. He surprised Melissa by saying that he had a number of them. Had I? he wondered.

Oh, sure, I said. Late one night in the African bush an African had pushed a gun muzzle into my face and began screaming at me. I described how I had started gibbering.

'That's not an anxiety attack,' Harrison said – not looking at me, still chinning himself slowly, his deltoids swelling, his lats spreading. 'That's scared shitless.'

He then volunteered the information that he often worried about his performance as Allie.

'You shouldn't worry,' I said. 'You're doing everything right. You're Allie Fox. Listen, that's from the horse's mouth.'

He frowned at me. He said, 'Don't tell me not to worry. I worry all the time. Does Allie Fox worry? Right. That's why I worry.'

He had another home-grown Allie Fox characteristic. He wouldn't say much, he would chin himself, or wrap himself around a chair and do isometrics; and then he would pipe up only to correct you.

I had been saying something about Peter Weir being a good listener.

'He listens,' Harrison said. 'He hears. But that is all.'

Weir was so highly respected on the set that he could give an order without raising his voice and it was instantly acted upon. I never saw him lose his temper or even get flustered. You might say, Why should he? But it was humid, and the temperature in the high eighties. The sandflies were tortuous, the roads terrible, the machines on the set temperamental. Because children were involved in the filming, the working hours had to be somewhat limited. Some of the actors hardly spoke English.

Several years before, Paul Schrader had told me, 'The hardest films to make are those with scenes on ships, or ones set in the tropics, or ones with a lot of kids. This one has all three obstacles.'

Peter Weir was imperturbable. He said there was a good analogy for directing *The Mosquito Coast*. 'It's like being captain of a ship. Not a small vessel, but a ship of the line, with an enormous crew. I don't do it alone. John [Seale, the cameraman] is my first mate. Jerry and Saul are the owners. My second mate is . . .'

This was another way of describing Allie, too: as a sea captain. In fact, I had given Allie a number of nautical expressions to suggest this very aspect of his character.

Any writer must be humbled when something he had dimly imagined and put down in a few sentences is brought to life: it is like magic – a conjuring trick – the words creating something solid. Surely the thrill of movie-making has something to do with these apparitions? I could write, 'Father built a tall ice house and filled it with a wilderness of iron pipes,' and then I saw the crew doing that very thing. It seemed rash, and expensive, and such an effort; but it worked! 'He cleared thirty acres and put up a settlement' – and they went at it, cleared virgin jungle and did the same thing. 'One day Fat Boy blew up,' I wrote. The Special Effects crew said, 'We're going to blow off the sides first, and then get those structures 180 feet off the ground. We can do so many things here with explosives, it will be a national event.' I loved their eagerness. I wrote the book alone in a room; but to make the movie they had to do exactly what Father did – go into the jungle and colonize it and make ice. I am not understanding my role. I had dreamed it all. But they had to tangibalize it, as Father Divine used to say. You have to agree with God: in the beginning was the Word, and the Word was made Flesh. It is not always an easy transition, but that is cinematic transubstantiation, the making of movies out of novels.

Kowloon Tong

Kowloon Tong did not percolate from my past the way most of my fiction has seemed to, but struck me suddenly one day in Hong Kong. I saw the story whole. I made notes, like a painter urgently sketching, and then back home I sat down and wrote it, confident that I was fulfilling an artistic as well as political intention. I feel awkward using the word 'artistic' though. All I mean is that I was guided by my imagination and being myself.

I had been in Hong Kong for an extended period, working on another project, spending my afternoons walking the back streets. That day I was walking through Kowloon in a cold spring drizzle in a northerly direction from Mong Kok up Lai Chi Kok Road – just prowling. Not knowing what I was looking for, I looked at everything. A Union Jack flapping on a tall pole at Sham Shui Po Police Station caught my eye. Soon after a red van sped by, on its side the British crest and the gold letters *Royal Mail*. A large truckload of doomed squealing pigs was driven into the abattoir on Fat Tseung Street. Nearby, on the western side of Kowloon, an enormous land-reclamation project was under way; the bridge to the new airport was being finished. Moody Mong Kok was scheduled for demolition. And all the newspapers were full of stories about the coming of the Chinese; in the bookstores there were dire titles, *The Fall of Hong Kong*, *The Last Colony*, *The Last Days of Hong Kong*.

And people were talking. They were thinking out loud in the most un-Chinese way. In this interim period, while the British government was being ineffectual, and the People's Republic was quietly maneuvering, and it was business as usual in Hong Kong, people were behaving somewhat out of character. Great events bring people together and make them talkative as, with the dire forecast of a storm, people chatter, comparing what they know, which is usually very little. Their sense of being ignorant and vulnerable makes for intimacy.

I was not interviewing people: such formal questions, with my taking notes, made for self-consciousness and equivocation – on both my part and theirs. The way to the truth was the humbler route of anonymity, faceless me striking up conversations with strangers. I did it all the time in Hong Kong, and nearly always the person said: *It's all right for rich people here, they can go anywhere, but I have to stay, and I am worried, I am afraid for my family, I don't know what will happen, the Chinese will not be like the British.*

Shop clerks, taxi drivers, people at the herbalist's, the women in the fresh-squeezed-juice stand, newspaper vendors, schoolchildren, the pimps in the karaoke lounges, the mama-sans in the girlie bars, the shoe-shine boys, the camera dealers. They didn't know who I was.

I think it will be bad when the Chinese take over, they said. *The Chinese are not clever. With the Chinese it is just money, money, money*, which was exactly what a woman from Beijing said to me about these Hong Kong critics, adding, *They are refugees. They live in the present, they are politically naive, and very few of them are interested in democracy.*

It had been that way in Hong Kong for the past year, and if anything people had become more garrulous as the wind had begun to rise.

The Hong Kongers were worried, they giggled with apprehension. I had the feeling that on July 1, 1997, their voices would be stilled.

Looking ahead, I realized that this would be gone: not just the Union Jacks and the mail vans, and old buildings – indeed, whole districts; but also this revealing talk, the apprehension, and all the maneuvering. In the Hong Kong Club the businessmen seemed hearty: many had grown rich on joint-ventures with China. I wanted to capture all those feelings and the landscape, before it was lost forever. 'Albion Cottage' exists on the Peak under another name – a friend of mine lives in it. After I finished the novel I went back to Hong Kong and saw this friend and said, 'By the way, I put your house in my novel.' She laughed sadly and told me that she had just been asked to vacate it. It was on valuable land; it would be torn down soon after the hand-over.

Other People's

Robinson Crusoe

Robinson Crusoe, an adventure story of the ultimate castaway, is so established in most people's minds that even those who have not read it know some details of the novel. Shipwreck. Desert island. Goatskin jacket and funny hat. Hairy umbrella. Talking parrot. Shocking footprint. Man Friday. Cannibals. Rescue. The book is all so familiar as an apparently simple, wonderful tale of survival that it is easily read as a great yarn.

Crusoe is too human and accident-prone to be truly heroic – this may be another reason for his enduring appeal. But the setting is also a compelling feature of his story, for the island as a microcosm of the world has been used imaginatively in works as diverse as Shakespeare's *The Tempest* and Golding's *Lord of the Flies*. Crusoe is more stubborn than brave, and his first-person narrative, the more believable for being defiantly unliterary, can be appreciated as the account of a man's twenty-eight-year ordeal of loneliness, hunger, and physical threat; the fate of a man who ingeniously succeeds against the odds. But it is all so assured and so filled with plausible episodes and peculiar wisdom, it helps to be reminded that it was written by a man nearly sixty, who resembled his fictional creation in his need to scheme in order to survive. Defoe was a master of improvisation, and he had to be, for his life was a chronicle of ups and downs – which is a fair description of this novel.

Daniel Defoe (1660–1731) was, in the words of one critic, 'a shrewd, shifty, ingenious man, much mistrusted and frequently imprisoned.' He was jailed for debt as well as for his satirical writing, and his reverses included bankruptcy and the failure of get-rich-quick schemes, of which raising civet cats (their glands were used for perfume) for ready cash was just one. He was a journalist, publisher, poet, businessmen, and sometime secret agent, whose novel – the first in the language – was a huge hit, running into many editions and being quickly pirated and imitated.

One of the reasons for the success of this piece of fiction was that it was taken for fact. It is utterly vulgarly modern in that sense. In the Preface, Defoe, wearing the mask of Editor, wrote, 'The Editor believes the thing to be a just History of Fact; neither is there any Appearance of Fiction in it.' Defoe (who took the view that fiction could be a low and subversive trick that encouraged mendacity) had hit upon an idea that persists to this day – that if a book is said to be true it is somehow more important and authentic. 'A true story, based on actual events,' runs the assertion in the made-for-TV movie. 'It really happened!' the person says, who urges you to read such a book. That was also what Defoe wanted people to say in 1719, when *Robinson Crusoe* was first published; and they did say it and believed it.

The story is sensational – even today a story about such a castaway would be front-page news. But with time and rereading this adventure deepens in meaning, and the longer you live, the more impressive an achievement *Robinson Crusoe* becomes, turning from an amazing tale to a subtle study in innovation, a metaphor for human survival, and ultimately one of our own mythical tales, almost biblical in its morality: Robinson is as vivid and unambiguous a character as Job or Jonah, two people he specifically mentions.

And surely it is significant that the very first English novel is a desert island story, just one man in the middle of nowhere, with almost nothing, who survives to create a whole world. In this sense the novel is like an allegory of the history of humankind. The narrative emerges from chaos, with no society or props to speak of. A whole metaphor of creation is described in this book, which is as surprising in its action as in its intelligence. Its contradictions are the contradictions in the lives of many people; it embodies many of our discontents and dilemmas. No women figure in its drama; there is no passion and though there is affection there is hardly any love. But in its understated way the novel discusses just about everything else – materialism, isolation, arrogance, travel, friendship, imperialism, rebellious children, the relativity of wealth, the conundrum of power, the ironies of solitude, learning by doing; it is about faith, atonement, and the passage of time. It is also as practical as a pair of shoes. No sooner is the ordeal over than Crusoe is back, founding a colony and counting his money; and in the same way, the Crusoe idea continued, producing sequels and parodies, giving words to the language – Crusoe is a byword for castaway, as Friday is a synonym for helper.

Robinson begins life as a disobedient and hubristic if accident-prone boy. He is given any amount of advice by his sententious father, the German immigrant to England Herr Kreutznaer, who anglicized his name to Crusoe. The name-change is a nice touch in a book full of detail which is the more plausible for its being strange and even somewhat unnecessary. But as it happens, Defoe also changed his name, Frenchifying it, for his father's name was plain Mr. Foe. Daniel Defoe was anything but average, but he chose to write about a pretty ordinary, though arrogant, young man who (ignoring his father's Teutonic and pedestrian sermon on the safety of staying home) leaves home and finds himself involved in extraordinary events, beginning just days after his departure when on his first voyage his ship sinks. He is not deterred, and not even put off by a fairly prescient man who looks him in the eye and says that wherever he goes he 'will meet with nothing but Disasters and Disappointments.'

Soon after, battling sea monsters, Crusoe is saved by his servant Xury; instead of rewarding him for his efforts, he sells Xury into slavery, and it is only when he is a harassed planter in Brazil that he regrets selling Xury, for he realizes that he could use a slave to help him in his work. He thinks of Xury again in this way on the island. That crudely human logic is one of the most plausible aspects of the novel; and it frequently gives rise to Crusoe's refrain that he can't seem to do anything right. He even claims in this early stage that as a tobacco farmer in rural Brazil he is living 'like a Man cast away upon some desolate Island, that had no body there but himself.'

A few pages later, in one of Defoe's calculated ironies, Crusoe is shipwrecked on a slaving expedition, and begins to understand the reality behind his desert-island hyperbole, as he becomes a real cast-away on an island of real desolation. There is no question that Defoe intended a morality tale, but as a prolific writer (400 works bear his name) he was well enough acquainted with the public taste to know that for his story to be believed it needed persuasive detail. Crusoe is not high-minded. He is a rebellious son who is attracted to the risky and the morally doubtful. He is inexperienced, not a Londoner but a young provincial, a Yorkshireman. That he is from a reasonably well-off family makes him seem out of touch and a bit innocent; he keeps reminding us how average he is in being incompetent ('I had never handled a tool in my life') and accident-prone ('I that was born to be my own destroyer'), and he is not at all religious until he finds a Bible among the tools and seeds and paraphernalia he had rescued from the smashed ship.

He survives by growing and maturing; but he does more than survive – he ends by ruling the island, by becoming if not wise then sensible; by acquiring power and using it with understanding. He progresses from being an almost-victim to an almost-dictator. One of the most satisfying aspects of the novel is that in order to prevail over the natural obstacles of his island Crusoe has to learn the rudiments of civilization. For this to happen he must become acquainted with the paradox that his desert island is both a prison and a kingdom – he uses those very words. Early on, he calls himself a prisoner and describes his anguish. Later he speaks of 'the sixth year of my Reign, or my Captivity, which you please.' After some time passes and his confidence grows, his hut is a 'castle,' and with the appearance (and conversion from cannibalism) of Friday he thinks of himself as a ruler. At last, with his rescue of the Spaniards and Friday's father, he says, 'My island was now peopled and I thought myself very rich in subjects; and it was a merry reflection which I frequently made, How like a King I looked.' And he thinks of himself as an absolute ruler and even a despot, but a benevolent one.

Whenever the subject of *Robinson Crusoe* comes up, the name Alexander Selkirk is mentioned. Selkirk (1676–1721), a Scotsman from the village of Largo in Fifeshire, was a contemporary of Defoe. He was a seaman and notorious for his pugnacity – well known for his having thrown his father down a flight of stairs. During a voyage on a privateer in the Pacific, he quarreled with his captain and demanded to be put ashore on the remote (and deserted) island of Juan Fernández, off the coast of Chile. There he remained for over four years, 1704–9. He became a popular hero on his rescue and return to Britain. Details of his life as a castaway were published: his living off the land, his thatched-roof huts, his goatskin wardrobe. He said that he hankered for the tranquility of his simple life on the island. The celebrated essayist Richard Steele interviewed Selkirk and used him as a living illustration of the maxim 'that he is happiest who confines his wants to natural necessities.'

There is no evidence that Defoe ever met Selkirk, but as a journalist he obviously knew the story and Selkirk was undoubtedly the inspiration for *Robinson Crusoe*. But though Selkirk was apostrophized as a simple-lifer he was in effect no more than a survivor in extraordinary circumstances. The differences between Crusoe and Selkirk are more significant than the similarities. Selkirk's story is a fairly simple tale of survival on a barren island, while Crusoe's is at once a story of atonement and colonization; it is about becoming civilized – at least in eighteenth-century terms, when forcible conversion and slave-trading were regarded as elements of civilization.

Selkirk was a pirate who remained a pirate. Crusoe, also an unruly son, is supremely disobedient; his experience on the island (at the mouth of the Orinoco) is both his punishment and his reward, as his island prison is transformed into his kingdom. Crusoe epitomizes perspective. The issue of survival is secondary to the whole debate circling around the matter of point of view, which is summed up in his stating that, on the island, 'I entertained different Notions of Things.' Ambition and arrogance and greed got him into this fix; rationalism gets him out of it. When he sees the futility of riches on the island, the meaninglessness of money, the vanity of hoarding, and reaches the conclusion, 'That the good Things of this World are no farther good to us, that they are for our Use,' he is on the way to salvation.

The odd thing is that Selkirk is usually represented as a kind of marvel and of course he isn't. He is just the singular fellow who returned to tell his tale of solitary survival. Crusoe insists that the reader see him as unexceptional but a vivid warning, a living example of the ills of man, beset by hubris and discontent. 'I have been in all my Circumstances a Memento to those who are touched with the general Plague of Mankind . . .'

Crusoe is only solitary for part of his ordeal. The dramatic, and poignant, appearance of the footprint, together with the serious meditation that follows, is one of the episodes that lifts this novel to another level of meaning. It also shows Defoe as someone who could speak in the plainest and most convincing way about tools and seeds and grape-growing while at the same time being capable of the most profound rumination about the invasion of solitude and society and the definitions of space and time. Crusoe had lamented his solitude earlier, but no sooner has he conquered it and prevailed over his isolation than he has to reckon on the complexities of human company. The footprint is the beginning of this test of his understanding and the end of his Eden. What follows is like an allegory of the Ascent of Man, for he has to cope with cannibalism, aggression, warfare, and the competitive instinct. By overcoming these obstacles, Crusoe grows stronger. And yet, though he is a hero in a literary sense, he is not heroic in his deeds. His most persuasive quality is his humanity; he is the congenital bumbler who is challenged by circumstances to become competent. And one might add that though the Bible strengthens him he does not become visibly religious until Friday appears, and then he is sanctimonious.

If *Robinson Crusoe* were a story about holding out against the odds, then everything would hinge on Crusoe's rescue. But this is not the case. By mastering himself, Crusoe masters the island and makes a world of it. He progresses in an almost evolutionary sense from a lowly creature precariously clinging to life at the edge of the island to being the dominant species on it; he moves from castaway to colonizer. At the end, Crusoe is both, as he says, a king and a 'Generalissimo.' Defoe's point is that Crusoe does not need to be rescued, and it is emphasized by the fact that no sooner has he been scooped up and told his story than he returns to the island and prospers. It is a success story – of fall and rise; it is also a narrative of purification, with the most downright details as well as something approaching the spiritual. Not surprisingly, this novel has been in print and popular for almost 300 years.

Thoreau's *Cape Cod*

We are constantly told how normal and honorable Thoreau was, and yet it seems to me that we would get much further in understanding him if we began by conceding that he was an odd fish, full of peculiar conceits. He was a loner, and like many loners he was capable of a kind of horrid humor. I think Henry James was mistaken when he described Thoreau as 'imperfect, unfinished, inartistic; he was worse than provincial – he was parochial.' But the judgment contains some truth. Thoreau himself said he was possessed of a 'crooked genius.'

With his irritating self-assurance, no sooner has Thoreau intimated that he is down to earth and interested only in the habits of woodchucks than he begins to quote Homer, in Greek, and sometimes at great length (eight Homeric excursions in this little Cape Cod book, for example). He frequently talks of country matters in a way that makes him sound pedantic. Few of his jokes are truly witty. He affects not to like other people or human settlements and can, in saying so, sound misogynistic. He is surprising; he can also be swiftly persuasive.

Some of these qualities characterize *Cape Cod* and are what makes it such an unusual and interesting book. It is unusual even by Thoreau's standards, because it is good-natured about the bleakest of subjects, only glancingly about the Cape (its real subject is the sea), and contains more reverie than actual experience. It appeals to me especially for its location, my own home – which was very near Thoreau's – and, among other things, that is the most difficult of all travel subjects: the journey near home. Concord is only about sixty-five miles from the Cape. It was a form that Thoreau excelled at – *Walden* is another example. Few travel writers have managed this well. Its spirit is summed up in Thoreau's deliberate pronouncement, 'I have traveled a good deal in Concord.'

Given its modest intention, it is surprising that so much criticism has been leveled against *Cape Cod*. This seems especially cruel since the book is hardly known to the general reader of Thoreau's work. I would suppose that many people who have read *Walden*, and know that Thoreau made pencils for a living, and that he influenced Mahatma Gandhi in his essay on civil disobedience, and that his dying words were 'Moose . . . Indian,' are completely unaware of the existence of *Cape Cod*.

All the criticism of the book is posthumous, since the chapters that comprise it were articles that were collected only after Thoreau's death (of TB, at the fairly early age of forty-five). James was out of sympathy, and dismissive (but what did James know of the outdoors?). James Russell Lowell simply reached the wrong conclusions: 'Thoreau had no humor, and this implies that he was a sorry logician.' Those who knew Thoreau – except for Ellery Channing, his boon companion – found the man a difficult friend and his trips somewhat mystifying. Although cautiously appreciative, Emerson found Thoreau aggressive and in his essay on the man explained it in a forthright way: 'There was something military in his nature not to be subdued . . .'

The subtlest and most eloquent dissent regarding Thoreau's life and his writing is Leon Edel's 1970 pamphlet examining Thoreau's personal mythology, stylistic formulas, and his ambiguities. Edel sums up Thoreau's as a narcissistic personality. This essay, on a par with the similarly persuasive one by Robert Louis Stevenson, questions the very foundations of *Walden* – how Thoreau was seldom really alone, nor in the wilderness. Thoreau 'had access to his mother's cookie jar in town and enjoyed sundry dinners elsewhere.' But Edel, who uncovers distinct pathological traits in Thoreau, only mentions *Cape Cod* in passing.

The book has been criticized for containing too much undigested historical material, and alternately for being too lightweight and too learned. At best the critical praise of *Cape Cod* has been patronizing, and it has not become less so with the passage of time. Even eminent Thoreauvians have sniffed at the book. 'Cape Cod is Thoreau's sunniest book – and least profound,' Walter Harding has written. 'Too deliberately directed at a vulgar audience to represent him at his best,' wrote Joseph Wood Krutch. Thoreau, who was fascinated by queer names and bad puns, would undoubtedly have taken his revenge on the critic and made a wooden-crutch joke of his name. In *Cape Cod* we get two groaners – a play on 'littoral'/'literal' and a bit of meaningless fun with the Viking 'Thor-finn' and the American adventurer 'Thor-eau.'

But if it were so woeful and inadequate a book, would it have remained in print for over 100 years and – more to the point – if it were so badly written would Robert Lowell have bothered to plagiarize it for 'The Quaker Graveyard in Nantucket'? (Lines 4 to 12 of that prize-winning poem are a direct steal from a brilliant paragraph in the chapter 'The Shipwreck.') The book is certainly cranky. It is enjoyable for that reason, and for another – its unexpectedness. The narrative contains the first mention of broccoli growing in America (in 'The Wellfleet Oysterman'), and though it was not written as a book, but rather ten pieces based on three short trips, it has an unshakeable unity. It seems convincingly like one trip, in the way that *A Week on the Concord and Merrimack Rivers* seems convincingly like one full week. (It was in fact two.)

'I am very little of a traveler,' Thoreau once wrote to a friend. It was true. His trips were short, and the distances not great. The farthest he went was to Minnesota. Emerson and Hawthorn got to England and the Continent, Melville to the Holy Land; and Thoreau was well aware that other writers were roaming in India and Turkey. He could be annoyingly defensive: 'I know little about the affairs of Turkey, but I am sure that I know something about barberries and chestnuts of which I have collected a store this fall.' From time to time Thoreau writes a sentence to which the only response is, *So what?*

He would probably not have left Concord had it not been necessary for him to find material for his articles and lectures. He did not go very far afield. At the time of his Cape travels in 1851, he was supporting himself by lecturing in Medford. His subject: Life in the woods at Walden Pond.

Another spur to his going to Cape Cod was his agreement with *Putnam's Magazine* to supply five pieces for publication. He tells us on the first page of his book that in all he spent three weeks on the Cape, which seems like nothing; but Thoreau was able to make the most of very little – that quality is the essence of his life. In 1857 he returned to the Cape for another few weeks, but he did not write about it except in his journals. On that last trip he went alone. On the trips that make up this book he was accompanied by his friend Ellery Channing (who, with Sophie Thoreau, edited the book after Thoreau died). It was not arduous travel. It seems for the most part to have been little more than an energetic sort of loafing – rambling and writing about whatever he stumbled over. Thoreau was mistaken for a tramp, for a peddler, and at one point for a bank robber on the run. It is not to belittle his travel to say that it was largely a kind of bumming around; that was the impression he wished to convey.

And yet he was serious enough about the trip to burden himself with two large reference books – Volume 8 of the *Collections of the Massachusetts Historical Society*, and a gazeteer. From internal evidence it seems he had a Bible, too. And it is possible that he carried editions of Homer's *Iliad* and Virgil's *Eclogues*, because at this time in his life he had resumed his reading in Greek and Latin.

He avoided the towns and the settlements of any size. When he wanted a bed he headed for a lighthouse on a cliff or an isolated farm or fishing-shack. He liked the undemanding company of Channing. 'I feel it wholesome to be alone the greater part of the time,' he had written in *Walden*. 'To be in company, even with the best, is soon wearisome and dissipating. I love to be alone.' He was self-possessed to the point of sounding selfish, and one gathers that if pressed he would probably have said that most people behave like fools. He hated walking in settled areas, 'but when I come out upon a bare and solitary heath I am at once exhilarated.' One of the things that pleased him most about the Cape was that there were so few people there, but he had his objections to them, too. 'Some of the inhabitants of the Cape think that the Cape is theirs and all occupied by them,' he wrote in his *Journal* on his 1857 visit, 'but in my eyes it is no more theirs than it is the blackbird's.'

He went to the Cape out of curiosity, but in the course of his travel a great thing happened: Thoreau, the woodsman and landlubber, discovered the sea. 'Wishing to get a better view than I had yet had of the ocean,' was his stated objective in heading for the Cape. It was a modest wish, but its fulfillment gives this book power, and it seems to me that it is also why it is such a rhapsodic book and so joyous. Thoreau discovered that the sea was a true wilderness and that the only way to know it was to study it from the shore. In the narrative he seems to raise beachcombing to a priesthood.

This is also the subject of a poem he wrote after his Cape experiences:

> My life is like a stroll upon the beach
> As near the ocean's edge as I can go;
> My tardy steps its waves sometimes o'erreach,
> Sometimes I stay to let them overflow.
>
> I have but few companions on the shore:
> They scorn the strand who sail upon the sea;
> Yet oft I think the ocean they've sailed o'er
> Is deeper known upon the strand to me.
>
> The middle sea contains no crimson dulse,
> Its deeper waves cast up no pearls to view;
> Along the shore my hand is on the pulse,
> And I converse with many a shipwrecked crew.

It is a clumsy poem, but the point is plain in the egotistic certainty of the apostrophizing narrator: the man on the shore has the most intimate knowledge of the deep sea. Can this be so? In Thoreau's terms it is likely, because he is not dealing with surfaces – not the sailor's preoccupation with storms, winds, and currents – but with inner states, and depths; the bottom of the sea. The last line of the poem is literally true, for the first chapter of *Cape Cod* is scattered with shipwrecked corpses.

After the dry observation of the Cape landscape, Thoreau moves his travel narrative nearer the water and begins to write a hymn to the seashore. He must have known that in travel terms this was virgin territory and that his insights were quite original and striking. 'Objects on a beach, whether men or inanimate things, look not only exceedingly grotesque, but much larger and more wonderful than they really are.' Far-off rags look like cliffs, and human bones are enlarged and imposing, and one particular corpse he saw 'had taken possession of the shore, and reigned over it as no living one could . . .'

In an almost perverse way he seems to celebrate the grotesqueness of what we now call 'found objects.' He makes a majestic surrealism of the experience. He is not calling for a mere acceptance of the grotesque but rather much more; we must find it beautiful: 'I saw that the beauty of the shore itself was wrecked for many a lonely walker there, until he could perceive at last, how its beauty was enhanced by wrecks like this, and it acquired thus a rarer and sublime beauty still.'

And there are other moods of the grotesque, too: the Pilgrim Father theology he finds ridiculous in 'The Plains of Nauset,' the comic castaways and the freakishness in 'The Wellfleet Oysterman' (they are the human equivalent of the flotsam and jetsam he finds in the tidewrack), and the lengthy description of the fish that swallowed a certificate of church membership in 'The Beach Again.' He seems to be describing scenes from another world, and one can imagine that a great deal of his enthusiasm arose from the fact that this strangeness was so close to home.

But scenes like these disturbed his editor at *Putnam's*, George William Curtis, who felt that Thoreau was belittling Cape Codders. And he found Thoreau's religious discussions 'heretical.' Thoreau sent the articles to Curtis in 1852, but Curtis was obviously fussed by them, because he demanded cuts, and dithered until 1855 before starting publication. When Thoreau saw that Curtis had made further cuts on his own initiative, he reacted snappishly and withdrew the balance of the pieces. Only three installments had appeared. He had partly fulfilled his intention: his Cape Cod lectures were among his funniest and best received. We have Emerson's word on that: 'The Concord people laughed till they cried.'

It is impossible to tell which single trip of the three inspired in Thoreau the notion that he was writing about the sea, not the land. The book unifies his impressions. After the articles began to be serialized he was writing to his friend H. G. O. Blake, 'Come by all means [to North Truro], for it is the best place to see the ocean in these States.' By then he had just about abandoned his botanizing and bird-watching, and had become a beachcomber and gazer at the sea. In a definite sense he had turned his back to the land. It is a very Cape Cod stance, this eternal watching from the shore. When people say the Cape is small and insignificant, the Cape Codder laughs, because he knows that the Cape is vast – it includes all the sea around it.

Almost from the first page of the book, Thoreau seems to be casting around for a subject. So he interests himself in everything. The wrecked ship of Irish immigrants furnishes him with a motif, but he moves on to other matters: the useless facts in guidebooks, the contradictions of organized religion, the derivation of words (though he is wrong about 'gulled'), the occurrence of algae and kelp. At first he is looking for the grotesque in a rather forced way; but he was fortunate in the shipwreck and he was fortunate in meeting the Wellfleet oysterman. Yet people are not his subject. He seems to be on the track of something much odder.

By 'The Beach Again' he has become more reflective. He is enchanted by the power of the sea and its relationship to the shore. That is his great discovery – that the shore is the only way to understand the sea: not a voyage in the open sea, but a stroll on the sand. There, everything is revealed. 'The sea, vast and wild as it is, bears thus the waste and wrecks of human art to its remotest shore. There is no telling what it may not vomit up. It lets nothing lie . . .'

Watching closely, he sees that the sea is not blue, but every other color – purple, green, dark and even 'wine-colored,' as his favorite author proclaimed. The land is vulgar, but the sea is subtle; it inspires reveries of distant places, and Thoreau becomes lyrical. It has depths. This commonplace Thoreau turns into a nuance, and he relates it to Walden Pond ('more than one hundred feet deep'), and he concludes, 'The ocean is but a larger lake,' echoing the last line of Walden, 'The sun is but a morning star.'

What land there is on the Cape is ideal, because it is neutral, barren, and seems to encourage reflection. At times it seems that the Cape is not a real landscape at all, but rather a trembling mirage. Here, in this insubstantial place, a person may stand and view the subtlety of the sea. He does not say so plainly, but toward the end of the book Thoreau implies that Cape Cod is little more than a beach. That is its chief glory, its only importance.

I think this is the reason the book is not better known. People have read Cape Cod hoping to confirm their impressions of the place, wishing to follow the progress of the traveler, looking to compare the Cape today with what it was over 100 years ago. And what does Thoreau give them? Waves breaking on the shore, and seaweed, and some corpses: flotsam. It was only by turning his back to the Cape that he discovered his real subject, but in that way he lost any chance for a wide readership, for he had ceased to be topographical.

And yet by concentrating on the sea his imagination was enlivened, and he explains the bewitchment of looking seaward from a beach. A beach is a place of ceaseless activity and sudden surprises and of drama. 'Even the sedentary man here enjoys a breadth of view which is almost equivalent to motion.'

There can be no question of the attraction that the sea had for Thoreau. He makes this clear in the chapter 'The Sea and the Desert,' which is the high point in the book – the last chapter, 'Provincetown,' is flatter and no more than an extended epilogue. Thoreau was a man with one foot in Eden. He liked the idea of wilderness, of the untampered-with landscape, of virgin forest. The revelation that makes this book special among travel books and unique in Thoreau's own work is that its subject is the sea, because the sea is a wilderness. It was the wilderness that Thoreau could not quite match in any of his travels and it made him revise his opinions of what wilderness actually is. He is specific on this point:

I think that [the ocean] was never more wild than now. We do not associate the idea of antiquity with the ocean, nor wonder how it looked a thousand years ago, as we do of the land, for it was equally wild and unfathomable always . . . The ocean is a wilderness reaching round the globe, wilder than a Bengal jungle, and fuller of monsters . . .

The subject, the point of view, the hyperbole – and even the imagery – make this journey-near-home extraordinary and bring Thoreau closer to his exact contemporary Melville. It is not only the darkness and strangeness of the sea that excite Thoreau's mind, but also the fact that he is writing about it with such simplicity and innocence; it is the voice of Ishmael in *Moby-Dick*, another loner. And when at the end Thoreau says of the Cape, 'A man may stand there and put all America behind him,' he is expressing the yearning of Ishmael. That most un-Thoreauvian sentiment is the statement of a man longing to get away. In this trip more than any other, Thoreau discovered a sense of freedom. To him, Cape Cod was not a territory to be explored; it was a vantage point.

A Dangerous Londoner

At first, Joseph Conrad did not dare to call his book a novel. He traveled to Montpellier in February, 1906, with his small family, telling himself that he was composing a short story, entitled 'Verloc,' the name of the central character. As always, he wrote slowly, in a stubborn mood of exasperation and uncertainty, laboring in a foreign language.

When he sat down furtively to begin, Conrad was forty-eight years old. Long ago he had been in the French merchant marine. He now lived in England and spoke English and had been married for nine years in a sort of mismatch to Jessie, a dull and bovine Englishwoman (whom he had met while lodging in her mother's boarding house). A novelist, and former ship's captain, he was an unlikely candidate for domesticity. He was a remote and somewhat unwilling father of a sickly boy.

Verloc, 'a man well over forty,' was furtive and foreign. Long ago, he had been in the French artillery. He now lived in England and spoke English and had been married for seven years in a sort of mismatch to Winnie, an incurious and silent Englishwoman (whom he had met while lodging in her mother's boarding house). An *agent provocateur*, and former prison convict, he was an unlikely candidate for domesticity. He was a remote and somewhat unwilling foster father to his wife's younger brother, a hypersensitive boy.

This fictional Verloc was a fairly amorous, not to say priapic, individual and his sentimental nature had been his undoing more than once. He had made frequent trips to France. So had Conrad – to write – and, just before setting out on this particular trip, Jessie had disclosed to him that she was pregnant. This news embarrassed him ('at my venerable age'), as though a secret of his sexuality had been revealed.

The short story 'Verloc' developed into a long story, a kind of thriller, became a series of episodes, grew to something resembling a novel, was retitled *The Secret Agent*, and serialized in a magazine at the end of 1906, then elaborated to its present form – and in its expansion it became not just plumper but somewhat misshapen. It was published as a book in 1907. It concerned a plot to blow up Greenwich Observatory in south-east London, and was based on an actual event that took place in 1894, when Conrad, living in London and working on *Almayer's Folly*, read about it in *The Times* and the

Morning Leader. The book received a mixed reception from the critics and it sold badly. Conrad called it 'an honorable failure.'

But at one point, quite late in the action of the story, a character says, 'From a certain point of view we are here in the presence of a domestic drama.'

It is easy to see why, and it is wonderful to reflect on how in writing what was in effect the world's first political thriller – spies, conspirators, wily policemen, murders, bombings, and in a London wearing a suitably gloomy expression for these misdeeds – Conrad was also giving artistic expression to his domestic anxieties: his overweight wife and problem child, his lack of money, his inactivity, his discomfort in London, his uneasiness in English society, his sense of exile, of being an alien. It is also a portrait of Russian wickedness, and that had a deeply personal resonance for Conrad, too. He had reasons to regard the Russians as satanic.

'It is essential to emphasize and remember the most crucial facts of Conrad's early life,' Jeffrey Myers writes in his biography, *Joseph Conrad*, speaking of Conrad's reasons for leaving Poland for good and going to sea. This was Russian Poland in 1874. 'The Russians had enslaved his country, forbidden his language, confiscated his inheritance, treated him as a convict, killed his parents and forced him into exile.'

There is a certain lurching quality to the narrative. The story is told in fits and starts and flashbacks – years summed up on some pages, while a number of chapters concern a single day: the day of the bombing. Conrad had as much trouble conveying the passage of time as he had using prepositions. Yet the plot is less complicated than it appears. The book begins with a description of Verloc's shop in Soho, with its grimy window of grubby merchandise – lurid books, girlie pictures, soft porn, bottles of patent medicine that we assume restore male potency, and envelopes and small cardboard boxes which in Conrad's original manuscript contained condoms ('superfine Indiarubber'). Verloc sets off that morning for a foreign – that is, Russian – embassy in Knightsbridge and we soon learn that his squalid shop is a cover for a shady operation in which with the embassy's sanction he encourages a small group of revolutionaries, who do not know that he passes their secrets back to his diplomat-contact.

But after eleven years of this cynical espionage, Verloc has grown lazy – he sleeps late, he does very little intelligence work, he is bored with the foolish talk of the conspirators. The diplomat, Vladimir, insults him, berates him, and demands that he produce an outrage – a great symbolic bombing – to frighten the British government and discredit all revolutionaries in exile. Although annoyed at being hectored like this, Verloc skulks away and waits for his chance. He despairs of rousing the silly revolutionaries to action. He devises a plan for blowing up Greenwich Observatory. We learn in the course of the narrative that Verloc's story started more than seven years earlier, when he was released from prison after serving five years for stealing secret designs of French armaments. He had been turned in by one of his girlfriends – he is susceptible to pretty women and has a fatal predilection for trusting women he has seduced. He becomes a lodger at a boarding house run by Winnie's mother, widow of an abusive man, and because Winnie has been disappointed in love (rejected by the son of the local butcher) and both she and her hysterical (perhaps autistic) brother need looking after, Verloc is seen as a good bet. They are married on June 24, 1879.

The year is now 1887, and in those intervening years of marriage Winnie has never questioned how Verloc has made his living – his seedy shop, his late hours, his visits to the Continent. Beneath her portrait, so to speak, Conrad has provided the caption, 'She felt profoundly that things do not stand much looking into.' All in all, she appears to be the perfect wife for a secret agent. Verloc has not looked very deeply into Winnie, but Conrad has, and he has arrived at a fascinating conclusion, in one of the novel's best *aperçus*: 'Curiosity being one of the forms of self-revelation, a systematically incurious person remains always partly mysterious.'

Winnie is satisfied that Stevie has Verloc to model himself upon – after all, Stevie is nervous, excitable, idealistic, and frail, and he is described in animal imagery, as a kind of neurasthenic pet – a dog or cat. Verloc is his antithesis, solid, ironic, fatalistic, and strong ('his thick arms . . . like weapons'), and seeing them together Winnie thinks with satisfaction that they look like father and son.

Winnie helps run the shop, she is loyal and obedient, she puts up with Verloc's late sleeping, his 'wallowing in bed,' his habit of seldom taking off his hat, and is especially tolerant and cooperative when Verloc's pulse quickens with a sudden fever of amorousness. Verloc has a tendency to wake, pull the bedclothes to his chin, gaze meaningfully upon his wife with heavy-lidded eyes and sleepily beckon her. Conrad was prudish both as a result of his strict – not to say traumatic – upbringing in Poland and his rather ascetic life as a seaman, yet

The Secret Agent was ahead of its time in showing a husband and wife in bed – two memorable scenes, as well as some coming and going. The couple can be observed both conversing about the day's events as well as indulging in sexual by-play of a verbal kind, the private euphemistic language of sex partners.

Feeling that she is in the way, wishing to give Stevie some latitude with Verloc, Winnie's mother takes herself off to an almshouse – a ponderous cab ride recommended by some critics for being properly 'Dickensian.' My feeling is that it is quite the reverse. Conrad has none of Dickens's affection for the homely (and often darkly comic) details of grubby London, but rather, as an exile and a master mariner and a cottage dweller in rural Kent, regards the city with pure horror. London in this novel is a sink of drizzling darkness and filth and slime, in which 'pests' (such as the posturing political fanatics, the Professor, and Ossipon, and Michaelis) can lose themselves in the crowd. London mobs and London gloom are convenient, though, for this monochrome novel of secrecy and shadows: the Verlocs' home life is enacted in a house 'nestling in a shady street behind a shop where the sun never shone.'

With compassion for her hypersensitive brother, Winnie urges Verloc to take him with him whenever he goes out. Verloc uses these maternal urgings as an excuse for the boy to accompany him on his bombing mission to Greenwich. The boy is dumbly loyal and eager to please – perfect as the bomb-carrier, for even if he is caught (Verloc reasons) he will say nothing to the police. Everything goes disastrously wrong. A scrap of cloth with his address on it is found near Stevie's dismembered corpse. Verloc is visited by a policeman, who delivers the awful news ('I tell you they had to fetch a shovel to gather him up with') as Winnie listens in horror at the keyhole. Verloc reminds Winnie of how she had asked him to look after the boy; in reply, he accuses her of being equally to blame for Stevie's death. More than that, sleepy, hungry, and libidinous, he changes the subject and indulges in the only foreplay he knows, the ambiguous verbal command to his wife, 'Come here.'

Consumed by grief, and hearing his unfair accusation, and the invitation to sex which follows it, she fatally stabs him. In the last portion of the book, Winnie considers suicide, is briefly rescued by Alexander Ossipon, one of the opportunistic revolutionaries, who promises to save her, but instead robs her, abandons her, and leaves her in despair so profound she jumps to her death.

Conrad maintained, both in writing and in speaking of the novel to friends, that Winnie was the central figure in the narrative. She does not seem so – we do not see much of her in the book, and we learn very little about her. But you know what Conrad means. In a thriller about a bomb outrage, with international implications, Winnie Verloc is the only character who is truly outraged. She has been true to herself and to her husband, a good wife, an attentive sister, a dutiful daughter, uncomplaining; the still center of the action – and what does she get for it? A brute of a husband. Her mother gone. Her brother senselessly murdered. And after all that, her husband goes on abusing her. You can almost hear her barrister at her murder trial recommending clemency and saying, 'My Lord, hasn't this poor woman suffered enough?'

Yet the peculiar passion and the violence in the novel appear very un-English, and Conrad must have been aware of that, because he seems at pains to highlight the strangeness of his characters and the alien nature of their urgencies. He concluded that this was a failing in himself when he reflected on the poor reception of the novel: 'There is something in me that is unsympathetic to the general public . . . Foreignness, I suppose.'

It does seem that entering this book one is in a distant land, a London borrowed and distorted as though reflected in a mirror – an elaborate but tarnished hand-mirror, made in Poland, framed in France, buffed up in England. The city is badly lit and dripping and much of it, and the novel, has the perverse logic and derangement of a dream, yet not an English dream. The sense of place is vivid but slightly askew. Setting off in the morning, Mr. Verloc perceives the sunshine as golden, and then coppery, and finally producing 'a dull effect of rustiness' – which is less a meditation on the meteorology of sunbeams than on metallurgy. Ten pages later, the sunshine is emphatically 'rusty' and 'Mr. Verloc heard against a window-pane the faint buzzing of a fly – his first fly of the year – heralding better than any number of swallows the approach of spring.'

This droll but faintly repellent observation, like a Polish joke, is that of someone new to London – indeed, new to England. Later in the novel London is compared to 'a slimy aquarium from which the water had been run off' – and you have to think hard to conjure up this image. Soon after, London is 'an immensity of greasy slime and damp plaster.' The celebrated cab ride produces this grim description: 'Night, the early dirty night, the sinister, noisy, hopeless, and rowdy night of South London –' This nocturne is experienced by Winnie's mother in the cab, but it is as though London is being seen by someone new to the city.

The strangeness of Conrad's language only adds to the reader's sense of dislocation. Much of it gives Conrad's prose its originality; but occasionally clumsy, often creaky and obsolete, it is sometimes plainly wrong. We can smile at a novel set in 1887 that contains a player piano – not invented until ten years later – but there is something about phrases such as 'the age of caverns' or 'a success of esteem' that smacks of translation. Conrad's writing is notorious for its unconscious Gallicisms.

Polish was his first language, he was raised speaking French – he could have become a French writer, he said. He was enormously well read, particularly in French literature, and he admired Flaubert above all (the influence shows even in *The Secret Agent*: the description of Ossipon's returning home after ditching Winnie, at the end of Chapter 12, echoes the famous passage in *Madame Bovary* when Léon and Emma spend most of the afternoon canoodling in the closed carriage). It was as a sailor in the British merchant fleet in 1878 that Conrad first encountered English and began to speak it and read it. He was then twenty years old. It was the opinion of everyone who ever heard Conrad speak that he never managed to pronounce English correctly. And (a personal detail he included in his story 'Amy Foster') he raved in the Polish language whenever he was feverish.

Non-native speakers of English tend toward repetition, overcorrectness, unconscious translation, and the use of arcane words. *The Secret Agent* abounds with examples of these quirks. Conrad was self-taught. He used words he had read in books he treasured. The books might have been French. How else to explain 'charabia' or 'villegiature'? They might have been very old English ones, which would account for 'paynim' – regarded as archaic even in Conrad's time. And then there are 'hebetude' and 'mansuetude,' 'frequentation' and 'uncandidness' – items in Seaman Korzeniowski's notebook, 'How to Increase My Word Power.' The effect of these usages is sometimes that produced by a person telling a story in a heavy accent – distracted by the cadences, the listener loses the narrative thread.

But this language matter is seldom a question of correctness in Conrad's case. The fact is that Joseph Conrad wrote like Joseph Conrad, and because of the setting and subject of *The Secret Agent*, this lexical flavoring, and the clumsily truncated time-scheme, give this particular book originality and power, and intensify its strangeness. It is not an English novel – it doesn't look like one, nor does it sound like one. It strikes me as laughable that the critic F. R. Leavis included it in *The Great Tradition*, for while it may have initiated the tradition of the thriller ('a very artificial form of writing which realism rarely redeems from its fundamental fantasy,' V. S. Pritchett wrote when discussing Conrad's book), it seems to me a hybrid in both structure and tone, without any specific English antecedents, and outside of any tradition. Of course it confused and irritated the English (like 'an excellent translation,' Kipling said of Conrad's prose), but it has a definite appeal to any expatriate living in London. The foreigner often sees in London what the Londoner misses, and by the same token the émigré writer is capable of producing hilarious howlers.

Everyone in the novel seems to languish in exile, not only the obvious characters – Mr. Vladimir, and the other diplomats at the (Russian) embassy, and the ranters Ossipon, Karl Yundt, and Michaelis – but also the Professor, whose 'parentage was obscure.' Verloc explains that although he is a 'natural-born British subject' his father was French. His wearing his hat constantly – even indoors, even when he is eating – is explained as a continental habit he learned from frequenting 'foreign cafés.' At the end of the novel it is revealed that Verloc's secret bank account is kept in a fictitious name, 'Prozor' – and you immediately think that 'Smith' or 'Jones' would be less likely to arouse official suspicions. Even London-born-and-bred Winnie has a taint of foreignness. Her stout wheezy mother claimed to be of French descent and 'Traces of the French descent which the widow boasted of were apparent in Winnie, too.' The Assistant Commissioner is English, and familiar, but when he sees his reflection in a window glass he is 'struck by his foreign appearance.' He visits Sir Ethelred and he looks 'more foreign than ever.'

The exiles are grotesque. And because of the tone of the novel, its relentless irony frequently coarsening into sarcasm, nearly all of the English characters tend toward caricature – the charlady Mrs. Neale, Sir Ethelred, and 'Toodles,' his assistant. But in the lady patroness Conrad has produced someone both familiar and beautifully realized, the plutocrat, 'above the play of economic conditions,' isolated from society and yet taking her pleasure in toying with it, being social, condescending, making promises, arranging introductions, a temptress, more a meddler than a fixer. It is she who makes Conrad's London so believable and who gives the book structure and a sense of order. Her guests are 'Royal Highnesses, artists, men of science, young statesmen, and charlatans of all ages and conditions.' Many of the important characters in the novel are known to her, they have met in her drawing room, and all would be welcome there. There is not a character in the novel who is not accessible to her. The lady patroness gives an English uniqueness to the book (her drawing room is not a foreign land) and makes much of the drama possible – after all, the Assistant Commissioner met Mr. Vladimir at her house, and he knows the slob (squat, 252 pounds) Michaelis to be a special friend. The lady patroness secured a contract with an English publisher for Michaelis to write his memoirs for an advance of 500 pounds. This was not a random number, but rather one of Conrad's bitter details (ten times more than he was paid for *Outcast of the Islands* in 1896).

The drawing room of the lady patroness gives London in the book the sense of a small world where chance meetings are possible, and it makes the coincidental encounters outside the drawing room seem less contrived, as when Chief Inspector Heat bumps into the Professor – cop meeting criminal again – or Ossipon meets Winnie just as she has decided to kill herself. Anyone who has lived in London for any length of time recognizes this cozy quality of the city. It is a vast city but a horizontal one with relatively few great thoroughfares and meeting places – Soho, Piccadilly Circus, Trafalgar Square, Hyde Park, the theatres, the large railway terminuses – and it might have been said in Conrad's time, as it is said now, that if you linger in Oxford Street long enough you will meet most of your London friends. In *The Secret Agent*, London seems less like the largest city in the world (which it was) than a very small dark village, inhabited by folks who know each other.

Repeated in the novel is the idea that these people, no matter how different they appear, resemble each other deep down, and in some cases are interchangeable. What is taken to be yet another irony in a novel packed with ironizing seems plainly cynical, but it is explicitly insisted upon. Is it true, or is Conrad being provocative?

'The terrorist and the policeman both come from the same basket,' says the Professor. In another context, Chief Inspector Heat says something similar: 'the mind and instincts of a burglar are of the same kind as the mind and instincts of a police officer.' When Conrad describes the respectable Assistant Commissioner awaiting Verloc's return, he lingers 'as though he were a member of the criminal classes.' And for Verloc, 'Anarchists or diplomats were all one to him.' Just as the Assistant Commissioner physically resembles a foreigner – as though he is surrealistically blending in with the rest of the exiles – Verloc and Stevie, unrelated by blood, are 'like father and son.'

To passersby, Winnie looks exactly like Stevie. This is not odd, since they are brother and sister, but what is unusual, since Stevie has a pathological horror of violence, is that Winnie becomes most like her brother when she is about to plunge a knife into her husband's heart: 'As if the homeless soul of Stevie had flown for shelter straight to the breast of his sister . . . the resemblance of her face with that of her brother grew at every step, even to the droop of the lower lip, even to the slight divergence of the eyes.'

These likenesses, this blended sense of small world – coincidences and common ground – convey an ambiguous aura of moral lassitude, but at the same time give the novel a family atmosphere, its 'domestic drama.' In that respect it is the simple tale of Conrad's subtitle. Not an English family, but a nest of exiles, fatalistic and unhappy, but dangerous only to themselves. But speaking of likenesses, surely the great but unintentional irony of this ironic masterpiece is the way in which the Verlocs are so like the Korzeniowskis.

The Worst Journey in the World

The heroic soul who wrote *The Worst Journey in the World* was physically rather frail and had terrible eyesight and everything happened to him while he was still in his twenties. It was as though, in having survived the near-death experiences of Antarctic exploration and World War I, he had incurred a huge debt which he spent the rest of his life repaying. He was broken mentally and physically. He once wrote, 'It falls to few men to do something which no one else has ever done. To have done so before the age of thirty is astonishing; the combination of opportunity, ability and motive power is extremely rare.'

Apsley Cherry-Garrard, the youngest member of Captain Scott's ill-fated 1910–13 expedition to Antarctica, made that observation about Lawrence of Arabia, whom he knew. He might have been writing about himself. The essay is included in a little-known collection of reminiscences, called *T. E. Lawrence by His Friends*. This piece is the only other example of Cherry-Garrard's writing I have ever found. There are no published letters or diaries, no reminiscences;

there is no biography. He volunteered first for the polar risk and then volunteered for World War I. He suffered and wrote about his experiences at the pole. He did not write about the war, though he said that for bravery and ideals no soldier he had seen in combat could compare with the Antarctic explorers he had known.

In that same T. E. Lawrence essay he wrote, 'To go through a terrible time of mental and physical stress and to write it down as honestly as possible is a good way of getting some of it off your nerves. I write from personal experience.'

It seems that *The Worst Journey in the World*, brilliant as it is, did not get enough of the stress off Cherry-Garrard's nerves. While writing his book and afterwards, he endured a number of nervous breakdowns. Yet everywhere in his writing his voice is clear, articulate, and humane, and sometimes startling.

'Polar exploration is at once the cleanest and most isolated way of having a bad time which has been devised,' he wrote. It is an unexpected and oblique observation but characteristic of this neglected polar explorer.

He had the older English gifts of understatement and stoicism, a dignified refusal to fuss or exaggerate, yet his experience was so horrific he wrote, 'This journey had beggared our language; no words could express its horror.'

The experience he speaks of was his five-week trek to Cape Crozier, in the polar winter (June–July) of 1911, to study the emperor penguins. Cherry-Garrard's epic (and successful) trip, which became known as the Winter Journey, was overshadowed by the tragedy of the later polar party, which he accompanied only part of the way. Scott spent more than two and a half months battling to the pole through blizzards, only to discover that Roald Amundsen had reached it a month earlier. Scott arrived to find the Norwegian flag flapping over the pole. 'Great God, this is an awful place,' he confided to his diary. He still faced a return trip to his base of 800 miles. On the way back he and his team of four men were stranded by storms only eleven miles from shelter. In dying of cold and hunger, the Scott team became national heroes and a lasting example of British fortitude. The British needed just such a symbol, for World War I began very soon afterwards. Cherry-Garrard went home from Antarctica and enlisted in the army. It was not until the war was over that he was able to begin his book.

The Worst Journey in the World was first published in 1922 and reissued with additional material in 1951. It goes in and out of print; but it is indestructible, because it is a masterpiece.

When people ask me (I get the question about twice a month), 'What is your favorite travel book?' I nearly always name this book. It is about courage, misery, starvation, heroism, exploration, discovery, and friendship. It vividly illustrates the demands of science and the rigors of travel. It is a record of the coldest, darkest days that can be found on our planet. It is written beautifully but not obviously, with a subtle artistry. It recounts a diabolical ordeal. It was composed by a man who was very kind and not particularly strong. He was one of the bravest men on the expedition.

Recently graduated from Oxford, where he had read classics and modern history, Cherry-Garrard was the youngest man, just twenty-four, when he set sail on Scott's expedition ship *Terra Nova*. His classical education stood him in good stead, providing comparisons for the almost mythic horrors he was to encounter. One night at a remote camp in Antarctica, Cherry-Garrard's Fahrenheit thermometer read minus 77.5. 'The day lives in my memory as that on which I found out that records are not worth making.' And he goes on to say, 'I will not pretend that it did not convince me that Dante was right when he placed the circles of ice below the circles of fire.' After the Winter Journey he wrote:

Such extremity of suffering cannot be measured. Madness or death may give relief. But this I know: we on this journey were already beginning to think of death as a friend. As we groped our way back that night, sleepless, icy, and dog-tired in the dark and the wind and the drift [death in] a crevasse seemed almost a friendly gift.

The title of the book is slightly misleading. Although this is a thorough account of Scott's effort to reach the South Pole, the Worst Journey was that Winter Journey, on which Cherry-Garrard and two other men, Edward Wilson and Henry ('Birdie') Bowers, searched for the remote nesting place of the emperor penguin. No human being had ever ventured in the winter to Cape Crozier, the site of the penguins' rookery. It was suspected that the male penguins tended the eggs – but how? And when did the eggs hatch? No scientist on earth had ever retrieved, much less dissected, the egg of the emperor penguin.

There was a very good reason for this. Until then, no one had seen the penguins' eggs in situ. For the several months that the birds nested at Cape Crozier, they were in complete darkness, obscured by the sunless Antarctic winter. The winds were gale force for much of the time. The temperatures were the lowest in the world. Deep and deadly crevasses cut across the route along the ice shelf. Scott preferred ponies to dogs (that preference was another reason his expedition failed), but neither dogs nor ponies would have been much use over the sixty-three miles of broken ice and cliffs that separated the scientists from the emperor penguins. Accordingly, the men had to split their 790 pounds of food and gear among three sledges, which they man-hauled. This they did, in appalling conditions, for the three-week journey out. They endured frostbite, nightmares, near-starvation, and exhaustion. 'And then we heard the Emperors calling.'

The birds were 'trumpeting with their curious metallic voices' in the darkness – hundreds of them. Cherry-Garrard and his two companions gathered scientific information, noting the strong protective instinct of the males: how they balanced the egg on the upper part of their feet to keep it off the ice, and warmed it further by plumping it under a tuck of their belly. With three eggs safely stowed in the sledges (two other eggs had broken), the men set off on the return journey, near death on many occasions. This eighty-page chapter is the most harrowing I have ever read in a travel book, and it easily vies with Poe's *The Narrative of Arthur Gordon Pym* for menacing weather and mounting terror.

The close attention to detail, to mood, to pace, and to the very shape of the sentences that makes Cherry-Garrard's Winter Journey chapter so powerful a piece of writing also characterizes the rest of the book. It is rare to find a person who is at once such a great traveler, recounting an overwhelming experience, and also such an accomplished writer. (This is one of the reasons we are still ignorant of what space travel or lunar exploration is like: no astronaut has shown any ability to convey the experience in writing.) This book is an almost unparalleled account of courage. Even if it were clumsily written, as many histories are, the book would be worth reading, for its story alone. But Cherry-Garrard gives aesthetic pleasure as well and his prose style is so efficient and even-tempered – never depending for effect on the quick-to-fade colors of hyperbole – that when he uses a word like 'horror' or the expression 'death as a friend' he means just that. Each word he writes is perfectly judged.

Here is his account – he was on the search party – of finding Scott's last camp six months after the men died:

That scene can never leave my memory. We with the dogs had seen Wright turn away from the course by himself and the mule party swerve right-handed ahead of us. He had seen what he thought was a cairn, and then something looking black by its side. A vague kind of wonder gave way to real alarm. We came up to them all halted. Wright came across to us. 'It is the tent.' I do not know how he knew. Just a waste of snow . . .

It was not a sense of misplaced masculinity that fueled Scott's expedition and drove them onward, Cherry-Garrard said. It was the desire for knowledge. Amundsen's expedition was a classic of national competitiveness; Scott maintained disingenuously that his was essentially a scientific endeavor. The Antarctic represented the unknown, and so it had to be investigated thoroughly, in spite of the risks, because, as Cherry-Garrard wrote, 'Exploration is the physical expression of the Intellectual Passion.'

This clear-sightedness, which reflects truthfulness and modesty and a capacity for portraiture, is well illustrated in his subtle sketch of Captain Scott in the book. It begins, 'England knows Scott as a hero; she has little idea of him as a man.' Cherry-Garrard first makes the point that Scott could be charming when he wanted to be. He then says of this complex man that he was both domineering and much more reserved than anyone could possibly guess.

'Add to this that he was sensitive, femininely sensitive, to a degree which might be considered a fault, and it will be clear that leadership to such a man may be almost a martyrdom.' Cherry-Garrard enumerates Scott's other limitations: he had continual indigestion, an unstable temperament, and 'moods and depressions which might last for weeks.' That last is a frightening-statement when you consider what weeks of depression might mean to the other members of an Antarctic expedition. In a last crushing judgment, Cherry-Garrard says, 'He cried more easily than any man I have ever known.'

Yet Cherry-Garrard maintains that Scott was heroic, and it is characteristic of his book that this subtlety is so memorably conveyed. It is in contemplation of these negative aspects of Scott – his weaknesses – that the heroism of his men can be truly appreciated. He had many triumphs, Cherry-Garrard says, and goes on, 'Surely the greatest was that by which he conquered his weaker self, and became the strong leader whom we went to follow and came to love.'

Scott's leadership qualities have been questioned. Scott has been depicted in other accounts variously as a blunderer, an enigma, and something approaching a villain, with a merciless ambition. But it is for the compassion in this apparent paradox that I have read *The Worst Journey* again and again, because among many other things it is a book about overcoming enormous odds, while at the same time preserving civility and humanity. Cherry-Garrard was quite specific in asserting that conventional heroism is essentially a display of foolishness. It is fear and faint-heartedness that make a person truly brave. He writes similarly of T. E. Lawrence:

The fact that in the eyes of the world Lawrence lived the bravest of lives did not help him prove to himself that he was no coward. For we are most of us cowards, and had not Lawrence been a coward to himself he would have had no need to prove his bravery. The man who is not afraid has no feelings, no sensitiveness, no nerves; in fact he is a fool.

It was also a satisfaction to Cherry-Garrard that at the worst moments of the Winter Journey his comrades still said 'please' and 'thank you' and kept their tempers – 'even with God.'

He was of ancient lineage, and lived with his wife on his family estate. They had no children. In many ways he seemed a sort of lord of the manor, but the causes he championed were uncharacteristic of that role. In his later years, Cherry-Garrard became interested in animal rights. He was part of a vocal opposition to the destruction of penguins; he stood firm and made himself unpopular by campaigning against fox-hunting. He saw himself as weak and near-sighted but regarded these apparent handicaps as a lasting source of strength.

He was always philosophical, his feet firmly on the ground. As he writes in his last chapter, entitled 'Never Again:'

And I tell you if you have the desire for knowledge and the power to give it physical expression, go out and explore. If you are a brave man you will do nothing; if you are fearful you may do much, for none but cowards have need to prove their bravery. Some will tell you that you are mad, and nearly all will say, 'What is the use?' For we are a nation of shopkeepers, and no shopkeeper will look at research which does not promise him a financial return within a year. And so you will sledge nearly alone, but those with whom you sledge will not be shopkeepers: that is worth a good deal. If you march your Winter Journeys you will have your reward, so long as all you want is a penguin's egg.

RACERS TO THE POLE

What most people know of the conquest of the South Pole is that Captain Scott got there and then died heroically on the return journey; that when the polar party lay tent-bound and apparently doomed, Captain Oates unselfishly said, 'I am just going outside and may be some time' – and took himself out to die, so that his comrades might live. That Scott represented self-sacrifice and endurance, and glorious failure, the personification of the British ideal of plucky defeat. Scott's expedition was essentially scientific; he was beset by bad weather. Roald Amundsen is sort of an afterthought: Oh, yes, the dour Norwegian actually got to the pole and planted his flag first, but that's a detail; he was very lucky and a little devious. So much for the pole.

Roland Huntford, in his *The Last Place on Earth* – its original title was *Scott and Amundsen* – proves all of this wrong, and much more to boot. Thus, the kerfuffle.

It is a measure of the power of this book that when it first appeared in Britain, it caused an uproar; and a few years later, a television series that was adapted from it created a flurry of angry letters to newspapers and a great deal of public discussion, in which the book was rubbished and its author condemned – even vilified in some quarters for suggesting that Fridtjof Nansen was engaged in a sexual affair with Kathleen Scott while her husband lay freezing in his tent.

The polar quest was not just exploration, a journey of discovery, it was indeed (although Scott tried to deny it) an unambiguous race to be the first at the South Pole. National pride was at stake – Norwegian and British; two different philosophies of travel and discovery, skis versus trudging, dogs versus ponies, canvas and rubberized cloth versus fur anoraks and Eskimo boots; two cultures – Norse equality ('a little republic' of explorers, as one of the Norwegians wrote) versus the severe British class system; and two sorts of leadership, more particularly, two different and distinct personalities, Roald Amundsen's versus Captain Scott's.

The great surprise in the book is that Amundsen is not a moody, sullen Scandinavian, but rather a shrewd, passionate, approachable, thoroughly rational man who tended to understate his exploits, while Scott – quite the reverse of the British stereotype – was depressive, unfathomable, aloof, self-pitying, prone to exaggerate his vicissitudes. Their personalities determined the mood of each expedition: Amundsen's was spirited and cohesive, Scott's was confused and demoralized. Amundsen was charismatic and focused on his objective; Scott was insecure, dark, panicky, humorless, an enigma to his men, unprepared; and a bungler, but in the spirit of a large-scale bungler, always self-dramatizing.

'It was Scott who suited the sermons,' Mr. Huntford writes. 'He was a suitable hero for a nation in decline.' Amundsen had made the conquest of the pole 'into something between an art and a sport. Scott had turned polar exploration into an affair of heroism for heroism's sake.' Mrs. Oates, who was privy to a running commentary on the Scott expedition through her son's letters home – Oates was throughout a remarkable witness – called Scott the 'murderer' of her son. As for Oates's opinion, 'I dislike Scott intensely,' he wrote in Antarctica.

Far from being a belittler or having an ax to grind about the phlegmatic British, Mr. Huntford merely points out that Britain took Scott as a necessary hero; it is not the British character that is being assailed in this book, but the process by which Scott took charge of the disastrous expedition. Scott was the problem. Though he knew little of actual command (and was unsuited to it), Scott was ambitious, seeking advancement, even glory, in the Royal Navy. He was a manipulator, he knew how to find patrons – which he did in Sir Clements Markham, a wonderful sly subsidiary character in the narrative – vindictive, pompous, queenly, attracted to Scott more for Scott's being strangely epicene. The femininity in Scott's personality was remarked upon by one of Scott's own men, Apsley Cherry-Garrard – the youngest in the expedition; Cherry-Garrard also mentions how they had erroneously rated Amundsen 'a blunt Norwegian sailor' rather than as 'an explorer of the markedly intellectual type,' sagacious and weather-wise.

The weather has always been regarded as the determining factor in Amundsen's success and Scott's failure. Yet it offered little advantage: conditions were pretty much the same for both expeditions; the fact was that Amundsen was far better prepared, and Scott left no margin of safety for food, fuel, or weather. In a journey of four months Scott had not allowed for four days' bad weather. Parallel diary entries in a given period show Amundsen hearty and bucked up as he skis through fog, and just behind him Scott's diary shows him fatigued, depressed, complaining, slogging along. Mr. Huntford sees this as a difference not in style but in approach:

Scott ... expected the elements to be ordered for his benefit, and was resentful each time he found they were not. This was a manifestation of the spiritual pride that was Scott's fatal flaw.

The difference between the two rivals is expressed in the way each called on the Deity. Scott did so only to complain when things went wrong; Amundsen, to give thanks for good fortune. In any case, Scott was an agnostic and believed in science; Amundsen was a Nature-worshipper. For that reason alone, Amundsen found it easier to accept the caprice of blizzard and storm. He and his companions were in tune with their surroundings; they were spared the angst that tormented Scott and, through him, pervaded the British expedition.

The Norwegian expedition, though vastly underfunded, were all of them skiers, had a better diet, simpler but more sensible gear, and the bond of friendship. Skis were a mere novelty to the non-skier Scott, whose class-ridden expedition had plenty of money and patrons. He had planned to depend upon ponies and motorized sledges, but when these proved useless he was reduced to hauling sledges by hand. In the base camp, long before Scott's party set out for the pole, one of Scott's men – significantly it was the one Norwegian, Tyrggve Gran – wrote, 'Our party is divided, and we are like an army that is defeated, disappointed and inconsolable.'

Amundsen had heart and compassion but could also be an odd fish in his way. He had a prejudice against doctors. He wouldn't take one on an expedition. 'He believed that a doctor created sickness,' Mr. Huntford writes, 'and, because of [his] priest-like role, meant divided command.' On the other hand, his men were master navigators. Only one of Scott's men could navigate and he was not taken on the polar party, though at the last moment Scott decided to take an extra man, which meant that rations would inevitably be short.

The long shadow over the quest for the pole was cast by the towering figure of Fridtjof Nansen, the greatest polar explorer, who was in fact bipolar – that is to say, manic-depressive. Nansen dismissed his heroic first crossing of Greenland as 'a ski tour.' Nansen 'demythologized polar exploration.' It is worth looking at him for a moment, to understand his importance in the race to the poles. It hardly matters that Nansen never actually managed to stand on either pole. Without Nansen's pioneering use of skis and dogs, Amundsen would not have made it to the South Pole; and Nansen was Amundsen's inspiration in his airship crossing of the North Pole. (It is now pretty much agreed that Robert Peary was telling a whopper when he claimed that he and his African-American partner, Matthew Henson, were first at the North Pole.)

Nansen began as a pioneer neurologist, a scientist, and a researcher. The polar regions were not the only unknown places in the world in his time. The human body also had its mysterious regions. The erroneous so-called 'nerve-net' theory of the central nervous system had not yet been disproved. Nansen's descriptions of the mechanisms of the nerves were revolutionary, and correct. 'His role was that of the often underrated historical figure; the enunciator of principles. He was one of the great simplifiers,' Mr. Huntford writes. But Nansen went further as an imaginative scientist, prophesying that the tangle of nerve fibers would be proven as 'the true seat of the psyche.'

His own psyche was complex and disturbed. His father was a stern, remote, and difficult man, and Nansen grew up having to prove himself. Nansen was also a stern and remote father, which is perhaps not surprising. But bringing his micro-managing and fuss-budgetry to exploration changed the whole business entirely and made it much more successful. Nansen, a passionate skier, saw this as the way to conquer the poles. He was unorthodox in expedition-planning: he opted for lightness and speed. He invented a new sort of cook-stove, a small sleeping bag, warmer clothes; he even devised a different cuisine. He invented a small landing craft; he came up with a brilliant solution to polar winters in designing the *Fram*. As an oceanographer he accurately predicted how a team might float north on current-borne ice. He was undoubtedly the first polar explorer to see the kayak as the marvel it is, and to use it.

Like many priapic men, he was essentially solitary, a fantasist, a loner, a non-sharer – though he slept with many women, from the Valkyries in his native land to the Duchess of Sutherland and Kathleen Scott. He was romancing Mrs. Robert Falcon Scott even as her husband was pegging out and breathing his last on his homeward journey, writing a pathetic note to the faithless woman. Nansen was a fussy and exasperating lover, and marriage and love affairs could throw him – later in life he begged Mrs. Scott in vain to marry him; but he was dauntless in exploration.

The Age of Discovery ended with the attainment of the South Pole. The trouble with exploration firsts is that they are nearly always generated by the meanest and narrowest demands of nationalism. Norway, emerging from Sweden's shadow in the last decades of the nineteenth century, needed heroes. Nansen was willing and he was well equipped. He was physically strong, a true athlete, an intellectual, a scientist; he was handsome and humane, he was well read – loved Goethe, spoke English well. He was something of an Anglophile.

That he was a legend in his own time made him more attractive to the ladies and got him invited to Sandringham, where he hobnobbed at Christmas-time with King Edward VII (and noted with hot eyes that Mrs. Keppel was in residence, as well as Queen Alexandra); he played bridge with the Queen of Spain and his own Queen Maud and the Duke of Alva; and he went further – paddled palms and pinched fingers with Queen Maud. 'Now don't you go and fall in love with Queen Maud!' Nansen's wife wrote from Norway. The Nansens seldom traveled together; the marriage, which produced five children, was unhappy, and Eva Nansen's early death produced a guilty grief in Nansen that was like madness. Remarriage did not ease his spirit.

Seconded to serve as a diplomat, he dealt directly with Lenin, who instructed his cronies, 'Be extremely polite to Nansen, extremely insolent to Wilson, Lloyd George, and Clemenceau . . .' Nansen was never less than a hero. But as he grew more famous he became ever more distracted and sadder. For his inventiveness and his energy and his fearlessness, he is for me the greatest of the polar explorers.

Because of Nansen's many accomplishments, he has been described as the 'Renaissance ideal of the universal man.' I don't think that is pushing it at all, because it is clear that Nansen succeeded – as so many people do – precisely because of the weaknesses in his character, not just his impatience and his questionable leadership qualities, but also his fear, for fear is a necessity that prevents the best explorers from being foolhardy. Nansen saw himself as Faustian and his biographer describes him as a 'driven and tormented man who, in spite of his triumphs, felt strangely unfulfilled.'

The loan of Nansen's ship, the unsinkable, the uncrackable *Fram*, was an immense benefit to Amundsen; Scott's creaky *Terra Nova* was no match for it, and indeed the *Fram* ultimately had the distinction of sailing both Farthest North and Farthest South. The *Fram* was crucial, for Amundsen needed a seaworthy and powerful purpose-built, expedition-tested ship – his mission was secret, he left home much later than Scott, and he had almost no patronage. Yet in almost every instance Amundsen made the right, most astute judgment and

Scott the wrong, most ill-informed one, which is why this book seems to me so valuable, for it is a book about myth-making and heroism and self-deception, the ingredients of nationalism.

The Last Place on Earth was a sensation when it first appeared. Rereading it twenty years later I still find it an engrossing and instructive narrative, with vivid characterization and a mass of useful detail. When you finish it you know much more about human nature, for it is more than a book about the South Pole. It is about two leaders, two cultures, and about the nature of exploration itself, which is to me a counterpart to the creative impulse, requiring mental toughness, imagination, courage, and a leap of faith. Most of all, this book about a race, which was the last great expedition that ended the Age of Discovery, is a study in leadership.

Prairy Erth

Any nation's literary history is rich in phantom pregnancies. Many writers produce a first book, worthy in every respect, and while there is often a muttered mention or a breathless hush regarding a second book, the thing never appears – phantom pregnancy. Isn't there a celebrated scholar in New Haven, sounding as desperate as a woman in a paternity suit, who is always threatening to publish his masterpiece? But it's a common condition. And I think most people, reflecting on the silence since *Blue Highways* appeared in 1982, believed – and who could blame them? – that William Least Heat-Moon's excellent book would not have a successor.

Yet that had also struck me as peculiar, because there must have been any number of publishers cooing into telephones, urging the man to repeat the formula. 'Why not try the blue highways of Russia or Brazil? Or what about the back roads of Italy, Bill?' you can almost hear them saying. 'Listen, they got plenty of blue highways in Australia.' In the simple act of writing a travel book about your peregrinating along back roads, you sort of lay claim to every back road on earth, or so people think. In that same spirit, it is sometimes felt that the world's railroads, and all their splendors and miseries, belong to me and that anyone else who writes about them ought to be shot for poaching.

With the appearance of *Prairy Erth* it is immediately obvious what Mr. Heat-Moon has been doing for the past almost ten years, and that is researching and writing this densely printed 624-page book. It is not on the face of it a travel book, any more than is Gilbert White's *The Natural History and Antiquities of Selborne* – a work it much resembles in form and intention. The subtitle, 'A Deep Map,' is not much help, being at once idiosyncratic and gnomic (I suppose he means the invasive procedures of writing about an alien landscape). But *Blue Highways* proved beyond any doubt that Mr. Heat-Moon is nothing if not gnomic. This one is travel in eccentric circles, but the word eccentric in the sense of off-center is also somewhat inappropriate since the landscape of Mr. Heat-Moon's book, Chase County, Kansas, is at the geographical center of our country. 'I have traveled a good deal in Concord,' Thoreau said, and in this book Mr. Heat-Moon has covered just about every inch in the 744 square miles of Chase County, met most of its people, noted most of its Burma Shave signs, and disproved the scribbled graffito, 'Living in Kansas is a contradiction.'

It is a wonderful and welcome book and has the distinct virtue of being completely unexpected. It is different from *Blue Highways*, as any book is likely to be, but obviously written by the same man, who is thoroughly friendly and patient, rather self-conscious, slightly pedantic (he knows the words 'forb' and 'chert' and you don't), something of a loner, a trifle old-fashioned, a bit mystical, and just as much at home in the tall grass prairie as on the far side of a cracker barrel. He is also something of a naturalist, though he is lacking in the misanthropy that characterizes that calling – nature-lovers are so often people-haters. Chase County has a total population of 3,000, and on Mr. Heat-Moon's reckoning there is not a bad egg among them. To his great credit, he is lavish in reporting the Kansas idiom: *He's been around the sun bettern fifty times*, and *All I ever caught was a limb in the face*, and the man *who wasn't worth a bushel of damn hedgeballs*, and, in a more sinister vein, *The other guy shot the colored boy in the back of the head and got off on self-defense – convinced the jury the guy used to wear his hat backwards*.

'In a purely metaphysical sense I am a turnip,' a Kansas clergyman once wrote – and you don't quite grasp his meaning until you learn his name, William Quayle, quite obviously a distant antecedent of our own political vegetable. Of the living heroes and just plain folks Mr. Heat-Moon finds, there is the cowboy 'Slim' Pinkson, 'a character shaped by the bovine nature of the animals he spends his days with;' Larry Wagner, crippled by polio, who is eloquent in his attempt to save the all-grass prairie; Linda Thurston, whose café went bust: 'We never did get the farmers to eat alfalfa sprouts. They know silage when they see it. Maybe we should have tried it with gravy;' Fidel Ybarra, who remembers every spike he has driven and every railroad tie he has set; Lloyd Soyez, who perhaps saved De Gaulle from being assassinated by snipers in Paris; and a nameless but memorable diner in the Strong City Café, who described his Kansas encounter with a history prof in Hush Puppies from Back East: 'Couldn't tell a sycamore from a cottonwood, hadn't the least idea of what kind of tree to cut a wagon axle out of. He wasn't exactly sure what an ox is. He didn't know how to make hominy, hadn't ever skinned a squirrel or milked a cow – and he got paid 50,000 a year to tell college kids about the West.'

This is rural Kansas, but a far cry from the grim lunacy of *In Cold Blood*, from the fantasy of *The Wizard of Oz*, or from Ian Frazier's vivid but shapeless *The Great Plains*. It is all prairie, and mostly pleasure – nothing here that smacks of the prairie fear felt by such natives of it as Willa Cather, who had an absolute horror of grassland. If *Prairy Erth* has a fault it is that it is almost entirely a celebration, even when it does not mean to be. It is a good-hearted book about the heart of the country. Mr. Heat-Moon does not make much of the xenophobia he encounters, nor does he explore the racism – the anti-black and anti-Hispanic sentiments he hears. He takes people as he finds them, and they put up with his note-taking. Nagged for drinking a beer with his lunch in a cemetery ('This isn't a tavern'), he just smiles. 'You'll be tolerated even if they do think you're about a half-bubble off plumb,' a woman tells the author, making him feel he has been complimented. I kept wondering why he apparently spent all his time in motels. If these people are the salt of the earth, why didn't they offer him a bed? And while I am quibbling, why was it that few showed much concern about the greater world beyond Kansas? I have recently been in the Solomon Islands, and I heard more intelligent political talk and global concern from one naked Melanesian than Mr. Heat-Moon heard from a whole county of Kansas farmers.

It is risky for any book to attempt to be exhaustive, and this is as true for *Moby-Dick* as it is for *Prairy Erth*. The risk is that lengthy extracts can break the spell of reading, and because such a book – as shuffling and pot-bellied with undigested stuff as the Kansans it describes – may quickly become nothing more than a database, something to sort and study. The catalog, the long digression, the essay-within-the-text, the scrapbook, the potted history, the portrait gallery – all of this served up as narration – can blunt the edge of reading.

Kansas is the way we were, and it is the way many people in this country still are. By concentrating his scrutiny on this small area of rural America, where families have been settled for generations, where folks are folks, and there is a strong sense of attachment to the land; by accumulating a vast mass of detail, and querying whether the West was won in quite the way we felt it was, Mr. Heat-Moon has succeeded in recapturing a sense of the American grain that will give the book a permanent place in the literature of our country. I mean to say that in its doggedness, its thoroughness, and its ingenious design, the book – in its intentional crankiness – has value both as historical document and as personal testimony.

Looking for a Ship

When, in *Looking for a Ship*, John McPhee explains in his characteristically lucid way the difference between ullage and innage, and the subtleties of the plimsoll mark, and the length of a Trident class submarine, and the manner of a Fathometer tracing the contour of the sea bottom, it is hard not to think of him as 'Doc,' the plain-spoken polymath, the voice of experience. Doc is methodical and thorough, even to the point of being a teeny bit ponderous. While the rest of us are generalizing like mad and cracking feeble jokes, Doc is simply nodding and taking notes. He has the sort of patience that makes people nervous, and an almost exasperating sanity.

In this voyage with a purpose, an account of the current decline of the United States Merchant Marine, Doc doesn't get rattled when the pirates board at Guayaquil; Doc understands the anxiety of a seaman eager to be employed: 'If his neurons seemed hyperactive, they had some reason to be' – and isn't it just like Doc to put it like that? When the storm blows the ship sideways Doc doesn't say exactly how he felt but rather enumerates the things that fell onto the deck – the alarm clock and all the rest of his clobber. In Chile, Doc reads Charles Darwin. En route he reads Bowditch and takes pulses. He knows the age of everyone on board. He is patient – no record here of his losing his temper; and he is restrained – only eight obscenities, all told, in this account of the Merchant Marine. (I find Doc's habit of enumerating to be infectious.) When the ship is moored in the steamy Colombian port of Buenaventura, another man might have gone boozing and roistering in the waterfront dives with the crew – I certainly would have seized the chance to watch this bunch of level-headed sailors lose their marbles – but Doc heads for the hills: 'We wanted to see the jungle rising to the Cordillera Occidental.' Typical!

Good-hearted, frugal, truthful, fluent, decent, and humane, John McPhee is Doc to his fingertips. In the past I have trusted him on tennis champs, geology, physics, Alaska, camping, the construction of the birch-bark canoe and a score of other subjects. In an interview in a recent issue of *Sierra* (official magazine of the Sierra Club), McPhee was reported as saying, 'My next book could be about a ketchup manufacturer . . . my next book could be about anything.' As it happens this, his next book, is about the sorry state of our Merchant Marine. Why shouldn't I trust him on that subject too? If John McPhee says the Peru–Chile trench is steep and the continental shelf is extremely narrow, I believe it. If he reports an exasperated man as saying, 'Another day in the life of Walter Mitty. Heavens to Murgatroyd, we're stuck in the lock,' I believe that McPhee reported it correctly. When a man says, unchallenged, 'Five more years, there won't be no Merchant Marine. It's going down the guts' you have to take it more or less as written – this is the last gasp of the Merchant Marine. McPhee allows himself to be fanciful only now and then. *Now* is his reference to the fact that his Spanish is purely functional and his grammar 'tartare'; *then* is a passage beside which I have marked 'joke' in the margin of my copy – I found no others. The sentences read as follows: 'The author Alex Haley is noted for riding on merchant ships as a way of isolating himself from distractions and forcing himself to write. He could write a book called *Routes*.'

Surrendering to his subject while remaining somewhat obscure himself, a technique he has just about perfected, McPhee follows the progress of a seaman named Andy Chase, who is looking for a ship. After quite a lot of hullabaloo, Andy lands himself a berth on the *Stella Lykes*, bound for the west coast of South America. McPhee also boards, but as a paying passenger, and he ranges over the ship reporting on the moods and experiences of the rest of the crew. It emerges that Andy is the great-great-great-grandson of Nathaniel Bowditch (of Salem), father of modern navigation and author of the basic text. But even this cannot make Andy Chase colorful enough to occupy the center of the book, and Andy is nudged aside in favor of Captain Washburn, the *Stella Lykes*'s skipper, who is both a superb captain and a self-made eccentric on a heroic scale. A poor student, a runaway, a circus performer (he walked on glass and did fakir tricks), and an amateur boxer, Captain Washburn earned his master's certificate the hard way under the tutelage of skippers such as Dirty Shirt Price and Terrible Terry Harmon. Here is Terrible Terry in a storm: 'Do you know how to pray? . . . Then try that. That's the only thing that's going to save us now.' Washburn has a delightful gift for the non-sequitur. He understands Columbus and is sympathetic: 'He [Columbus] did not produce, and that was the bottom line. He was a maverick, an adventurer; he was not a follower of the party line. Come to think of it – not to compare myself with Columbus – some of those adjectives kind of fit me.' McPhee obviously agrees, and a few pages later quotes rather a nice Washburnism (the captain speaking from the bridge): 'I would rather be here for the worst that could be here than over there [on land] for the worst that could be there.'

I would be happy to read a whole book about Captain Washburn and cannot think of a better man than McPhee to write it. Unfortunately the captain is somewhat incidental to McPhee's purpose, which – to state his intention crudely – is to use this voyage on the *Stella Lykes* in order to give an idea of the state of the Merchant Marine. He writes about the ill-assorted cargo, about stowaways, piracy, and flags of convenience. It is all wonderfully set out, but McPhee makes it clear that the boat and its crew will soon be museum pieces.

'Russia is going to have 5,000 merchant ships in ten years,' the captain says. 'And we are going to have none.' Another crewman says, 'We can't compete with countries that pay sailors one dollar a day and feed them fish heads and rice.' The enjoyment of reading this book is dampened by its lugubrious message: these people are more endangered as a species than the whales and green sea turtles they sail among.

McPhee is often praised for his economy of phrase and description. Certainly there is a patented McPhee simile, unusual and animal (and it probably helps to be wearing L L Bean clothes when you're reading it), like the men who 'fanned out around the office door like fish at the mouth of a tributary stream,' or the ship that had its end open 'like the mouth of a sucker,' or 'big backhoes that look like thunder lizards.' This is writing that might send some readers searching for an illustrated volume of natural history. There is no question that

McPhee knows what he is talking about, but beyond that there can be few writers today – I think Edward Hoagland and Peter Matheissen are two exceptions – who would use the phrase 'graceful as an alligator' with the certainty that they had hit the nail on the head.

Economy is a virtue in magazine writing. In a book it can seem like meagerness and insufficiency. These chapters all appeared as articles in the *New Yorker*. What is it about that magazine? It seems to do with ink and paper what morticians do with formaldehyde. When *New Yorker* articles and short stories are reprinted in book form I always get a sniff of the clean inky smell of the magazine and can sense its cool, smooth paper, and I hold the book differently, as though afraid I will be gouged by a loose staple.

I would have preferred *Looking for a Ship* to sprawl more; I could have had more of the captain and more of the crew – McPhee visited them at home but gives us only the merest glimpse of their family lives. That business about McPhee looking at the snowcapped peaks while the crew was drinking and misbehaving and – who knows? – using the Christian Science Reading Room. Had he conceived this as a book, I think he would have seen the necessity of including such boisterous scenes. What looks like prudence and humility could be journalistic economy. McPhee has written thumping big books, and he has reprinted shorter articles between covers. This is an example of the latter. I wanted more. That might sound like criticism. I mean it as praise.

Part Seven

Escapees and Exiles

Chatwin Revisited

BRUCE'S FUNERAL

When I think of Bruce Chatwin, who was my friend, I am always reminded of a particular night, a dinner at the Royal Geographical Society, hearing him speak animatedly about various high mountains he had climbed. And this struck me as very odd, because I knew he had never been much of a mountaineer.

I was some way down the table but I heard him clearly, for Bruce had a voice which carried sharply and always rose above any others in a room, like a chattering bird-call. That night he spoke in his usual way, very rapidly and insistently, stuttering and interrupting and laughing, until he had commanded enough attention to begin speech-ifying. Being Bruce, he did not stop with the peaks he had scaled. He had plans for further assaults and expeditions – all of them one-man affairs, no oxygen, nothing frivolous, minimum equipment, no delays, rush the summit – and as he appeared to hold his listeners spellbound (they were murmuring 'Of course' and 'Extraordinary' and 'Quite right'), I peeked over to see their faces. On Bruce's right was Chris Bonington, conqueror of Nanga Parbat and numerous other 20,000-footers, and on his left, Lord Hunt, leader of the first successful expedition up Everest.

'Chatter, chatter, chatter, Chatwin,' a mutual friend once said to me. He was smiling, but you could tell his head still hurt. Bruce had just been his house guest for a week. 'He simply never stops.'

This talking was the most striking thing about him, yet there were so many other aspects of him that made an immediate impression. He was handsome, he had piercing eyes, he was very quick – full of nervous gestures – a rapid walker, highly opinionated, often surpris-ingly mocking of the English. Of course Bruce talks a lot, people said. It's because he's alone so much of the time. But he wasn't: his official biographer, Nicholas Shakespeare, demonstrated in 1999 that Bruce was seldom alone, and nearly always traveled with a friend. Because Bruce was given to sudden disappearances, everyone assumed he was alone. In any case, I believed he talked to himself, probably yakked non-stop, rehearsing his stories and practicing funny accents and mimicry: it is a habit of many writers and travelers. I am sorry I never asked him whether he did this. I am sure he would have let out his screeching laugh and said, 'Constantly!'

Chatwin's funeral remains for me the most significant single literary event I knew as a writer in London. It was a cold bright day, Valentine's Day, 1989. Bruce was such a darter he seldom stayed still long enough for anyone to sum him up, but when he died many people published their memories of him – and the portraits were so different. It was amazing how many people, old and young, many of them distinguished, a number of them glamorous, gathered to mourn him, in the Greek Cathedral of Santa Sophia in London in a ceremony rich in religious fetishism. Every English writer I knew or had heard of turned up. Writers, especially London writers, look so odd, so pale, so twisted and defenseless in the open air. Salman Rushdie sat in the pew in front of me with his then wife. Just the day before, the Ayatollah Khomeini had condemned Salman to death – I thought it was a hollow condemnation, and I joked about it. Judging from the congregation, Bruce had known everyone – the aristocracy, the gentry, the editors, the art crowd, the auction people, and the riffraff to which most of us as writers belonged.

In the Order of Service, we joined in the Kontakion, which contained the lines, 'O Lord, give rest to the soul of Thy servant Bruce, in a place of light, a place of verdure, a place of repose, whence all pain, sorrow and sighing have fled away.' It was the sort of place he never wrote about, nor did any of us writers who traveled.

There was no buzz in the pews. In life, Bruce had flitted from one to another, keeping everyone separate, making a point of not introducing us but often dropping our names.

He did not merely drop Francis Bacon's name, he went one better and mimicked him – which suggested how intimately he knew the great painter. 'Oh,' he would say, with an epicene hiss, 'a million quid for one of my paintings – I'll just spend it on champagne.' Bruce could get two or three boasts into a single statement, as in, 'Werner Herzog and I just hiked 200 miles in Dahomey,' or 'David Hockney told me that his favorite painter is Liotard, an eighteenth-century

Swiss. He's brilliant, actually. I often go to the Rijksmuseum just to look at his work.' (This must have been true, because one day in Amsterdam Bruce showed me a Liotard painting.)

Postcards are the preferred medium for many self-advertisers, combining vividness, cheapness, and an economy of effort – something like a miniature billboard. Bruce was a great sender of postcards. He sent them to me from France, from China, from Australia, and from the artists' colony Yaddo. *Feverish lesbian sculptors doing vulvaic iconography in plastic*, he wrote from Yaddo. He encapsulated a theory about an Italian writer in Yunnan. From Australia he wrote, *You must come here. The men are awful, like bits of cardboard, but the women are splendid.* And on another postcard from Oz (this one of a bushranger), *Have become interested in an extreme situation, of Spanish monks in an Aboriginal mission, and am about to start sketching an outline. Anyway the crisis of the 'shall-never-write-another-line' sort is over.*

In terms of writing he was in a state of permanent crisis. Perhaps he had started to write too late in his life, perhaps he lacked confidence. A writer talking to another writer about the difficulty of writing is hardly riveting – you just want to go away. Bruce was at his least interesting bemoaning his writer's block, and I often felt that he was not really bemoaning it at all, but rather boasting about the subtlety of his special gift. His implication was that it was so finely tuned it occasionally emitted a high-pitched squeal and seemed to go dead; but no, it was still pulsing like a laser – it had simply drifted a fraction from his target. I had no such story to tell. I was producing a book a year, turning the big wooden crank on my chomping meat-grinder. How could I talk about a literary crisis, when all I had to do to continue was grab the crank and give it a spin?

Bruce did write like an angel most of the time, but he is never more Chatwinesque than when he is yielding to his conceit. In *The Songlines* he mentions how he happened to be in Vienna speaking with Konrad Lorenz (in itself something of a boast) on the subject of aggression. Considering that Lorenz was the author of *On Aggression*, this was pretty audacious of Bruce; but he was unfazed in the presence of the master, and went further, cheerfully adumbrating his own theory of aggression, with much the same verve as he described his mountaineering exploits to Lord Hunt.

"'But surely,'' I persisted, ''haven't we got the concepts of 'aggression' and 'defense' mixed up?''' Bruce asks pointedly, implying that

Professor Lorenz has been barking up the wrong tree in sixty-odd years of scientific research. Bruce then boldly sketches his Beast Theory: Mankind needing to see his enemy as a beast in order to overcome him; or needing to be a 'surrogate beast' in order to see men as prey.

It seems astonishing that the world-renowned zoologist and philosopher did not find Bruce's Beast Theory conventional and obvious (as it sounds to me). Instead, 'Lorenz tugged at his beard, gave me a searching look and said, ironically or not I'll never know, "What you have just said is totally new."'

Bruce claimed to have the usual English disdain for flattery and praise, which is odd, because he adored it, and of course – praise is cheap and plentiful – it was lavished upon him. To need praise is human enough. Bruce solicited it by circulating to his friends bound proof copies of his books, prior to publication. We would read them and scribble remarks in the margins. I remember the scribbled-over copy of *The Viceroy of Ouidah*. My remarks were anodyne but some other snippets of marginalia were shrieks of derision: 'Ha! Ha!' or 'Rubbish!' or 'Impossible!' He said he didn't care. But he was at his most unconvincing when he was dismissive of praise.

Here he is in Dahomey, in conversation with an African soldier, in his sketch 'A Coup.'

'You are English?'
　'Yes.'
　'But you speak an excellent French.'
　'Passable,' I said.
　'With a Parisian accent I should have said.'
　'I have lived in Paris.'

Much of Bruce's reading was in French, usually obscure books. It would be something like Rousseau's *Des rêveries du promeneur solitaire* (*Reveries of a Solitary Walker*), Gide's *Nourritures terrestres*, Rimbaud's *Les Illuminations*, or – one of the strangest travel books ever written – Xavier de Maistre's *Voyage autour de ma chambre* (*A Trip around My Room*). When he found a book that few other people had read he tended to overpraise it. He might dismiss a book precisely because it happened to be popular.

His ability to speak French well was of course part of his gift for mimicry, and it delighted me, though it irritated many who felt that Bruce was showing off. When Bruce appeared on the Parisian literary

TV show *Apostrophe* he was interviewed in French and he replied with complete fluency, talking a mile a minute.

He was full of theories. One was highly complex and concerned the origin of the color red as the official color of Marxism. This theory took you across the ocean to Uruguay. It involved butchers in Montevideo, peasants on horseback, Garibaldi, and the Colorado Party. I think I've got that right. The theory then whisked you back to Europe, to Italy, to Germany, to Russia and the adoption of – was it a red apron? was it a red flag? It was all very confusing, though Bruce told the story with precision, and always the same way. I know this because I heard him explain the theory at least four times. He told it to everyone. It was tiresome to hear this theory repeated, but it was even more annoying to realize that he had not remembered that he had told you the story twice before.

That was something his friends had to endure. If he couldn't recall that he was repeating something to you verbatim – shrieking each predictable thing and looking eager and hopeful – that seemed to indicate that he cared more about the monologuing itself than about you. The worst aspect of monologuers is their impartiality, their utter lack of interest in whoever they happen to be drilling into. Because it hardly matters who they are with, everyone is a victimized listener, great and small.

Bruce was a fairly bad listener. If you told him something he would quickly say that he knew it already, and he would go on talking. Usually he was such a good talker that you didn't care that he alone bounced the conversational ball.

But while most of us knew his stories, there were always great gaps in between them. There is a nice English quip to express befuddlement, *Who's he when he's at home?* Exactly. Everyone knew Bruce was married – we had met his wife, Elizabeth. But what sort of marriage was this? 'A *mariage blanc*,' a friend once said to me, pursing his lips. Bruce was in his way devoted to his wife, but the very fact of Bruce having a wife was so improbable that no one quite believed it.

One night at dinner, just before he left the table, I heard Bruce distinctly speak of his plans for the near future and say, 'I'm going to meet my wife in Tibet.' Afterwards, one of the people present said, 'Did he say his wife was dead?' and another replied, 'No. He said his wife's in bed.'

He was not so much reclusive as selective. We heard the colorful stories of a born raconteur. But what of the rest of it? We wondered what his private life was really like, and sometimes we speculated. His first book, *In Patagonia*, embodied all his faults and virtues. It was highly original, outrageous, and vividly written. He inscribed a copy for me, writing generously, *To Paul Theroux, who unwittingly triggered this off* – and he explained to me how a book of mine had inspired him to go to Patagonia. But his book was full of gaps. How had he traveled from here to there? How had he met this or that person? Life was never so neat as Bruce made out. What of the other, small, telling details, which to me gave a book its reality?

I used to look for links between the chapters, and between two conversations, or pieces of geography. Why hadn't he put them in?

'Why do you think it matters?' he said to me.

'Because it's interesting,' I said, and thought, *It's less coy, too.* 'And because I think when you're writing a travel book you have to come clean.'

This made Bruce laugh, and then he said something that I have always taken to be a pronouncement that was very near to being his motto. He said – he screeched – 'I don't believe in coming clean!'

V. S. Naipaul felt that Bruce was trying to live down the shame of being the son of a Birmingham lawyer. I challenged this facile theory.

Naipaul said, 'No, you're wrong. Look at Noël Coward. His mother kept a lodging house. And he pretended to be so grand – that theatrical English accent. All that posturing. He knew he was common. It was all a pretense. Think of his pain.'

This might have been true in a small way of Bruce, but I think that he was secretive by nature. It kept him aloof. It helped him in his flitting around. He never revealed himself totally to anyone, as far as I know, and in this way he kept his personality intact. In any case he never struck me as being thoroughly English. He was more cosmopolitan – liking France, feeling liberated in America, being fascinated by Russia and China, something of a cultural exile.

I am skirting the subject of his sexual preference because it does not seem to me that it should matter. Yet it was obvious to anyone who knew him that in speaking tenderly of marital bliss he was always suppressing a secret and more lively belief in homosexuality. That he was homosexual bothered no one; that he never spoke about it was rather disturbing.

In an ungracious memoir, the writer David Plante refused to see Bruce's sense of fun and perhaps even deeper sense of insecurity. Plante wrote at length about how they had gone to a gay disco in

London called Heaven, but it is typical of the memoir's dark hints and hypocrisy that Bruce's behavior is regarded as sneaky and insincere, while Plante himself never discloses his own motive for going to the gay hangout.

I wanted to know more about his homosexual life, not because I am prurient but because if I like someone I want to know everything. And while Bruce was secretive himself, he was exasperated by others who kept their secrets. He never wrote about his sexuality, and some of us have laid our souls bare.

When he called me he always did so out of the blue. I liked that. I liked the suddenness of it – it suited my life and my writing. I hated making plans for the future. I might not be in the mood that far-off day. I might be trying to write something. If he called in the morning it was always a proposal to meet that afternoon or evening. And then I might not hear from him for six months or a year.

It surprised me that he had agreed to give a lecture for the Royal Geographical Society, but he had done it on one condition – that it be a duet. Would I agree? I said okay, and I quickly realized that we were both doing it so as to seem respectable among all these distinguished explorers and travelers.

Working together with him to prepare the lecture we called 'Patagonia Revisited,' I realized how little I knew him and what an odd fish he was. He was insecure, I knew that, it had the effect of making him seem domineering. 'I can't believe you haven't read Pigafetta in full,' he would say, and he would put the book in my hand and insist that I read it by tomorrow – and the next day, instead of talking about Pigafetta, he would say, 'Our talk's going to be awful, it's hopeless, I don't know why we agreed to do this,' and later on would say, 'By the way, I've invited the Duke and Duchess of Westminster.'

I found this maddening. I felt it was a task we had to perform and that we would do it well if we were decently prepared. Bruce's moods ranged from rather tiresome high spirits to days of belittling gloom. 'No one's going to come,' he said. 'I'm certainly not inviting anyone.'

We got in touch with a dozen members of the RGS who had photographs of Patagonia, and we assembled eighty or 100 pictures of the plains, of glaciers, of penguins, of snow and storms.

When the day came it turned out that Bruce had invited many people, including his parents – his big beefy-faced father had the look of a Dickensian solicitor – and he was miffed that the Duke and

Duchess had not been able to make it. The lecture itself I thought was splendid – one of the high points of my life in London – not so much for the text but for the atmosphere, the Victorian oddity of it. We gave the talk in the large paneled amphitheater in Kensington Gore, where so many distinguished explorers had reported back to the society; and we stood in the dark – a little light shining on our notes – while big beautiful pictures of Patagonia flashed on the screen behind us. This was thrilling – just our voices and these vivid Patagonian sights.

There was loud applause afterwards. Bruce, who would have been a wonderful actor – who perhaps was a wonderful actor – was flushed with pleasure. He had been brilliant and I realized that he needed me to encourage him and get him through it.

And when I heard him at dinner afterwards regaling Lord Hunt and Chris Bonington with his mountaineering exploits I thought, *He's flying!*

He traveled. We ran into each other in various places – in America, in Amsterdam. When he wanted to meet someone I knew well he simply asked me to introduce him. Graham Greene he particularly wanted to meet. But Bruce was disappointed. He thought Greene was gaga. He could not understand the mystique. He loved Borges. Later he needed glamour. He let himself be courted by Robert Mapplethorpe. He liked the thought of his portrait appearing in Mapplethorpe's notorious traveling exhibition, along with women weight-lifters and strange flowers and even stranger sexual practices.

He went to China – just a magazine assignment, but Bruce made it seem as though he had been sent on an expedition of discovery to an unmapped place by the Royal Geographical Society. I admired that in him. He took his writing assignments seriously, no matter who he was writing for. He was the opposite of a hack, which is to say something of a pedant, but a likeable one, who was fastidious and truly knowledgeable.

When he fell deathly ill soon after his China trip the word spread that he had been bitten by a fruit bat in Yunnan and contracted a rare blood disease. Only two other people in the entire world had ever had it, so the story went, and both had died. Bruce was near death, but he fought back and survived. And he had another story to tell at dinner parties – of being bitten by a Chinese bat. He recovered. A tall plummy-voiced resident of Eaton Square called me to say, 'I just saw Bruce walking through the square carrying a white truffle.'

But the rare blood disease returned. 'I was warned that it might pop up again,' Bruce explained. What kind of bat was this exactly? Bruce was vague. He became very ill. Seeing him was like looking at the sunken cheeks and wasted flesh of a castaway. That image came to me again and again, the image of an abandoned traveler – the worst fate for travelers is that they become lost and, instead of reveling in oblivion, they fret and fall ill.

When I visited his bedroom in Oxfordshire – a pretty, homely farmhouse that Elizabeth kept ticking over, and she also raised sheep – his hands would fly to his face, covering his hollow cheeks.

'God, you're healthy,' he would say sadly. But later he would cheer up, making plans. 'I'm going to Arizona to see Lisa Lyon. She's fabulous. The woman weight-lifter? You'd love her.' And when I prepared to go he would say, 'I'm not ready for *The Tibetan Book of the Dead* yet.'

'He expected to get better, and when he got worse he was demoralized and just let go,' Elizabeth told me. 'He was in terrible pain, but at the height of it he lapsed into a coma, and that was almost a blessing.'

Hovering in this fragile state of health he died suddenly. He had been handsome, calculating, and demanding; he was famous for his disappearances. His death was like that, just as sudden, like Bruce on another journey. We were used to his vanishings – his silences could be as conspicuous as his talk. It seems strange, but not unlike him, that he has been gone so long.

What Am I Doing Here

Our friendship began, like many friendships between writers, with a good review. I liked Bruce's *In Patagonia* very much, I said so in print; he sought me out. He said that after he read my *Great Railway Bazaar* he was inspired to chuck everything and just clear off to South America. It surprised me that he needed any help at all in anything related to his travel. He was by instinct nomadic, he believed in what he called 'the sacramental aspects of walking,' and he had more of Ariel about him than anyone I have known. But he also liked the sweet life, he enjoyed glamorous company ('Jackie Kennedy's actually quite nice . . .'), and betrayed his provinciality by being a bit of a snob. He also had worked at proper jobs, at Sotheby's and the *Sunday*

Times, the sort that allowed him to rub shoulders with the likes of Beatrice Lillie and Diana Vreeland and Noël Coward and others like them – the sort of strangely enameled celebrities that make you hanker after the company of a Yaghan Indian or an Aborigine, which of course represented the other side of Bruce's social life. Either the drawing room or the bush – there was nothing in between, or at least nothing that Bruce would admit to.

Very early on he asked me – a very Chatwinesque question – what I did *not* like about his Patagonia book. I said straight off that it bothered me that he never explained the difficulties and in-betweens of travel – where he slept, what he ate, what kind of shoes he wore – and too many sentences of his were like this one: 'From Ushuaia it was a 35-mile walk along the Beagle Channel to the Bridges' estancia . . .' Twenty-odd miles is a good day's walk, so was this thirty-five miles easy or hard for him; did it take a day or more (he suggests a day – surely not possible in Patagonian wind and cold), and where did he stop? Bruce just laughed at me, because he was an inveterate leaver-out of things. I said I believed that a travel book ought to give the reader enough information to be able to take the same trip. He didn't think so. I also liked having the right equipment – shoes, poncho, water bottle, sleeping bag, whatever. No, no, he said. Leave it out. He liked making everything connected with travel and his life a bit of a mystery.

There is a fragmentary quality in all his writing, but not in a random sense, more in the deliberately isolated way that a paragraph or incident was a sort of collector's item he had found and worked over and buffed up, in the way he must have dealt with the pretty and precious objects that came his way all the time at Sotheby's auction rooms. He was essentially a miniaturist and, with that, a parer-down of description, of emotion, sometimes eliminating it entirely. Even after you have read his six unclassifiable books you still don't know him – though you know a lot about his world. I think this is true of that other traveler and outsider and oblique snob, Wilfred Thesiger.

His posthumous collection *What Am I Doing Here* (the question Arthur Rimbaud asked himself in Ethiopia after he had abandoned poetry), because it is more ragged than anything else Bruce wrote, tells us more about him – his interests and friends, if not his passions. He writes of his mother and father, of his friend the distinguished painter Howard Hodgkin, and his tête-à-têtes with André Malraux and Nadezhda Mandelstam – you see what I mean by having the right job placing you cheek by jowl with luminaries?

At his best he gets a really bizarre bee in his bonnet, such as the rumor of a 'wolf-boy' in India, or a Chinese *feng shui* geomancer in Hong Kong, or the notion of looking for a Yeti. Then he sets off on a quest to establish the truth of the rumor. Much of his travel is Bruce's search for an unholy grail – something freakish, plainly an excuse, like the dinosaur fragment at the beginning of *In Patagonia*, and off he goes, and the piece is a winner.

More than half the pieces in the book are winners, and the others can be classified as Anecdotes, Fragments, Assignments, and Bits of Odd Lore. This last category is a Chatwin specialty. He loved to explain the Nazca Lines in Peru – those gigantic ideograms on the mountainsides. And what about Joseph Rock in Yunnan, who inspired some of Ezra Pound's dottiest cantos? Or the charade of an African coup (this one in West Africa) – Bruce gets it all down, how he was slapped, pushed around, imprisoned, robbed, put on trial, starved, and finally released. He leaves with wonderful images and memorable lines and never tells us whether he suffered.

Scattered in these pages are mentions that he contracted a rare blood disease in China. 'I was bitten by a bat,' he told me enthusiastically, after he recovered – it was something of a thrill to him that a bat had sunk its fangs in him, that he had been near death and only survived through a number of blood transfusions. The unusual in travel mattered to Bruce, because this was the stuff of travelers' tales. But travel is also ordinary, monotonous, exasperating: Bruce never mentions that. Nothing of meals or hotels. No tickets, no money; only the Ariel-like comings and goings, and the dazzling summaries. I think of this as an English way of traveling – the ability to make one good story stand for a vast messy ordeal. But such a way of writing can be misleading, because it is also about style and, hiding so much, it is often the opposite of the truth.

Just as seriously – and this is another problem for the English raconteur – the obsession with anecdotes lends a fragmentary quality to Bruce's writing. Narrative structure is sorely lacking, there is little forward movement, there seems to be nothing at the center – perhaps no real motive. I think Bruce himself suspected this. He hated the term 'travel writer' and he was at his happiest mixing fact with fiction.

'What makes Malraux a great figure is not necessarily his verbal performance or his writings,' Bruce says in one of the best pieces in this collection. 'His life is the masterpiece.'

One can see a real affinity in the young Chatwin talking to the old Malraux in 1974. Revolution, De Gaulle, Mao, China, suicide, history, war, travel, the Bomb, student revolt – it is a wonderful and wide-ranging conversation. And clearly Chatwin admired the man who was a gentleman, a fine writer, a statesman, a socialite, and – best of all – a man of action, not an *homme de bibliothèque*, the worst sort of French intellectual. Malraux was also suspected of being a bit of a fraud, of having a dubious side. *So what?* Bruce would have said. Shady aspects thrilled Bruce and made him more attentive.

Anatomy of Restlessness

Early death is frequently seen as a sort of martyrdom. Bruce Chatwin's tragic death in 1989 at the age of forty-nine is often depicted that way, and the acolytes who have gathered round his flame have proven to be pretty passionate in advancing the solemn personal myth that Chatwin sometimes helped along and sometimes mocked. Smirk even for a moment at the stained-glass window these people have put together out of ill-assorted chunks of colored glass and you risk being attacked, as I was, for the little portrait I wrote of Chatwin a few years after his death, 'Bruce's Funeral.' In it, I suggested that he was something of a mythomaniac and had a screaming laugh and bizarre conceits that provoked him to such behavior as monologuing to the mountaineers Lord Hunt and Chris Bonington about great climbs he had made.

His audacity was part of his crazy charm. How else could he have gotten on with the likes of Werner Herzog and Robert Mapplethorpe and (so he reported) Georges Braque? I enjoyed him for his contradictions, but I found that the more he admired someone, the more he talked. I liked being with him and I was exhausted and grateful when he hurried away – to see a woman weight-lifter in Capri or a fruit bat in Madagascar or (as he tells us in this last collection of pieces, *Anatomy of Restlessness: Selected Writings 1969–1989*) to hold 'a conversation with André Breton about the fruit machines in Reno.'

Chatwin insists here and elsewhere that he spent his life flying by the seat of his pants (a poor student, a muddler, a bit of a con man as a Sotheby's art valuer). You have the impression he wants you to contradict him, and yet I have no trouble seeing him airborne, whizzing skyward, propelled by only his pants. I think nervousness, not arrogance, made him a poseur. 'I aired my scanty knowledge of the French Impressionists . . . I particularly enjoyed telling people that their paintings were fake,' he said.

It was not strange that such a restless person was a traveler. Some of us are so much happier alone. He was self-conscious in the company of others; he wanted to impress you with something you didn't know (he giddily corrected my pronunciation of Gouda and in this present book we are told, 'The word fetish derives from a Portuguese expression *feticceio*' – not a lot of people know that, you see). He talked – nervously, interestingly – boasted, joked, gossiped; his mind was always teeming. And then he would need the respite of solitude, or else new listeners.

Needy, and yet also self-sufficient, he was mad about contradictions. The beauties of *In Patagonia* and *Utz* and *The Songlines* are their oddities – the odd lore, the unexpected incident, the queer etymologies. Of course, Bruce tended to recycle his discoveries. In this collection, surely the bottom of the Chatwin barrel, for the umpteenth time Bruce tells us how he figured out the source for the name Patagonia. It was one of Bruce's etymological coups.

Quite often Bruce got the wrong end of the stick, but he still managed to build a whole edifice upon it. Nomads interested him. He worshipped the nomadic impulse. One of his longest and most complex historical essays on the traveling spirit is built on the fact that 'the word Arab means "dweller in tents."' But anyone with an Arabic-English dictionary could have told him that, etymologically, Arab means 'people who express themselves' – derivations from the root *'arab'* mean Arabic, a clear speaker, clarification, an expression – nothing to do with tents. Bruce goes on 'as opposed to *hazar*' – a man who lives in a house – 'with the original implication that the latter was less than human.' This again is misleading and untrue.

He had an unstoppable energy for curious inaccuracy. I agree that such waywardness at first blush makes better reading. But, in the long run, the truth is usually very weird indeed, which makes his judgments merely lame. He says that Robert Louis Stevenson is 'a second-rater' and *Treasure Island* is 'second-rate.' In fact, his elliptical description of Stevenson is like a self-portrait. In one essay he goes on endlessly about the Hsiung-nu, a nomadic Central Asian people, but nowhere does he add that they were the avatars of the Huns. Had he done so, he perhaps would not have written, as he does here, 'Nomads rarely, if ever, destroyed a civilization.'

Anatomy of Restlessness is not a book for people coming to Chatwin for the first time. Those readers ought to start with *In Patagonia* and work onward from there, taking the books chronologically. They are wonderful books. And it hardly matters how Chatwin lived his life, except that it was a great deal odder and more interesting than the keepers of his flame seem willing to admit. It seemed that he was either the life and soul of a London party or else he was living in a tent in Wagga-Wagga. Of course, the real Bruce – hidden, calculating, intensely perambulating – was somewhere in between.

Greeneland

GRAHAM GREENE AS OTIS P. DRIFTWOOD

'When they were writing in the Sunday papers about the death of the last Marx brother, one of whose film characters was Otis P. Driftwood,' Vivien Greene – Graham's former wife – told his biographer, 'I thought, "That's the name for Graham" – never staying in the same place for more than weeks together.'

It is a rum idea, the greatest living novelist as the fifth Marx brother, wearing a funny hat and flapping shoes, with a false nose and an exploding Bible, tripping all over the world – today Berkhamsted, tomorrow Haiti, next week Budapest; Otis P. Driftwood the ambidextrous writer, scribbling novels with his right hand and travel books with his left, and occasionally doing a lifelike imitation of Gustave Flaubert in the French writer's most notable feat, of copulating with a woman, writing a letter, and smoking a cigar *at the same time*. After all, wasn't it Greene himself who pointed out in a preface to a volume of his plays how near tragedy is to farce?

There is something rather farcical about an authorized life of Greene – indeed about having an official biographer. Professor Norman Sherry was once a lecturer at the University of Singapore. I know this because I inherited his office there, and some of his students were passed on to me. Stories were told in the Staff Club (and by the way this is the tone Sherry himself adopts when writing of Greene) of how, researching the background to Conrad's novels, Sherry would set off for Surabaya, to make sure whether there had been a real-life prototype for, let us say, Axel Heyst's cook, 'Wang,' in *Victory* or whether there had been three mysterious strangers like those in the novel. Actually, Conrad had nicked those three villains from a minor R. L. Stevenson novel, *The Ebb-Tide*. Sherry was less interested in literary antecedents than those he might find in Equatorial back streets, and Sherry's eagerness to embrace little-visited countries, strange people, and the possibility of amebic dysentery so impressed Graham Greene that, on the publication of *Conrad's Eastern World*, he got in touch with Sherry and eventually authorized him to write his biography.

The years of a writer's struggle and failure often spell success for the biographer. There is no question but that in his following in the footsteps of Greene's life, and in possession of all the Greene papers, Professor Sherry has, as they say in Texas, where the Greene archive is held, lucked out: he has a career, a subject, an income, and he is sole proprietor of the official life.

If *Graham Greene, a Biography* were not so long, so plodding and so odd, it would not be necessary to raise these points. At this moment, Greene himself is stonewalling the publication of a racier – unofficial – biography by one Anthony Mockler. Professor Sherry's life of Greene is one of those monumental works which appear to be so exhaustive that you are almost certain that something crucial is being left out. William Faulkner's biographer also took two long volumes to anatomize a life in which he mentioned every insignificant detail imaginable yet failed to find space for the fact that over a period of about thirty years Faulkner was an ardent adulterer and had a long-standing affair with a woman who apparently mattered very much to him. It is impossible to read Sherry's book without thinking that a similar sleight of hand is being practiced.

A large proportion of this first volume of Greene's life (1904–39) is given over to the courtship between Graham and his future wife, Vivien. Am I alone in finding it comic that Greene's hundreds of love letters have been sold to and solemnly catalogued by the University of Texas. Sherry offers us many lengthy and gushing passages from these letters (showing a tender and romantic and vulnerable side to the novelist most people regard as a cold fish), but he does no more than suggest that at the same time Greene was living quite a different life – with 'tarts,' girlfriends, and drifting women. Indeed, any reader of Greene's work can easily guess that he is well acquainted with the one-night stand as well as the protracted affair, and that his libido has had quite a workout over the years. Where it is possible to document Greene's comings and goings, Sherry gives us great helpings; but clearly there have been many episodes Greene had not wished to discuss with his biographer, and so we are forced to witness the sorry sight of the biographer reading Greene's diary and reporting, 'The rest of this entry has been torn out' – or scribbled over or amended or whatever – reminding me yet again that there are often more lacunae in a long book than in a short one.

Greene's selective autobiographies, *A Sort of Life* and *Ways of Escape*, were wonderful in their way, but I also felt they suffered from being somewhat elliptical. I felt that Greene had the strongly self-dramatizing steak that characterizes travelers more than it does novelists, and I never quite believed those seemingly well-polished stories about Russian roulette, failure, and school bullying. As for the nervous breakdown – it seemed to me that Greene's interest in dreams would lead him to a psychiatrist out of sheer curiosity quicker than it would from the result of neurosis. Greene tells many stories about how he hated and suppressed certain books he wrote in his early years – and I felt these stories, too, to be exaggerations for effect.

This biography not only substantiates these facts in Greene's life but adds detail to them. The suicide attempts were real, the manic-depression was actual, the sense of failure was repeated, and the suppressed novels apparently quite dreadful. After struggling with poetry and even publishing a book of it, *Babbling April*, Greene turned to journalism and the novel, made a success of his first novel, *The Man Within*, and then suffered the ignominious fate of writing one dud after another, culminating in his writing a life of Lord Rochester that lay unpublished for more than thirty years. Down and out is not merely a glib phrase to describe Greene's early writing life, for at various times he ponders the alternatives to writing – perhaps teaching in Bangkok or Norway or Japan or Burma; and he sees the folly of his having chucked his well-paid subeditor's job at *The Times*.

With the writing of what he felt was his pot-boiler, *Stamboul Train*, Greene achieved popular success, but it was to be short-lived. This first volume of Greene's life tells two stories, the first about Greene's courtship and marriage, the second about his first ten years as a novelist. Vivien said that Greene had a splinter of ice in his heart – it was that which made him so objective and vivid a writer. By the end of the first volume Greene appears to be coming to the end of marriage and just beginning to find real fame as a writer; and the splinter of ice is now a dagger-like icicle.

Greene's decision in 1935 to walk through the hinterland of Liberia was crucial. The oddest feature of it was that he chose as traveling companion his cousin, Barbara. This young socialite proved amazingly equal to the task, nearly as tough and resourceful as Graham, and her own account of the trip, *Land Benighted* (reprinted as *Too Late to Turn Back*), should be read alongside *Journey Without Maps*. Going to Liberia proved to Greene that he could endure hardships, that he could be brave and take risks, that there was an attraction in squalor and seediness, and that – having put his mind to it – he had convinced himself that he had something of Jim Hawkins as well as Stevenson in him. One of Greene's most attractive traits is his willingness to put himself on the line. In the quietest sort of way he is a man of action, making the most of any experience. At the end of this first volume, after his five weeks – only – of travel in Mexico, he produced two of his best books, *The Lawless Roads* and *The Power and the Glory*.

The unhealthiest aspect about a burning curiosity to know every last detail of a writer's life is that it often signals an utter indifference to a writer's work. Do we understand Greene's books better or like them more after knowing (as Professor Sherry tells us) about the brothels and prostitutes in San Antonio in 1938, complete with names and addresses, adding, 'No doubt some of those girls were still living there when Greene went to explore the street'? I am not convinced of this. Yet I found this biography fascinating in the same way that Greene must have found Lord Rochester fascinating, and I read it with the same enthusiasm that animated Greene when he went to a freak show in San Antonio to see two dead gangsters (mummified), Siamese-twinned sheep, and 'a frog baby born to a lady in Oklahoma' – in other words, impure enthusiasm.

GRAHAM GREENE: THE CONSPICUOUS ABSENTEE

'I'm afraid that at the moment my health is pretty lousy,' Graham Greene wrote to me from his hospital bed in Vevey. 'I am not supposed to drink at all, which is painful, and my days seem taken up with blood transfusions, vitamin injections, and four different kinds of pill. I suppose one could expect worse at my age.'

True – he was eighty-six years old. But even reading that dire description I felt he was still indestructible, and I did not seriously fear for his life. He was unlike any other writer I have known in his being physically fit, without effort. When anyone asked him how he managed to stay in such good health he said that he ate and drank whatever he liked, and he boasted (to – among others – Fidel Castro) that he never took exercise. In fact he was an energetic walker his whole life, but he loathed outdoor types and he was rather stuck on the idea of being dissolute. 'I'm in the mood for a pipe,' he sometimes said, after a good lunch, meaning a puff of opium.

Meeting him, I had the idea that he was someone who had had everything he had ever desired, and that it was perhaps this abundance that made him romanticize loss and failure. Certainly he disdained success. The idea of noble ruin appealed greatly to him, I think, because it implied struggle. He often spoke of his writer's block, yet he was immensely productive. And nearly all his fifty-four books are in print. But he did not want anyone to think that his achievement had been easy for him. I am quite sure he didn't care about not winning the Nobel Prize – in any case, he had a sworn enemy ('Over my dead body,' the man supposedly said) on the judges' panel. He was much more famous for not having won it. But since the prize is awarded on what the English call the Theory of Buggins's Turn ('Isn't it time for an Albanian?'), what is it really worth? 'I see the Nobel People are at it again,' V. S. Naipaul said to me the year a Nigerian won it, 'pissing on literature, as they do every year.'

The first impression you had of Greene was almost heroic, a man overwhelmingly tall, staring with a sort of imperious boredom straight over your head. But who had actually laid eyes on him? He was a conspicuous absentee, like Robert Louis Stevenson in Samoa ('My cousin,' Greene said, and it was true. Christopher Isherwood was another cousin). Greene liked to be in Nicaragua or India when any of his books appeared. He hated television, loathed guest appearances, and never promoted his books. He disliked celebrity, but I think he fancied being outrageous, even notorious. Any literary interview with him was done on his terms – and he deliberately made himself a bit mysterious. Once he appeared on a BBC TV interview in a darkened room, his face obscured for the duration of the program.

'He's very, um,' and then John Le Carré searched for a suitable word – we were preparing a program to discuss Greene's work, 'um, *slippery*, isn't he?'

Greene hated public speaking and the few times he was persuaded to do it in London his audience was disappointed, as though they had attended a seance at which there were no rappings nor any ectoplasm produced.

He was larger than life in a specific sense: six foot four, the handsome, even dashing young adventurer having become distinguished and statesmanly. His eyes were in a class with Madame Blavatsky – there is no paler nor more penetrating gaze in literature. They were almost unbelievably intimidating, and it is hard to imagine anyone lying into those eyes. Graham's brothers, Raymond and Hugh, were also tall, and equally robust. Hugh was a bureaucrat, Raymond an endocrinologist and a mountaineer who had known Aleister Crowley, the diabolist; but they didn't have the eyes.

Greene's photographs show a severe face, befitting a Companion of Honour, but those who could call him a friend knew his solemnity was a mask. He laughed often, and his laughter was deep and appreciative. He was an unusually good raconteur, and he had a fund of stories, mostly travelers' tales, that had never found their way into print. A great one of these, about multiple murders in Argentina, had as its refrain, 'And I was told, nothing happens in Cordoba . . .'

Greene's comic side was so profound it verged on sadness and touched mania. In his autobiography, an otherwise highly selective book, he was frank about his mania, and he went further and described how he was a manic-depressive. He said his bipolar personality was responsible for novels as diverse as *Travels with My Aunt* and *The Heart of the Matter*, giddiness on the one hand, gloom on the other. I think his comic vein deepened as he grew older.

One of his biographers made much of the fact that Greene sought psychoanalysis, as though in seeking help he feared for his sanity. But I am sure he was as much an observer on that couch as he was a patient. He was a man who seldom wasted an experience (although he traveled to Samoa and Tahiti and never wrote about those places). He did not regard madness as a weakness or a moral fault; it was another way of seeing the world, another form of inspiration. 'Much madness is divinest sense' – that sort of view. He was also a tremendous quoter of poetry stanzas – Browning, Kipling, and, his favorite, the scurrilous and obscene Lord Rochester.

I think Greene's conversion to Catholicism was an act of rebellion against a family (and a country) which saw Catholics as exotic and suspect and sinister. Belief also gave him a sense of sin, so his villains are not simply wrong – they are wicked and evil. The theological side of his work I find the least interesting, the most schematic. As a convert he wears his theology heavily – it is often a millstone in his novels – yet there is no question but that in the English novel of his time his religiosity set him apart.

He liked thinking that he lived (to use one of his favorite lines from Browning) 'on the dangerous edge of things' – politically, morally, emotionally. But was he living there? It seemed to me that he was pretty safe – well heeled, connected – and that all this business of his being furtive, the spy-bore side of his personality, opium-eater, and ponderer of Damnation, was rather a pose. Perhaps he really had played Russian roulette as a young man (he wrote several different versions of it), but if so he got a hell of a lot of mileage out of it. Dicing with death – I do believe it was as corny as that – is much more romantic, and it gives a biographer something to puzzle over. But, at bottom, isn't playing games of shoot-yourself-in-the-head also very, very silly?

In his outlook and in his manners, in the way he ran his literary life, in his lingo and in his pleasures (he seems to have had quite an active libido), he was an Edwardian – and an impressionable ten-year-old when World War I began. Most of his literary heroes were still alive when he began to read them – Conrad, Saki, Ford Madox Ford; he was precocious enough to have ventured upon Henry James before the Master died in 1916. But Greene's man-of-letters outlook was combined with an extraordinary zest for life. Edwardian though he may have been in most respects, he still relished flying to Paris or New York on Concorde, first class, at supersonic speed.

I avoided reading him for a while, because in our early married life my first wife had a great fondness for him and his work. I resisted. I was envious, I irrationally demanded her attention. What about me and my writing? This was in Africa. Eventually I read him and I was so bewitched I began to inhabit his world. That could not last, but I saw hope for myself as a nomadic writer, never writing about home. He inspired me and gave me heart.

I was asked to interview him once in the 1970s. We met at the Ritz and drank. I saw him several more times. Then I realized that it was an impossible task, and that to write about him in the way of an assignment I would be taking advantage of his generosity, invading his privacy, and letting the world in. In doing so, I feared losing his trust. I wanted to go on being his friend, so I turned him into a fictional character and put him in my novel *Picture Palace*. He laughed about it and we remained friends. He liked his mask, he preferred being a fictional character.

Just the other day, in Hawaii, I reread *The End of the Affair*. His sense of place is so precise and appreciative, I began to miss south

London, and to wonder, in a premonition of his death, what the world would be like without his gaze upon it. Temperamentally, he was much like the central character, Bendrix – a lonely man, capable of great sympathy, but with a sliver of ice in his heart.

GREENE'S REFLECTIONS

'It is time to close the quarry,' Greene said, when a huge and seemingly exhaustive biography of Rudyard Kipling appeared some years ago. After reading *Reflections*, a collection of essays, snippets, open letters, occasional poems, book reviews, and Sunday magazine pieces, I think it may be time to declare the Greene Quarry officially closed. Surely nothing of much value can possibly remain, and some of these pieces that have just been disinterred are of questionable literary value. And yet anyone who is interested in Greene ought to be interested in everything the man has written. Sixty-seven years ago, Greene wandered through Dublin, making notes on the Irish. The piece he wrote about it for the *Weekly Westminster Gazette* is here, one of the best in the book, with a good Greene ending about Dublin: 'Like that most nightmarish of dreams, when one finds oneself in some ordinary and accustomed place, yet with a constant fear at the heart that something terrible, unknown and unpreventable is about to happen.'

That brooding, nameless-terror side of Greene is in great contrast to the puckishness that one also finds in his writing. I suppose puckishness and terror are a cozy way of describing manic-depression, but Greene has confirmed that his writing is, as we amateur psychiatrists say, bipolar. 'Stop that fucking noise, you bugger,' we find the Companion of Honour shouting at the door of a British professor in China. Greene believed the prof to be out of order; in fact, the horrible noise was that of some Chinese chatting amiably in the kitchen in their own language. Later in the same trip, Greene, requiring a little something for a weekend, asked his male guide about contraceptives.

'In this village, for example, there would be a chemist shop?'
    'Yes. Yes. In all places.'
    'Where a man can buy a sheath?'
    'Yes, yes, of course.'
    'Would you mind going and buying one for me?'

He hesitated a long while before he found his reply. 'That I cannot do. You see, I do not know your size.'

A novelist's collection of occasional pieces can often seem like an archive for his or her fictional ideas. Many of the pieces here are like diary entries, but written for magazines and newspapers. Greene goes to a place out of curiosity; he is fascinated by the place, and he writes a piece about it with all the gory details. Nearly all the places eventually form the background for a novel. So there are a number of pieces here about Vietnam, one on Haiti, one on Paraguay, several on Cuba. He makes a point of calling this 'reporting,' not 'journalism.'

Some of the pieces are portraits – Greene's heroes. One quartet is made up of Charlie Chaplin, R. K. Narayan, Henry James, and Ho Chi Minh. Yes, it would make an odd bridge party, but a reader of Greene's work would be startled to find this foursome repeatedly mentioned. I was reassured by the fact that Greene often gets the lowdown on a place from his taxi driver ('"Money speaks," my driver said, "but it shouts in Mexico."') That is what reporting is. A journalist on the other hand talks to a taxi driver and writes of, 'Informed sources.'

Some of these pieces we have read before in a different and more finished form. Others, particularly those concerned with cinema, have not appeared before, not even in Greene's collected film criticism in *The Pleasure Dome*. He expresses gratitude, good sense, and some regret when speaking of all the times he spent writing screenplays and watching bad films. But he is a wonderful film critic and at his best here in three or four essays when he is reminiscing or reflecting on films or film-making.

The scariest and saddest pieces concern Indo-China – specifically Vietnam in the 1950s. One part I found more horrific than the episode it inspired in the subsequent novel, *The Quiet American*. Greene is on a bombing raid with a French pilot. After dropping bombs into the unknown they head for home, into the sunset, but not before sighting a victim in a sampan.

Down we went again, away from the gnarled and fissured forest towards the river, flattening out over the neglected rice fields, aimed like a bullet at one small sampan on the yellow stream. The gun gave a single burst of tracer, and the sampan blew apart in a shower of sparks; we didn't even wait to see our victim struggling to survive, but climbed and made for home. I thought again, as I have thought when I saw a dead child in a ditch in

Phat Diem, 'I hate war.' There had been something so shocking in our fortuitous choice of prey – we had just happened to be passing, one burst only was required, there was no one to return our fire, we were gone again, adding our little quota to the world's dead.

Inevitably, a collection that spans so many years – 1923 to 1988 – contains some contradictions and awkwardnesses. In several pieces Greene takes a side-swipe at J. B. Priestley, and in another he extravagantly praises him. He expresses an opinion about thieves or Catholics or Americans, and you don't know whether he is teasing or naive or in one of his puckishly manic moods. He extols Cuba in 1963 and then three years later writes, 'Things had improved since 1963.'

But the strangest effects in the book are those produced by the mere passage of time. In 1928, as an undergraduate, he writes a piece about pushing a barrel organ across Hertfordshire with Claude Cockburn. The piece is not bad but it is rather stiffly jaunty and colorless. Returning to the same episode in a book review forty years later he gives different details, quite funny ones, about being dressed as tramps, and mistaking a cow disturbed at night for an invisible coughing figure who tried to attack them, and finally how at one stage of the trip both men wore Halloween masks that were so silly and irritating that they parted company. This collection describes why Greene didn't mention those details the first time by showing how he grew in confidence and accomplishment.

GREENE'S DREAMS

The most horrible thing he could imagine as a boy was to feel an ice-cold hand laid upon his face in a pitch-dark room when alone at night; or to awaken in semi-darkness and see an evil face gazing close into his own; and these fancies had so haunted him that he would often keep his head under the bed covering until nearly suffocated.

No, the young haunted writer is not Graham Greene but rather Edgar Allan Poe, in Jeffrey Meyers's biography. But that was the sort of ghoulishness I had hoped to find in Greene's *A World of My Own – A Dream Diary*. Unfortunately, there is nothing in Greene that even remotely resembles the ice-cold hand or the evil face.

'Another thing lacking [in the book] is nightmare,' Greene explains in his Introduction. 'Never terror, never nightmare.' What kind of serious writer has no nightmares? And my heart sank early in the Introduction when Greene wrote, 'The erotic side of life may seem oddly absent from this record but I do not wish to involve those whom I have loved in this *World of My Own . . .*'

Dry dreams and nocturnal omissions: perhaps this is the key to Greene – that he was not tormented at all and that his libido had ample latitude. This book is a personal selection of Greene's best dreams from 1965 to 1989, listed under general topics, such as Travel, Reading, Science, Animals Who Talk, and of course Brief Contacts with Royalty – it has been said that there is not a man, woman or child in Britain who does not at some time dream of the Queen. Greene's royal dream seems fairly standard: 'Then Prince Philip entered. I was not surprised at all that he was wearing a scoutmaster's uniform, but I resented having to surrender my chair to him. As I moved away the Queen confided to me, "I can't bear the way he smiles."'

Early in his life, on the suggestion of one of his psychoanalysts, Greene jotted down the details of his dreams. Later on, he resumed the practice for his own amusement and edification, accumulating over this twenty-four-year period (he says) 800 pages of dreams. You would have thought Greene's dreams would be highly enlightening. On the contrary, I knew less than before. It is as though, in one of the current American expressions for deliberate obfuscation, Greene is 'blowing smoke.'

I have always felt the story that Querry tells his lover in *A Burnt-Out Case* to be one of the weakest parts of the book. The story was a dream that Greene had while writing his novel, and he says that much of his work was derived from dreams. 'In dreams begin responsibilities,' as Delmore Schwartz once wrote.

The trouble is that Greene in these dreams spends such a lot of time hobnobbing with popes, with dead writers (Henry James, T. S. Eliot), with Edward Heath ('an agreeable evening'), Castro, Ho Chi Minh, Oliver Cromwell. I think it might be true to say these dreams reveal a distinct power mania, but nothing serious. He meets Hitler. They talk until the cows come home. But 'I can't remember the subject of our conversation.' His memory seems to fail him in other dreams. This is Greene's entire dream entitled 'D. H. Lawrence' – 'It was the Duke of Marlborough who introduced me to D. H. Lawrence. I found him younger and better groomed than I had expected. He was quite friendly towards my work.'

All the words that have been written about Greene since his death have made him seem to me a simpler and more remote figure. And here is the man himself, indulging himself in one of the most revealing and intimate activities anyone can attempt, and the result is a quite startling banality. There is a little comedy in the dreams, some satire, a touch of paranoia, a smidgen of *folie de grandeur*, but none of the tragic, harrowing, horripilant experiences that visit the average person – me, for example – in his dreams. Greene is never chased – never pursued at all. He is never naked. Never seriously injured. Never regretful. Never guilt-ridden. After finishing the book I decided that, on the basis of his dreams, Greene was the most normal man in the world. And then I reflected on what was missing and thought the opposite.

V. S. Pritchett: The Foreigner as Traveler

You only have to do a little arithmetic to see that V. S. Pritchett, who recently died at the age of ninety-six, was older than George Orwell and Evelyn Waugh, a year younger than Hemingway, an impressionable teenager (and young adult) during World War I, old enough to read Henry James while James was still alive, and the same for Joseph Conrad, for Kipling, for D. H. Lawrence, for Joyce. He was middle-aged when H. G. Wells died in 1946; indeed, he knew Wells, and his lower-middle-class background on the shabby genteel fringes of London was also similar. As with Wells, these suburbs were the origin of his frustration, which found release in his clear-sighted satire.

As perhaps the last writer on earth who could accurately be called a man of letters, Pritchett wrote insightfully about his numerous literary contemporaries in his five collections of essays; he also wrote of his literary forebears (and heroes, Turgenev and Chekhov among them) in biographies. His criticism was as inventive, and as witty as fiction. But if you asked him about his influences he smiled and named the Spanish short-story writer Pio Baroja (whom he knew) or how important it had been to him to have skipped almost all formal education (he left school at fifteen) and learned the leather business. Afterwards he sold glue and shellac in Paris. 'I half wished I had spent my life in an industry,' he wrote. 'The sight and skill of traditional expertness are irresistible to me.'

Small and sturdy – he had walked across Spain, he had traipsed through the American South – he was half Londoner, half Yorkshireman, 'as old as the century,' he often said, the title of a poignant essay he wrote on turning eighty. He liked his initials – his wife referred to him as 'VSP' – and hated the name Victor, hating being photographed wearing glasses. He smoked a pipe his whole life. He drank wine; he had been denied the pleasure by his unpredictable father. He worked six days a week for most of his life. He called himself 'one of the non-striking self-employed.' V. S. Naipaul once told me that Pritchett's happiness and productivity were signs of his second-rateness, but that's contemptuous and probably (being an English judgment) envious. He worked slowly, and he was confident. Like Joyce and Nabokov and very few others, he knew he was a wonderful writer.

It is impossible to tell V. S. Pritchett's story better than he told it himself in his two volumes of autobiography, *A Cab at the Door* (1968) and *Midnight Oil* (1971) (probably the only books you'll find of his in an American bookstore). It is equally impossible to paraphrase his short stories, many of which are masterpieces of the form – and not just the early and middle stories, but ones from his later years. 'The Camberwell Beauty' and 'Blind Love,' written when he was in his seventies, come to mind. His novels, too, defy summary, because they are not at all plotty and their structure is so subtle it is hardly apparent. But all his work is of a piece. Read it and you know him and his world, this whole century.

England might have been a trap for him. It has been for many others who tried to emerge from his social class, who had a similar lack of education. The utter disorder of the Pritchett family (Micawberish failure-prone father, excitable gabbling mother) was both comic and grotesque – hilarious in the telling, but hell for the poor soul who has to endure it. A classic way to succeed in England, if you come from the wrong class or have a bad accent, is to leave the country and go far away. That was Pritchett's solution – and it worked for him, as it has for many other English writers. His first success as a writer came when, in his early twenties, he was working in an office in Paris. France gave him a second language and inspired his short stories. Travel in Spain came soon after. He learned Spanish, met Baroja, and published his first book, *Marching Spain*, which he ended up hating. He rectified this with his superb study *The Spanish Temper*. His first foreign travel was crucial – because he had no money and he could not go back until he had realized his literary ambition. 'I became a foreigner,' he writes at the end of *A Cab at the Door*. 'For myself that is what a writer is – a man living on the other side of a frontier.'

There is more about writing, less about family, in *Midnight Oil*, in which he describes a writer as 'at the very least, two persons. He is the prosaic man at his desk and a sort of valet who dogs him and does the living.'

The morning I heard that Pritchett had died I picked up his 1951 novel, *Mr Beluncle* (like most of his books, out of print), and reread it with intense pleasure. Pritchett said that it concerned his 'obsessive subject,' Christian Science, but it is also about the semi-detached weevil-life of the inner suburbs of London: the secrets, the hurts, the whispers, the stifled lust; the almost Asiatic obliqueness of English middle-class manners, the pompous vacuity of organized religion, the savagery of the workplace, and eternally twitching curtains. It is impartial: no villains, no angels in Pritchett, only English people peeking out the window and sizing up their neighbors. *Mr Beluncle*, like *Dubliners*, is also about suffocation, and it is full of Pritchett's precise description, such as, 'Then Ethel appeared in their rooms, with her hair dividing over her cheeks, and looking out from it like a savage peeping in terror from an old tent.'

Mr. Beluncle is a version of Pritchett's father, and young Henry Beluncle is a version of Pritchett as a boy, and Mrs. Parkinson is a version of Mrs. Eddy. Beluncle lectures his son on Divine Love as adumbrated by Parkinsonian creed: 'Love was getting up when you were called, not making a mess in the bathroom, coming when you are sent for, being prompt, punctual, tidy; not shutting yourself up unsociably with books . . . getting to know nice people, seeking first the Kingdom of Heaven . . . not kicking the furniture . . .' It is the lower middle class at prayer. Smiling at rather than mocking Christian Science, Pritchett wrote in his autobiography:

Insofar as Shakespeare or Homer approached Christian Science beliefs they were considered good, yet sadly lacking. It was disappointing to see that Christian Scientists were quick to 'give up' things. They gave up drink, tobacco, tea, coffee – dangerous drugs – they gave up sex, and wrecked their marriages on this account, and it was notoriously a menopause religion: they gave up politics; they gave up art but, oddly, they did not give up business.

During World War II, when he was too old to go soldiering, he worked on the *New Statesman*. Newly published books were rare because of the paper shortage, so Pritchett reread the classics – English, American, Russian, French, Spanish – and wrote a weekly essay for the magazine. He had kept on writing short stories, and after *The New Yorker* began publishing them he had some money. He lived precariously by his writing, in that respectable little cul-de-sac off Grub Street, the address of literary quarterlies and political weeklies and poetry magazines; where a writer can get by, writing like a grown-up. Twenty years ago he told me that one of the things he liked about England was that money was fairly unimportant – it was a measure of nothing, it bought nothing, and few people had it. That had been true for most of his life, though he survived to live in a greedier, more money-conscious age. It is still a mystery to me how Pritchett, who ultimately lived at the edge of Regent's Park, kept body and soul together. If I had ever been so discourteous to raise the matter, he would have laughed and said, 'That's an American question!'

When I lived in London I saw Pritchett whenever I could. He was a repository of literary history. He was the most widely read man I have ever known; and he had been personally acquainted with many of the great writers of this century. He wasn't social. He seldom went to parties. Happily married, he was always home writing, or reading.

Pritchett wrote in a small room at the top of his tall house. I know this. He is the only great writer I have ever seen in the act of writing. I was delivering something to him and his wife, Dorothy, said, 'Go up,' and waved me upstairs. I climbed three narrow flights of stairs and came up behind him and looked over his shoulder. Even then I was thinking, *I have never seen this before!* He was at a tiny desk, canted back in a chair, holding on his knee a clipboard with a piece of paper that was a muddle of blue ink, not much text, mostly blobby balloons and cross-hatched lines and words struck out, like a demented message, layers of it on the page, almost pictorial in its density. He was chewing his pipe, struggling with his pen, yet he smiled when he saw me, seemingly very happy. He had once described writing as 'a labor delightful because it is fanatical.' He was happy and he was also fanatical.

William Simpson: Artist and Traveler

William Simpson, the first war artist (it was the Crimea), was born poor and raised in a Glasgow slum, but he was one of those indestructible Scots whose life was shaped for the better by his disadvantages. The man never stopped working, and he was brilliant at what he did. Unlike most self-made men, he had a sense of humor; and he was modest – not a ranter, not abrasive. He seems to have been very tolerant and easygoing – rare qualities in someone who was obviously a workaholic. He started life with nothing – he had no standing, no influence – and he got little help. His education lasted just over one year. This condition gave him a peculiar hunger and curiosity. The Victorian age produced many wonderful artist-travelers, and Edward Lear was the best of them, but Simpson (who ranged farther afield) came very close – truthful, intrepid, and very talented. He took nothing for granted.

If he had a fault it was his intense sense of privacy, but this is not unusual in someone who seemed to come virtually from nowhere. Such people often develop a habit of secrecy, for why should anyone want to know of the dullness, the sadness, the humiliation of having nothing? The habit is unhelpful for anyone writing about Simpson, because there is so much in the foreground and so little in the background – and come to think of it, his pictures are a bit that way, too.

But of course, starting nowhere with nothing is impossible. Although he says little about them, the details he lets drop must convince us that his family was loyal and kind, that his father inspired him, and his grandmother taught him. In a very likeable appendix to his autobiography he describes life in a Glasgow 'land' or tenement in the 1820s – his friends, his fun, the children's songs and games. One can see that he had close friends and that people were kind to him, and that all this helped give him a good beginning.

But the fact that he gave instructions for his autobiography to be published after his death is evidence of his judiciousness, and it can only have been an unnecessary delay: the book covers the high spots of his career – nothing personal, and no revelations. Yet this in itself is revealing, for who is more welcome as a friend and fellow traveler than a person of tact and discretion? He did not mutter, he did not whisper, he did not dine out on his stories about the grand and the glorious – and he could easily have done so, because he traveled in the close company of aristocrats and royalty, and most palaces were open to him. Nothing is more revealing of character than the experience of travel. For example, just after the Crimean War he journeyed through Circassia with the Duke of Newcastle; but typically he tells us only about Circassia and the Circassians. No gossip, no trivia, no broken confidences, no froth: that decency he had brought from the Glasgow tenement.

Still, a little detail would have been welcome. We know from the chance remark of an editor that Simpson married late in life; but we don't know when or where that was, we know nothing of the courtship, and we don't know the woman's name. The marriage is not even mentioned in Simpson's entry in the *Dictionary of National Biography*. There is a single allusion to the wife in Simpson's autobiography, but that book is dedicated to his only child, his daughter, Anne Penelope. The tenderness in the dedication suggests he was devoted to the child. He arrived in London when he was in his late twenties, but travel took up so much of his time that he did not buy a house and settle down until he was in his sixties. This was in Willesden – no trace of him there.

His books are out of print, his pictures hardly known. Poor Simpson! Yet one suspects that Simpson would be very philosophical about this, for he had plenty of pride but he was a man who had no vanity at all.

As the first war artist, Simpson was the first painter to follow soldiers into battle, with the intention of recording it for the press – in this case the *Illustrated London News*. In a sense we know more of the Crimean War from Simpson's lithographs than from Alexander Kinglake's many volumes of official history. But Simpson was also a prolific writer, a journalist, amateur archeologist, and a watercolorist of distinction. Above all, he was an eyewitness in an age of great events. His career spanned the triumphant and turbulent years of Victoria's reign, from the war in which he earned the name 'Crimean'

Simpson, to the Queen's Jubilee, just a few years before he died. He went everywhere, he saw everything, he met everyone; and he was not a snob, so 'everyone' meant just that – dervishes, kings, princesses, pioneers, camel drivers, mad Irishmen, predatory Kurds, the Shah of Persia and the King of Abyssinia. He was particularly skillful at talking to – and sketching – rebels and outlaws. He had courage, and a strong stomach and a nose for what the public wanted. When he was touring San Francisco in 1873 he got wind of the war between the Modoc Indians and American troops – this was near the Oregon state-lane. One of the pictures he supplied to his employer, the *Illustrated London News*, was of an odd tangled and uprooted-looking thing like an oversize divot whacked out of the ground by a very strong, very bad golfer. The description reads, 'Scalp of Scaur-faced Charlie, Modoc Chief . . .'

He was also very interested in religion. He wrote a book about symbolism in the story of Jonah and the whale – and other stories in which men are swallowed by sea creatures. He wrote a learned book about the Buddhist praying wheel, and about wheel symbolism and 'circular movements in custom and religious ritual.' While covering the first Afghan War and sending back sketches of battles and marches, he also managed to carry out pioneering excavations. He was fascinated by mounds, and tombs, and caves. He went to Jerusalem to look at digs, and unearthed part of ancient India, and reported on Schliemann's Troy – indeed, he was practically alone in disputing Schliemann's claim that the mud dwelling in Troy could be King Priam's palace. He was one of the first to suggest what many people said later – and he was right – about Schliemann being rather bogus and impatient.

Simpson's father was a poor working man, but it was a stroke of luck that he toiled in a printing shop, because it meant that his son would do something similar, and that led the boy into lithography. Young William had a glimpse of better things, and wanted them. He was apprenticed to a lithographer and that highly specialized skill inspired his drawing and painting. From the age of fifteen or so he was saving his dinner penny, and instead of buying baps he bought tubes of watercolor paint. He sketched from nature and later drew pictures of all the old houses of Glasgow – that was the beginning of his lifelong interest in history and archeology. After the houses were pulled down, only Simpson's pictures remained as a record of old Glasgow, in Stuart's *Views of Glasgow* (1848) – posthumously reprinted as *Glasgow in the Forties*. He read poetry and literary criticism, attended night classes somewhat fitfully, and became a devotee of Ruskin. He spent his days working as a lithographer and his time off hiking and sketching. In *Meeting the Sun* (1874), he wrote:

My first love in art was a Highland mountain, and I have been a mountain worshipper ever since. Fate has privileged me to visit many shrines of this faith, – the Alps, the Caucasus, the Himalayas, the mountains of Abyssinia; now I can add to this list Fuji-yama in Japan, and the Sierra Nevadas of California, where I have seen Mount Shasta and the Yosemite Valley. I think that a valley, however beautiful it may be, never could have become a sacred object, such as mountains seem to have been all over the world. A great high peak, soaring up into Heaven, with its garment of snow, white and pure, often lost in the clouds, as if communing with those above, its icy barriers setting it apart like consecrated ground where the profane must not tread – these are the features of the higher mountains, which may have impressed men and produced that religious veneration of which we have evidences from the most remote antiquity.

He sold his first watercolor, *The Braes of Lochaber*, in 1850.

Naturally ambitious and seeking a challenge, he set off for London in 1851, and in the metropolis found work in a large firm of lithographers. He was at pains to point out in his autobiography the importance of lithography. It was exclusively pictorial, concerned with people and events ('Now it is all done by photography,' he said in 1893). Of lithography he wrote, 'The startling thing is that it was a class of work which came into existence, lasted only a quarter of a century, and has entirely vanished.' And he remarked on how lithographers frequently became artists, while engravers seldom did.

The Crimean War gave him his first great break. In London he had been sketching pictures of battles for readers, basing them on newspaper accounts. He read the papers and mugged up the topography and tried to depict the action. He kept wishing he was there at the front. He said to his employers, 'Here they are making gabions, fascines, and traverses. What are these? No one knows. If I were there I could send sketches of them, so that everyone would understand.'

He was sent, and two days before his thirty-first birthday he was under fire at Balaclava. He was very brave; he sketched while being shelled. But he was not foolish – just very rational and downright. 'If a shell is coming towards you,' he said, 'it becomes instantly visible, as a black speck against the white smoke of the gun which fired it, and before it reaches you there is plenty of time to go under cover.'

He earned the respect of Lord Raglan, who allowed Simpson to use the official letter-bag for sending his pictures back to London. And he learned the paradoxes of war. He discovered that it was essential that he see battles for himself, because often two officers in a skirmish would disagree on the details and conduct of the action. And at the battle of Tchernaya he noted that in spite of heavy shelling and numerous casualties there was no blood visible on the battleground. The uniforms and dust absorbed it. During the war he was able to spend three weeks at Kertch, visiting and sketching mound tombs – one of his passions. He did not see Miss Nightingale, he said (she was at Scutari), but he did see the elderly mulatto Mrs. Seacole, and an odd Irish man, one of the casualties of the Crimea. It is characteristic of Simpson's interest in the unusual and out-of-the way that he gives a brisk description of the British commanders yet offers a vivid portrait of this madman:

He had wrought himself into a state of madness. In the village he had picked up a long stick – a wooden hay-fork formed by the natural branch of the tree. With this clenched in both hands and his eyes staring wildly out of his head, he was rushing about, exclaiming, 'I smashes whatever I sees;' and whatever could be smashed with the hay-fork was destroyed by this maniac. Glass windows were special attractions to him. I saw him chase a very small fowl, and each time he failed to catch it he became more excited. At last the miserable chicken, exhausted with the chase, fell into his hands, and when this took place the wild fool did not know what to do with it. In an incoherent way he expressed himself as wishing to know what could be done, and at last, grasping the bird by the neck and squeezing it with all his strength, he said, 'Die! Die! Die!'

Another memorable portrait (and of course Simpson sketched these people as well as wrote about them) was that of the Kurd he met near Batoum (now the Soviet city of Batumi) on the Black Sea. This Kurd had a face that was 'vile, wicked and cruel,' and when asked what he was doing there he said simply, 'killing people.'

'Who do you kill?'
   'Travelers.'
   'How do you kill them?'
   'I watch the road, and when I see travelers coming I hide behind a rock and shoot them as they pass.'

'How many have you killed?'

'Thirteen, and five Russians.'

He did not explain the reason why he made a distinction in the case of Russians. It may have been perhaps some patriotic sentiment. He was then asked what he was doing in Batoum. To which he replied, 'Some business.'

'Where are you going when you leave this place?'

'Back to the mountains, where, please God, I hope to shoot some more travelers.'

Simpson had amassed an enormous number of pictures, including rarities, for he had recorded the fall of Sebastopol and had traveled in unknown Circassia. He was able to publish a pictorial history of the war (two folio volumes, eighty plates) and his reputation as a war artist was made.

He was something of a novelty, too, though in a different respect. He had grown a beard. He was mocked for his beard. People saw him and bleated like goats or else called out, 'Doormats!' because, 'anyone with a beard was looked on as a Jew or a foreigner.'

After the Crimea, whenever there was a great event to be depicted in a lithograph for the London weekly papers, Simpson was sent. He made pictures of everything that came his way, the opening of a canal, a tunnel, or a bridge; wars and uprisings; weddings, coronations, funerals, state visits, or following a royal progress. Simpson faithfully recorded these events, but he did much else besides – sketching ruins and back streets or simply picturesque views. In Japan, later in his life, he tramped around doing views of Fuji.

When Simpson was sent to India to record the aftermath of the Mutiny he had in mind a large-scale project, so that he might do for India what his fellow countryman David Roberts had done for the Holy Land. He had a grand scheme and envisioned four large volumes with something like 250 plates.

He was at it seven years – almost three years in India and over four years working his sketches into finished pieces. He had traveled all over India – to Lahore and Peshawar and up the Khyber Pass; to Simla and sixteen marches beyond it, to Sutlej. He sketched Thugs in Jubblepore and then set off in a dooley (a sort of light palanquin) for the wild in-between places ('It is in these spaces that the real India exists'). He traveled to Bhilsa, to find Buddhist architecture, and to the source of the Ganges in the Himalayas, and to out-of-the-way

Chittore, before the railway. All the while, he was sketching. He estimated that in his Indian journey he covered 22,570 miles.

The project was an almost total disaster, and I think that its failure is one of the reasons that Simpson is so obscure a figure today. It was Simpson's awful fate that his Indian pictures remained unpublished. His putative publisher, Day's, had gone bust, but the firm regarded Simpson's pictures as their property, and they were simply sold off – flogged as bankrupt stock. In spite of this reverse, Simpson kept on.

If the Crimea had made him a war artist, the India trip of 1857–9 made him an artist-traveler in the manner of the Daniells, George Chinnery, Edward Lear, Zoffany, William Purser, Henry Salt, and so many others who made their name bringing pictures of India and the Far East back to England. Some of these were greater artists than Simpson, but no other traveler had more stamina, and none was so fastidiously truthful. Simpson's counterpart today is the inspired photographer who roams widely and reports on places that are little known and dangerous.

Travel also vindicated Simpson's fair-mindedness. He believed he held 'exceptional' views on the subject of national character: in a word, he was not a racist, and he felt very strongly that it was politicians who whipped up feelings of nationalism and xenophobia. He said that as a child he had always been told of the 'superiority of the Scotch.' But it was all prejudice and political humbug. He was not taken in: 'I saw that each country remembered only its own virtues, and saw mainly the vices of its neighbors and, by contrasting the good features of its own character with the bad of the others, reached what was to it a satisfactory conclusion.' His humanity made him clear-sighted, and this shows in his pictures. His 1876 album *Picturesque People* depicts individuals not stereotypes. It was one of his great virtues that he traveled around the world without any preconceived notions of who or what he would find; and this absence of cant and bigotry in his nature made him a brilliant observer.

I long ago came to the conclusion that there is more resemblance than difference among the various people of the world, and here is what I take to be a characteristic example. In passing through the palace [of the Maharajah Runbir Singh] . . . I had to cross an open court. On the first day I saw a boy mending a defect in the pavement with a *chunam* or *kunkur* of some kind. The hole was only about six inches or a foot in size, and the boy sat there pounding the *chunam* slowly into it. I think I spoke to him in passing. Next day I again found him slowly beating away at the same hole.

I said something about such a small hole not being yet finished, and his reply was, '*Ha Sahib, Sircar ke-kam hai*' – 'It is Government work, sir.'

It struck me on hearing those words that it was not the first time I had met that boy.

Simpson made two more visits to India, but by this time he was 'special artist' on a retainer from the *Illustrated London News*. This picture magazine was for most people a window on the world, and under its auspices Simpson went as far afield as Afghanistan (he covered the First Afghan War and later the Afghan Boundary Commission) and China; and in 1873 he went completely around the world, the journey he recorded in *Meeting the Sun*, a delightful travel book full of excitements and adventures, off the beaten track (up the Yangtze River, among the Modoc Indians in northern California) and on the beaten track (the marriage of the Emperor of China and Niagara Falls).

Simpson was happier among outlaws than he was among royalty. As a guest of the Prince of Wales in a royal residence, he worried that the servant assigned to him (because he had none) would take a dim view of his darned socks and his plain old hairbrushes – and he cringed at the thought of 'a gorgeous creature in blue plush breeches' unpacking his portmanteau. He preferred the dervish in the caravan-serai or the floor-mender in Kashmir. This is the reason his pictures are full of telling detail, and it also accounts for the fact that Simpson – not a natural writer – produced good travel books. Simply, he talked to everyone and reported faithfully what they said.

That Modoc business turned him into a listener. It was a bitter war and it was particularly bloody for its being so far from any large settlement. But Simpson was not put off by the remoteness of this bloodbath. When the railway ran out, Simpson took a stagecoach, stopping at settlers' log-houses on the way. He met all the usual settler belligerence, but typically Simpson reported it with irony.

In one place, an old settler expressed the usual warm desire to see the Modocs exterminated, and included the whole race of Indians in the same merciful sentiment. When he came to the place first there were lots of Indians about – they were as plentiful as ground-squirrels, and every fall white men used to go out and shoot a hundred or two of them. At the present moment he was sorry he could not get away . . . I reported this valiant warrior's wish at the camp, and there was a great regret that such valuable services were not to be had.

That twinkle and tone of voice and light touch, and even some of the expressions, are very Kiplingesque. Though their paths did not cross, Kipling and Simpson traveled many of the same routes in the world, and their enthusiasms, their pawky humor, and the colors they favored are very similar. Kipling and Simpson shared an interest in biblical history and classical scholarship, and they were each machine-mad, too – loving the mechanisms of locomotives and tunneling equipment.

Although Simpson was born almost forty years before Kipling, their experience of India overlapped, and their sympathies were much the same – not the pink, princely India, but India outdoors, in its streets and hills and bazaars. Kipling's father illustrated some of his son's work, but how much more appropriate Simpson's pictures would have been. In his passions and sympathies, as well as his limitations and his quirks, William Simpson is the Kipling of watercolorists.

Rajat Neogy: An Indian in Uganda

We made our introductions through our work, and met in person later, which is the right sequence for writers to get acquainted. Rajat's magazine, *Transition*, had recently begun in Uganda, I was writing poetry and fiction in Malawi. Africa was a small place then – or so it seemed, because it was one place where writers were eagerly signaling to each other: Chinua Achebe and Wole Soyinka and Chris Okigbo and Ulli Beier from Nigeria, Cameron Duodu from Ghana, Dennis Brutus and Nadine Gordimer and others from South Africa, Ezekiel Mphalele and James Ngugi from Kenya, David Rubadiri and I from Malawi, and yet others in the Sudan, Ethiopia, Zambia, Tanzania. Nearly all these signals were directed toward Uganda, where Rajat edited them for publication in *Transition*.

It is hard to imagine a little magazine that was so generally influential on such a vast continent, but that is what happened with *Transition*. Rajat began his magazine at just the right time and it became a rallying point throughout the 1960s. It helped that Rajat was a local boy, with Africa inside him as well as the experience of a British university. It all showed in the way he spoke, moving from Swahili, to Hindi, to English. Kampala then was a small green city, and Uganda was prosperous and full of distinguished people: in 1966, Chinua Achebe, V. S. Naipaul, Ali Mazrui, Ezekiel Mphalele, and distinguished artists (Michael Adams, Jonathan Kingdon) and anthropologists (Raymond Apthorp, Colin Turnbull) from Makerere. Rajat had lived through Uganda's later colonial years, through its independence and hopeful years; he was also to experience its disintegration and terror.

He was brave, he was forthright and funny, he was a tease; he had tremendous confidence, not the ranting and fearful bravado that was common among some Ugandans, but a stylish poise that was both intellectual and social. He was handsome, clever, and young. He used all his gifts. He traveled across Africa, and to London and New York. His magazine mattered. He liked me, he published my work – he was the first publisher of my work – and I felt lucky to know him.

One of the strangest requests to me – but typical Rajat – was that I agree to sign a paper saying that I had committed adultery with his Swedish wife, Lotte. This was 1965. Adultery was grounds for divorce in Uganda, and it had to be proven. 'I wouldn't ask this of anyone else,' he said. 'I am asking you because you're my friend.' Well, that was true, but Kampala was such a small place that I was afraid of the social consequences; I was not married, and I did not want to be known in town as 'a co-respondent,' the legal term for the adulterous party. Rajat said that he had excellent contacts at the printers of the *Uganda Argus* – the printers also worked on *Transition* – so he would see to it that my name would not appear in the Court column, where divorces and criminal convictions and bankruptcies were listed, once a week in very small print.

Although I had never laid a hand on the woman, I agreed to be named as co-respondent and said that I had slept with her on three occasions. I was soon served with papers. I was warned by Rajat's harassed attorney that this was illegal – connivance, in fact. In court, the magistrate said, 'This Theroux chap – isn't he supposed to be a friend of yours?' Rajat admitted this was so. Magistrate: 'Some friend!'

In spite of Rajat's promises, my name appeared in the *Argus*, and afterwards, when I showed up at parties, people – expatriates or leathery ex-colonials – smiled at me knowingly. At the age of twenty-four, I had my first experience of celebrity. It was also one of the happiest periods of my life. I fell in love. Rajat approved of the woman, Anne Castle. He was a witness at our wedding – his elegant signature on our marriage certificate. Rajat married two more times and fathered six children, who are now scattered around the world.

In those years, because we were friends, because we were in Africa, I saw him every day. (I had started out as a lecturer at Makerere; a few years later, because of the rapid departures of expatriates, I was Acting Head of the Adult Studies Centre. 'We have no one else in the pipeline,' the Chancellor, Y. K. Lule said.) Rajat's natural element was at a large table – City Bar on Kampala Road was one, the Staff Bar at Makerere was another, an austere vegetarian restaurant, Hindu Lodge was also one. He sat, he talked, he teased, he encouraged; he then went back to his office and worked on his magazine. We all assumed that Uganda would just get better. Naipaul disagreed. The politicians were clearly opportunists and crooks, he said: 'This country will turn back into jungle.'

We did not really know what would happen. You never do. But it got worse; many of us left. Rajat stayed and got thrown into jail for sedition — criticizing the Ugandan government, something he had been doing for years. His detention in prison might have broken him. Or was it disillusionment? It was revealed that for some years the magazine had been partly funded by the CIA, the grubby money dispensed by the clean hands of the Farfield Foundation (*Encounter* magazine was another recipient). He brought *Transition* to Ghana in 1970 and edited it for two years. He then went to the United States, and he just about vanished. I saw him once: he looked frail, unsteady, and he had no interest in pursuing any conversation. He was found dead on December 3, 1995, in the San Francisco hotel which had been his home for a number of years. He was fifty-seven. After he left Africa, he was not the same. But when I knew him, thirty years ago in Africa, he was brilliant and his friendship meant everything to me.

The Exile Moritz Thomsen

I

A travel book may be many things, and Moritz Thomsen's *The Saddest Pleasure* seems to be most of them – not just a report of a journey, but a memoir, an autobiography, a confession, a foray into South American topography and history, a travel narrative, with observations of books, music, and life in general; in short, what the best travel books are, a summing-up.

Thomsen, the most modest of men, writes at one point:

Though I have written a couple of books I have never thought of myself as a writer. I had written them in those pre-dawn hours when the land still lay in darkness, or in days of heavy winter rains when the cattle huddled in the brush dumb with misery . . . I had always considered that all my passion was centered around farming.

The books he refers to are *Living Poor* (1971), the best book I have yet read on the Peace Corps experience, and *The Farm on the River of Emeralds* (1978), which is a sort of sequel, and describes a maddening and exasperating series of reverses as part-owner in a farm (with an Ecuadorian) on the lush and muddy coast.

To my mind, this farmer is a writer to his fingertips, but he is an unusual man and his writing life has been anything but ordinary. Writing for him is a natural and instinctive act, like breathing. It is obvious from this book and his others that he loathes polite society and shuns the literary world (meeting Joao Ubaldo Ribiero in Bahia he is meeting a kindred spirit). He is no city slicker, he is not possessive or acquisitive; he mocks his physical feebleness, he jeers at his old age and his sense of failure. He wishes to write well and honestly, he is not interested in power. A great deal of foolishness or a little wickedness makes him angry. He always tells us exactly what he thinks, in his own voice. He is the least mannered of writers, and he would rather say something truthful in a clumsy way than lie elegantly.

I liked him the instant I met him, and even then, eleven or twelve years ago, he seemed rather aged, frail and gray-haired, wheezing in the thin air of Quito. I could see he was a good man and that he was tenaciously loyal and that he was a serious writer. He was in his middle sixties and had published his Peace Corps book, and he mentioned that he was working on several others, including a memoir of his father. He hated his father, he said, and since literature is rich in such hatreds, I encouraged him in his memoir.

Moritz tantalized me with stories of his father's odious behavior – the time he hanged his wife's pet cat, the time he tied a dead chicken around a collie's throat with barbed wire because the collie had been worrying the hens. In addition to this sadistic cruelty, his father was also a poisonous snob and a liar; this pillar of the community – for indeed he was – made poor Moritz's life a misery. Clearly it went on for some time. We read in this travel book of how, at the age of forty-eight, Moritz was still being berated by this paranoid maniac for joining the 'communistic' Peace Corps. The only other person I have met in my life who hated his father as much was a German who told me that his father had been a member of the precursor of the SS, the SA – *Sturm Abteilung* – and, long after the war was over, was still ranting. Thomsen Senior and this Nazi would have got along like a house on fire.

I am happy to see this monster in the narrative. Whatever else travel is, it is also an occasion to dream and remember. You sit in an alien landscape and you are visited by all the people who have been awful to you. You have nightmares in strange beds. You remember episodes that you have not thought of for years and but for that noise from the street or that powerful odor of jasmine you might have forgotten. Details of Thomsen's life emerge as he travels out of Ecuador, through Bogota and around Brazil – his childhood dreams, his shaming memory of a shocking incident one long-ago Halloween, his years in the war (twenty-seven combat missions flown in a B-17 in 1943 alone), his father's death and funeral, his disastrous farming ventures, and the outrages he witnessed in various coastal villages in Ecuador.

By the end of this book, you know Moritz Thomsen intimately, and, what is more important, he is a man well worth knowing. In many respects this is a self-portrait, but in this case the artist is painting himself naked. He is candid. He withholds nothing. When we get a glimpse of his body he is never sentimental: he describes poor, weak human flesh. In Rio, for example, he is in a room with a mirror. He has no mirror in Quito. 'I am looking at myself for almost the first time in ten years, and can see at last that I had been truly broken by that time in the jungle and that old age.'

He was sixty-three at the time of the trip, but he had been very ill beforehand. His illness and his sense of failure make him morbid, but also ghoulishly humorous. He gives most people a lot of latitude, but he is always hard on himself. He laments that he doesn't look Latin. He reflects on his own appearance: 'Pure gringo, but more bum than working man.'

Moritz Thomsen is rare in an important way. He is a true Conradian, and his distant literary ancestor is someone like Axel Heyst in *Victory* – although I should quickly add that Axel Heyst's father was a different sort of devil from the elder Thomsen.

In the 1960s many middle-aged men and women joined the Peace Corps. It was not unusual for a man in his forties or fifties to head off to Africa or South America to teach school or show people how to raise chickens. Three little old ladies and an elderly gent were in my own Peace Corps group, which left the States in 1963 bound for Nyasaland in Central Africa. People at home said, 'Lordy, I don't know how they do it,' but the fact was that they didn't do it very well. Moritz Thomsen underplays his Peace Corps successes, but the records show that he was an exemplary volunteer. That is not his rarity; he is rare in having stayed on, and twenty-odd years later he is still in Ecuador, still committed to the place and the people, still an anarchist at heart, and still poor.

He is the man – there are not many in the world – who stayed behind. Americans seldom do. You meet the odd German, the tetchy Englishman, the panicky Hindu, the refugee Pole, or whoever; but seldom do you see the cultured, civilized, widely read American in the Third World boondocks. Throughout his books, Thomsen says – but never so explicitly as I am putting it now – that going away made him a person, made him a writer, sharpened his sensibilities. His subject is not suffering humanity, but rather loneliness and fellowship. He sees himself as the ultimate tramp, but then so was Henry David Thoreau, so was W. D. Hudson, so was Gauguin, so, for that matter, is Wilfred Thesiger, in spite of his Eton tie.

Because Thomsen stayed behind, he saw the dust settle, the sun drop behind the mountains, and another generation of vipers appear in the government. He is watchful, patient, and, in his way, very strong. He remembers everything. His writing is not that of someone who is merely visiting, but that of a man who has taken root; and after the initial uneasiness he feels in traveling – his hatred of planes, his superstitions, his irritation with other passengers or officialdom, his worry about lack of money, his deep loneliness and isolation – he begins to drift and relax, and he begins to encounter Brazil.

In this sort of travel there is catharsis, but few travelers are so honest in their reactions or so skillful in documenting them. Moritz is happier in the hinterland and on the river; his writing begins to sing. It is not a coincidence that it was on his river trip that he described the diesel rhythm of the boat as 'slow and languorous, like the heartbeat of a sleeping woman.'

I should have declared my own interest at the outset – he is a good friend of mine. I am glad he used a line of mine as a title for this book. It occurs in my novel *Picture Palace*, in a conversation between the photographer Maude Pratt and the writer Graham Greene:

'I'm going to wind it up. Call it a day.'
'Whatever for?' Greene said.
'I'm too old to travel, for one thing.'
'Which Frenchman said, "Travel is the saddest of the pleasures"?'
'It gave me eyes.'

Our friendship is, I suppose, characteristic of many Moritz must enjoy. We met in Ecuador twice in the late 1970s and have corresponded irregularly since. He goes on boasting of his ailing health, his failing fortunes, his insignificance. For these reasons and many others I am proud to know him. There are so few people in the world like him who are also good writers.

2

When he was forty-eight, and faced with a farm that was going bust (he had been raising pigs in California), Moritz Thomsen joined the American Peace Corps and went to Ecuador – more farming, but this time in profit, earning the Peace Corps wage of fifty dollars a month. He stayed for twenty-five years and died in Guayaquil, on August 28, 1991. I thought of Moritz Thomsen as the vanished American – the man who stayed behind. The hardest thing about being an expatriate, he used to say, was that everyone else eventually went home.

Because of a promise to an Ecuadorian friend, Moritz stayed in the country, in the coastal province of Esmeraldas, to continue farming. The farm was a miserable failure; Moritz was robbed, taken advantage of, lied to, and browbeaten. As he had done in *Living Poor*, Moritz turned misery into literature. The result of this failed attempt to farm at the coast was his second book, *The Farm on the River of Emeralds*. In 1991 Moritz published a travel book, *The Saddest Pleasure*, and finished a third book on the farm in Esmeraldas where nothing ever seemed to go right.

Events that would devastate most of us made him smile. He was one of those fatalistic people for whom misfortune was a kind of tonic that confirmed his view that the world was generally arbitrary and unfair, and only wicked people ever succeeded. 'See, I told you so!' he would say, when the worst happened.

But he kept writing, which itself is a kind of optimism. And writing is for its practitioners a fair profession; it only seems perverse and unrewarding in the short-term. Anyone who cared about Ecuador, expatriation, suffering humanity, and travel cared about Moritz's books. Like many who have chosen to observe the doctrine of silence, exile and cunning, Moritz was sought out in his seclusion in Quito. He pretended not to notice how he was admired. He was a constant reader, a responsive letter-writer, and had a great heart.

Finding the thin air of Quito hard on his already damaged lungs, he moved to sea-level Guayaquil. He continued to write, and it was a considerable satisfaction to him when a small press began reissuing his books in Britain. His emphysema worsened to the point where he could not leave his room, and at last he was bedridden. In August he came down with cholera. Knowing he was dying, he refused to go to the hospital, nor would he allow himself to be treated, feeling it would just prolong his agony.

Still, he suffered and he died alone, in a city he disliked, in a country he often despaired of, and he died poor. His cremation was delayed because the oven was unworkable. Meanwhile, the bill for his corpse occupying the shabby mourning room was mounting up. His name on the signboard was spelled wrong. There were six mourners. One of them, his Ecuadorian doctor, subsequently sent his executors a bill for the hours she had spent in the room where Moritz lay dead and at the cemetery, charging the dead man for mourning him.

'Moritz would have appreciated that,' one of Moritz's friends told me.

Yes, he would have cackled. He was alive and unselfish in everything. The opposite of love is not hate, Moritz Thomsen said; it is boredom.

Part Eight

Fugues

Unspeakable Rituals and Outlandish Beliefs

One of the excitements of travel is the chance to become acquainted with bizarre customs, unspeakable rituals and outlandish beliefs, many of which have perhaps never been described before. In my thirty-five years of wandering I have recorded many such encounters, some uniquely unpleasant, others mirroring practices we believe to be peculiar to our own lives. The Gond people of south-central India clean their teeth with fresh brushlike twigs of the *neem* tree and say the green (chlorophyll) keeps them bright. The Naulu people of Amboyn smoke their dead like kippers to preserve them. That sort of thing. But I have a greater interest in the odd, the irrational, and the truly monstrous.

That I had no prior notion such people existed was my main reason for making scrupulous notes; another was that on further investigation I learned that the people in question had been ignored in anthropological studies, or that they had been so inadequately described that they had been seriously misrepresented.

There was also the question of correctness – 'Let's skip over this ritual, since it might be used as ammo by bigots' – or of taste: certain practices were obviously regarded as so shocking that a detailed description was thought to be out of the question. Such considerations are beneath my notice. My only ambition is to be faithful to what I have seen, no matter how strange or sad.

I have written elsewhere of the Urine Ceremony of the Baciga; the Jon Frum Cargo Cult on Efate, in Vanuatu; the harvest bingeing on Three-Penis Wine in rural Shandong; the riotous Bachelor Houses of the Trobrianders; the diet of lightly cooked caribou droppings among the Naskapi Indians; Ritual Fellation among the Asmat; Wife-Inheritance, or *Chokolo*, among the Sena people of the Lower Shire River in Malawi (and how the widow in question is required to engage in sexual intercourse with the male relative while the husband's corpse is adjacent), and the manner in which people generally in India wag their heads negatively to mean yes.

'In Mali, best friends throw excrement at each other,' Robert Brain writes in *Friends and Lovers*, 'and comment loudly on the genitals of their respective parents – this to us unnatural and obscene behavior is proof of the love of friends.'

Rather than being exceptional and thus misleading, I think of such supposed oddness as the most telling, arising out of the heart of the culture. What ought to interest us is the enduring nature of the customs and beliefs; that they have not changed at all, nor are likely to, as long as the people remain isolated and wholly themselves. An Englishman, wishing to be contemptuous, expressed a tolerance greater than he intended when he wrote of the Chinese, 'These people are unlike any others on earth and can therefore be judged from no known standpoint, and not even from their own, if it can be found.'

With regard to the odder practices, I prefer not to disclose the extent of my own participation, though an old motivating memory of mine is the line in *Heart of Darkness* which speaks of how Mistah Kurtz would 'preside at certain midnight dances ending with unspeakable rites.'

I also kept a record of such customs because in general they seemed to bear no relation whatever, even metaphorically, to the way we live in the United States.

THE MOUSE MISSIONS OF THE PLASHWITS

Among the Plashwits, a pastoral people in Central Asian Turkestan, the ability to carry a live mouse in one's mouth for a great distance without harming the creature is regarded as an essential skill, acquired in the passage from boy to man.

A Plashwit boy becomes a warrior by feeding flesh from his own body to the mouse, and once the mouse is fattened in a way that impresses the commander of the Plashwit army, the animal is eaten.

The male organ in Plashwit is also known as a mouse. Plashwit women are forbidden to look at a mouse or even to utter the word.

THE SMOKE SICKNESS OF THE BALUMBI

In order to prove their strength the Balumbi, who are the dominant pygmoid people of the Ituri Forest, on the lower slopes of the Mountains of the Moon, enter Smoke Houses, where they remain for long periods, inhaling the smoke of a vine peculiar to their part of the forest, in groups of fifty or more. The Balumbi are well aware that the vine is noxious, that the priests who administer it are corrupt, and that far from being a proof of strength it is addictive and leads to a fatal condition known as 'smoke sickness.'

THE BOWL CULT OF BAOJIANG

What began in the antiquity of Baojiang as an annual feast to which bowls of food were brought has become a ceremony of display in which latterly the bowls alone take precedence.

Only women, known as Votaries, take part in the ritual of presentation. The Votary carries her bowl, always a clay pot, and shows it to the others, who sit in a circle.

What makes the cult especially unusual is the intervention of a master potter and the fact that clay is unknown in the sandy Baojiang desert of Qinghai. The potter supplies perfect bowls at great cost.

One other curious feature is that Baojiang is also an area where famine is common, though this has far from diminished the Cult of the Bowl. It could be said to have enhanced the cult, since bowls, some of them very lovely, with a sort of scrimshaw worked into the cranial bone, are occasionally fashioned from the skulls of those who have died of starvation.

BODY SCULPTURE AMONG THE MONGONI

The first Mongoni I saw I took to be the victim of a tragic accident. This was in the early 1960s, in an isolated district of Nyasaland, where I was a Peace Corps Volunteer. On closer acquaintance with these remote and deeply insecure people, I learned that it was the result of deliberate mutilation. As one group will prize the accumulation of muscle and flesh, the Mongoni notion of beauty is skeletal: physical contours are the more beautiful for being unnatural.

The Mongoni cut all excess flesh from their bodies – chunks from their calves and buttocks, lumps from their cheeks and arms. Scars are prized. A merely thin person is far less attractive than one rendered thin through the flesh being carved from the body, the skin itself scraped so that the face is cadaverous.

To display their wounds and their lacerated bodies, the Mongoni wear hardly any clothes, just a wrap-around. No power is derived from this ordeal, only the notion of beauty. The chief of the Mongoni I remember as monstrous, his wife carved almost to bits, and it was common also for the Mongoni to hack off their fingers and toes.

THE CAT TOTEMS OF MOTO TIRI

At one time, all over Oceania, dogs were raised and eaten, and still are in many places. Dogs are also found in the meat markets of South East Asia and throughout China. Instances of cat-eating are rarer, chiefly occurring in Alotau in Milne Bay in New Guinea, and in some outlying islands in the Philippines.

But in Moto Tiri cats are universally eaten, and every part of the cat is used – its meat forming a significant source of the islanders' protein, its fur as decoration, its bones fashioned into needles and hair fasteners, its teeth into jewelry. The cats are wild. They feed on the island's dwindling bird population.

Butchered cats are displayed in the Moto Tiri markets – the legs, the haunches, the back meat; some are sold dressed or stuffed. They are coated with sauce, they are smoked, or salted. Cats are the essential ingredient in stews; they are fried, poached, baked; they are served *en croûte* with taro crust.

I mentioned to a man in Moto Tiri that cats are house pets in much of the world. He laughed at such a novel concept and in the course of our conversation I learned that pigs are the house pets of Moto Tiri. They always have names, they are petted and made a fuss of. Pigs are never eaten. On chilly nights, pigs are often taken to bed by the natives and embraced for warmth, a practice which has given rise to the affectionate name for the pig on the island, being called 'a Moto Tiri wife.'

THE LIVING STONES OF HANGA ATOLL

The local legend has it that the stones had swum to Hanga Atoll on their own from the distant land of Honua, which means stone. The Honua granite matches the stone, which is not found anywhere on Hanga.

The stones are the size of humans, but of course are much heavier, being solid rock, and many have been carved into the rudimentary shapes of humans.

Each person on Hanga is responsible for one stone: the stone bears the name of that person. When the person dies the stone passes to the eldest child in the family and the name of the person changes to that of the stone. If there is no child the stone goes to the nearest living relative.

Some people have no stones; many have one; a number of people have many. Incidentally, one of the meanings of the Hanga word for stone is the same as that of the word 'stone' as it is used in the biblical Book of Deuteronomy, meaning testicles.

Stones are wealth in Hanga, but the predicament of the 'owner' (ownership is reversed – in effect it is the stone that owns the person) is to keep the stone moving, clockwise around the atoll. Someone with many stones will spend a great deal of time moving the stones, often most of the day, every day, totally preoccupying the person with a granitic ordeal.

A stone may be 'killed' by moving it to a cliff at the south side of the island, but if a stone is disposed of a family member must go with it. That is a sad occasion, yet it is the stone that is mourned and remembered, not the person.

THE FIRST NIGHT COLORS OF THE MULVATTI

The term 'First Night' indicates the time when the Mulvatti man and the Mulvatti woman consummate their marriage. It is not the wedding night or anything like it. Months and sometimes years pass before the Mulvatti couple make love, though no one I met was able sufficiently to explain to me why such a long period of time passed between the marriage ceremony and the act of love. There is no specific expression for sexual congress, only an ambiguous Mulvatti word meaning 'It is happening.'

Perhaps it is shame, perhaps it is their low sexual charge, or their instinctive Puritanism. The Mulvatti have one of the lowest birth-rates in the world, a minus figure. Mulva is a lozenge of land the size of Delaware, tucked into the south-eastern border of Yakutsk.

The normal Mulvatti home is a tent of felt. Animals share the single room, peat and dung are burned in the fire, and the Mulvatti worship wolves, believing that they are descended from a wolf. Mulvatti women are so lupine in aspect that this bizarre belief seems eerily accurate.

The 'First Night Colors' refer to those vegetable dyes that are painted on the private parts of the Mulvatti man and woman on the night they enjoy sexual congress for the first time. They present themselves on the night wearing aprons, and when these are removed and their painted parts displayed they lie down. Innocence is greatly valued among the Mulvatti. Either party expressing surprise at the lurid colors – the purple penis, the green vulva – is taken to be an unmistakable sign of previous sexual experience and vicious behavior, and such an outcry can be used in a subsequent annulment of the marriage.

THE ELEPHANT PROTOCOLS OF THE SHAN STATES

In Upper Burma the Shans, a hill people, live adjacent to the Marins, who are traditionally the mahouts, or keepers, of the Shan elephants. But the Marins have degenerated into an isolated folk without animals or income, living precariously as subsistence farmers. Still they revere the elephants, and they retain a memory of having managed these majestic creatures. They hold that the creator of the earth was an elephant and that the earth itself is the interior of an elephant's body – that we all live within an elephant, the First Elephant, and that the curved dome of the sky is the elephant's body cavity.

In the Marin belief system, humans are nothing but an insignificant aspect of the elephant. This reverence is ritualized every four years when the Marins raid the haunts of the elephant and steal their great muffins of dung, removing this excrement to their villages, where it is baked into their wheels of bread known as 'protocols.' These are consumed on a certain day, specified by the Marin priests. There is no word for dung in Marin. A clod of elephant dung is universally known as a record of a transaction, or a 'protocol.'

I have almost no clue to the significance of any of this. And as though deliberately to confuse me further, a Marin woman told me that the elephant is a symbol of unity, prosperity, and fertility. 'The elephant head is male,' she said – meaning it resembled a penis – 'The elephant hind-quarters are female' – meaning it resembled a pudendum. She was amused when I told her frankly that I did not see this at all and that in my culture an elephant was an animal that had a long memory.

THE FEASTING DONKEYS OF QUEVALO

In a time of great antiquity in Quevalo, in eastern Ecuador, a group of people, lost and starving, heard the braying of a donkey and were rescued. The Feasting Ceremony conducted every four years commemorates that deliverance.

All the donkeys of Quevalo are rounded up and herded into the village and ritually bathed. They are washed and brushed, carefully groomed, their tails and manes braided, their hooves painted, and each is brought to a hut and fed cakes and tid-bits prepared especially for the occasion. Money in the form of notes of high denominations is sometimes baked into the cakes the animals are urged to devour. For this period the donkeys are continually fed all sorts of delicacies, they live in the house, and their members are stroked by the Quevalo women until they are huge and tumescent. Although I asked repeatedly I was not privileged to acquire more detail, although from the giggles I suspected that there was a great deal that was withheld from me. An old woman told me bluntly that ejaculation occurred; however, I never learned how it was accomplished.

The paradox of the fine food is that it seldom agrees with the donkeys. It is so much richer than the normal diet of grass that the donkeys swell with gas, they break wind, they cramp, they bellow with discomfort. Yet the attentions are unceasing, the donkey is fed and stroked until it is so stuffed and nauseated and excited that it finally vomits copiously, and the entire family feeds on the vomit.

In the event that the donkey does not vomit the family pokes a stick into its gullet, forcing the creature to regurgitate, and this is gratefully eaten, as occurred to the lost family of Quevalo, long ago.

THE MEMORY PRIEST OF THE CREECH PEOPLE

One person alone, always a man, serves as the memory for all the dates and names and events of the Creech, the hill-dwelling aboriginals of south-central Sumatra. (The word is also written Crik, Krich, Kreetch, and so on.) This person possesses an entire history of the people and may spend as much as a week, day and night, reciting the various genealogies.

This Memory Priest reminds the Creech of who they are and what they have done. He is their entertainment and their historian, their memory and mind and imagination. He keeps the Creech amused and informed. The Creech have no chief or headman, and so the Memory Priest serves as the sole authority.

The Memory Priest is awarded his title at birth: an infant is chosen. As soon as he is able to communicate, he is given to understand that he is the repository of all the Creech lore.

History begins with him. His is not an easy career. He must memorize great lists of family names and he must be able to recite all the events that took place from the moment of his birth.

The Creech are an outwardly placid people, occasionally displaying fits of violence. Biting themselves in order to show remorse is not unknown, and clawing their own faces is commonplace. They are also untruthful and unreliable, prone to thieving, gossiping, gambling, and sudden spasms of the most aggressive behavior.

What the Memory Priest knows, the immensity of his storehouse of facts, is nothing compared to the one fact that he does not know, a secret that is withheld from him in the conspiratorial silence of the entire population: that after thirty years have passed, and he is old by Creech standards (possibly toothless, almost certainly wrinkled and shrunken), a meeting is convened, he recites the Creech history, and at the conclusion of this he is put to death, and finally roasted and eaten by every member of the Creech, in a ritual known as the Ceremony of Purification.

The next male child born to a Creech woman is designated Memory Priest, and elevated; history begins once again. Nothing that has taken place before his birth has any reality, all quarrels are settled, all debts nullified.

So the Memory Priest, now an infant, soon a man, learns his role, believing that history begins with him and never aware that at a specified moment his life will end. Yet it is the death of the Memory Priest that the Creech people live for and whisper about, the wiping out of all debts, all crimes, all shame and failure, and so they eagerly anticipate the amnesia his death will bring. Throughout his life, though he is unaware of it, less as a supreme authority than a convenient receptacle into which all the ill-assorted details of the Creech are tossed, he is secretly mocked for not knowing that it will all end in oblivion, at the time of his certain death.

THE ORNAMENTS OF THE WAHOOLI

The Wahooli people of the Rumi River in north-west New Guinea made first contact with outsiders only in 1973 and after that they vanished – moved deeper into the forest, which was odd and perhaps inconvenient for them, since they were a fishing community and there were far fewer fish in the area they fled to. But they had their reasons.

I heard about them from an Australian gold-seeker on the Rumi. He said that he had thought of writing their story but that he did not think he would be believed. He also felt – so he said – that the proper way for the story to circulate was as the Wahooli themselves might pass it on. That is, verbally.

The Wahooli do not write. That is not remarkable – the world is full of people who have not found any need for written language. But the Wahooli are unusual in having no pictures, or symbols, absolutely no decoration of any kind. In fact, all ornamentation is derided as suspect and wicked, and anyone found in possession of any decoration is punished severely. The Wahooli believe that all such designs are meant to cast spells. Only the devil – in Wahooli cosmology an elaborately costumed demon – would approve of such designs.

The Wahooli go utterly naked. They feel no shame. Clothes are pomp, feathers a vice, even a skirt of dead leaves is vain. In every encounter, the Wahooli make a practice of peering very closely at each other's bodies; and their ritual greeting is a snorting or a sniffing, for even the odors of flowers or any perfumes are a despised form of ornamentation.

Weapons among the Wahooli are generic, the simplest spears and daggers, the most straightforward nets and fishing tackle. Much of their fishing is accomplished by damming various reaches of rivers and streams and making fish ponds in which the fish are easily caught by hand.

The Wahooli sleep in trees on roofless sleeping platforms, in family groups, one to each shelf. Although the Wahooli have names, they use them with great reluctance. They have no words for please or thank you, no equivalent of good morning or farewell. No colors are recognized, and for all intents the Wahooli world is achromic. Their language is almost without adjectives, although 'useful' and 'harmful' are two of their chief categories; 'edible' and 'inedible' form another. The word for stranger is 'inedible,' while enemy is 'edible.'

The Wahooli are noted for their silences. They eat what they kill. Nothing is kept overnight, nor is anything stored. They do not use feathers or shells. It is a people without texture or design.

They have no leadership at all and hardly any social organization. Women are equal to men and though the infant mortality rate is enormous even children have specified rights in the Wahooli code. But then so do animals and birds and even fish, all of whom the Wahooli communicate with, often holding lengthy conversations.

All this I learned on my first visit. On my second visit I found that the Wahooli had utterly disappeared, perhaps having fled deeper into the interior.

THE RAT ROOMS OF RONDOK

The Rondok people of the Aru Sea inhabit the almost inaccessible heights on one island and have thoroughly resisted any attempt to become integrated with neighboring Indonesia. Indeed, to save face – because the island has repelled all invaders and has remained unconquered – the Indonesians leave Rondok off their maps. Melville wrote of Rokovoko, Queequeg's island, 'It is not down on any map – true places never are.' As is the case with many people who have remained steadfast in their beliefs, the Rondok people are fierce and well governed and neither missionaries nor soldiers have made any lasting impression upon them.

It is a tradition that no outsider has survived a single night on the island; anyone who has not departed the island by sundown vanishes in the darkness of the island, is 'swallowed' – literally, so I was assured in the short time I spent there, just a matter of hours, having gone ashore in the tender of a passing yacht on which I was a passenger. I wanted to see the 'fish-hogs', a sea mammal that inhabits the island's inner reef.

From a Rondok fisherman who had wandered to the edge of the lagoon I learned two facts.

The first was the one I have just mentioned, the disappearance of anyone who remains on the island overnight (there were many instances, owing to the obscurity of the island).

The second was the manner in which the Rondok people conduct elections to their highest office. Anyone may be a candidate, any number of volunteers are invited. In the initial caucus, various tests of strength are given, and they involve both mental and physical ability – running, jumping, feats of memory, repeating poems and songs, floating in the lagoon with arms and legs tied ('down-proofing'), throwing heavy objects. Rondok women are not excluded.

The volunteer cannot withdraw, but must persevere in the tests until he or she is either eliminated or attains the level of Candidate. This may take months. When there are about a dozen Candidates remaining they are individually locked into cylindrical pits called Rat Rooms, like shallow man-holes, sealed with heavy covers or lids.

Each Candidate shares his or her small underground space with thirty or forty furious squealing rats. There is no light in the Rat Room, there is no bed, and because of the low ceiling the Candidate cannot stand and would not want to sit. There is water but it is in a basin, at floor level, in what is known as the Tank, available to the rats and the Candidate alike.

Some Candidates, already exhausted by the selection process, and undone by the sheer misery of the situation, sometimes fall to the floor and are gnawed to death. These Candidates are mourned. Another category comprises those who, starved and imprisoned, eat the rats. On their release they are put to death. The successful Candidate is the one who emerges unscathed, who has neither been bitten nor eaten any of the rats, who has found a degree of harmony in the Rat Room. This person is made head of the people, given the title of Rat Chief, and when he or she dies the tedious selection process begins again.

Gilstrap, the Homesick Explorer

The tamarind trees hummed with the evidence of baboons, Gilstrap had noticed, because the noisy creatures loved squatting in the branches, cracking a tamarind seed, and a smile, with each bite of their doggy teeth.

You could not camp within fifty feet of a tamarind. But Gilstrap was not dismayed. 'There it is!' he said, with cheery fatalism, and tugged his mustache. He was on a quest.

The Two-Toed Tumbo People were the object of this quest, yet as an explorer he knew that such a journey was a continuous series of startling confrontations of which the baboons chewing in the limbs of the tamarind were just one. This was the Zimbaba, the lower river.

It was not Mudford, the home he had left too long ago even to remember the names of its trees, nor any of the people there, except the ones who had tormented him as a youngster, and the woman who waited for him in vain. Her name was Elveera Howie. Mudford was the past and like all such distant memories it was unreal and a little absurd, a sort of toy-town he had abandoned, when he was Freddie Gilstrap from Webster Street.

Gilstrap the explorer had a taste for hardships but could not abide nuisances, which was why he had fled Mudford and why he had stayed away. Elveera was just an encumbrance, because she would not leave the hideous town.

Christmas was coming. Good! He was where he wanted to be, on the other side of the earth, in Central Africa, beneath the tamarinds and winterthorns of the Zimbaba banks. Gilstrap knew that had he been anywhere else he would be yearning to be back here on the Zimbaba.

Sometimes, trekking alone in the heat along the riverbank, he was able in his stupor of satisfaction to recover his dislike of Mudford. There was first of all Elveera Howie, supporting herself by giving music lessons in the parlor of her house near Craddock Bridge, adjacent to the Interstate; and the Interstate itself, looming over the town, illuminating Mudford with its glaring lights at night; and with that traffic, drowning the music of Elveera's strings, Mudford was never silent, nor ever dark.

The pillars of the Interstate attracted graffiti, and beneath the arches were strange encampments of drifters and drunks. Then there were Gilstrap's hatreds: the litter, the filthy back seats of a Mudford taxi and the meaningless smile of the driver. Someone at a soda fountain slurping a drink or loudly chewing ice. Circus animals, baseball hats on backwards, the exultant insincerity of the *Mudford Messenger*. Dirty hands, cold eyes, billboards, bad breath, most flags. The person who rested a damp drinking glass on a book cover, and bus fumes, and the idiot laughter of someone watching TV. Mayor Mazzola, Dr. Enid Hugo the dentist, Hump his neighbor's Lab – just one of Brimble's slobbering dogs, Elveera's cat Morris, most children, and – in this season – everything to do with Christmas, from the Christmas carols monotonously repeated in elevators and the over-stuffed Santa ambushing him from every Mudford street corner to the top-heavy Christmas trees on their wobbly stands.

Gilstrap craved new sights and in Africa he was thrilled when he reflected, *I have never been here before*, and better, *Nor seen anything like this before*.

Even better, *Nor has anyone else*.

He was altogether a satisfied man. He was more than fifty but could pedal that many miles on his bike in half a day, and not only could do that number of push-ups as well but often did. On any quest, he said, the principal thing was never to look back.

His bearers saw him down the Zimbaba from Chambo in dug-outs – the river was down, the heavy rains were not due until mid-December – and just above Kawaba he paid off his bearers and sent them back and struck out on his own, the low scrub smacking his puttees.

And while Gilstrap marched he heard a child's bratty voice call out, 'Go away!'

'On the contrary.'

He spoke pompously, to make his point, yet was somewhat self-conscious at finding himself replying to a bird in a tree. It was of course a go-away bird.

'I am staying.'

Because, Gilstrap reflected, it was a land without Christmas trees, nor any suggestion of home; it was in a word not Mudford. He had spoken indignantly and it seemed significant that there had been no answer, so the bird had quite seen his point.

One afternoon he pitched his tent and, squatting to tidy the tent pegs, could not rise from his heels. He toppled forward, used the last of his strength to zip the flapping door, and there he lay, under canvas, twitching like a monkey. He was very cold. He shivered. He grew warm. His brain ached, his skin was scorched, he panted, he slept, he saw doggy demons with chewed fur and red eyes; he saw cranky birds on black trees with beaks like scissors; then he saw nothing, for he felt that his eyes were being boiled in their sockets.

When the fever finally passed, Gilstrap crept from his tent weak and thirsty, and knelt at the riverbank. He saw a troop of baboons all tangled in the tamarinds. The baboons joined him, scoop-splashing the water to their mouths as Gilstrap did – the Zimbaba was clean enough to drink.

Ranged on the bank, the baboons regarded him with dripping faces, but what struck Gilstrap most of all was the way the baboons separated into little families, mother and child and frowning father, just the way Mudford families picnicked at Hickey Park or rested by the banks of the Mystic River, near Craddock Bridge, at Christmas. Now he remembered that fragment of Mudford and sighed.

Resuming his hike, he saw a crocodile on a sandbank with its mouth wide open, and a white-feathered egret approached it, and Gilstrap was put in mind of Dr. Enid Hugo the dentist and her long legs and white smock. The egret did a most dentist-like thing, tilted her head and drilled expertly between the crocodile's teeth, foraging as she cleaned them. He remembered the garrulity of Dr. Hugo, though perhaps her questions were no worse than the squawks of this insistent egret.

A roly-poly hippo not far away raised itself before Gilstrap and seemed to smile, and Gilstrap was put in mind of a well-padded Santa shaking with laughter on a Mudford street corner. But the Santa was the more harmless of these buffoons.

Even trotting busily along the banks the hippos looked like shoppers and they munched in the herbage like mothers at lunch.

'Go away!' he heard, and it was repeated.

He knew it was another go-away bird, yet now the command made him pensive.

Gilstrap pushed on, picking the odd guava and watching the slow-footed progress of his dusty boots, to the doubtful encouragement of the monotonous lark and the screech of the racquet-tail roller in their tumbling acrobatics.

Toward nightfall, camped by a kopje, he felt a pair of eyes upon him – a wart-hog receding, indeed backing directly into his hole. Yet Gilstrap did not see the tusks and the hairy nostrils, the bristly face nor the oversized head, but the sweeter and sillier face of Hump the Lab settling into his dog bed with the same tentative inquiry of his hindquarters. Not twenty feet away another wart-hog was also reversing; this one with a snout like a hood ornament looked like an old Chevy, specifically that of Ed Brimble, Gilstrap's Mudford neighbor, as he fastidiously backed into his garage.

Gilstrap woke and crawled from his tent to see Aunt Tom at breakfast, nodding at her spinster sisters, Grace and Trudy. But no: though they had many Gilstrap features – solemn and long-faced and leggy – it was a trio of marabou storks at work on the remnants of the food Gilstrap had unwisely left out last night. They had just about finished his provisions and had punished the hoard of guavas he had gathered.

Put distinctly in mind of Mudford at that juncture, he saw something Wagnerian in the Cape buffaloes, which looked like an entire cast of *Parsifal* at the Mudford Opera. Reminiscing in this way, Gilstrap hardly noticed the eland beneath their horns, so lyre-like you half expected the phantom hand of a lovely woman – Elveera's, perhaps – to reach out and pluck them and fill the air with the plangency of this chord.

Yet there was no music here. There was all of Africa and not the chirping of birds but their sudden utterances, the go-away bird with its command, and even more orders from the mourning dove, which repeated, 'Work harder, work harder!' and at noon, 'No farther, no farther!' and at nightfall, 'Drink lager, drink lager!'

In his already crapulous state, Gilstrap heard and obeyed, and listening for more heard the laughing dove laughing and a spotted hyena yakking like a boasting child. Stumbling in the darkness he shone his torch and saw a porcupine like a pot-scrubber and a night ape lurking like Mayor Mazzola, and a large ripe artichoke. The artichoke made him hungry – and a bit homesick, too, for the last artichoke he had eaten at Elveera's in Mudford – but before he could feast on this one he saw it revealed as a pangolin.

Onward in the morning on more reluctant feet, he saw a squirrel and he was back in Hickey Park, but it was just a bush squirrel, not as glossy or as well fed as the Mudford squirrels. He saw more families of Mudford picnickers, but they were troops of chacma baboons. Nor was that creature Morris the cat but instead a frolicking clawless otter, drying itself on a rock; that coiled coach whip an Egyptian cobra, that coat rack on the pretty patterned carpet a goliath heron standing in a backwater in a small sea of hyacinths.

'Go away,' cried the go-away bird.

He glanced up and saw a fish eagle and for an instant was in the Mudford post office standing under the American eagle getting his mail, which at this season would have been a stack of Christmas cards.

Yet the hooded vulture was a hooded vulture, the tsetse flies were tsetse flies, and the crocs crocs, the bats bats, the sunlight's shattering flash like the swipe of a golden sword. Gilstrap knew he ought to have been nearer to the object of his quest, and yet he seemed no nearer.

He turned inland away from the riverbank in desperation and what he saw made him pine for Mudford: as far as he could see were Christmas trees.

Pine trees here? Yes, the trees were gorgeous – their green boughs beautifully decorated with bright trinkets. Gilstrap wept at their symmetry and their color, and even at the way they so explicitly wobbled on their stands.

Through his tears of homesickness, how was Gilstrap to know that these were the Two-Toed Tumbo People in their ceremonial cloaks, which were contrived from the feathers of the green-backed heron and the green sandpiper, the emerald cuckoo and the olive bee-eater; and hung with ornaments.

'Go away,' cried the go-away bird.

This time Gilstrap obliged, leaving his tins and his camp stool and his puttees and his tent, and fled upriver to Chambo, and caught the night bus, the first of many journeys that brought him back to Mudford and his love.

The Return of Bingo Humpage

The morning room of Thorncombe Manor was thick with artifacts, ancient skull racks, canoe prows, tortoise paddles, dog-tooth necklaces, nose cones. His islanders would swap almost anything they possessed for the fruit lozenges Humpage brought them in tins – anything except the crocodiles they venerated.

This made Humpage livid.

'There's money in wallets,' he said, winking horribly, 'and even more in handbags.'

The skull rack served for hats, of course. Near it a framed photograph showed a fashionably obese islander and a small boy.

'Who is that, Bingo?' Wetherup squinted.

Humpage was 'Bingo' to those who thought they knew him.

'One of my chiefs,' he said.

The obstinate chief lived near Humpage's bungalow by the muddy lagoon. Obstinate because he would not hear of crocodile handbags or wallets.

'And who's that next to him?' Wetherup indicated the child.

'His lunch.'

Back on the island, hilarious on grog, Humpage repeated this offensive exchange to the chief himself.

The chief gnawed a betel nut and then spat. Islanders could be impassive. This encouraged Humpage, and he shouted the story throughout the archipelago all that year, showing his teeth.

In return for lozenges, the islanders crafted wicker visors and gathered loofahs that Humpage sold in Burlington Arcade.

Humpage trusted them without liking them much, nor could he contemplate their passion for dog meat without thinking of his own Monty. Crocs were more numerous – there were now twice as many crocs and half as many islanders since his first visit. Why not eat those accumulating beasts instead, and use their hides for handbags?

The islanders muttered that they had reasons.

449

At night while Humpage sat with Monty chucking dollops of chunky marmalade to the crocs he longed to skin, the islanders crouched in their windowless huts. For them the night was alive with creatures – there was no finality in death for an islander, but only rebirth, new lives, new forms, not always human.

Humpage jeered at their savagery and twitted the chief with his monotonous humor ('I said, "That's his lunch!"') and brought their artifacts back to England on the December mail boat in time to be sold as stocking fillers.

Now all that was the past, for this year on his return to the islands Humpage was informed of the death of the chief.

Humpage missed him in the resentful way a bully misses his victim. Nevertheless, he drank, and red-faced with grog he rubbished the chief and spoke with renewed hope of handbags.

The night was too black to reveal any listener.

Humpage flipped marmalade into the lagoon, and he awaited the mail boat and Christmas at Thorncombe.

One day soon after, the lagoon was heaving with crocodiles. These were the estuarine variety, thriving in salt water, and as sturdy and sleek as the islanders who venerated them.

In previous years the creatures had seemed grateful for a spot of jam, and so it was odd when one fat beast made straight for Humpage.

Monty went rigid.

In a single gulp the reptile bolted the Lord of Thorncombe Manor and then sank beneath the muddy lagoon. All that night there were bubbles and the agreeable sounds of digestion.

The mail boat was a day late, though not late enough to explain the crocodile, impassive and upright upon the jetty. Nor was Monty anywhere in sight.

Without a word, the crocodile boarded the mail boat, occupying Humpage's usual cabin; and it was this same creature – green and enigmatic, but with a tremulous dignity – that stepped off the 11.37 from Waterloo in the snow at Thorncombe Halt, causing talk and twitching curtains in the village.

On Christmas Eve, the crocodile joined in the trimming of the tree, hooking on an ornament peculiar to the island, and standing just ahead of the Wetherups and the Pratts, and Sasha, and little Algy, as Bingo had done in years past.

Bibliography

'Being a Stranger' is based on a lecture I gave at Michigan State University in March, 1999.

'Memory and Creation: The View from Fifty' I wrote off my own bat to console myself on turning fifty. A shorter version was printed in the *Massachusetts Review*, in 1991. 'The Object of Desire' first appeared in *Vogue*. 'At the Sharp End: Being in the Peace Corps' appeared in a Peace Corps book entitled, *Making a Difference* (1986) and also in the *New York Times*. 'Five Travel Epiphanies' was written for the fifth anniversary issue of *Forbes FYI*. 'Travel Writing: The Point of It' I wrote after the Tiananmen Square massacre, when I reflected on what waspish reviews my book *Riding the Iron Rooster* had been given. The reviewers' line was that I had been beastly to the Chinese authorities. After the massacre my book was seen as prescient; in fact I had just written truthfully of what I had seen over the course of a year in China, and writing the truth can sometimes seem like prophecy.

An earlier version of 'Fresh-Air Fiend' appeared in *Worth* magazine. 'The Awkward Question' formed the Introduction to *Alone*, by Gérard D'Aboville. Soon after 'The Moving Target' appeared as an op-ed piece in the *New York Times*, a woman jogger was beaten and raped by a gang of boys in Central Park – a notorious example of the sort of thing I discussed in the piece. 'Dead Reckoning to Nantucket' appeared first in *Condé-Nast Traveler* and 'Paddling to Plymouth' in the *New York Times*. 'Fever Chart' appeared under a different title in *Condé-Nast Traveler*, and formed the Introduction to Dr. Richard Dawood's book *Travelers' Health* (1994).

I am not a diarist. In general a diary is a waste of a writer's time. I kept one-week diaries in London and Amsterdam at the suggestion of different editors, one at the *Guardian* in 1993, the other at *Handelsblad* in 1990. 'Farewell to Britain: Look Thy Last on All Things Lovely' I wrote for *Islands* magazine. 'Gravy Train: A Private Railway Car' was published in *Gourmet*. 'The Maine Woods: Camping in the Snow' appeared in the German edition of *Geo* magazine, 'Trespassing in Florida' in *Travel & Leisure*, 'Down the

Zambezi' in *National Geographic*, 'The True Size of Cape Cod' in *Outside*, and 'German Humor' in the *New York Times*.

'Down the Yangtze' was first written as a short piece for the *Observer* in 1981. I then expanded it to include the whole trip. Under the title *Sailing Through China*, I published this at my own expense, in a limited edition, with illustrations by Patrick Procktor. This little book appeared in a commercial edition and after it went out of print resurfaced as a Penguin book under the present title. As it is no longer in print – perhaps it was too small to survive? – I have included it here. 'Chinese Miracles' is the account of an extensive trip I took in 1994 through newly prosperous South China for *Harpers*. 'Ghost Stories: A Letter from Hong Kong on the Eve of the Hand-Over' was published in a somewhat different version in *The New Yorker*.

'The Other Oahu' appeared first in *Travel Holiday* magazine, 'In Molokai' in the German edition of *Geo*, 'Connected in Palau' in *Condé-Nast Traveler*, 'Tasting the Pacific' in *Vogue*. *Outside* magazine published both 'Palawan: Up and Down the Creek' and 'Christmas Island: Bombs and Birds.'

'The Edge of the Great Rift' was the introduction to the Penguin edition of my three novels with an African background: *Fong and the Indians*, *Girls at Play*, and *Jungle Lovers*. The piece 'The Black House' appeared in the *Independent*, and 'The Great Railway Bazaar,' 'The Old Patagonian Express,' and 'Kowloon Tong' appeared in new editions of those books. 'The Making of *The Mosquito Coast*' appeared first in *Vanity Fair*. 'Robinson Crusoe' is the Introduction to the Signet paperback edition of the novel; 'Thoreau's *Cape Cod*' is the Preface to the Penguin edition; 'A Dangerous Londoner' is the introduction to the Everyman edition of *The Secret Agent*; 'The Worst Journey in the World' is the Introduction to the Picador edition of that book; 'Racers to the Pole' is adapted from my Introduction to *The Last Place on Earth*, by Roland Huntford. 'Prairy Erth' and 'Looking for a Ship' first appeared as critical pieces in the *New York Times*.

'Chatwin Revisited' was the Introduction to the book *Nowhere is a Place*, and when it appeared it greatly angered some of Bruce's friends, who felt it was too breezy and disrespectful. After biographies of Bruce began to appear, my portrait was seen to be accurate. 'Greeneland' is a gathering of four separate pieces published in various places; 'V. S. Pritchett' I wrote for the *New York Times* on Pritchett's death; 'William Simpson: Artist & Traveler' was the introduction to the English edition of a book by Muriel Archer about this little-known painter, the first war artist. 'Rajat Neogy' was published in a newly revived series of the magazine *Transition*. 'The Exile Moritz Thomsen' is my Introduction to his travel book, *The Saddest*

Pleasure – a title he found in my novel *Picture Palace*; but it was actually a line spoken to me by Graham Greene, quoted in the novel: 'Which Frenchman said, "Travel is the saddest of the pleasures"?'

'Unspeakable Rituals and Outlandish Beliefs' appeared in *Granta*, 'Gilstrap, the Homesick Explorer' in the *Independent*, and 'The Return of Bingo Humpage' in the *New York Times*. These last three pieces I wrote while traveling, to amuse myself; I think of them, as I often think of my travels, as fugues.

For various reasons (off the subject, repetitious, insubstantial, being saved for later), I decided to exclude a number of pieces from this collection. In the interests of bibliographical completeness I am listing them. Anyone who wishes to read further may find these pieces on the shelves of a good library:

'Beijing in the Year 2040,' *Omni*

'Big Sur,' *Bon Appetit*

'Carnival in Brazil,' *Bon Appetit*

'Christopher Okigbo: Nigerian Poet,' Introduction, *Collected Poems*

'Crossing Nantucket Sound,' *Sea Kayaker*

Diana, by Carlos Fuentes, *New York Times Book Review*

'D. J. Enright: Portrait of a Poet,' *Life by Any Other Means*

'Doctor Sacks,' profile of Dr. Oliver Sacks, *Prospect* (London)

'Hong Kong: The Persistence of Memory,' *New York Times*

'It's About Time: The Work of Daniel Brush,' *Gold Without Boundaries*

'James Lewton Brain, Anthropologist,' *Independent*

'Nurse Wolf,' profile of a dominatrix, *The New Yorker*

'Return to Malawi,' *National Geographic Magazine*

Waldo, Introduction

'What about Salman Rushdie?' *New York Times*

'Why I Write,' *Nouvel Observateur*

Woman in the Mist: Dian Fossey, by Farley Mowat; review